# American Towns

# American Towns

## AN INTERPRETIVE HISTORY

# David J. Russo

*Ivan R. Dee   Chicago*

The author and the publisher gratefully acknowledge those institutions and individuals that granted permission to reproduce illustrations in the text, as identified in the captions. Every effort has been made to locate those parties who hold the rights to the illustrations reproduced.

Library of Congress Cataloging-in-Publication Data:
Russo, David J.
    American towns : an interpretive history / David J. Russo.
      p. cm.
    Includes bibliographical references and index.
    ISBN 1-56663-348-6 (alk. paper)
    1. Cities and towns—United States—History. 2. City and town life—United States—History. I. Title.

HT123 .R86 2001
307.76'0973—dc21                                  00-052399

*For Deerfield, Massachusetts,*
*my hometown*

# Contents

# *Preface*

BY "INTERPRETIVE HISTORY" I mean that I have focused on the *patterns* of life among those who have lived in American towns—what connects them rather than what separates them. I am interested in what town dwellers have shared, what has made their lives and communities similar. Behind each of my observations is a multitude of stories, a vast array of incidents and personalities, the endless particularities of the life of each town and town dweller. Each town is unique, and its story could be rendered in a descriptive narrative filled with the details that would give such uniqueness its shape. But each town also shares with other towns various patterns of life, and it is these patterns that have attracted my attention.

I have chosen to investigate these patterns by dissecting the lives of those who have lived in towns. Instead of creating a continuous, all-embracing narrative, I have examined the major dimensions of town life over four centuries—the founding and building of the towns, and their inhabitants' political, economic, social, and cultural lives. This analytical approach, this separation of the dimensions of life as experienced by individuals and communities, is a standard academic way of dealing with a subject. But the idea of smashing apart time and space and examining a subject from various perspectives has a much wider, popular resonance as well. Modern technology allows us to repeat and replay happenings on film, tape, disc, telephone, and computer, happenings that have occurred once in real time and space. We are used to playback, flashback, zoom-forward, stream of consciousness, and multiple perspectives in various combinations in sporting events, feature films, novels, short stories, drama, song, music, and dance. Human life is portrayed in various fractured ways, not only in scholarship but in art, entertainment, and recreation.

The following chapters may be read separately as distinct essays, but they are meant to add up to a coherent whole, a multi-faceted history of towns in what became the United States.

This book is a synthesis of existing scholarship on the towns. I have used the writings of historians but also of sociologists, anthropologists, geographers, and economists. Taken together, these writings are my "evidence," and I use them to substantiate my observations and conclusions. I have drawn on them freely and have relied on them to illustrate and particularize what I have to say about the towns, to concretize what otherwise would be vague or general. This scholarship is large and varied, but my synthesis is necessarily limited by the coverage of these writings. Surprisingly, almost never has this rather extensive scholarship led to historiographical controversy. Historians have continued to add detail and depth, but rarely have they taken serious issue with their predecessors. (A well-documented exception is the matter of certain aspects of life in early New England towns.)

Most Americans lived in rural neighborhoods or in towns into the twentieth century. Before this time, life as organized locally was more important than national or international life. Why and how the town lost to the city its primacy as the local community of greatest influence—something that occurred fairly early in the twentieth century—is one of this book's major concerns.

Most local communities have not grown into cities but have remained as towns, as places that have not been urbanized in any significant way. In a continuum of local communities, from the smallest to the largest, cities have stood as rare population centers at the apex of a hierarchy of local "place" communities, but their dominance is a recent historical development. Yet American historians did not seriously begin to study the history of towns until the 1960s, after the towns had clearly lost their place as the primary local community for most of the population. Surely the towns deserve to be studied historically with as much rigor and depth as cities.

What is a town? To say that towns are small local communities is to say something important about their essential character, but, as with any terms in a definition, "small" and "local" imply other questions: How small? What is local? Both terms imply a context. What was small and local in colonial America differed from small and local in the nineteenth century, which in turn differed from a modern, twentieth-century definition. What is perceived as a small local community has changed over time in the American context, as in any other. In the seventeenth and eighteenth centuries, towns typically embraced populations in the hundreds. By the nineteenth century this figure had risen to a few thousand. In the twentieth century it rose to anything up to, say, ten thousand. The U.S. Census Bureau has periodically changed its definitions of what constitutes a town and a city. State governments have differed over the population level to be reached before an erstwhile town is eligible for city status and thus a new form of (city) government. Other government agencies have not been consistent over time in their definitions of towns. And my historian's definitions are approximations only.

To further complicate matters, I argue that the shapes and sizes of towns shift, depending upon the feature of their makeup being examined (a Heisenberg principle of sorts). Towns can assume protean shapes, determined by whether an observer examines them from the standpoint of their founding; or as geographical territories or physical constructions; or from the perspective of their political, economic, social, or cultural activities.

Towns have a territorial definition in the sense that they occupy a space that is administered politically and defined by borders. Towns also have a topography that contains geographical features within their borders—rivers, ponds, lakes, meadows, woods, valleys, hills, and such. But towns also have a physical definition that consists of the entire man-made environment— buildings, artifacts, livestock, cultivated fields, and the extractive, industrial, or commercial operations situated upon their landscapes. The physical center of a town's life has been its Main Street, but what have been its outer limits, the shape of the various dimensions of town life?

The economic activities of town dwellers have usually embraced a territory greater than their town's political boundaries, as the inhabitants of towns have served the surrounding rural population in various capacities. Those who have lived in towns for a long time, perhaps for a lifetime, or those whose families have lived there for more than a generation, have tended to think of themselves as the only *true* inhabitants of the towns and have thought of others as "outsiders," whether recent immigrants from abroad or more transient citizens. In this social definition of the towns, the community has consisted of significantly fewer people than all those who have actually lived within the town's political territory at any moment. Towns have also typically been divided into educationally or religiously defined neighborhoods clustered around schools or churches. And yet a town's artistic activity and entertainment have usually involved performers and audiences from areas beyond the confines of a particular place.[1] Thus a town's "boundaries" expand or contract, depending upon the dimension of their existence that is examined.

There is no archetypal American town; there are only American towns, in all their variety and individuality. Nothing sharply distinguishes towns in America from those of other nations or empires or city-states, whether in adjoining Canada and Mexico or farther away. The life of towns in America has not been unique to the mainland North American English colonies or, later, to the United States. Economic, social, and cultural patterns do not follow political boundaries. What has united American towns from the seventeenth century onward is that they have existed within the wider political contexts of colonies or states, regions, and an empire or nation. Towns in the United States have shared much of a nonpolitical character with towns in other parts of the world and have, among themselves, exhibited local and regional variations of many kinds.

A full awareness of regional variations is of crucial importance to an understanding of American towns, and so I have indicated regional distinctions in the nature of the towns founded and developed in New England, the mid-Atlantic states, the South, the Midwest, the Plains, the Rocky Mountains, and the Pacific coast. Different geographic settings attracted different groups of settlers with different objectives and ways of adapting to distinctive landscapes.

I have also included assessments of particular *types* of towns founded with a special purpose: towns founded by ethnic, racial, or religious immigrants; religious and socialist utopian towns; mill towns and factory towns and company towns; cattle and mining towns and fishing villages; county seats, state capitals, and forts and military bases; railroad towns; college towns; resort towns and retirement villages.

My main concern is with settlement across the North American continent, initially by the English colonists and, later, by a more ethnically and racially varied American population. I also refer more briefly to the towns developed by the Spanish colonists throughout what later became the American Southwest, to the native civilization that the English colonists encountered, and to the slave quarters and, later, black towns that were developed by forced African migrants and their descendants. The activities of these groups lay outside the main settlement process but occurred on the same continent, during the same centuries.

Dividing the towns' history into discrete periods is difficult because so many different kinds of towns have existed at so many stages of development at any given time. The most appropriate divisions are those based upon economic functions, because most towns were founded and developed in response to material and economic activities. In the seventeenth and eighteenth centuries, towns were service centers for farmers when agriculture was overwhelmingly the leading economic activity; in the nineteenth century, towns were the earliest factory centers at a time when industrial production was based chiefly upon water power; and in the twentieth century, towns became the setting for various combinations of local and national or global economic activities and organizations. These periods I have designated are approximations only, but the extent of change in American towns at the turns of particular centuries is quite remarkable.

The following chapters are divided according to this periodization. But the sections on the seventeenth, eighteenth, and nineteenth centuries are longer than those on the twentieth century. The reason is that during the first three of these centuries the towns were the primary community for a largely rural population and were the locations for early industrial production; thus they were of great historical importance. By contrast, in the twentieth century the towns lost their primacy to the cities as the urban population became ever more dominant.

Occasionally passages in the text from the autobiographical writings of town dwellers personalize my general observations. These writings were fairly common from the late nineteenth to the early twentieth centuries. It was a time when many inhabitants of towns moved to urban centers and felt compelled, late in life, to reminisce about their earlier lives in their hometowns, which they looked back upon with unmistakable nostalgia.

Both towns and cities are types of local communities that are situated along a hierarchy. It is difficult to separate them cleanly and neatly and to make generalizations that hold for all of them. What is more, some small communities have shown evidences of urbanization, and some communities in urban complexes have exhibited characteristics typical of town or rural life. Nonetheless in brief introductions to the chapters I try to indicate both commonalities of and distinctions between towns and cities.

# Acknowledgments

I WISH TO THANK the staff at the Local History and Genealogy Room of the Library of Congress and the Interlibrary Loan Department of Mills Library at McMaster University for so dependably locating and making available for my use the vast numbers of published materials upon which this book is based.

I also wish to thank the editorial and production staffs at Ivan R. Dee for their attentiveness throughout the publication process, and especially Ivan Dee himself, who has been a superb editor for me, in every way.

D. J. R.

*Hamilton, Ontario*
*March 2001*

*American Towns*

ONE

# Foundings

THE NORTH AMERICAN continent was inhabited for thousands of years before the arrival of white European migrants, beginning around 1500. The semi-nomadic elements of the native population typically clustered together in small settlements, but these settlements were not usually "permanent" in the same sense that European towns were meant to be. Many of the Indian tribes created villages—along the Northwest coast, in the Rocky Mountains, across the southwestern plateaus, and in many parts of the eastern woodlands. In most areas of the continent, these settlements were only seasonal: temporary quarters for semi-nomadic agricultural, hunting, and fishing tribes who settled in one area during the growing season and another during the cold-weather months. Only in the Southwest of what later became the United States did tribes build permanent settlements. These tribes were probably influenced by those farther south who had developed complex civilizations with large urban centers.[1]

During the seventeenth and eighteenth centuries, the villages founded by white European migrants to North America were sometimes located on sites that earlier native villages had occupied. But, in contrast to the practice of most of the native tributes, the English, French, and Dutch colonists planned or developed permanent, not seasonal, settlements. In the broadest sense, the Europeans who migrated to North America usually rejected the classic peasant village (with homes in town and farms in fields arrayed outside) and favored instead the "open-country neighborhood,"[2] living in individual farmsteads somewhat beyond a community setting of any kind.

This was as true of the semi-feudal agricultural systems established by the Dutch along the Hudson River or by the French along the St. Lawrence

River as it was of the English farmers who settled in the river valleys along the Atlantic coast from the Bay of Fundy to the Florida peninsula. The English colonists in particular extended a practice that became increasingly common in England and elsewhere in Europe during the seventeenth, eighteenth, and nineteenth centuries. When the "strip-field" pattern of land holdings surrounding peasant villages were "enclosed" or consolidated, the farmer-owners of the new, enlarged lots moved out to their fields, leaving the villages to farm laborers and craftsmen. In North America the abundance of usable land made possible similar but even larger holdings.

Even though the white European migrants dispersed onto farmsteads, fished off the coasts, logged the forests, and mined the mineral veins of a resourceful land and its adjoining seas, they also founded towns as settlement moved across the continent. A dispersed population still had need of milled and crafted products and of professional services, both of which could be most effectively delivered in clustered settlements. In founding towns, the white pioneers drew on European experiences, adopting them to the altered conditions of a new continent.

Of course, all settlements were founded as towns. But a few of these towns grew during the seventeenth and eighteenth centuries into port cities, and rather more of them emerged during the nineteenth century into inland urban centers. Indeed, in the early and mid-nineteenth century, as settlement spread through the great Midwestern valleys and plains, some town founders hoped that their settlements would grow quickly into cities. The vast majority of towns, however, remained towns. Some grew into small cities; others neither grew nor shrank significantly; still others declined or even vanished, became ghost towns. The combination of a favorable location and stimulative economic circumstances, which together fostered the emergence of urban centers, was a rare phenomenon. Most local communities did not experience transformative urbanization.

In the twentieth century most Americans came to live in these relatively few urban centers, which became the standard location for a population that had been dispersed in rural settings for the past three centuries. Neither before nor after did most Americans reside in towns: at first they moved out to the countryside, then they swarmed into the cities. Most of them have never been town dwellers, but they have always needed towns, even if they have not lived in them.

## · I ·

THE ENGLISH who settled in North America drew on their experience of settlement in Ireland, England's first colony. Across the Irish Sea, the English "transplanted" themselves onto resourceful land, displaced and removed rebellious natives whose land was forfeited, and attempted to convert native Catholics to Anglicanism.[3] The English—far more successfully than the French, Dutch, Spaniards, or Portuguese—promoted mass migration to the lands they claimed in the Americas, repeating many of the patterns that Irish colonization had assumed by the seventeenth century. As in Ireland, so in North America: the native population was perceived as wild and uncivilized; transplantations called for the invasion, subjugation, and displacement of the natives; colonization was sponsored by either proprietors or trading companies; occupiers and natives had to be kept physically separate, to make more space for newcomers and to increase the chance for homogeneity in the colonizing population.[4]

Large numbers of Englishmen migrated to North America during the seventeenth and eighteenth centuries, dwarfing in number those who emigrated from other parts of Europe. Migrants from particular regions of England tended to stay together and settle in particular areas of the North American Atlantic coast. The Puritans who settled New England came mainly from East Anglia. Those who settled in the Southern colonies tended to come from the south and west of England. Migrants to the Delaware Valley were from the North Midlands. Those who went out to the frontier and settled in the backcountry came from the northern Borderlands. But though there were regional variations in the way these transplanted Englishmen lived, with respect to their linguistic dialect, religious practice, architecture, family relationships, old age, childhood, education, sport, leisure, food, and dress,[5] there were no discernible regional differences—either in England or in North America—in the way they settled on the land. In North America this was mostly in dispersed farmsteads but also in an array of clustered settlements, varying in size from crossroads hamlets and mill hamlets to full-scale villages or sizable towns and, in the case of a few coastal ports, early urban centers. The urge to move out to land that could be farmed was a powerful cause of dispersion, but a rural population nonetheless needed community services, and that need explains the emergence of a variety of settlements.

The land actually used for town formations was obtained in one of two ways throughout the English colonies. In New England, "proprietors" owned the land granted free by the colonial legislatures. They divided up some of their acreage among themselves and gradually sold off the remainder to subsequent settlers, having set aside lots for common lands and a meeting-house. Elsewhere in the colonies, land for towns was sold directly to the original settlers by the colonial legislatures. Land lots were a commodity easily bought and sold, though, and, at least in the planned communities of the middle and Southern colonies, a few lots were usually set aside—as in early New England—for public purposes.

As the English colonists divided the land they settled on, they exhibited a deep-seated land hunger, a territoriality that was revealed by the fact that land was viewed as a marketable commodity from the beginning, something that began to be bought, sold, and traded shortly after its original distribution. During the seventeenth and eighteenth centuries, only very small areas were surveyed and laid out into towns. The vast areas beyond, used for agricultural, extractive, and milling activity, became a visually chaotic arrangement of parcels. In New England, New France, and Louisiana—places where the residents had a strong desire for community-wide rules—there was regularity in the way parcels in the open countryside were surveyed and sold. But elsewhere there was a mixture of large and small lots. Although many colonists became family farmers and owned quite limited acreage for that purpose, a landed elite also emerged, an elite that owned large land areas for speculation or for staple crop agriculture.[6]

The northernmost English colonies, which came to be known as New England, were settled by Puritan migrants. The Puritans were a group of separatist[7] and reformist[8] Anglicans who sought an asylum of sorts within the transatlantic territories claimed by England. The Puritans, both the Separatists of 1620 and the Reformists of 1630, secured charters as trading companies, by then one of two common ways of sponsoring colonization. Although seeking religious sanctuaries within which to profess unmolested their reformed Anglicanism, the Puritans also aimed to improve their economic situation. They came from the middling elements of an English population whose commercialization of agriculture, craft production, and trade was the most advanced in Europe. Thus, in addition to their undoubted religiosity, the Puritans were imbued with a commercial, entrepreneurial spirit. These two passions—spiritual and material, religious and economic—when fused were inseparable.

One manifestation of this duality was the Puritans' decision to migrate as a trading company, with shareholders and members, whose purpose was to be a profitable resource for the colonization and settlement of like-minded Puritans who wished to start again in a new land. Another was the early decision, in the form of colonial legislative procedures, to disperse into small local communities which could be indefinitely expanded in number and thereby kept small as religious and civil entities, but to found these towns under the aegis of land corporations, with all the hallmarks of the very trading company that had sponsored their own colonization to the new land. In short, even in their founding of towns the Puritans embarked on an enterprise that was as entrepreneurial as it was religious in character. In a further dualism that marked this notably intense and passionate group, the Puritans were practical, community-building utopians, the first great town builders of English colonization anywhere in the New World.

The places the Puritans chose for their town-founding enterprises were, without exception, the most blessed with resources—along the coasts and major inland river valleys. In Connecticut, settlers turned first (from 1635 to 1675) to the seacoast and the Thames River system, the Connecticut River, and the Naugatuck and Housatonic rivers. Later migrants (1686–1734) settled in the interior uplands and secondary river valleys. Only then did further settlers move into the least desirable northwestern areas of the colony and fill in elsewhere (1737–1761).[9] Similarly, in Massachusetts Bay, Plymouth, and Rhode Island, towns were founded first along the coasts and then along inland river valleys, and then only in the hills and plateaus. In more northerly New Hampshire and Maine (as a district under Massachusetts Bay's control), this pattern of town foundings persisted.[10]

By 1800, towns covered the entire territory of southern New England and a significant portion of New Hampshire and Maine as well. Much of New England's land, the portion beyond the coastal plains and inland river valleys, was quite marginal for agricultural purposes. But the mania for town founding continued unabated from the seventeenth to the nineteenth century. From the beginnings of settlement, it is clear that the Puritan migrants and their descendants wished to sustain their faith but also to further their economic well-being. They did both in towns located throughout the region they dominated.

The device the Massachusetts Bay colonial legislature chose to supervise numerous town-founding enterprises was to create in each instance a town or land corporation that behaved much like a trading company or any limited-liability business corporation of the time. Like a trading company, these land corporations had shareholder members who were the proprietors of the common land that the legislature gave to the corporation or association. Shareholders were sometimes prominent colonists who had the contacts, expertise, and financial resources to supervise settlement within the new town and thereby realize a profit on their land. The legislature wanted the land "improved"—settled on and developed; it did not want land simply held, unimproved. The legislators' goal was to populate the landscape as expeditiously as possible.

Prominent Puritans could most effectively choose and survey sites, purchase the land from the native tribe that had occupied it, lay out lots, build roads and bridges, and lure settlers to populate the new town. Individuals like these were an indispensable part of the founding of towns in colonial New England. Some of the shareholders of these town corporations were not themselves actual settlers; some of them were shareholders of a number of such corporations; and the shareholders of some town corporations founded—as a group—other towns and thereby became shareholders of more than one town corporation. Deerfield, Massachusetts, for instance, was founded by the proprietors of Dedham, Massachusetts, none of whom became actual settlers in Deerfield. As many as one-fifth of the towns founded during the seventeenth century were launched by older towns.[11] Profit came to shareholders when they sold off their land to subsequent settlers.[12]

Leading entrepreneurial town founders appeared throughout early New England: the ubiquitous Pynchons, William and John, in the Connecticut River Valley; John Winthrop, Jr., in southwestern Rhode Island and southeastern Connecticut; James Fitch throughout Connecticut; Humphrey Atherton in Rhode Island; Thomas Willett in Plymouth colony; Joseph Dudley in the Merrimac region of Massachusetts Bay as well as in south central Massachusetts and northeast Connecticut; and Richard Wharton in Maine and New Hampshire.[13] But there were also lesser-known town promoters who were deeply involved in the process. Frontiersmen such as Cornelius Waldo, Solomon Keyes, and James Parker moved from one frontier town to another, becoming involved with several over their lifetimes. Political leaders such as Joshua Fisher, Eleazer Lusher, Andrew Belcher, Sr., and Thomas Danforth did not settle in the towns they helped found. Others knew and could deal with the native population, either as traders and neighbors or as military experts: Joseph Parsons, Sr., John Prescott, Simon Willard, Jonathan Tyng, Daniel Denison, and Daniel Gookin.[14]

Land or town corporations or societies were formed when the shareholders made formal agreements. These agreements or contracts might be a town covenant or articles of association or town orders. Whatever they were called, they organized the shareholders of the land granted by the colonial legislature into a society for the purpose of designating a tract of land on which a town was to be formed. The agreements required the shareholders to perform certain common tasks, such as dividing the land, settling the lots, paying taxes, and maintaining the commons. In some cases shareholders who

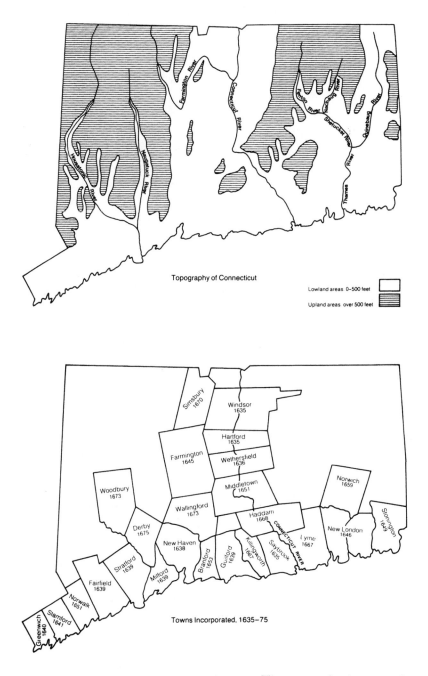

TOWN FOUNDINGS, COLONIAL CONNECTICUT. The connection between the economic viability of the land and the pattern of settlement can be clearly seen in these maps of the topography and early settlements of colonial Connecticut. [Bruce Daniels, *The Connecticut Town*]

were settlers signed the agreement. In other cases absentee shareholders, nonresident proprietors, drew up the agreement, especially if the shareholders of an established town corporation were founding a new corporation somewhere else. In some cases the agreements preceded actual settlement; in other cases they followed it.[15]

Once an agreement was made, the shareholders of a land or town corporation became the sole owners of the land on which a town was founded. A leading objective of the corporation was to entice settlers to become residents of the new town and to sell lots to them, both house lots and the fields beyond. But these residents were not necessarily admitted as shareholders of the new corporation. In a great majority of the early towns in New England, the resident population were not proprietors, as shareholders typically closed off admission to the corporation after the first years of settlement. Although they were property owners, nonshareholding residents could neither participate in nor benefit from the further sale of the remaining common land.[16]

Two well-documented cases illustrate the wide variations in circumstances in which particular towns in New England were founded. Dedham, Massachusetts, was founded in 1636 when the colonial assembly of Massachusetts Bay colony granted about thirty families two hundred square miles between Boston and the Rhode Island border. The native population was persuaded to relinquish their claim over the territory for a small sum. The settlers composed a town covenant, which pledged everyone to practice Christian love in their daily lives, limited residence to those who shared their faith, required all in dispute to submit their differences to binding meditation, commanded all to obey the rules agreed upon for the benefit of a harmonious and orderly community life, and obliged all future inhabitants to sign the covenant as well. By the end of 1656, the seventy-nine men who had been allowed to sign the covenant (all but the original settlers having undergone a public inquisition for suitability) constituted themselves as the proprietors of the public lands of Dedham, and only these men, their heirs, or approved newcomers were entitled to take part in periodic divisions of land.[17] By contrast, the shareholders of Springfield, Massachusetts, signed articles of agreement, also in 1636, but instead of a long list of religiously oriented statements, Springfield's town covenant consisted mainly of formulas for allocating land.[18]

The only other settlers in the English colonies like the Puritans were the Moravians. Both were groups of religious refugees who tried to form settlements that were meant to be exclusively for themselves. The Moravians were far more organized than the Puritans but far less widespread or numerous. They carefully planned their towns, starting with Bethlehem in the

Pennsylvania colony in 1741, followed by Nazareth (1742) and Lititz (1757). A second series of towns was founded in North Carolina, where in 1753 the Moravians acquired a 100,000-acre tract. Economy was established in 1753 as a village for farmers, whereas Salem, founded in 1766, was intended for crafts. Others were Bethabara, followed in 1759 by Bethania.[19]

While in New England the earliest significant migration took place in 1620, in the Southern colonies settlement began even earlier under the auspices of another trading company. Group settlement in Virginia began as early as 1607, in Jamestown. But the Southern colonists, unlike the Puritans, did not become committed town founders. The Southern colonies contained the largest and most productive area for agricultural production in all of the mainland colonies, with broad and contiguous river valleys cutting through a wide tidewater and piedmont (or foothills) landscape. A warm climate and a long growing season promoted extensive agricultural production.

The failure of the English colonists to found towns on a regular basis throughout the South has an economic explanation. In Virginia and Maryland the emergence of tobacco as a staple crop, and of plantations as economical and efficient large-scale farming operations, led to the development of private dock and port facilities along the long, deep, navigable rivers of the area.[20] A notably dispersed rural population occupied plantations and adjoining smaller farms and relied for community services on crossroads churches, courthouses, and markets. These constituted a kind of "shredded community" and served as scattered focal points for farming, trading, politics, and religion.[21] In Maryland, mills and smiths' shops dotted the countryside, and even churches and schools were not always in clustered settlements of any kind.[22] In Georgia such bits of community existed at crossroads or at a particularly good location on a trade route, such as at a good spring, at a ford on a river, or at a trading post or inn.[23]

But the pervasively rural nature of Southern settlement coexisted during the seventeenth and eighteenth centuries with continuing efforts by colonial authorities in Maryland, Virginia, the Carolinas, and Georgia to create towns as marketing centers. The trading company that founded Virginia issued instructions to the first group of settlers to found a town well inland on a navigable river, in a location that had the trading advantages of a coastal location and that could be easily defended against attack by the native tribes. Jamestown, Henrico, and Hampton were all early, fortified settlements at the outset of English mass colonization, when survival was precarious.[24]

Thereafter the imperial government in London pressed the colonial assembly to enact legislation setting up procedures for the founding of towns. From a transatlantic perspective it seemed essential that the colonists have towns to serve as tax-collection points and trading depots. In 1662 the royal governor in Virginia induced the assembly to pass town-founding legislation that included a method for creating new towns. A tobacco tax was to be levied as a fund for the rebuilding of Jamestown and the building of new towns on the York, Rappahannock, Potomac, and Accomac rivers, with the towns to serve as ports of entry through which all shipments were to pass. Such ports would ensure that the imperial government could collect all legitimate taxes on the colony's trade. Compliance was erratic and slow, however, and in 1680 the legislature was again induced to pass port-of-entry town-founding legislation. The new act directed each county's authorities to buy fifty acres of land on which to found a town, specifying the price to be paid for each town site as well as the price to be paid for each building lot, with added inducements, such as tax abatements, for the settlement of craftsmen. County sites were to be chosen for their accessibility and popularity. The act was, in fact, unpopular because of the expense planters and farmers would have incurred transporting and storing tobacco and because of the restriction of their trade to designated places. So many lawsuits arose that the English authorities suspended the act, which even the commissioners of customs denounced as being too rushed, too restrictive of trade, and too lacking in the needed infrastructure for both trade and taxation.

In 1691 the legislature was induced to act again, refining the procedures of the previous legislation and emphasizing the need for a dependable means of collecting revenue. This act was also repealed, probably because of opposition from both English merchants and Virginia planters. In 1706 the legislature was prevailed upon to act for what turned out to be the last time, reducing the number of towns to fifteen but otherwise providing for similar inducements to settlement and continuing to emphasize the channeling of trade and the necessity for tax depots. Once again, though, the commissioners of customs opposed the act as being restrictive of trade, and it too was disallowed.[25] Nonetheless some towns such as Yorktown (1691), Marlborough (1691), and Tappahanock (1706) were founded under the terms of these acts during the brief time they were in effect.

In Maryland the colony's proprietor, Lord Baltimore, instructed the earliest Catholic migrants to plat or survey a town, which became St. Mary's (1634). Later, Maryland's colonial government followed the lead of Virginia's with a governor's proclamation (1668) and town-founding acts (in 1683, 1684, 1686, and 1706) even more ambitious in scale than Virginia's: fifty-seven sites, each to be built on fifty acres of land designated in the legislation of 1680.[26] Vienna Town (1706), Oxford, and Wye were founded and planned as a result of this legislation. But, once again, legislative fiat did not produce the requisite number of town foundings. Just seventeen towns were established between 1680 and 1708. And some of them gained only a few lot owners before disappearing, with prior economic activity sometimes continuing on the former town sites.[27]

Carolina colony, founded by a group of proprietors in 1663, was settled in a way that contrasts quite sharply with the character of settlement in the more northerly colonies of Virginia and Maryland. By 1672 the proprietors had instructed the governor of the new colony to found a town on the peninsula between the mouths of the Ashley and Cooper rivers. Named Charleston, the new town occupied the best harbor in the southern part of the colony. The proprietors, in exercising their control over the pattern of settlement, concentrated their resources on this one location, with the result that no town anywhere in the Southern colonies attained the size of Charleston at any time during the seventeenth and eighteenth centuries.[28] The development of rice production along the tidewater coastal area as a second staple crop in the South meant that the planters who came to dominate this production naturally clustered in Charleston and the surrounding sea islands. Unlike the tobacco planters to the north, in Virginia and Maryland, settlement in early Carolina was more compact, constricted to the coastal area around a steadily growing port town.

Planning extended to colonial capitals when Governor James Nicholson of first Maryland and then Virginia persuaded the colonial legislators to pass legislation that authorized, first, the planning of Annapolis as Maryland's capital city in 1694 and, second, the planning of Williamsburg as the capital of Virginia in 1699.[29]

By the eighteenth century the pace and scale of town founding significantly increased throughout the Southern colonies. These colonies became steadily more populated over a progressively wider area and developed a more varied and commercialized economy. Between 1728 and 1751, twenty-three towns were founded under special legislative acts in Maryland. And the Virginia assembly acted in the same manner (Alexandria originated on this basis in 1748, for example).[30] By the 1780s there was a veritable flood of thirty-eight separate acts for the establishment of towns passed by the Virginia colonial assembly. Those who petitioned the legislature for enabling legislation cited the stability that incorporation would bring to the settlement process. Some cited the prior existence of a courthouse and sought to encourage settlement around it and, thereafter, the conferring of county-seat status. Others sought to lure craftsmen to settle through the attraction of owning a house lot, which met the property-holding qualification for voting. Still others stressed the importance of developing trade centers as commercial, agricultural, extractive, and craft production increased, and pressed for state aid to transportation as well as for the establishment and incorporation of towns. Agrarian hostility in the legislature markedly diminished as sentiment grew that a republican polity should be based upon a commercial temperament, that an agrarian population should not continue to consist of isolated frontiersmen relying on subsistence farming.[31]

Although it was settled later than Virginia, the North Carolina colony (which separated from the original Carolina) contained a geography quite similar to Virginia's. In the younger colony, deep, wide estuaries flowed into coastal Albemarle and Pamlico sounds. Even though the coast was somewhat obstructed from ocean commerce by sand bars, the colonial assembly in North Carolina designated six planned port towns—New Bern (1710) on the Neuse River; Bath (1712) on the River Tar; Brunswick (1739) and Wilmington (1739) on the Cape Fear River; and Beaufort and Edenton (1712) along the coast itself. New Bern was founded by a Swiss nobleman, Baron Christopher de Graffenried, as a settlement for Swiss and Palatine refugees. Wilmington began its existence six years before being incorporated and designated as a port town. But other ports, such as Edenton, originated through acts of the general assembly.[32]

The Georgia colony was founded in 1732, when a group of proprietors, called "trustees," planned a novel, philanthropic colonial undertaking by promoting a settlement that would benefit those in England imprisoned for debt (who would be allowed to emigrate) as well as persons of modest means who were religiously or economically oppressed. To prevent land speculation and wide divergences in wealth, the trustees prohibited anyone from owning more than five hundred acres of land, and limited the land grants to colonists transported and settled at the trustees' expense to fifty acres, which could not be sold and which could be inherited intact only by a male heir. James Oglethorpe, the most active of the trustees, accompanied the first expedition of migrants, and, assisted by Colonel William Bull, attempted to locate and lay out the towns.

In 1733 Oglethorpe founded and planned Savannah, inland on the Savannah River. But the Georgia trustees wished to develop other settlements and extended their charitable aid to a group of Protestant Salzburgers who had been religiously persecuted. Oglethorpe selected a site for a town near Savannah in 1734, and when this site proved unsatisfactory, he granted them another site nearby. The town came to be known as Ebenezer, and, later, New Ebenezer. The Georgia trustees also settled a group of Scots south of Savannah in 1735, at what was named New Inverness. They founded Frederica in 1735 as a garrison to strengthen the defense of the colony against the

Spaniards. Minor, privately sponsored settlements included Joseph Town, Abercorn, Thunderbolt, Highgate, and Hampstead. Oglethorpe and his associates carefully planned many aspects of their enterprise, and they certainly sponsored settlement with town foundings firmly in mind.[33]

Between 1738 and 1776 more than twenty little inland or back-country towns from Maryland to Georgia were started—at crossroads and ferry crossings, near mills at fall lines, at county courthouses. They were located along the main north-south or important east-west post roads or at the head of navigation (the "fall line") and served as stopover places for travelers and as neighborhood centers for artisan, marketing, and governmental activity. Frederick Town was founded in 1745 and settled by German Palatines. Winchester was also founded in 1745 by German immigrants, on Openquon Creek, the gateway to the Valley of Virginia, and became a trade depot through the Blue Ridge gaps. Salisbury (1753) was a center for trade in the surrounding valleys in western North Carolina. Pine Tree Hill (ca. 1750), renamed Camden in 1768, became a principal trading center for the North and South Carolina backcountry.[34]

In the backcountry of Virginia and North Carolina—in the Piedmont Southside and Great Valley of Virginia and in the Piedmont of North Carolina—twenty-eight towns were established from 1744 to 1776 as administrative or trade centers.[35] Even in the tidewater area (particularly in Maryland), where bits of community had coalesced during the seventeenth century around churches, courthouses, crossroads, and landings, by the eighteenth century small settlements appeared, developing also around stores and ordinaries (or taverns) and storage houses at landings. Such hamlets served a rural population for five miles around, within a circumference of an hour's horseback ride.[36]

Many of the inland towns were planned, but many were not, at least not at the time of their initial settlement. They grew from tiny clusters—unplanned and unfounded. Whether their settlements were planned or unplanned, the Southern colonies and then states had, by 1800, a network of hamlets, villages, towns, and a few urban centers. This network of settlements was linked to the growth of three great staple crops: wheat, rice, and tobacco. The size and spatial pattern of the region's ports and hinterland towns was linked to the peculiarities of marketing that were distinctive to each of the three staples. The exportation of wheat throughout the region stimulated the growth of port towns supplied by an array of interior settlements. But the rice port of Charleston did not generate a constellation of hinterland towns, as rice production was restricted to coastal areas. By contrast, the coastal tobacco towns of the Chesapeake remained small trade depots, though similarly unconnected to a hierarchy of settlements.[37] By the close of the eighteenth century the South still had a relatively greater rural population than any other part of the United States, but it also contained irregularly spaced settlements of the same kinds that existed elsewhere. In their settlement pattern, Southerners differed in degree, not in kind.

Among the early proprietors of the mid-Atlantic colonies that developed into New York, Pennsylvania, New Jersey, and Delaware during the 1660s, 1670s, and 1680s, William Penn, proprietor of Pennsylvania, became the most committed planner and founder of towns. Penn believed that the settlers to his colony should live in neatly laid-out villages in the midst of rural, agricultural settings. He proposed that farmers and craftsmen inhabit villages in the manner of the classic peasant village of Europe. Such an arrangement would provide the settlers with an orderly and satisfying life, he believed. Penn wanted individual holdings to extend outward from the village center, but, unlike the open-field system of scattered strips that predominated in Europe, farms would be of one piece, with contiguous fields. Penn publicized various schemes, spelling out the size of the holdings and the number of purchasers. He in fact sold blocks of land to his fellow Quakers as "First Purchasers," and during the first two decades of the province's history (from 1681 to 1701) he was able to maintain some aspects of his plans. In 1682 he ordered Thomas Holme to survey the land for settlement, and, as surveyor general until his death in 1696, Holme controlled the disposition of land. Surveys preceded occupation, and even speculative holdings were laid out in regular rectangular fashion. But even with all this surveying and planning, most settlers did not cluster in villages. In this early period, only three villages survived: Germantown, Newtown, and Bucks.[38] Germantown was founded by Francis Daniel Pastorius, legal representative of the German-based Frankfort Land Company, as well as by a group of Dutch Quakers.[39]

As elsewhere in the colonies, most settlers wanted to move onto dispersed farmsteads in the open countryside, not in villages, planned or otherwise. Settlers in colonial Pennsylvania established farms and raised a variety of grain crops and livestock; but it made no economic sense for them to establish large-scale, plantationlike operations, as in the Southern colonies. Like Southern colonists, however, rural Pennsylvanians satisfied their need for community by dealing with haphazardly located institutions in the countryside, with churches, schools, craftshops, mills, stores, and taverns scattered about. Again, like the South, many unplanned hamlets developed at crossroads or around taverns, mills, and ferries.[40]

The Penns and others were far more successful in planning county seats. Early centers outside Philadelphia such as Bristol, Newtown, Chester, and New Castle were planned villages. Bristol was established by the provincial government after residents on the site petitioned the assembly. New Castle had been founded by the Dutch when they took over Swedish settlement in the Delaware Valley. Chester was an outgrowth of Upland, the place from which the Duke of York maintained jurisdiction over the Swedes in that same valley. These administrative centers stagnated until after the Revolutionary War, largely because of the growth of Philadelphia, which dominated a large hinterland.[41] But farther west, county seats often became market towns as well, secondary centers outside the direct domination of Philadelphia. Most of the newer county seats were founded by Thomas Penn, who arrived from England in 1732 and reorganized a confused proprietary administration. Sites for new county towns were carefully considered as the Penn brothers and their surveyors and agents stressed centrality, accessibility, and distance from other county centers and from Philadelphia. The Penns combined their own sense of the matter with petitions from inhabitants, hoping to select sites of optimum benefit for both political and economic activity in the surrounding county. York, Reading, Carlisle, Easton, Bedford, and Sunbury were all founded as a result of these efforts.[42] Other towns—Chambersburg, Lebanon, and Gettysburg—were founded as private undertakings by others.[43]

During the course of the eighteenth century, Pennsylvania became blanketed with clustered settlements. Many small ones were often unplanned, but a substantial number of larger ones were often deliberately planned. Even in the mountainous sections of Pennsylvania, towns such as Bellefonte were planned and founded, in this case near a spring, with an iron ore deposit nearby. By 1800 Bellefonte was selected as its county's seat and its iron ore was mined, thus assuring the town a future.[44] As in the South and in New England, an expanding population and the progressive commercialization of the economy led agricultural and extractive workers to require services that were most effectively provided in clusters, in villages.

South of Pennsylvania, in Delaware after 1760, villages grew as important focal points at crossroads, connecting the Chesapeake Bay and the Delaware River—places such as Middletown, Glasgow, Odessa, and Noxontown. The first planned town, designed as a trading center, was Port Penn, founded by Dr. David Stewart, who partitioned his own farm and envisioned a flourishing port, an economic funnel through which trade into and out of the region would flow.[45]

North of Pennsylvania, in New York, individuals and groups petitioned the colonial and then the state government for grants of land on which to found towns. In the case of Beekmantown, near Lake Champlain in the northeast corner of New York, Dr. William Beekman, a New York City merchant and investor in urban property, and various associates, most of them relatives, petitioned New York's colonial governor in 1768, for thirty thousand acres of unoccupied, uncultivated land. Such grants were limited to one thousand acres per individual, so group petitioning was required for a tract of this size. The government agreed to issue a patent for a fee, after which Beekman devised a plan to settle families in a town. But it took the absentee proprietors eighty years to dispose of their entire grant. They hired agents to survey the land, to advertise its availability, and to collect from those who rented, leased, or bought portions of the grant. The proprietors vainly tried to import tenants from Scotland, to unload their property on other investors, and to get what income they could from sales and rentals while waiting for an influx of settlers to populate a town or the surrounding land. Meanwhile, because of competition from other, nearby land sellers, the Beekmans chose not to foreclose on the many settlers on their grant who were delinquent in their payments.

The activities of the Beekmantown proprietors contrasted sharply with what the owners of the nearby Plattsburg grant were able to accomplish. Plattsburg's proprietors were men with experience in rural and town life. They did not rely on hired managers but gave personal on-site supervision to their business. And rather than wait passively for purchasers or tenants to materialize, they invested heavily in businesses that would help attract settlers.[46]

On New York's western frontier (along the Niagara frontier, around what is now Buffalo, from the Pennsylvania state line to lakes Erie and Ontario), a group of Dutch investors who formed the Holland Land Company, with headquarters in Amsterdam, bought three million acres of land in 1792 and 1793, and, after several years of planning and surveying, in 1800 opened the land to settlement. The investors struggled to entice settlers to migrate to their grant and were compelled, like the Plattsburg proprietors, to invest in the region in order to make the grant appealing to potential settlers. Company land surveys reshaped the landscape into an orderly succession of townships and lots. Company-sponsored villages—Batavia, Buffalo, Mayville—were established as centers for the emerging rural population. And company-constructed roads connected settlers to one another and to the world beyond.

The Holland Land Company was the largest of a number of sizable land-settling operations in western New York. The Wadsworths sold land around Geneseo in the Genesee River Valley. Oliver Phelps and Nathaniel Gorham were involved in the same activity near Canadaigua. Before the Dutch investors acquired the Holland Purchase, the largest land agency managed the Pultney Purchase, just east of the Holland, with its agent Charles Williamson situated at Bath, on a tributary of the Susquehanna River. The Dutch investors who bought the Holland Purchase initially hired Theodore Cazenove as their agent, working out of Philadelphia. John Linklaen was their agent for another of their purchases, in the area surrounding what became the village of Cazenovia. Other purchases in Pennsylvania contained a rather poor quality of land and were thus not significantly developed.

The resident land agent was the key figure in these company-managed improvement schemes. Joseph Ellicot served the Holland Purchase for more than twenty years in this capacity, supervising the laying out of villages and the construction of the roads and sale of land and town lots, even offering incentives to millers, shopkeepers, and craftsmen.[47] He was a trained surveyor, having worked in his family's milling operations before accepting a position as land agent.[48] Using company funds, Ellicot created newspaper ads, handbills, and maps. The ads were seen in faraway eastern settlements; handbills were displayed in taverns and meetinghouses; and maps provided a graphic picture of the land grant. The ads described the purchase, stressing its fertility. Liberal credit policies lured those with little cash. Special provisions for group settlement enticed whole neighborhoods to migrate. Descriptions of villages and roads created the impression that the grant was accessible to existing settlements. At his office (in Batavia), Ellicot provided prospective buyers with further information on the location of lots, the assessed land quality of a given parcel, its price, and terms of credit. If existing settlers agreed to assist prospective buyers, Ellicot supplied them with the necessary information, even allowing them to sign contracts if they agreed to register them with him, and giving them a small commission in cash or land.[49]

Ellicot carefully chose sites for seven villages, scattered through the Purchase. Batavia was his land-selling headquarters and occupied a strategic location at the eastern boundary of the company's lands, where the main pathway through the region forked—an obvious gateway trading depot. New Amsterdam (soon renamed Buffalo) was situated at a point where Lake Erie funneled into the Niagara River and had great potential as an interregional trading entrepôt. Ellicot's only failure was Manila, on the shore of Lake Ontario, north of Batavia, meant to be a convenient shipping point for travelers and settlers arriving from the lake. Other sites were situated in the southern part of the purchase. Cattaraugus Village was located at the mouth of Cattaraugus Creek, which flowed into Lake Erie, at a point that could become a transshipment center. Mayville and Portland were located at each end of a portage route connecting Lake Erie and the Ohio River watershed. Ellicot Village was located in a central point on river valley bottomland amidst the hills of the southern part of the purchase, on the east-west roadway being built across southern New York. In short, Ellicot chose sites that either had already attracted settlers or were situated along portage routes, transshipment points, or road junctions—all places with potential for becoming commercial centers or trade depots.[50]

Ellicot also persuaded the Holland Land Company to help finance elements of the infant economy. He recognized that settlers expected certain services to be available upon their arrival, especially saw and grist mills, and to a lesser extent tavernkeepers and storekeepers. In Batavia, where his land office was located, Ellicot supervised the building of mills, which the company owned for the first decade of settlement. He bought mill parts and equipment from newly established merchants in the village. Laborers were hired to construct the mill race, the mill dam, and mill buildings. They were paid both in cash and in land. Local inns and taverns were paid on a weekly basis to feed and house the mill workers. But the more common policy was to assist others who were willing to build mills on their own with company loans or discounts on land sold to the prospective miller. Ellicot gave craftsmen free village land and even made loans to them as they set up their shops. Similar loans were made to storekeepers upon their arrival. To prevent speculation and assure that the towns would be populated by genuine settlers, the more lots a buyer purchased in the villages, the higher was Ellicot's price— the exact opposite of his price-discount policy for large purchasers of rural lots outside the villages.[51]

Not all investors in land companies came from Europe. Enterprises similar to the Holland Land Company were also launched by investors in the Atlantic coastal states. For instance, in 1801–1802 a colonizing association called the Scioto Company was formed in Massachusetts and Connecticut. Colonel James Kilbourne, a member of the company, traveled to the Ohio territory shortly afterward and selected sixteen thousand acres of land on and near the Oleantangy River in Franklin County. In their Articles of Association the members of the company agreed in writing to found a town, which they named Worthington. They chose a site on which there was a flat till plain, a good water supply, intermingled tracts of forest and prairie, and a nearby navigation head, which provided a site for mills.[52]

British settlers were not the only town founders on the territory that later became the United States. Spanish colonists founded hundreds of towns throughout South and Central America and into the Southeast and Southwest of the later United States. They did so in a manner prescribed by

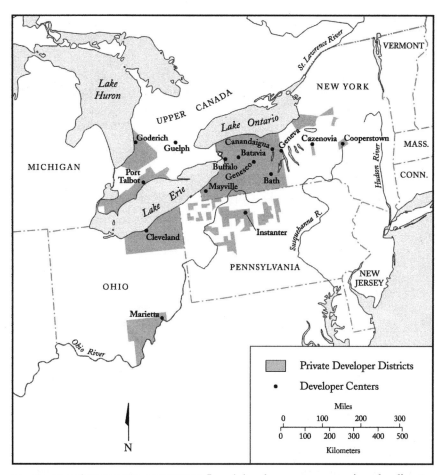

DEVELOPERS' FRONTIER DISTRICTS. Land development companies, the direct descendants of the town corporation of early New England, owned and developed not single towns but entire districts in frontier areas. This map shows a variety of such efforts at the turn of the eighteenth century in New York, Pennsylvania, Ohio, and Upper Canada. [William Wyckoff, *The Developers' Frontier*]

Spain's Laws of the Indies, proclaimed in 1573 to establish uniform procedures for colonial settlement.[53] From the 1500s to the 1700s the Spanish colonists founded three types of settlements: presidios (or military forts), pueblos (or civilian towns), and missions (centers of religious missionary work). In practice these different types of settlements were not always kept separate but were sometimes melded in a single location.

In 1556 St. Augustine was founded along the Florida peninsula as a military garrison to offer protection against privateers and pirates; as a civil settlement for trade, farming, and crafts; and as a center for missionary work. Similarly San Antonio (Texas) combined these functions, as neighboring mission, fort, and town, amalgamated into one settlement, from 1718 to 1730. Galvez (Louisiana), begun in 1698, showed Spanish, French, and British influences, as the Louisiana Territory was at various times a possession of all three European powers. Santa Fe (New Mexico) was founded in 1609 by Don Pedro de Peralta as the capital of the most northerly of the Spanish provinces. A sustained attempt to settle California came only in 1769, when sea and land expeditions left Mexico to establish both presidios and missions. The Spanish established four presidios, or military forts: San Diego (1769), Monterey (1770), San Francisco (1776), and Santa Barbara (1782). The governor of the province, Philip de Neve, founded pueblos in San Jose (1777) and Los Angeles (1781), with square land tracts outside the towns.[54]

The Spanish monarch granted land to individuals (*poblador principal*) or groups who wished to found new communities, but colonial governors were given broad power to supervise the laying out of towns. Town founders had to abide by the regulations or could legally be forced to give up the land they had been granted. Spaniards had long been town dwellers, but in the northern provinces of Spain's American empire, outside the rich Pacific coast valleys, the land was either prairie, mountains, or semi-arid plateau, and in these settings settlement became dispersed, as was the case with the European colonists elsewhere in North America. For instance, in colonial New Mexico there were only four formal *villas* (or full-fledged towns)—Santa Fe, Albuquerque, Santa Cruz, and El Paso. *Plazas* were far more numerous. They were loosely grouped *ranchos* (or farmlands) in the form of hamlets or even rural neighborhoods. Fortified or restricted plazas were the dwelling places of single extended families. Plazas usually were strung out along waterways, in the midst of the best farmland.[55]

In the communities planned and laid out according to regulations, *suertes* (or farming plots) were laid out in rectangular fields outside of town. The settlers were not given title to their land, which could not be sold, but rather held their plots as long as they cultivated them. Certain farm tracts were reserved to the Spanish monarch; others were retained for subsequent settlers; still others were rented, with the income devoted to community purposes. In certain respects, Spanish land policy resembled that of early New England's, with its common lands. Both the Spaniards and the Puritans had a concept of collective land ownership and communal land management. But whereas the Puritans favored a private land corporation, in the case of the Spaniards the town itself exercised communal control.[56]

French colonists also founded towns, particularly military garrisons, on territory that later became the United States. During the seventeenth and eighteenth centuries, French explorers, traders, and missionaries moved into the great central lake basins and river valleys of North America, establishing a string of forts and missions, with occasional settlements large enough to be civilian-dominated towns. With its far-flung trading and missionary activity, the French colonial empire depended heavily on water transportation as its only means of speedy and effective communication and trade, and so its forts and missions were usually founded on waterways. The French favored long narrow farm plots that extended back from river fronts, whether along the St. Lawrence River or outside of Detroit, Fort Duquesne (Pittsburgh), Fort St. Louis (1691–1692), Cahokia (1699), Prairie du Rocher and Kaskaskia (shortly thereafter), Ste. Genevieve (1732), and New Orleans (1763). Pierre Laclede, whose company was given a trade monopoly of the upper Missouri valley, founded St. Louis. Pierre Bienville, appointed governor of Louisiana in 1706, founded Mobile (Alabama) in 1711 and New Orleans in 1722, as the province's capital city.[57]

Even though town founding during the seventeenth and eighteenth centuries involved Spanish and French as well as English elements, it remained an essentially English phenomenon, as the vast majority of towns founded in this period were originated by the English colonists. One distinction to be made in the small local communities founded by English migrants during these years is between those that were planned and those that were unplanned. Several proprietors of particular colonies, such as William Penn of Pennsylvania and James Oglethorpe of Georgia, attempted to plan settlement in their colonies. The legislatures of the several colonies—those in Maryland, Virginia, and the Carolinas—enacted laws concerning the founding of towns. Such efforts at planning reflect an awareness on the part of colonial officials of their earlier European experiences with consciously designed habitats. Many of the towns founded during the seventeenth and eighteenth centuries did not start in a haphazard, unplanned manner, but many others did. In the Southern colonies, crossroads villages grew up without prior planning, where post roads intersected in the midst of counties and took on the functions of government and market centers. At the fall lines of the rivers flowing from the Appalachians into the Atlantic Ocean, other unplanned villages coalesced around mills located to harness waterpower. And everywhere in the colonies—through the backcountry of the mid-Atlantic provinces of Pennsylvania and New York and in the hill country of New England—wherever there were mills, often there were also craft-oriented mill villages, growing here and there around the only existing power source for machinery.

Another distinction to be made among English colonial towns is between special and ordinary communities, that is, between towns with one overriding purpose and those whose inhabitants exhibited a variety of purposes. One type of special town was religious in character. In New England the Puritans tried to found towns whose inhabitants would sustain a purified form of Anglicanism. Elsewhere pietistic Protestant sects, such as the Moravians, founded similar kinds of religiously oriented towns. Other special towns were political or administrative centers, in particular the capitals of the various English mainland colonies or the numerous county seats (or capitals) of the counties within each of those colonies, as well as the military forts constructed at various times by the British for the defense of the empire. But many other colonial towns were founded with no special purpose and grew in response to a need for some mixture of trade or crafts or milling and certain governmental activities, whether administrative, judicial, or penal. These were towns whose fluid, multi-faceted character differed from the all-encompassing special purpose of early, religiously oriented villages or planned political centers or fortifications on the frontier.

## · II ·

BY 1800, settlement in the original states—those east of the Appalachians—had fairly well covered the inhabitable land, either in the form of dispersed rural homesteads or clustered settlements. Town founding as an enterprise moved inland, across the continent, as the newly formed United States became a continental nation with astonishing speed. As a result of a series of diplomatic successes and the quick, successful war with Mexico, the United States added in broad brush strokes on the map: (1) all the territory from the Great Lakes to the Gulf of Mexico west to the Mississippi River, from Britain in the peace treaty that ended the Revolution in 1783; (2) Louisiana, which extended deep into the mid-continent plains beyond the Mississippi River, from France in 1803; (3) Florida, from Spain in 1819; (4) Texas, which had already established its independence from Mexico, in 1845; (5) Oregon, ending a joint occupation with the British, in 1846; and (6) California and New Mexico from Mexico, in the 1848 peace treaty at the end of the war with Mexico.

In the Midwest until the 1870s, towns were typically founded by the speculator-owners of the land they were laid out on. These town founders acted under the terms of the Northwest Ordinance (1785), which provided for the sale of public land in rectangular lots or in sections of 640 acres throughout the vast territory from the Appalachian Mountains to the Mississippi River, north of the Ohio River—a large portion of the territory granted by the British in the peace treaty following the Revolution. When this territory and that of the Louisiana Purchase (1803)—which ranged far beyond the Mississippi River—were actually settled, towns were usually founded as service centers for the rich farmlands of the huge Ohio and Mississippi and Missouri river valleys, and were typically spaced at regular intervals, at distances that horses and wagons could travel in a single day.[58]

The migrants who founded these towns brought a mixture of town-founding experiences with them—at first from New England, the mid-Atlantic, or the South; later from more easterly portions of the Midwest itself, so that there was variation in the process of forming towns, whether by groups or syndicates, or by individuals.

From the veranda of the Woodson Hotel in Waverly, Kansas, in 1855, Eliza J. Wiggin, saw a "broad wagon road with its traffic and bustle, carried now and then by slow moving ox teams, or long lines of canvas-covered wagons of the countless home seekers. These wagons were filled with furniture and bedding, weary women and sunburnt children. Sometimes a stove pipe protruded through an opening in the canvas telling of an attempt at warmth and comfort when the prairie winds blew cold. Buckets and pails dangled underneath and the faithful dog plodded along behind; often there were cattle and horses driven by shouting men on horseback; well booted and spurred, while boys of all ages, usually barefooted and shaggy of hair, closed the familiar and never-ending procession."[59]

The German Count Bauddisin, while touring Missouri during the 1850s, concluded that "[the] most profitable business on earth ... is to found a town, and innumerable towns have the spirit of speculation to thank for their rise. If a farmer has in his possession somewhere a favorably situated place, and he proposes to found a town, he first goes and gets the permission of the court. This will be given without formalities, and the farmer made to understand that he must be willing, for the establishment of a town, to lay out his land in house lots (each ¼ acre in size). . . . If the immigrant from Europe has the luck to have settled in a place which grows up fast, then he becomes a wealthy man through the possession of a single house. . . . Americans, as a preference, seek out the newly founded towns; but if the new town does not thrive in a hurry, they vacate house and yard and take themselves on to another place which promises more advantage. For this reason one finds in nearly all towns half and wholly fallen down houses, the owners of which are often completely unknown."[60]

As an example of one method of town founding, Jacksonville, Illinois, was founded and planned in 1825 by the county commissioners of Morgan County, Illinois, when the commissioners decided to create a new town as the county's seat, or capital. The settlers who bought the land that the government chose for its site shrewdly donated half their holdings to the county, thus assuring a quick beginning.[61] Abilene, Kansas, was laid out in 1861 by a sole proprietor, a townsite speculator, who saw the site's possibilities for future growth, and, in a fierce competition, the hoped-for town became the Dickinson County seat a year later.[62] Ellsworth, Kansas, was planned in 1866 by a group of businessmen who formed a corporation in January 1867—the Ellsworth Town Company—and took advantage of an undeveloped agricultural area and a likely rail depot.[63] Wichita, Kansas, was founded by another business group in 1867 on the site of a Wichita tribal village vacated as a result of a treaty with the U.S. government. The group formed the Wichita Town and Land Company, whose members looked to the emerging cattle trade as the basis for their town's future.[64] Dodge City, Kansas was started as a military garrison in 1865 and was developed as a town by the post commander, local merchants, and army contractors when they formed the Dodge City Town Company in 1872.[65] Caldwell, Kansas, was created by real estate deals in 1870–1871 in the midst of the cattle trails.[66]

Town founding or "jobbing" was a major occupation of the earliest settlers throughout the Northwest Territory and the Louisiana Purchase. Little capital was required, and those involved merely cleared title to the land to be surveyed and paid for both registration fees and the surveying itself. If the township lots sold, huge profits could be realized, considering the original cost of the land. Town founders usually promoted their proposed towns, advertising in local and eastern newspapers, and posting broadsides at travelers' way stations. The advertising created a picture that was typically quite exaggerated and distorted. Essential elements in these efforts to woo potential settlers were an easy payments scheme and a site that contained mills, had a potential for industrial development, and was situated in an area containing fertile land for agriculture.[67] Still, many such promotions failed, and many town "foundings" never took place. But many other promotions did succeed, and the towns founded as a result of these efforts became successful, durable communities. The crucial factor was a proposed town's economic viability, something that varied widely. Important too was a town's designation as a county seat, which brought benefits of governmental activity.

Town founders performed a variety of tasks. Harriet Bonebright-Closz remembered that her father, as founder of Newcastle, Iowa, "located claims, advised for business ventures and improvements, and in swapping land to satisfy any disgruntled settler."[68]

In Illinois during the 1830s, the legal procedure for town founding was for a proprietor of land to obtain the services of a county surveyor or his deputy. After surveying the town, the county official drew a plat or map of town lots, and filed the plat with the county recorder, who entered the transaction in the current deed book. Stiff fines were prescribed for distorting the lot layout of the plat when the lots were offered for sale, but there were no restrictions as to lot size, lot shape, or town plan. This procedure was quick and cheap. Towns were founded at the critical margin between forest and prairie, where most farmers first settled. Promotional literature commonly mentioned that sites were near timber. Most town proprietors in early Illinois founded only one town, and many stayed on even if the town failed to develop.[69]

In Kalamazoo County in Michigan during the 1830s, the earliest settlers were farmers. Town promoters sought to provide services and chose what they thought would be the most advantageous sites—those with waterpower for mills; or in central locations so that the resulting town would be chosen as a county seat; or at the heart of a dense farming population in order to make possible the development of a future retail center. Titus Bronson sought a site that would serve as a county seat, and the county commissioners chose his town site because it lay on a navigable river, between two prairies, and was well situated for roads. Horace Comstock tried to win the county seat away from Bronson and invested heavily in land. Comstock chose a site in the center of the county, near Bronson, and helped build the infrastructure for a town. But the county's settlers met and voted to leave the county seat at Bronson (renamed Kalamazoo). Lucius Lyon, a surveyor and land speculator, sold information to prospective settlers and speculators and bought a good deal of federal land in the area including some of the best farmland. Like Comstock, Lyon chose a town site that he hoped would become the county's seat, a site located in the densest farming area of the region. He went on to found a town there, but it too failed to become the seat.[70]

The Boonslick area of Missouri, where forest and prairie meet, surrounds the navigable Missouri River as its branches off from the Mississippi. Towns developed in this rich agricultural area. A steady flow of settlers, first from the upper South, and then from the North, with immigrants from Germany too, arrived first by keelboat and flatboat and then by steamboat in the 1820s, as well as overland by the Boonslick Trail. Towns were founded along the Missouri River—the earliest settlements in Missouri beyond St. Louis—at Jefferson City, Providence, Rocheport, Boonville, Arrow Rock, and Glasgow.[71]

Similar foundings occurred in Nebraska and Kansas, both of which contained vast plains and much fertile land for agriculture. As in Missouri, the early towns of Kansas and Nebraska were located along the Missouri River. By the time the Kansas-Nebraska Territory was established in 1854, land speculators had moved in, and a frenzy of town building began. Promoters published elaborate maps, advertised the sale of town lots, and freely criticized the location and prospects of rival towns. Town founding went ahead at a faster tempo in Kansas than in Nebraska because the Kansas River was navigable to an extent that Nebraska's shallow Platte River was not. More early towns were established in the interior of Kansas than in Nebraska, and no town in Kansas dominated settlement the way Omaha did in Nebraska.

Many early Kansas towns originated from the efforts of organized, militant pro- and anti-slavery groups. Leavenworth and Atchison were leading pro-slavery towns founded by settlers from nearby Missouri. Pro-slavery settlers, already on the Missouri frontier, found it relatively easy to found towns. The anti-slavery settlers, many from New England, were unfamiliar with the frontier and faced the expense of transporting supplies and outfitting their group at inflated prices after their arrival. Both Lawrence and Topeka were sponsored by the Emigrant Aid Society from New England, whose officials hoped to cover the territory with New England–style settlements.[72]

Sometimes the process of founding a town could be quite open and democratic, involving groups of actual settlers acting together. In Kansas Territory in 1858, Chelsea was founded by such a group. Under the provisions of the Pre-emption Act, it selected a site along the Walnut River in Butler County, in the southwest corner of the early settlements, in a forested, watered area. The group immediately organized itself into the Chelsea Town Company and laid out the town. Official sanction of these actions came in the form of an act of incorporation by the territorial government, which gave the company the authority to buy up to 320 acres of land to be laid out as a town.[73]

Throughout the Midwest, early settlers clustered along rivers and then moved slowly into the interior during the 1820s, 1830s, and 1840s. North of St. Louis, farmers sent enormous amounts of produce to St. Louis via outposts along the river system: Quincy, Keokuk, Burlington, Davenport, Dubuque—all these towns developed and competed for access to the steamboat transport system, for control of the river trade, and for the role of leading secondary entrepôt north of St. Louis.[74]

Town foundings in the early Southwest, that is, in the territory between the Appalachians and the Plains south of the Ohio and Missouri rivers, occurred in much the same general fashion, even though the land was not surveyed and packaged for sale in the same manner. As settlement moved inland from the Atlantic coastal region, cotton became the leading staple crop in the region. The large-scale production of cotton sustained the plantation system and a dispersed, rural population, just as tobacco had earlier along the Atlantic coast. But the smaller cotton farming operations needed a gin machine, which storekeepers typically provided. These stores became the basis for unplanned settlements, often at crossroads, as before. And all cotton growers, large and small, need shipping centers.

As settlement spread westward, Southerners created towns, especially at sites with water connections, along rivers and particularly along the Gulf coast. The process of town founding did not differ significantly from what was occurring during the same years in the old Northwest. New town fever, a town-founding boom struck Kentucky and Alabama during the years just after the War of 1812, with the launching of such towns as Florence, Athens, Demopolis, Marion, Muscle Shoals, Owensboro, Newport, and Covington.[75] Townsite advertisements from Texas, Louisiana, Mississippi, Alabama, and Florida during the years 1835 to 1837 fixed their locations in the minds of potential settlers by emphasizing a high and dry site, transportation links, the fertility of the surrounding land, and the natural beauty of the setting—much like the advertisements of town promoters to the north.[76] But large numbers of unplanned, random, scattered hamlets, villages, and towns, for example in Louisiana, were also strung out along bayous and rivers or clustered around crossroads, most of them little more than "receiving and dispatching stations" for supplies and produce.[77]

As settlement moved away from the rivers of the mid-continent and fanned out across the plains and into the Western mountain ranges and plateaus and valleys, towns continued to be founded by individual or group promoters. Some towns also emerged without planning, growing up around a merchant's store or at a crossroads, much as towns had sometimes emerged without planning or founding during the eighteenth century, as the population grew and moved inland from the Atlantic coast. Merchants often opened stores near settled, wooded areas before the arrival of well-developed road systems or a railroad line. Craft shops and mills sometimes located at water sites in the midst of settled areas. The government set up post offices at anticipated focal points of settlement. Such positioning of vital but scattered services represented the initial "thickening" of settlement in a rural area.[78] In the rural neighborhood called Sugar Hill, Illinois, the centers of community life were little more than the local church and the local school.[79]

In the plains, in a fourteen-county area of north central North Dakota, for instance, from the 1890s to the 1920s there were more than two hundred surveyed towns and another four hundred unplanned hamlets.[80] In Northeast Oregon—between the Blue Mountains to the north and west, the Snake River to the east, and the Burnt River to the south—in an area of fertile valley land, placer mineral deposits, and rich forests, fifty-two towns were founded between 1860 and 1915, with settlement proceeding rapidly off the Oregon Trail into the more productive areas, and slowing dramatically when expanding into the more difficult mining areas and onto lands with shorter growing seasons, poorer soils, less rainfall, and greater distances from markets. Of these fifty-two towns, forty-four were planned, surveyed, and registered at the county courthouses. All of them were service centers for farmers, miners, or loggers. At first they were travelers' service towns (such as Baker) situated at established resting spots (freighters' stations or stage stops), and were generally a day apart. Then towns emerged (such as Sumpter) that served areas where there were exploitable resources (particularly mining), often unplatted and located off major roads. By the 1870s there was a string of towns along the main through roads and a scattering of mining towns some distance from roads. Towns founded in the 1880s tended to be along new rail lines. There were also some hinterland service centers located a distance from rail lines, in agricultural areas, along secondary roads—towns such as Unity, Richland, Halfway, Langrell, Immaha, and Troy.[81]

The process was still flourishing in the late nineteenth century. For example, in Colorado in 1881, Grand Junction was founded at the mouth of the Gunnison River after the Utes tribe were removed from their reservation and the land was opened to settlement by the white population that had moved into the area. George A. Crawford, for twenty years the president of the Fort Scott Town Company, and with much experience in town founding, located a site for a new town, incorporating with other speculators as the Grand Junction Town Company, initially with six shareholders. The Rio Grande Railroad received half the company's stock in exchange for a promise to locate some of its operations in Grand Junction. By 1882 Crawford had approved a layout for the town and filed it with the county clerk.[82]

In Arizona Territory in the late 1870s and early 1880s, a flurry of town foundings further illustrates the process. In the fall of 1878, Amos Stone filed a homestead claim for 160 acres across from the Tombstone Mill and Mining Company's stamp mill on the San Pedro River and hired A. J. Mitchell, an engineer and surveyor, to lay out a town. It was named Red

Dog, then Charleston. The townsite company offered three-year free leases to anyone who would live there. Other towns started shortly thereafter were Fairbank and Contention City, located along the same river across from mining operations.[83]

Aside from these ordinary town foundings, a number of special types of towns were also founded in the nineteenth century. One was the railroad town, deliberately created by railroad companies, who from the 1850s to the turn of the century became the chief instrumentality for the founding of towns in certain areas. Rail transport, which had matured as a form of technology by the 1850s, became another basis beyond water sites for locating settlements. When the U.S. government, beginning in the 1850s, aided the development of a continental railroad system by granting corporations free public land along proposed routes, many railroad firms got into the business of sponsoring town foundings along their tracks. Rail transport was not limited by terrain or by season, as water transport was, and settlement in towns could occur anywhere that railroad officials and rural populations thought it should.

Many railroad companies became town founders. Collectively these firms developed a system that quickly assumed a pattern. A necessary prerequisite was the availability of public land, whether federal or state, in an area not yet filled with towns but already attracting settlers, particularly farmers who, though dispersed through the countryside, would need service centers. Railroad corporations that became active town promoters typically created subsidiary organizations to mask or ease their involvement in the process, usually because governments forbade the railroad firms from directly profiting from the development of towns, fearing public hostility to rail corporations receiving both land grants *and* profit from town promotion along their track. These subsidiary organizations acquired land in advance of the actual line construction at the most favored sites and used a variety of techniques to encourage the settlement and growth of their towns.

Some of these towns would eventually develop into durable service centers for the surrounding population. Farmers expected them to be created, and merchants expected a sufficient population to support their trade. So the railroads founded towns that settlers wanted, limiting the number of stations along the line at every seven to ten miles in order to discourage other promoters. The motive of the railroad firms was clearly to enhance their profits. In their early years they often earned greater profit from town promotion than from freight or passenger fares. Later rail companies learned from earlier companies' experiences. The risk was that new towns would wither once railroads had developed still newer towns farther along the line, a risk that was reduced with the realization that a large enough "catchment area" of farmers would need a service center *somewhere* within reach.[84]

The Illinois Central was the first to develop the technique. In 1850 Congress passed the first railroad land-grant bill to stimulate construction of the line from Illinois to Alabama. Promoters of existing towns in the area of the proposed routes were protected by a charter amendment that forbade the Illinois Central from founding towns itself. To get around this prohibition, some of the company's directors formed the "Associates" under the leadership of David Neal. Its purpose was to buy up the sections of public land that Congress had granted to the railroad, those sections that were near the locations where the company planned to establish new stations. The Associates in turn deeded to the railroad sufficient land for its regularly spaced stations, which they, as directors of the firm, helped to determine. As town promoters the Associates actively encouraged milling, lumbering, mining, and manufacturing enterprises to locate in their communities. They also tried to lure county and state governments to locate public institutions there. By 1855 the Illinois Central, with a further change of its charter, was no longer prohibited from founding towns along its tracks, and it became an active promoter, even selling town sites to other private promoters at deliberately low prices in order to stimulate economic activity. It continued to encourage industrial development by offering reduced freight rates to firms that would locate in their towns. The railroad corporation encouraged mining by converting its engines from wood fuel to coal burners, thus increasing the demand for coal. Public and private institutions petitioned for land as the price for locating in the firm's towns.[85]

Similarly the Hannibal and St. Joseph line, in Missouri, in the 1850s also became a town promoter. The founding of towns along its right-of-way constituted another source of income for the company. Town lots sold for proportionately more than farmland. Moreover stations and other sites were needed as transportation nodes, assembly points, and dissemination centers. The railroad bought newly available, cheaper government-reserved land rather than privately held land. Like the Illinois Central, the Hannibal and St. Joseph was barred from founding its own towns, so it created the Missouri Land Company to speculate in rural land and town sites. The company founded Brookfield in Linn County, selecting the site as a major division point for the line. Indirectly, through a complicated purchase and sale arrangement, it acquired the land for the town site.

Sometimes groups of investors founded towns on their own, without a direct connection to the railroad company or its townsite subsidiary—though these individuals tended to have information about the railroad's plans. Contractor John Duff and others bought government land and laid out Monroe City, Missouri, building a hotel and a store and attracting a crowd by putting on a free barbecue.

At other times individuals from outside the region were involved. George S. Harris, an Easterner, wanted to found a town that would be a New England colony in the West, a town that would promote education and Christianity and be slave-free. Harris and others formed the Kidder Land Company, using railroad company bonds as payment to the Hannibal and St. Joseph railroad company. The company accepted them at face value, even though their current market value was considerably less, doubtless because the rail line wished to promote settlement. In 1854 Albert G. Davis formed the Hamilton Town Company and the next year bought a section of government-reserved land. Davis, a surveyor, laid out a town. Then, using the inducement of free food and whiskey, the company held an auction before a large crowd. To encourage settlement, Davis built his own home in the town, Hamilton. He used his home as a hotel, and a stage line was soon established. In this way Davis made a town come to life.[86]

When Congress chose a transcontinental route in 1862, it was the most central of those proposed. The federal charter created two firms, the Union Pacific, to build the eastern portion, and the Central Pacific, to build the western portion. Congress granted the new corporations generous swaths of public land, with a right-of-way of four hundred feet. Both companies used granted lands for towns promoted by themselves or their associates. The transcontinental line was, in turn, connected to a number of smaller railroad lines that interlaced the plains and the mountains, either serving as connector lines or running north and south across the east-west axis of the main route. Some of these other rail corporations also were town promoters.

As these lines were constructed, temporary towns sprung up at the temporary terminal points, the sites of dormitory cars for the large crews of workers housed by the company. Track lines became dotted with dozens of such communities, which often quickly disappeared. The Union Pacific sometimes constructed railroad support facilities, which greatly increased the likelihood that the settlements so favored would become durable ones. Railroad "division points" were especially favored, as in these locations the railroad company built shops, roadhouses, yards and sideways, warehouses, and other buildings. Grenville M. Dodge, chief engineer of Union Pacific during the 1860s, became a leading town founder.[87]

Other lines parallelled the Union Pacific. The Northern Pacific railroad, beginning in 1870, constructed a line from Minnesota to the Dakota

Territory, in a straight line westward. Thomas P. Canfield was president of the Lake Superior and Puget Sound Company, a railway subsidiary that was established to found towns along the rail route. As construction moved into Montana, the Minnesota and Montana Land and Improvement Company organized towns: Bismark, Fargo, and Billings were founded by these town-promoting organizations. In the case of Billings, Herman Clark, head of construction for the rail corporation, founded this widely advertised site.[88] The Chicago and North Western railroad, which crossed the plains from Chicago across the middle of South Dakota, had as its subsidiary the Western Town and Lot Company. The Chicago, Milwaukee, St. Paul company also created many new towns in the late 1870s and early 1880s.[89]

The Central Pacific, building eastward from Sacramento, California, appointed Charles Crocker to oversee its construction projects. Reno, Nevada became the line's principal town and site of its major facilities, but Laramie, Wyoming, also became a center, particularly for agents of the line itself. Like the Union Pacific, the Central Pacific spurred the development of parallel or connector lines, which also became heavily involved with townsite promotion. Tacoma, Washington, was founded by Morton M. McCarver, a land speculator and townsite promoter with prior experience in Iowa and California, who wanted a site on Puget Sound. In 1887 the Great Northern railroad, under James J. Hill's leadership, became the chief rival of the Northern Pacific, founding such towns as Great Falls, Montana, and Pocatello, Idaho, which became a center for the firm's rail facilities. In the 1870s the Missouri, Kansas, and Texas, one of the smallest railroad companies in the West, aggressively pursued a policy of town promotion as it moved south and west through Kansas, Oklahoma, and Texas. Its general manager, Robert S. Stevens, was responsible for the creation of such new towns as Vinita, Muskogee, and Denison.[90]

Under General William Jackson Palmer's aggressive leadership, the Denver and Rio Grande line specialized in building its own towns and destroying or undermining those that already existed. Palmer hoped to profit from the rise in land values that rail transport brought as well as deriving revenue from carrying passengers and freight and creating spur lines to mining areas. His outstanding engineering and financial abilities were matched by his lack of ethics. The Denver and Rio Grande received no federal land grant subsidies, so Palmer was forced to finance his firm from other sources, notably local subsidies. Palmer's threat to build a nearby town when an existing town refused to cooperate turned into reality when he actually founded new towns near recalcitrant Pueblo and Durango.[91]

Texas, a state with its own public domain, supplemented federal land subsidies. The Texas and Pacific line planned towns west of Dallas and Forth Worth as profitable real estate ventures to help finance construction along the line itself and thus generate needed freight and passenger traffic. El Paso became a railroad support facilities center along the Rio Grande. Arthur Edward Stillwell conceived of developing a rail line from Kansas City to the Gulf coast. The Kansas City, Pittsburgh, Gulf railroad constructed track through Missouri, Arkansas, Louisiana, and Texas, and along this long route built dozens of new towns. In the territory of New Mexico, the long-awaited railroads provided the necessary impetus for the founding of towns. The Santa Fe railroad founded New Albuquerque, across from the old, and the new town became the most important settlement in the territory. The Santa Fe also founded towns elsewhere in the territory. In nearby Arizona Territory, an expanding rail system had a similar impact.[92]

Practice varied somewhat from line to line, though a clearly visible pattern also emerged. The Chicago, Rock Island, and Pacific established more than eighty-five towns between 1886 and 1889 across the plains into Kansas. The line built through already fairly populated, improved land, and founded towns as an economic proposition. Its main concern was not to establish a human community but to channel agricultural products to the company's lines for transport.[93] The Chicago, Great Western built the "Mapleleaf Route" in the mid- and late 1880s and was involved in the founding of more than a score of new settlements. The company formed the Iowa Townsite Company, allowing this group of landowners and speculators to divide agricultural land into town lots. The railroad encouraged its subsidiary to found towns at ten-mile intervals. It was sometimes cheaper to build around existing communities because of the expense of acquiring homes and businesses. The Iowa Townsite Company founded Lanesboro when it bought 280 acres from George Lane. It held an auction and attracted many buyers by offering a free lunch. The auction took place around a chalkboard showing the lot numbers and locations. Bidding was brisk. The company went on to lay out eight additional townsites and provide free transportation to each auction.[94]

During the 1880s the Northern Pacific's construction of rail lines across the Dakotas coincided with the settlement of the area. Colonization associations sponsored inexpensive group immigration to the plains, with migrants from both Europe—England, Wales, Germany, Russia—and from the eastern United States as well. The Northern Pacific's own colonization bureau organized local boards open to anyone (male or female) of good moral character. The rail company's central bureau investigated locations for settlement, obtaining transportation and supervising explorations of possible sites. But the local board chose its own site and picked out its own land. In this way such towns as New Salem, Glen Villin, Richardton, Mandan, Taylor, Gladstone, Dickinson, and Belfield were founded.[95]

The Northern Pacific's Land Department worked with townsite companies to found towns such as Sykeston (1883), Melville, Carrington, New Rockford, and Minnewaken. Typically the railroad company owned half the town lots, which were held in trust by the townsite company. The most successful of the townsite promoters who worked with the Northern Pacific were Comstock and White of Moorehead, Minnesota, who formed the Northwest Land Company and founded Minot, Towner, Rugby, Bottineau, and two dozen lesser places along the Great Northern line during the 1880s. Townsite agents such as Frederick Stoltze and David Tallman were information brokers for those who inquired about lots. Agents like these tried to connect the inquiries they received to the appropriate townsites and lots.[96]

In California during the 1880s the Southern Pacific became a town promoter in the San Joaquin Valley, south of San Francisco. It was lightly populated when the railroad built its line, which meant that land prices were lower than in, say, the Sacramento Valley to the north, where significant settlement preceded the construction of a rail line. Townsite acquisition and promotion were integral parts of railroad construction. Town sites were chosen with engineering considerations and a desire to build a straight line as major factors, which often meant bypassing existing settlements. If local business interests provided sufficient cash and land to the railroads, however, these considerations could be overlooked. But it was often more profitable for the railroad to found its own towns. The Southern Pacific used a variety of methods for obtaining land, but timing and secrecy in advance of actual construction were always important. Here as elsewhere, because of public hostility toward the railroad's being involved in its own town promotion, the Southern Pacific disguised its activity by creating a subsidiary organization, in this case the Pacific Improvement Company. The railroad organized auction lot sales and provided reduced passenger fares for those who attended. It also built and operated hotels and dining facilities and either gave away or discounted lots for schools and churches. Among the towns founded by the Southern Pacific were Fresno, Tulare, Modesto, Lodi, Hanford, Lemoore, Sumner, Newman, Porterville, Lathrop, Traver, Sanger, and Delano, all in California.[97]

The mining town that emerged during the nineteenth century was another special enterprise. Wherever discoveries occurred in the Rocky Mountain ranges, starting with the gold strikes in California in 1849, 1850, and 1851, and continuing with both gold and silver strikes in Colorado, Idaho, Montana, and South Dakota in later decades, mining camps sprang up, some of which were planned—that is, surveyed and laid out. Because they involved the most valuable of the minerals present in North America, a gold or silver strike created the most frenzied sort of migration to the sites, and the camps were characterized by their swift physical development. When the strikes had run their course, many prospectors left the camps, and those who stayed at the more promising sites typically were farmers and craftsmen.[98] Camps served both as places of residence for the prospectors and as supply centers. With such names as Whiskey Bar, Humbug Creek, Jesus Maria, Devil's Retreat, Jackass Gulch, Hell's Half Acre, Flapjack Canyon, Murderer's Bar, Shirt Tail Canyon, Red Dog, You Bet, Gouge Eye, Lousy Level, Gomorrah, and Rough and Ready, the camps were sites for a motley gathering of the hopeful, all animated by the possibility of instant wealth, all having "rushed" from places near and far: the Mississippi valley and the East Coast, but also Mexico, Australia, China, Hawaii, France, Britain, and Ireland.[99]

The camps that became durable towns tended to be well-situated supply depots that could serve migrants' caravans and miners over a wide area. Dozens of mining towns sprouted suddenly and just as quickly withered when the easily worked placer deposits became exhausted or when richer strikes occurred elsewhere. In Colorado, beginning in 1858, each successive gold or silver strike temporarily drained an already established center (such as Denver) as residents rushed off to a new camp. But as rushes declined in the frontier mining towns, people drifted back to the more established centers.[100]

In Idaho, gold strikes occurred in 1860 in the Snake River area. Lewiston, at the confluence of the Clearwater and Snake rivers, began as the principal supply center for the mining areas of northern Idaho. New gold deposits were then discovered along the Boise River valley in southern Idaho, and in 1863 silver was discovered along the Snake River in southwest Idaho, each strike leading to the sudden appearance of clusters of mining camps. Boise started as a planned town and as a major supply center for these newer strike areas.[101]

In Montana the earliest gold rush occurred in 1862. Butte grew swiftly as a rail transport connection, bringing in people and supplies and hauling out ore and refined copper and silver, and serving as a major supply and transportation center of the kind that made the many smaller mining towns viable. Benton, Bozeman, and Missoula became transfer points between different means of transport, outfitting stations for prospectors, and continuing sources of supply for the mining camps. Benton's location gave it an early advantage: it was the head of steamer navigation on the Missouri River and adjoined Fort Benton, a long-established fur trading post. But Benton's advantage declined as rail transport replaced steamboats. Bozeman became a rail center, as did Missoula.[102]

In 1874 gold was discovered in the Black Hills of South Dakota, the last remaining area in the mountainous West where mining exploitation was possible. In the rush that followed, Rapid City became the largest town in the region, serving as a major supply center, well situated between mountains and prairie and between the northern and southern Black Hills. Without the successive discoveries of vast mineral wealth in each of the mining regions, the pace of settlement and the creation of new territories and states and towns would have been slower and more orderly.[103]

As mining and lumbering improved technologically and became corporatized, another kind of special town emerged: the company town. In the more remote areas of the Western mountains, when corporations used mining and lumbering technology and gathered a large labor force to operate that technology in the mines and forests they developed, these corporations sometimes founded and built entire towns at the sites of their operations, and remained the owners of the towns they founded. Logging and mining camps sometimes evolved into company towns at a later stage of development, when corporations sought to recruit and retain sizable labor forces of workers who would not otherwise have migrated to remote and undeveloped settings.

Among company towns for lumbering operations were the Puget Mill Company's Port Gamble (1853), the Washington Mill Company's Seabeck (1857), the Manley-Moore Lumber Company's Montezuma (1910), and Bloedell-Donovan's Sappho (1924), all in Washington. In Oregon there appeared the Wauna Lumber Company's Wauna (1912), the Valsetz Lumber Company's Valsetz (1919), the Kinzua Corporation's Kinzua (1927), and the Gilchrist Timber Company's Gilchrest (1938)—and so on, with other lumber towns in California, Arizona, Montana, and Utah.[104]

Large-scale operations were required when corporations began mining low-grade copper at the turn of the nineteenth century, and some of the biggest and most durable company towns were copper towns. The Anaconda Copper Mining Company founded Anaconda, Montana, before the turn of the century and Conda (1921) and Weed Heights (1941) in Idaho afterward. Kennecott Copper Corporation founded and owned eight company towns in Arizona, Nevada, New Mexico, and Utah—towns such as Ruth and McGill, Nevada (both 1908). Phelps Dodge Corporation took over and developed as company towns such places as Ajo and Morenci and Bisbee, in Arizona, before and after the turn of the century.[105]

Company towns were founded at various sites where coal-mining operations flourished in Wyoming, Colorado, Utah, and New Mexico. Coal mining was often sponsored by corporations whose primary operations demanded a secure supply of fuel, so that company towns at coal-mining sites were often built to support firms whose primary interest lay elsewhere. For example, because the Union Pacific Railroad used coal as its fuel, its subsidiary, the Union Pacific Coal Company, founded and built Carbon (1868), Hanna (1889), and Cumberland (1900), Wyoming. In the coal fields of southern Colorado, the Colorado Fuel and Iron Corporation founded more company towns than any other company in the West.[106]

Special kinds of towns also included state-sponsored trade, college, or resort towns. Georgia was a particularly active state in the founding of towns. The new state government sustained the town-founding initiatives of the former colony's original proprietors. The state legislature directly planned and supervised the founding of trading towns, the state capital, county seats, resort towns, and college towns along the eastern seaboard. From the 1790s to the 1840s an activist state government started two trading centers, three different state capitals (at Augusta, Louisville, and Milledgeville), about fifty county seats, and a number of resort and several college towns. College towns (such as Athens and Oxford) were founded when a citizen, a church, or the state gave land for a school. The sale of lots generated funds used to build the campus. Resort towns (such as Indian Springs) were usually located at springs. Trade towns (such as Macon and Columbus) were strategically located to foster commerce across the state. County seats were centrally located within counties.[107]

Some special towns were "colonized" by groups from the Eastern United States or Europe who moved together to a new location farther west. Group migrations from particular towns in the East resulted in the founding of new towns named after the old in a number of states from the Atlantic coastal region to the mid-continent plains, even to the mountains and plateaus and valleys of the West. Other colonized towns were founded by groups of Europeans who migrated with the express purpose of founding their own towns, as the Puritans and Moravians had done in the seventeenth and eighteenth centuries. Groups of Swedes, Germans, Dutch, Poles, and Russians all migrated in this manner. Zeeland, Michigan, for example, was founded in 1847 by emigrants from the Netherlands who had been involved in a schism in the Dutch Reformed Church.[108] New Braunfels, Texas, was founded in 1845 by a philanthropic but entrepreneurial-minded group of German nobility as a center for German migrants to rural central Texas, where the noblemen sponsored emigration to land granted by an independent Texas government. The sponsors hoped to develop cotton production on the Texas plains and establish regulations for emigration to the land itself.

But they also founded a town and even foresaw a series of towns linking their grant to the Gulf Coast.[109] In Kansas, from 1876 to 1878, groups of German-Russians migrated from villages on the Volga River where their ancestors had moved during the eighteenth century; they established new villages, often with the same name as the former village in Russia. When they arrived, the colonists pooled their resources and collectively purchased sections of land from the state along a railroad upon which they founded their towns.[110]

By contrast, some colonized towns drew together migrants from various places, usually from within the United States, requiring only that the gathered share a common faith or ideal or race. The Mormons, the largest of the indigenous American Protestant sects that emerged during the nineteenth century, became notable colonizers. They carefully planned their communities under the close supervision of church officials, founding over more than five hundred towns throughout the great central basin of the Rocky Mountains. The original Mormon leader, Joseph Smith, planned several towns in the Midwest even before the Mormon trek to the Rockies. Nauvoo, Illinois, was the Mormon center before Brigham Young, Smith's successor, made the decision in 1845 to migrate farther west and begin large-scale colonization there in order to escape persecution. The Mormons considered Texas, Oregon, and California before settling on Utah because of its isolation and sparse population. Nauvoo became the base camp for the great migration, but the Mormons also built camps at intervals across the plains.

Young founded more than 350 new communities in Utah over three decades, under a detailed plan for settlement. Once a general location for a proposed settlement was determined, an exploring party was dispatched. This party decided upon the feasibility of settlement at the site and whether it was the most advantageous place in the area for a town. Only then were colonists "called" to the site itself. Young chose people with a variety of skills and trades and provided the group with tools, implements, and supplies. When the cadre of settlers reached the selected location, they cultivated their farms and constructed fortified enclosures to protect their temporary cabin homes. Only then did surveyors lay out streets and lots.[111]

Black freedmen colonized towns in this fashion in the years after the Civil War. Groups of blacks from various locations migrated out of the South in considerable numbers. Some went north to southern Indiana and Illinois and to rural Wisconsin, where they established their own farmsteads and tiny settlements within larger white towns.[112] In Kentucky after the Civil War, the owners of large horse and cattle and hemp estates set aside tracts of land at the backs of their properties for the resettlement of black freedmen. The land was sold at a low price or given to blacks who would work on the estates and settle in what turned out to be twenty-nine newly founded hamlets.[113]

But the main exodus of blacks was to the plains, to Kansas and to Oklahoma, where the black migrants joined the westward trek and attempted to form separate black communities. In Oklahoma, from 1889 to 1919, twenty-seven towns were founded in order to provide a separate setting for black pioneers. The town promoters believed that isolation from white Americans was the only solution to the difficulties blacks confronted. The most notable of these promoters, Edwin P. McCabe, even hoped that Oklahoma could become an all-black state. The Oklahoma Immigration Association was founded in 1889 at Topeka, Kansas, for the purpose of colonizing and founding such a state. The plan was to petition Congress for statehood for the Oklahoma Territory if the 1890 census there showed a black majority.[114]

But there were separate black towns in many states in the decades after the Civil War that mirrored the segregation of American society at large. In Nicodemus, Kansas, in 1877, six black Kansans and a white Kansan formed the Nicodemus Town Company. The Louisiana, New Orleans, and Texas Railroad Company hired black land agents, James Hill and Isaiah Montgomery, to found Mound Bayou, Mississippi, in 1887. William Eagleson and Edward P. McCabe, other black land agents, in 1890 founded Langston City, Oklahoma. A biracial trio of townsite speculators formed the Fort Smith and Western Townsite Company and in 1904 founded Boley, Oklahoma. The all-black California Colony and Home Promoting Association founded Allensworth, California, in 1908.[115]

Like other town founders, black promoters sought profit while they tried to help blacks escape from the pervasive racism of white Americans and to establish their economic independence through the ownership of property and land—which, such promoters argued, were the only bases for future citizenship. Black town promoters greatly exaggerated the attraction of proposed townsites, formed immigration societies, gave away lots, sponsored celebrations, arranged excursion tours, dispatched traveling agents, and mailed out booster literature—just like their white counterparts.[116] They distributed handbills, broadsides, and pamphlets; advertised in newspapers; sponsored round-trip excursions featuring reduced fares for Easterners; offered free land to churches and schools and subsidies to new businesses and even prospective residents—all time-tested promotional techniques.[117]

Newspaper editors in the black towns explained why blacks should emigrate. The *Herald*'s editor argued the "Langston City [is] the negro's refuge from lynching, burning at the stake and other lawlessness." In March 1895 the *Boley Progress* asked blacks to "come and help to prove to the caucasian race . . . that the Negro is a law-making and law-abiding citizen and help solve the great racial problem before us." Early residents also had explanations. One in an Oklahoma town thought that blacks came because "they was tired of the way white folks was treating them." Another thought that in Langston, Oklahoma, "no matter how little you be here, you can still be a man." Outside Boley, Oklahoma, one of its settlers claimed, "you always had prejudice to contend with," but inside the town "everybody can be somebody." Another thought that everyone in Langston "wanted to prove to the world that colored folks could run a town without white folks."[118]

Other colonized towns that gathered people from many locations were religious in character. Groups of Quakers founded such towns as Newport, Indiana, and Springdale and Salem, Iowa. Spiritualists founded Alton, Indiana. Similarly, temperance towns replaced a religious covenant with a secular one: a pledge to avoid alcoholic beverages was the basis in 1869 for the founding of the Union Colony in Greeley, Colorado, and the Chicago-Colorado Colony in Longmont, Colorado. Dozens of similar communities were founded in the years after the Civil War.[119]

But the most numerous of such communities were those whose founders sought to form communal havens in a world of private property. In these towns all property was held in common, which made them the most radically different kind of town established in all of the United States during the nineteenth century. Most of these groups selected sites in settled areas short of the frontier, sometimes moving farther west during succeeding generations. They wanted to be close enough to settled areas to proselytize new recruits, but they did not wish to risk being overrun with visitors.[120] The Shakers, who arrived in North America from Europe in 1774, founded twenty-seven towns during the century that followed. The Rappites, followers of George Rapp, formed the Harmony Society and in 1803 established themselves at Harmony, Pennsylvania. Followers of John Humphrey Noyes founded Putney, Vermont, and Oneida, New York. Adin Ballou and others in 1841 founded the Hopedale community in Massachusetts. In 1855 German Pietists established Amana in Iowa. Old Order Amish founded various communities of this kind.

Secular communist communities also drew on European models. The Owenite communities, inspired by the English social reformer Robert Dale Owen, flourished in the 1820s, not only Owen's own colony at New Harmony, Indiana (purchased from the Rappites), but similar towns at Coxsackie, Haverstraw, and Frankin in New York; Allegheny, Pennsylvania, Kendal and Yellow Springs in Ohio; Blue Springs and Forestville in Indiana; and Nashoba, Tennessee, as well as a half-dozen other places. The Fourierist "phalanxes" followed the prescriptions of Charles Fourier, an early French socialist. In the 1840s these phalanxes multiplied with remarkable speed: seven in New York, six in Pennsylvania, six in Ohio, one in Indiana, two in Wisconsin—thirty in all. Brook Farm in Massachusetts became the most famous. Individuals unattached to these models also founded such communities: in the 1840s John Collins started Skaneateles Community in upstate New York.[121]

In sum, throughout the nineteenth century, groups continued to found American towns with special purposes. Some were utopian in nature (though none dominated an entire region as the Puritans did for a time in colonial New England). Others were ethnic or racial enclaves. Mining corporations also planned and founded towns near their mines in the remoter parts of the Rocky Mountains, as did railroad corporations along their land grants across the central valleys and the Western plains and coastal valleys. Immigrant groups from the Netherlands, Sweden, Germany, Poland, and Russia founded towns after moving en masse from areas of Europe, as did groups from towns *within* the United States from along the Atlantic coast. So too did religious and secular communistic groups such as Fourierists, Rappites, Owenites, Shakers, and Pietists. Subscribers to a common faith or ideal from scattered areas came together to found still other towns, such as the dozens of temperance communities, or the Quaker and Spiritualist villages. Other towns became, as a result of a competitive scramble, political capitals of counties and states. And the American government continued the British practice of building frontier fortifications—in this case to defend the nation from America's own native people. Once again, such special towns were shaped by one all-encompassing purpose, in contrast to the fluidity and variety of ordinary small communities originated in response to mundane economic and social needs.

American towns continued to be planned during the nineteenth century, just as they had been during the seventeenth and eighteenth centuries. In the Midwest and the Plains, towns were typically founded and planned by the original speculative proprietors. But many other nineteenth-century towns grew unplanned—as earlier—around waterpower sources (before steam and then electricity developed into major alternative sources late in the century) or at crossroads.

## · III ·

BY THE TIME the twentieth century arrived, Americans had settled everywhere within their borders across the North American continent, from the Atlantic to the Pacific Ocean, from Canada to Mexico, whether in rural neighborhoods, hamlets, villages, towns, or cities. Town founding was thus a process that was part of the settlement of a continental nation. By contrast, during the course of the twentieth century the founding of towns was confined to the creation of planned communities in the midst of already settled areas.

During the depression of the 1930s the federal government encouraged the planning of new settlements when the Federal Emergency Relief Administration and then the Resettlement Administration were given authority to create whole new communities in an effort to resettle people who had been set adrift by the economic cataclysm. The director of the RA, Rexford Tugwell, favored suburban "greenbelt" communities rather than new towns in rural settings, as he thought the latter kind of community was becoming anachronistic. Tugwell managed to plan only three new communities, all on the fringes of urban areas, outside Washington, D.C., Cincinnati, and Milwaukee. He located them close to employment opportunities and encircled them with green countryside.[122]

In 1968 the Johnson administration induced Congress to enact the New Communities Act, under whose terms the federal government guaranteed the bonds of new communities founded by private developers. Supplemental grants followed to state and local agencies for water, sewer, and open-space projects. The grants were conditional upon the construction of a substantial number of housing units for low- and moderate-income persons. The 1968 act was extended in 1970. A 1968 survey found 53 new community developments in 18 states; by 1972 there were 151 projects in 30 states. Only 28 of these new communities had a population of more than 5,000 as of 1972. Unlike European and earlier American ("greenbelt") new towns, governments did not invest directly in the planning and construction of the towns. These new communities were private developments. The actual builders were financially backed by large corporations—Westinghouse, Goodyear, Humble Oil, large home-building and construction firms, and insurance companies as well as lenders and investors in land.[123]

Over the course of four centuries, what linked Puritan land corporations, Quaker "First Purchasers," Southern town planners, Midwestern land jobbers, railway subsidiary townsite companies, company town originators, and a variety of colonized town groups that founded towns is that they all performed essentially a real estate transaction—part of a general speculation in land, whether for agricultural, extractive, industrial, or commercial purposes. The founding of towns was meant to be a profitable enterprise, like any other real estate venture. And like the sale of any kind of "product," towns needed to be promoted, publicized, and sold. Their founders always tried to locate them in advantageous sites, places where they could enjoy a secure economic future. This was the case whether the town was founded as a service center for farmers and planters; a predominantly livestock, fishing, lumber, mining, or industrial town; a county seat or a state capital; a fort; or a colonized town under the auspices of a particular group. All towns that were planned, whether for a special purpose or a for a variety of purposes, had to have a basis for economic durability. Even those that grew unplanned from a mill site or a crossroads or a docking facility, or from the site of a single service (a store, a post office, a tavern, a church, a courthouse), needed economic viability.

Town founding flourished as Americans settled the continent. The creation of towns coincided not only with the settlement process but also with a time when most Americans were farmers. As a result, most towns were founded as service centers for farmers. The vast decline in agriculture and in the number of people working as farmers came after the continent was settled, after most towns were founded.

During three centuries of town founding, Americans dispersed into rural settings to farm. But they also clustered to mine, to raise livestock, to cut timber, to fish, to handcraft items or to mass-produce machine-made products, to provide professional services, and to sell goods already made. Towns became the sites for the activities that required clustering. The dispersed, rural population needed the services that a clustered community provided. Wherever the population reached a certain level in a particular rural "catchment" area, services that had been isolated or itinerant were more effectively centralized in a clustered settlement, whether planned or unplanned.

Americans of all kinds founded towns, usually for mundane economic purposes. Those small groups within a notably varied population that felt threatened or embattled and thus especially cohesive often founded towns that became their sanctuaries, protective settings where members of such groups felt they could live secure lives. Thus town founding mirrored the heterogeneous character of the American population, and the creation of towns became a kind of safety valve, providing an outlet for embattled minorities to find a place in what during the nineteenth century became a vast continental nation.

But many other towns were not founded, not planned. They just grew, originating around a particular service provided by a church, a courthouse, a tavern, a store, a mill, a post office, a fort. Many of these unfounded, unplanned places became genuine towns as well. Thus American towns can trace their origins to two very different kinds of beginnings.

## TWO

# *Sites*

W HETHER TOWNS were founded by a conscious act or simply grew
unplanned, they occupied unique sites, had particular street layouts, consisted of a variety of human constructs: buildings and facilities. In short, they
had a physical presence. Towns in this sense were human artifacts or constructions.

Little is known about the layout of the villages built by the native tribes
across North America during the many generations they engaged in agriculture before contact with European migrants. Much more is known about
their dwellings. Because most of their settlements were seasonal, the tribes
favored building materials—tree bark, reeds, grass, brush, or saplings—that
were light and portable. On the treeless plains they also used sod (as the
white settlers later did there) and sometimes used wood and made plaster
walls of clay (like the white settlers). So varied were the dwellings of the native tribes that in some cases they were the original designers of particular
kinds of structures that white settlers developed only much later. Long before modern Americans invented mobile homes, native tribes in the Great
Lakes region and on the Western plains and basins had easily movable wig-
wams and brush huts. Long before urban Americans built tenements and
apartment buildings, the Iroquois had huge longhouses which accommo-
dated many families. And long before twentieth-century Americans thought
of building below-ground bunkers as a protective shelter in times of natural
or military threat, tribes in the Rocky Mountains lived in pit houses, with
rooms three feet below ground to provide earth-sheltered insulation.[1]

White settlers shared with the tribes the use of wood and sod and plaster as building materials. But because the European migrants and their de-

scendants favored durability in their settlements, those who constructed buildings in the towns sometimes changed their primary material from wood to longer-lasting brick (which the native tribes did not know how to make) or cut stone, especially after the early years of a town's existence, at a time when the inhabitants of a town believed their community would endure. By the twentieth century, modern Americans also used concrete and metal and such synthetic materials as asphalt and plastic.

Although it is not known whether the native tribes had a conscious sense of design in the layout of their villages, what is clear is that during the seventeenth and eighteenth centuries the English colonists sometimes laid out towns with various forms of European town planning as models. By that time, well-established towns and cities in Europe were occasionally re-designed and rebuilt and enlarged as a result of careful, professional planning. It seems quite evident that the founders of many of the English colonies were aware of these efforts.

The most sophisticated designs included public circles as well as squares, and radiating street patterns as well as linear ones. But the basic layouts of the planned parts of European towns and cities carried forward a few basic features of town and city planning that stretched back to the ancient world: street patterns that were either a grid or linear (that is, with one basic "spine" street) in form, either of which enclosed some sort of public space, usually rectangular in outline.[2]

Among planned or designed settlements, the grid quickly won out over the linear design among both English and Spanish colonists. It was easier to survey or "plat" a planned settlement with a grid design. It could be endlessly expanded as a community grew. Its only obstacle was the town's topography. Thus location was an important consideration for town founders who favored a grid layout. The grid was as useful for settlements that grew into cities as it was for those that remained as towns. Certainly there was no distinction between the layouts of towns and cities. As settlement spread from coast to coast during the nineteenth century, planned communities everywhere—with great repetition and monotony—featured the ubiquitous grid.

The first challenge to the supremacy of the grid layout came only during the mid-twentieth century, when those who constructed mass housing developments at the edges of towns and cities introduced the curvilinear street pattern—streets that followed the contours of the land. To those who could afford large lots on such curving streets, it seemed they were experiencing the openness of the countryside while living in a clustered settlement. The curvilinear street layout became in the last half of the twentieth century as common a pattern of new community design as the grid had been for three and a half centuries before. But, again, there was no distinction between settlements that burgeoned into cities and those that remained as towns.

Similarly there was little to distinguish town dwellers from their urban counterparts in the design or style of the buildings and houses constructed in the settlements founded and developed by European migrants and their descendants. From the very beginning, mercantile and later industrial elites in port and then inland cities tried to emulate the latest European styles in house and building construction, and so too did the elites in the towns and in rural areas. This included not only the planters in their embryonic plantation communities but elites who lived in towns and dominated an area's economic activity, whether it involved fishing, forestry, livestock, grain, or minerals. Throughout the four centuries of white settlement, town dwellers, especially those who aspired to have status and to be proper, have tried to emulate urban architectural style. To the extent that there have been significant stylistic variations, they have not divided towns from cities but one region from another. Architectural detail has been quite specific to geographical region, sensitive to climate and topography and to the experiences of those who settled a particular area. But even these regional variations have been overridden by the mass design patterns that have predominated in the construction of houses and buildings during the twentieth century.

## · I ·

THE COLONISTS clearly drew on their homeland brethren's recent experiences in town planning, particularly the English colonization of Ireland. The earliest efforts at laying out towns along the Atlantic coast, from Virginia to New England, were patterned after recent town planning in Ulster.[3] This traditional military town plan was used at Roanoke and Jamestown in Virginia: simple triangular fortifications to enclose military camps, with semi-circular bastions surrounded by palisades or stockades. The plan of Jamestown was essentially that of a colonized town in Ireland. The homes of the settlers were huddled closely around a church, with the palisade, storehouse, and church the focus of the community. The Virginia trading company that sponsored the earliest settlement specified the design of the settlers' houses as well as their fields outside the village.

In New England, Boston was sited in a sheltered harbor with a fort constructed on one of the town's hills. In Connecticut, all the towns founded before 1645 contained closely laid-out house lots, and all were built on rivers or the coastline, in places good for defense as well as pasturage and farming. This was the case with Fairfield, Milford, Branford, Guilford, New London, and Saybrook. In the instance of Saybrook, the founder of the town hired Lion Gardiner, an engineer trained in continental military practice, to lay out the town, which was in the form of a grid at the point of land at the mouth of the Connecticut River, with the fort separated from the houses of the settlers.[4]

The colonial assemblies made town founders or proprietors responsible for surveying the lands in their town grants.[5] The proprietors (that is, the shareholders of the land corporations who became the owners of the land the towns were built on) carefully defined house lots, fields, and the common lands. Colonial assemblies further prescribed that all towns have a meeting-house (for both religious and civil gatherings) at the center of town, located on a "common," or public space.

But once an area ceased to be on the frontier and thus necessarily forti-fied, the predominant settlement pattern of the English colonists changed from clustering to dispersion. When it became clear that the English mi-grants were in North America to stay, the groups who first settled the towns that had been so systematically founded in New England did not typically create clustered settlements. They dispersed, as settlers did elsewhere in the colonies, occupying house lots scattered along roadways near their strips of farm land, which extended outward from the roads and houses. Although the Puritans were the great town founders of the colonial era, the "towns" they founded were typically dispersed settlements, with only a common and a meetinghouse to mark a center. Towns such as Norwich in Vermont; Salem, Walpole, and Francestown in New Hampshire; Meriden in Connecticut; and Dedham and Pittsfield in Massachusetts—all were settled in this man-ner.[6] In Connecticut, for example, ordinary towns were seldom larger than eighteen buildings, situated on one or at most two intersecting streets, some-times organized around a green, sometimes scattered about to the extent that there was no center at all.[7] In New Hampshire too, those who settled in Lon-donerry, Bedford, Peterborough, New Marblehead, New Amesbury (or Warner), Amherst, and Henniker all avoided small house lots in a compact area in favor of larger lots dispersed along roadways with farms directly attached.[8]

Only those towns that became substantial service centers or trade de-pots developed genuine centers, with a clustering of public and private struc-tures around the common. Towns that did develop in this way—and there

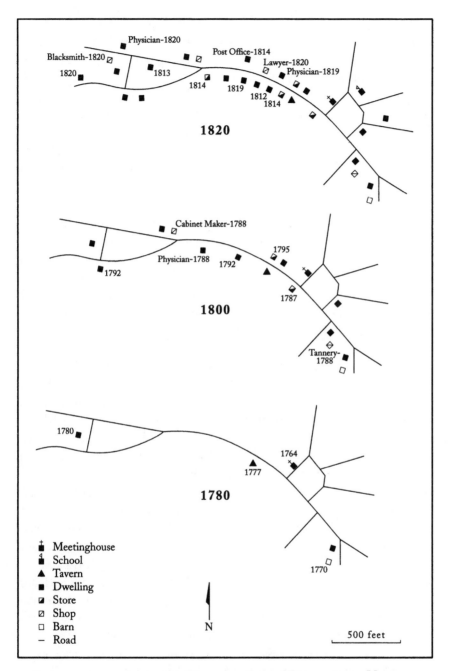

NEW ENGLAND TOWN GROWTH. These drawings of Francestown, New Hampshire, in 1780, 1800, and 1820 show a typical progression: dispersed settlement with only a meetinghouse as a focal point gradually develops into a clustered settlement as a small commercial center. [J. S. Wood, "Elaboration of a Settlement System in New England," *Journal of Historical Geography*]

were not very many before 1800, assumed either a grid or linear layout, with secondary streets connecting along its sides. In both cases these street layouts centered on a common with an adjoining meetinghouse. These rare centers included Cambridge, New Haven, and Hartford, laid out on a grid pattern. By contrast, Salem, Providence, Springfield, and Boston (which rather quickly became a coastal urban center) exhibited a linear pattern. So while the Puritans were the greatest English colonial town founders, they were conspicuous failures as town designers and town builders. Just as the Southern colonists were slow to react to legislative summons to *found* towns, the New England colonists were slow to respond to the commands of assemblies that they *build* towns centered on a common.[9]

In the Southern colonies, towns were also planned, surveyed, and laid out. The most common design was a simple grid pattern, sometimes with special squares for courthouses and churches. Typically a settlement was situated on a river or shoreline, with potential for later development farther inland. Towns such as Yorktown, Tappahonock, Marlborough, and Alexandria in Virginia; Vienna Town, Oxford, Wye, and Charleston in Maryland; and Wilmington, New Bern, and Edenton in North Carolina all assumed this kind of shape.[10]

James Oglethorpe created a more sophisticated design for Savannah as the center for his special colonial venture (Georgia), and Francis Nicholson provided equally sophisticated plans for two colonial capitals: Annapolis and Williamsburg. Both planners drew successfully on their awareness of European design theory and practice. Nicholson, who had a notably varied career as a colonial official, undoubtedly had absorbed the latest practices in town planning while in London. His plan for Annapolis, which became the capital of Maryland colony, included circles and squares and diagonal streets. For Williamsburg, built as the Virginia colony's capital under special legislation, Nicholson planned a principal street (Duke of Gloucester Street) with major buildings at either end and a market square and a palace green on either side of the street's midpoint.[11] Oglethorpe, who also had likely studied European town planning, designed and laid out the lead settlement of his and his fellow proprietors' Georgia colony. On top of a grid, Oglethorpe created a number of wards, each consisting of forty house lots, and at each ward center he provided an open square, on two sides of which were trustees' lots set aside for churches, stores, places of assembly, and similar public services.[12] Oglethorpe's Savannah became the prototype for other towns founded in Georgia before 1800. In sporadic legislation that created specific towns, the proprietors (or trustees), the later colonial government, and the still later state government continued to favor the Savannah plan.[13]

Another colonial proprietor who doubtless drew on his awareness of European town planning schemes was William Penn, who hoped that those who bought surveyed land for the founding of towns would lay out and design those towns in a rational fashion. His own proposal, generally ignored, was that settlers should lay out house lots along a grid around a square, with outlying farm lots contiguous to each house lot.[14] Actual town layouts in Pennsylvania were quite different in shape. In Germantown, a well-documented early village, the original settlers laid out a one-street town, with a row of houses and narrow gardens and fields strung out behind them. But, no "center" developed, no focal point for marketing, milling, governmental activity, religion, or education. Buildings of a public character were scattered throughout the area.[15] Like New England towns, those in the mid-Atlantic region usually failed to develop into well-designed communities unless they became substantial service centers.

Although he failed to generate much interest in his proposals for the laying out of ordinary towns, Penn was heavily involved in the planning of his capital city, Philadelphia, which was laid out in 1683 by Captain Thomas Holme, whom Penn had appointed as surveyor general of Pennsylvania. Philadelphia was designed as a grid but with a central square and subsidiary squares situated at intervals as the grid expanded. Later Thomas Penn and his brothers, as subsequent proprietors, laid out various county seats in the backcountry from the 1730s to the 1770s, selecting sites that were chosen either for the distance from Philadelphia, the capital city, or, in the western reaches of the colony, for their centrality.[16]

By the eighteenth century in New York too, towns were surveyed and laid out all the way from the Hudson Valley to the Niagara frontier. Both linear and grid patterns could be found. In the early eighteenth century a farm settlement of Palatine Germans dotted the King's Highway along the Hudson, forming a kind of "street village," with a glebe (or land reserved for the clergy) at the center. When others—English, Scottish, and Dutch settlers—joined them, the glebe was subdivided into a grid in 1752, creating the new river town of Newburgh. Another new river town, Lansingburgh, was laid out in 1770 along the Hudson as a real estate speculation for Abraham Lansing. The surveyor, Joseph Blanchard, designed a grid with a central village square. In 1783 twelve proprietors from New England laid out another town in a grid pattern at Claverack Landing along the Hudson. Other New Englanders prevailed upon Jacob D. Vanderheyden in 1786 to undertake a speculative subdivision of his estate south of Lansingburgh. Vanderheyden copied Lansingburgh's grid and created Troy. Farther inland, many of the towns that developed were not planned and laid out but began as crossroads hamlets, slowly expanding along highways without a plan. But the land companies who bought large chunks of the frontier toward the Niagara River tried to plan and lay out towns on their lands. Land agents such as Joseph Ellicott of the Holland Land Company usually designed towns with a relentless grid pattern.[17]

The only group in the English colonies to found and build their own towns according to strict specifications were the communalistic Moravians, who were carefully directed from the sect's headquarters in Herrndorf, Germany, where all plans had to be approved. Each town the Moravians built was planned around a central square and an open green, and was visually dominated by their church building. All their towns, whether as industrial or craft centers (Bethlehem), agricultural service centers (Lebanon or Emmaus in Pennsylvania, and Hope in New Jersey) or educational centers (Lititz in Pennsylvania), were carefully planned; all involved variations of the linear or grid patterns.[18]

In the English colonies a substantial clustering of settlement occurred only if a concentration of services made economic or political sense. The typical layout was grid or linear. It was rare for a town planner to design a community with more sophistication and beauty than was indicated for what was almost universally regarded to be a utilitarian real estate exercise. The names of Francis Nicholson, James Oglethorp, and William Penn were distinctive in this regard.

Still, most designed towns had a public space as part of their setting, which indicated that town designers saw a need for a place for public functions. Unless a town became a substantial service center, however, during the seventeenth and eighteenth centuries it had no clearly demarcated residential, commercial, and public areas. Houses in the towns were quite similar to those on farmsteads, that is, they frequently contained outbuildings on the house lots, and their inhabitants performed activities whose range was like those who lived and worked on farms. Of course, whether families lived in rural settings or in towns, they had to be largely self-sufficient. The chief difference was that, unlike farmhouses, houses in town were clustered on smaller lots and did not directly include fields for large-scale farming activity. Within towns, most craft shops were also the homes of the craftsmen, making for much overlayering of residential and commercial activity. Thus, in many senses, towns in the seventeenth and eighteenth centuries were admixtures of rural, residential, commercial, and public activities, all pursued within a setting not clearly divided into districts of any kind.

The English colonists were not the only European migrants who surveyed and laid out towns, nor the only group to rely on the grid and linear patterns. Both the Spaniards and the French were active town designers in the interior of the continent that would later become part of the United States. The best organized of all the European colonists, the Spanish by 1573 already adhered to regulations that had evolved in piecemeal fashion. Philip II's "Laws of the Indies" remained basically unchanged throughout the entire period of Spanish rule in the Western Hemisphere. These rules revealed an awareness on the part of Spanish officials of the evolution of European municipal design.

Spanish colonists were instructed to select generously sized sites on elevations surrounded by good farm land, with an ample water supply and with fuel and timber present. All towns were to have plazas, either near the shore or, if inland, in the center of town, situated with reference to the four points of the compass. The principal streets were to lead from the middle of each side of the plaza, with minor streets diverging from each corner. In other parts of the town there were to be open spaces for churches and other religious buildings, and sites around the plaza were to be assigned for the town hall, the customs house, the arsenal, a hospital, other public buildings, and shops for merchants. Settlers were to draw lots for sites. Outside the town, a common land was to provide space for recreation and the pasturing of livestock. Beyond the common were to be agricultural lands, with as many parcels as house sites in town, also to be distributed by lot. Remaining farm lands were reserved to the crown for distribution to later settlers. Other regulations dealt with the construction of houses, the planting of seed, and cattle breeding.[19] These prescriptions were not all followed in every town Spanish colonists built, for the colonists had to deal with local conditions, just as the English colonists did. But for more than two centuries these regulations guided town design through Spain's vast domains across much of the Americas.

The French also attempted to plan the shape of settlements in their New World empire. Whether in the form of compact grid layouts (Quebec City, Louisbourg) or expanded linear ones (St. Louis, Montreal), and typically with a *place d'armes* or public space open to the water, French planners (including Champlain, Laclede, and Bienville) established a series of military garrison communities—such as Detroit, Mobile, and New Orleans—which attracted missionaries, traders, and farmers, with narrow strips of farmland stretching back from the rivers or shores where these forts were located.[20]

The houses and buildings constructed by the inhabitants of colonial towns provided the immediate physical setting for individual families and small communities, but they also revealed social and economic meanings, roles, and functions.

The chief public buildings of colonial New England were the meetinghouses, focal points for both civic and religious life. Beyond the garrisonlike appearance of those built in the earliest towns, when defense was a priority, they were box- and barn-like structures, with entrances on one of the long-sides, opposite the pulpit, and had a bell tower attached almost as a separate structure, along one of the short ends.[21]

The most notable nonresidential building in the mid-Atlantic area was the mill, which often could be found at the center of small, unplanned, unde-signed hamlets and villages. Commercial farming involving grain crops and livestock spread through the valleys of this region during the seventeenth and eighteenth centuries, and mills ground grain into flour and spun wool into cloth. During this period the valleys of Pennsylvania, for example, be-came dotted with dozens of mill hamlets.[22] Mills were usually two- or three-story structures made of wood or stone, in which a water wheel turned by a "fall" of water was the energy source for the turning of gears that in turn moved grindstones or carding mechanisms.

In the South, as in New England, the most notable public buildings were civil and religious in nature. Unlike the New England meetinghouse scheme, however, religious and political activities occurred in physically sep-arate spaces, in courthouses and in churches which occupied central locations in towns but characteristically could be found at separate, isolated crossroads in rural areas. The physical layout of civic and religious structures further re-vealed the hierarchical nature of rural Virginia society. In Anglican churches the planter families were assigned pews toward the center of the church. The pulpit, from which ministers explicated the word of God, was also situated in the center of the church, raised significantly above the congregation.[23] Court-houses served as guardians of the law, which above all else secured property in land and slaves and dispensed justice under raised royal insignias and in the king's name, thus expressing that civil authority also came from above.[24] In this way, church and courthouse, the locations for religious and secular authority, confirmed the patriarchal nature of rural Virginia.

By contrast, evangelical Christianity and revolutionary republicanism, when they emerged in the late eighteenth century, both emphasized the im-portance of the individual as the basis for a just society, and in so doing they profoundly questioned the legitimacy of a patriarchal society, with all its obli-gations and duties. These two movements produced contractual communi-ties that featured houses with increasingly private spaces; new churches without pulpits and with graduated pews, organized as unstructured meeting halls; and courthouses shorn of royal authority and based upon written contracts or constitutions expressing the will of the people.[25]

In New England the typical colonial house was small, of one story, with little ornamentation. The earliest houses were sometimes one-room log huts or cottages and blockhouses or garrison houses in newly settled frontier settlements. When an area became secure, one- or one-and-a-half-story wood frame houses with several rooms became the norm, with wood paneling inside and clapboard outside. By the mid- to late eighteenth century, more affluent New Englanders built larger, two-story houses with architectural details borrowed from prevailing European styles, such as Georgian and a later American variation, Federal. Better-off New Englanders began to build homes not only for greater comfort but also as a measure of social status.[26]

In the mid-Atlantic colonies, in Germantown, Pennsylvania, for example, houses at their most primitive were either wooden huts (with dirt floor and ceiling, stone hearth in the gable end, wooden shutters over slit windows, and a clapboard roof), or houses of log or stone (with a steep German roof or gable and a garret above the main interior room), or an enlarged version of either of these (with full stone-walled cellars, entirely underground, and extra rooms tacked on). The larger houses were the traditional two-story English stone house with Germanic variations in detail (two stories high, with four windows, no outbuildings, but full stone cellars). Long, narrow, almost windowless frame buildings or tenements housed single workmen. Small, one-story frame or stone workshops stood beside their craft or trade owners' houses or at the end of the alleys behind them. By the end of the eighteenth century, as a significant craft center, Germantown had one hundred separate buildings for craftsmen and tradesmen who no longer worked in their homes. Most were small stone or frame workshops, usually one story and with dimensions of fifteen by sixteen feet. These shops crowded the edge of the road beside the owners' houses or at least were visible at the end of the alleys that ran behind the houses. Germantown appears to have been a town most of whose families were of middling circumstances. They lived in a few rooms, engaged in crafts or trades in shops separated from their homes, and sometimes employed others.[27]

In the South, in a rural area such as Middlesex County, Virginia, one could find so-called tobacco houses (long, narrow wooden structures for drying the main staple crop of the region) and rail fences (surrounding the cultivated fields) and farmers' houses (small, framed, with unpainted wood and pounded-in posts, and floors of earth or above-ground planks). Such houses did not have foundation walls, and deterioration was a constant problem. The white settlers built structures conducive to income rather than to comfort; stone was scarce, and bricklayers were few and expensive. But in the case of planters' estates, this simple and skimpy construction was augmented. More substantial homes contained (on the main floor) an inner room (a private room for husband and wife), a common room (for cooking, eating, and entertaining), and, upstairs, a windowless room (for children and maidservants). The homes of more successful planters included sundry outbuildings, with specific functions—cooking, for example—removed from the house altogether.[28]

In Virginia as a whole, the homes of ordinary farmers and small planters were built rather flimsily but with a regularity that suggests a "grammar" of folk architecture spread along with colonial settlement. The plain Virginia house was a one- or a one-and-a-half-story frame dwelling with two rooms on the ground floor and a chimney on the gable at one or both ends, sometimes made of brick but more often of wood with a clay lining. The house was covered with unpainted clapboards, and the windows sometimes had glass, sometimes wooden shutters. The great planters' houses, by contrast, became elaborate, overt physical expressions of social values. The large, main building, with many symmetrical dependent structures surrounding it, mirrored the patriarchal authority of the planter as head of an extended household. *Within* their largely self-sufficient rural communities, private, isolated planter families became communally oriented patriarchs. Similarly the slave settlements or quarters on the larger plantations were communal dwelling spaces. A continuation of the communal life they or their ancestors had experienced in African village society, the communalism of the slaves assumed physical form in their common, shared quarters. This was in sharp contrast to the communalism of the planters, who dominated their closed plantation communities from a house that contained only their families and their slave servants.[29]

Throughout the colonies most settlers inhabited small houses with few rooms or divisions of any kind. The home of the typical town dweller during the seventeenth and eighteenth centuries had a main room or "hall," usually with an additional back room and upstairs chamber. Space was not divided into rooms with particular functions. In the hall the family ate, bathed, worked, rested, learned, played, and even slept and engaged in sexual activity if the house was a one-room structure. Pieces of furniture had several uses and were moved to various positions depending upon the use at a given time. Varied utensils were used to prepare what the family needed for food and clothing, as most families approached being self-sufficient.[30]

The result was that most settlers, whether in rural areas or towns, lived in small, undifferentiated domestic spaces with little privacy. This lack of di-

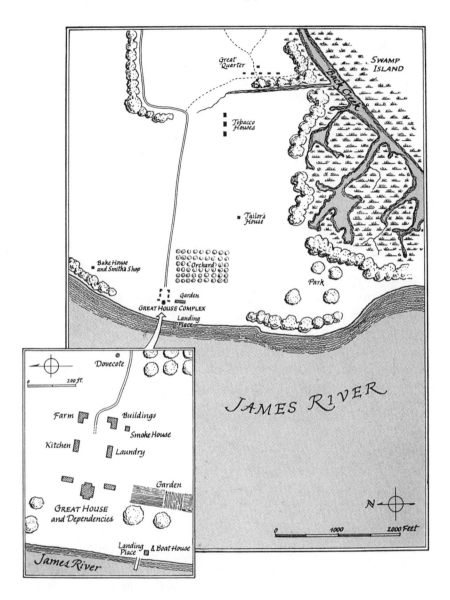

A PLANTATION SETTING. This drawing, based upon a 1742 surveyor's plat of the Carter family plantation, Shirley, shows the clustered settlement or village-like character of the plantations that emerged throughout the tidewater area of the Chesapeake Bay country during the seventeenth and eighteenth centuries. [Rhys Isaac, *The Transformation of Virginia, 1740–1790*]

vision according to activity or function in their domestic spaces mirrored the dispersed, undifferentiated way most colonists settled on the land and the poorly demarcated residential, commercial, and public spaces in their towns. In their land, their towns, and their houses, most settlers during the seventeenth and eighteenth centuries did not separate rooms or communities or farmsteads into functional divisions.

Among the groups in the colonies who tried to build their own utopias, the Puritans and the Moravians stood out. As the Puritans generally failed to lay out their towns, only the Moravians were designers of utopian settlements in various parts of the English colonies. The Moravians crafted distinctive buildings for their towns. In Bethlehem, Pennsylvania, the *Gemeinhaus* was a community center, a building that served as a church and church office, a town hall, and a hospice—like the Puritans' meetinghouse, only more so. Christian Reuter laid out Salem, North Carolina, in 1766, but did so under detailed instructions and a model plan sent to him a year earlier by Friedrich Marshall from Bethlehem, Pennsylvania. Marshall specified that, even though the group was communalistic in nature, separate houses should be built on separate lots, and the lots should be relatively small, so that the town would not spread out too much. When the Reverend David Zeisberger laid out Schoenbrun, Ohio, in 1772, his plan took the appropriate form of a cross.[31]

## · II ·

DURING THE NINETEENTH CENTURY, already-established towns in the East sometimes assumed a different form from the one they had had in the seventeenth and eighteenth centuries. In New England, by the early nineteenth century, in some of the smaller towns, the town center (where the meetinghouse and common were located) became a commercial service center, as the growth of economic activity and of improved road networks and postal connections made a clustering of services for farmers a natural development. Public activity grew around the meetinghouse lots, which abutted what became known as village "greens" (the old commons land). Unplanned, unplatted grid or linear layouts extended beyond these new centers, with stores, shops, offices, government facilities, academies, churches, and houses for the nonfarming population arrayed around what became much more significant focal points. An opportunistic, speculative quality characterized the growth of these service centers, as center village lots became a good investment, especially with the encirclement of the prime meetinghouse lots.[32]

As economic activity became more commercialized and village society assumed a more hierarchical shape, more elaborate houses turned into status symbols for a growing elite. A significant house rebuilding phenomenon occurred in New England at the turn of the eighteenth century as older one-story houses were enlarged into two-story dwellings, with domestic outbuildings—kitchens, woodsheds, washhouses—added to the main edifices. Wherever there was a density of the agricultural population or an intensification of market-oriented agriculture—such as along the Atlantic coast or up the Connecticut River valley—an array of two-story houses rather dramatically appeared. These palatial town houses were meant to enhance the prestige and influence of prominent villagers, to show their enterprise and good taste. As before, the towns lagged significantly behind the coastal cities in the diffusion of architectural styles. The most prestigious village houses incorporated details of the Georgian and then the Greek Revival styles, following the example of the coastal urban elite.[33]

Colonial meetinghouses were also commonly rebuilt at the turn of the eighteenth and in the early nineteenth century as churches and town halls became separate structures, reflecting the growing distance between the increasingly varied religious and civic lives of the towns. Many congregations in New England removed their colonial-style, boxlike meetinghouses or replaced them with classically proportioned churches. Sometimes these were built on new sites if the town center had moved away from the original common and meetinghouse. In new, classically designed churches, the entrances and the pulpits were shifted to the opposite gable ends of the building. There was also a marked increase in ornamentation and the addition of a spire. Most church designs reflected the builder's translation of Georgian, Federal, or Greek Revival styles into the vernacular. The town common, with its meetinghouse lot, evolved into a secular village "green."[34]

Within the mid-Atlantic region, a distinctive type of layout emerged by the turn of the eighteenth century in eastern Pennsylvania and into Maryland and a portion of Virginia, in both planned and unplanned towns, whatever their arrangement during the colonial era. The features of this distinctive design were (1) the presence of lots of compact row houses, with little space between the houses or between the houses and the street; (2) a lack of clear spatial division between private and public structures, between residences and shops or offices, with churches, cemeteries, schools, parks, and playgrounds consigned to peripheral locations; (3) the widespread use of red brick for all buildings, though there were some stone and stucco structures; (4) the frequent appearance of duplexes; (5) the inclusion of "diamond-shaped" public spaces (with a right-angle intersection of two streets at a central point, with the rectangular corners cut from the four adjoining blocks); and (6) a prevalence of narrow back streets or alleys, open to traffic, with buildings facing them.[35] These features suggest that in the mid-Atlantic area the tendency to differentiate town spaces into residential, public, and commercial was not as far advanced as in New England.

The evidence is similar for neighboring New York. In Kingston, a rural town in an agricultural area situated along the Hudson River, in 1820 just over half the shops and stores were also identifiable as the homes of their proprietors.[36]

By contrast, in the South, as in New England, rebuilding and redesigning appeared in established towns by the nineteenth century—though the direction, again as in New England, was toward a greater definition of public squares, commercial zones, and residential areas. This was the case, for example, in Columbia, Franklin, and Murfreesboro, three county seats in middle Tennessee.[37]

Not all the eastern seaboard states were fully settled by the nineteenth century, particularly in the South, where a rural population retained its dispersed character over the broad valleys of the south Atlantic region. In Georgia especially could be found undeveloped land, with considerable territory still occupied by native tribes. The Georgia state legislature maintained the active town-planning initiatives of the colony's original proprietors. Up to the 1830s the state legislature also created about fifty county seats as unoccupied lands were opened for settlement and as native tribes agreed to further land cessions.

The Georgia legislature appointed commissioners to oversee the actual laying out of the county seats, which were planned to center on a courthouse square. If a courthouse was to be situated on an already existing settlement on a trading route or on an important road, the courthouse was located facing the main existing thoroughfare. If newly planned, the courthouse was placed in a central square, with streets entering at either the sides or the center of the courthouse, as was already the case in Virginia and the Carolinas. As for layouts beyond the square, the commissioners favored the grid pattern but insisted that the focal point of the town be its courthouse square.[38]

As Georgia ended its initial practice of granting land for the establishment of county seats, the state's General Assembly passed specific acts for the purpose, with provisions for the appointment of commissioners and the amount of land they were permitted to buy. In the earliest acts, during the 1780s, the legislature carefully controlled location, lot size, and even the lots to be reserved for the courthouse, an academy, and churches when such towns as Washington, Augusta, Greensboro, Waynesboro, and St. Marys were laid out. In Washington the money derived from the sale of the lots was to be used for a courthouse, a jail, a school, and a cemetery. Waynesboro was located along an already existing settlement. In Greensboro it was hoped that the sale of town and farm lots would bring in sufficient revenues to start a university. In St. Marys, subscribers to lots had to build a house of a speci-fied size by a specified time or forfeit their lots.[39]

In both the New England and the mid-Atlantic regions during the nine-teenth century, a new kind of town emerged in already settled areas: the mill/factory village. In many locations scattered through New Hampshire, Massachusetts, Rhode Island, New York, and Pennsylvania, where water power was already harnessed for milling operations involving grain, lumber, minerals (iron), and livestock (wool), certain individuals, partners, or corp-orations sometimes set up a "factory," adapting or constructing a mill as the energy source for their machine-made product. At other times such in-dustrialists built entire villages—mills, housing, stores, recreational facili-ties—around new or existing mill sites, creating streetscapes and designing buildings.

There quickly came to be a recognizable appearance to mill villages. A roadway always followed the waterway along which the mill was built. The mill itself was a three-story structure with a clerestory or gallery along the shorter top floor, long rows of large windows on the larger first and second floors, a bell cupola or tower in the center (to signify work hours to employ-ees), and a doorway with an overhang and a pulley (so that material could be hoisted into or out of the building). Designers of mill factories drew elements from barns, churches, and existing mills, lifting design features from each to create buildings that would function well for a new purpose: machine-made products. The earliest large-scale machine production involving one contin-uous process enclosed within a single building was the making of cotton cloth, the first great mass-produced, machine-made consumer good.

Near the mill were workers' tenements made of brick or wood. Farther away were superintendents' houses, and farther still were the mansions of the owners (if they lived locally and were not absentee). In the Rockdale mill dis-trict south of Philadelphia, in Pennsylvania, the actual physical layout of seven adjoining mill villages mirrored the socially hierarchical nature of the local society in the sense that the workers' tenements were almost at mill level

while the superintendents' homes were on higher elevations and the owners' mansions on still higher ground.[40]

As mill/factory villages spread through the river valleys of New England and the mid-Atlantic regions during the time that waterpower was the only significant energy source for the operation of machines, a new kind of small local community came into existence, one with a familiar layout. An incubator of modern industrial enterprise, a place where large-scale machine production and concentrations of wage laborers as machine operators coalesced, the mill village was the only possible location for industry before the development of steam power and electricity, as one product after another be-

FACTORIES. The diagram of a factory mill village, above, displays the ingredients of a community that was organized socially and economically in hierarchical fashion but was physically quite compact. Opposite, the mill factory building, top, was an architectural amalgam of preexisting forms, with builders drawing on structural features of churches, barns, and mills to create a form that was practical and remarkably durable and unchanged. Owners of the early factories sometimes built workers' tenements, below, that in architectural detail did not differ greatly from the factory buildings themselves. [Above, Anthony Wallace, *Rockdale;* opposite, Serge Hambourg, *Mills and Factories of New England*]

came machine made and mass produced during the course of the nineteenth century.

Settlement moved beyond the Appalachian Mountains across the continent to the Pacific coast during the nineteenth century. Throughout this vast territory, towns that were planned and designed were usually laid out in a simple grid pattern. Just as Congress in its ordinances of the 1780s decreed that the vast Northwest Territory was to be surveyed and sold in rectangular lots, so too did town planners there and elsewhere almost automatically create grids for their new settlements. Both the sale of public land by Congress and the planning and sale of town lots by promoters were greatly simplified by a procedure that turned the landscape into equal lots, thereby ignoring completely the terrain's greatly varied topographical configurations.[41] But just as "squat-

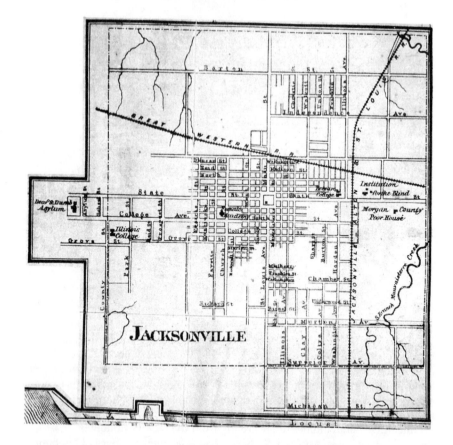

TOWN LAYOUT. By the mid-nineteenth century the street layouts of many towns were depicted in atlases. The common grid pattern can be seen in this map of Jacksonville, Illinois, in 1863, with its central courthouse square. [Henry Francis Walling, *Map of the State of Illinois*]

ters" settled within the natural contours of the land along the frontier, so too other towns just naturally developed, without design or plan, along roads and waterways, and rail lines.

Almost never was a "linear" alternative considered (as was the case in the seventeenth and eighteenth centuries) in a planned town. The grid pattern meant that the town could expand indefinitely, subject only to topographical obstacles. Since the design of planned towns was closely related to the interest of the original promoters in having a successful real estate venture, a design that was especially easy to survey and that could be indefinitely repeated had enormous appeal. As in the seventeenth and eighteenth centuries, so too in the nineteenth: exceptions to the prevailing pattern were rare.

The promoters and speculators of Franklinville and Lystra in Kentucky presented elaborate plans for each of their towns in 1796, drawing on the latest in European design and featuring circles, with sites for town halls, churches, colleges, and theatres—but there is no indication that either town was ever laid out.[42] In 1827 William Bullock, an English traveler and lecturer, purchased a tract of land and hired John Buomarotti Papworth as his town planner. Papworth's plan for Hygeia (as he called it) incorporated most of the building designs and street layouts developed in England during the preceding century: detached villas, semi-detached houses, terrace dwellings, small and large residential squares typical of Georgian and Regency builders, as well as an elaborate street layout with diagonal and even circular shapes, along with public spaces that were squares within circles and that were located in complicated places within the overall scheme. There was no clearly defined center; the public activities of the proposed town were to be located in buildings in unrelated parts of the plan. Such an elaborate scheme never led to an actual laying out of the town.[43]

Jeffersonville, Indiana, was laid out by the territorial governor, William Henry Harrison, in 1802 as a county seat in honor of the president and in response to suggestions that Jefferson himself had made for the design of a town. The town, laid out by John Gwathmey, featured a pattern of continuous squares and diagonal streets. So uncongenial did the actual settlers find this design, however, that, within fifteen years of the founding, the proprietors of the town lots persuaded the legislature to allow them to replat the town into a conventional grid pattern.[44]

When the county seat of Pickaway County, Ohio, was selected by three commissioners soon after 1810, Daniel Driesbach was chosen to lay out the town. Driesbach made use of the mounds that remained from a native tribal spiritual site and created Circleville, with the principal street a circle for a courthouse, and eight other streets radiating out from the circle. Once again, disgruntled owners of lots petitioned the legislature to permit the replatting of the town. The legislature created the Circleville Squaring Company, charged with the responsibility of gaining the consent of the owners to replat as a grid. The group accomplished this in stages over twenty years as Circleville gradually was transmogrified into a square![45]

Those who settled in planned towns typically came from states to the east. For example, Hudson, Michigan, was settled in 1834 by Daniel Hudson and others from New York. Chilton, Wisconsin, was first settled in 1845 by Moses Stanton from Rhode Island. Early settlers in Grundy Center, Iowa, in 1856 came from Ohio, New York, Pennsylvania, and New England. Daniel Miller of Lancaster County, Pennsylvania, in 1808 laid out Millersburg in the same state. Rockville, Indiana, was settled in 1824 by migrants from Pennsylvania, Ohio, Kentucky, and Tennessee. Petersburg, Illinois, was laid out in 1836, with settlers chiefly from Kentucky and Pennsylvania. By contrast, other towns were settled by groups from Europe. Hermann, Missouri, was created by the German Settlement Society of Philadelphia, which bought land with river bluffs that reminded settlers of their home in the Rhineland. Still other towns continued to be settled by land companies. Apalachicola, Florida, was laid out in 1821 in the usual grid pattern by the Apalachicola Land Company.[46]

A common sort of planned town throughout the South and Midwest in the nineteenth century was the county seat with its courthouse square. An important center in the rural areas of Pennsylvania and the Southern colonies during the seventeenth and eighteenth centuries, when it was typically the only substantial town in a given county, the county seat continued to be the largest town and trade center in the county as settlement spread inland, across the Appalachian Mountains into the Mississippi and Ohio valleys and onto the plains. As earlier, government officials sometimes selected a new site as county seat but might also choose an already forming, unplanned cluster of settlement which then became planned. The great heartland of the county seat stretched from Georgia, through Kentucky and Tennessee, then to Indiana and Illinois, Missouri and Iowa, and down to Texas. Its courthouse square, though ostensibly the location for the seat of county government, was also a great public place, used as a business center, as the focal point of social and cultural activity, and as a symbol of civic pride.[47]

Court house squares could be both overwhelming and monotonous to visitors. One who visited Missouri in 1902 said, "I've been in Missouri for six weeks now and every town I've struck had a square until I got sick of the sight of them. If you ask where the hotel is, 'It's on the east side of the square.' The bank is on the 'corner of the square,' and such and such a fellow lives a block or so from the 'square.' Everything is calculated from the 'square.' . . ."[48]

As in the East during the eighteenth century, so in the Midwest and inland South in the nineteenth century, builders of these squares and their courthouses copied from one another as fashions in layout and building design emerged. In Missouri, for example, the overriding consideration in the territorial and then the state government's choice of sites for county seats was centrality of location—that the site proposed by the county commissioners be equidistant for all residents of the county, with proximity to waterways and, later, railways a prime consideration.[49] As in the Atlantic seaboard states, the courthouse squares in Missouri were at the center of the street layout, with streets in the grid entering the square, either singly or doubly, at the ends or at the sides or middle of the courthouse, which was located in the middle of the central square.[50]

As for the courthouses themselves, the Missouri legislature, from its early territorial phase, beginning in 1820, governed the construction of county buildings. The county courts were responsible for choosing commissioners who in turn selected the lot for the court and jail, presented a plan, advertised for bids, contracted with builders, and even chose the materials. County commissioners were required to use funds raised from the sale of building lots in the county seat for the construction of the public buildings, or, if that proved insufficient, to raise taxes for that purpose. The courthouse as a building was typically a multi-purpose center, providing space for civic, social, educational, and religious activities. Courthouses sometimes contained separate quarters for women, especially those who had come into town on a day's outing. If the county government did not occupy the entire building, the courthouse might contain rental space. Sometimes jails were also located in the buildings.

An appointed courthouse commissioner usually drew up the plan for the building. Gradually, during the nineteenth century, these commissioners turned to trained architects to design the courthouses, usually choosing someone from the area. Courthouse builders also made use of architectural pattern books, such as G. P. Randall's *Handbook of Designs* (1868). When the county court approved a design, it opened the contract for bids and tried to stay within its funding once construction began. The favored building material was brick or stone.[51] The earliest architectural styles were in the vernacular, made of log and frame and then of brick. The classic style was the plain "four square," or nearly square, two-story building, but fancier variations occasionally appeared, influenced by neoclassical revival, Georgian, French, or Romanesque designs.[52]

Another kind of layout was adopted during the nineteenth century by the planners and promoters of railroad towns. Various railroad corporations and their ancillary townsite companies developed three basic designs for their towns with respect to street layout, placement of the business district, and the railroad station, whose presence created the need for a design that went somewhat beyond a simple grid. The "symmetric" design was the earliest, developed by the first railroad line to create railroad towns, the Illinois Central. The track itself provided the central throughway for the town, with a wide right-of-way for facilities such as lumber yards and grain elevators that needed direct rail access. Two business streets ran parallel to the track, on either side, one of which sometimes became the principal street. A somewhat

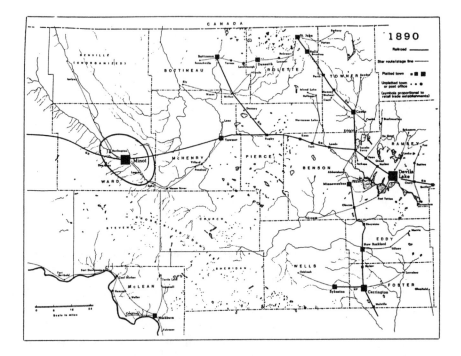

RAILROAD TOWNS. The dramatic impact of the railroads on the settlement of areas they built through can be seen in these maps showing settlement in North Dakota over a twenty-year period. Above, 1890. Opposite, 1900 and 1910. [John Hudson, *Plains Country Towns*]

later design, out on the plains, was the "orthogonal," in which the railroad company built a depot near the main street crossing in the middle of the townsite. A still later design was the "T," in which the main street began at the tracks, creating a T formation. In such layouts there was no central intersection, and the business blocks were typically located on a cross street down from the depot.[53]

Mining towns also assumed a special pattern that reflected their special purpose. They typically had densely built-up Main Streets crammed into a small, rugged space—a canyon or a hillside—with miners' houses as well as the mines themselves and attendant buildings all dotting the hillsides.[54] In the company towns built by mining and lumber corporations, layouts varied from unplanned, meandering sites that followed the typical canyon settings to well-surveyed grids on whatever relatively flat topography there was, depending on whether the company had taken over a randomly shaped mining or lumber camp or had developed a town from its inception. In either case, the uniformity of the structures built by the company for the town—not the

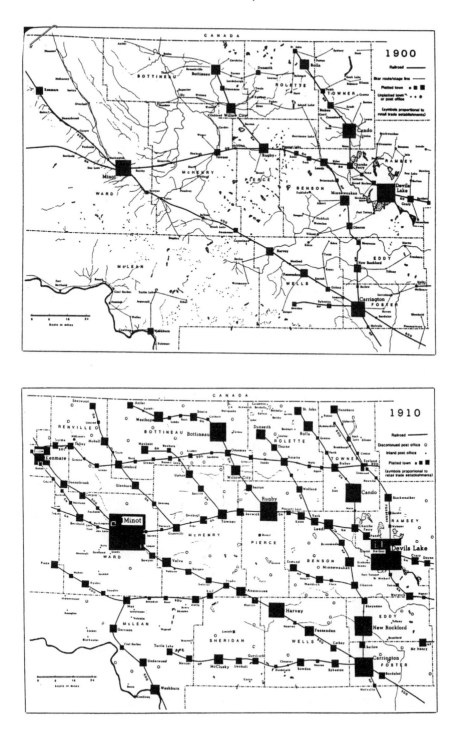

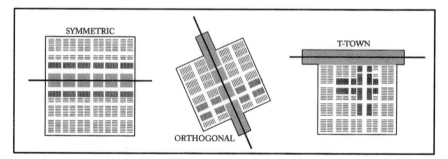

RAILROAD TOWN DESIGNS. The development companies that actually planned the towns along rail lines drew on three basic designs for their layouts. [Hudson, *Plains Country Towns*]

overall layouts, which were quite ordinary—made company towns distinctive in their appearance.[55]

Among the many groups who sought to build towns with a utopian purpose during the nineteenth century, none equaled the Mormons as designers. The Mormons drew up a plat for the idealized City of Zion, which was to be God's headquarters after his second coming. The plan indicated that the Mormons should live in a mile-square city laid out in a grid pattern, with central lots reserved for public buildings and uses and with farmlands surveyed outside the city.[56] The Mormons used this plan for many of their settlements, both in the Midwest and later in Utah after their trek across the plains.[57] Other utopian groups were less innovative in the layouts of their towns. The Harmony Society, led by George Rapp, used simple grid plans for its communities in Harmony, Pennsylvania, and Economy, Ohio. Robert Owen was an exception. He drew up plans for towns that he hoped his followers would build in America, but none ever did so, perhaps because the plans were so novel. Owen envisioned a quadranglelike enclosure, much like a fort or a garrison, with public squares repeated throughout the enclosure. Within the squares were public buildings, and on three of the four sides were family dwellings, with children's dormitories on the fourth side. Outside of the enclosure were buildings for crafts, farm buildings and stables, and, finally, agricultural land.[58]

Even the unplanned, tiny clusters of settlement (or hamlets) that emerged during the nineteenth century assumed recognizable forms, if not conscious designs or plans. Growing up around a post office, a mill, a general store, a church, or a school, such bits of community usually took on a linear form but also were "radial," that is, stretched out along roads that intersected, or in some cases along streets that had been added to the original roadways.[59]

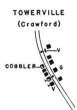

TOWERVILLE
(Crawford)

v

COBBLER G

Linear type of hamlet
not located at road in-
tersections.

RISING SUN
(Crawford)

CH

S. AND H.

BS

Linear type located at road
intersections.

0  ¼  ½ MI.

LEMONWEIR
(Juneau)

S

Complex
plan group.

BARRE MILLS
(La Crosse)

S

G

S

Linear type associated with
crooked roads.

TWIN GROVE
(Green)

V

S

V

TRUCK BARN

Radial type associated
with an intersection in-
volving four or more
roads.

NEWBURG CORNERS
(La Crosse)

S

CH

TH

Too tiny to have a
distinct ground
plan.

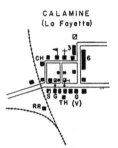

CALAMINE
(La Fayette)

CH
3
6

S G G
RR TH (V)

Some evidence of a
street pattern dis-
tinct from the high-
ways on which they
are located.

MARXVILLE
(Dane)

V
V
V

S

Radial type associated
with an intersection in-
volving three roads.

BLACK HAWK
(Sauk)

L

5

S(v)

BS

G
S

Binodal or two-cluster
plan.

LEGEND

■ NON-FARM RESIDENCE
■ GROUP OF RESIDENCES
⊠ FARMSTEAD
◪ COMBINATION RESIDENCE
   AND BUSINESS
⊥ FILLING STATION
S■ STORE
G■ GARAGE
▼■ SCHOOL
+■ CHURCH
C■ CREAMERY
CH■ CHEESE FACTORY

PO■ POST OFFICE
⊠ BLACKSMITH
BS■ BARBER SHOP
—■ TAVERN
▲ SAW MILL
▼ GRIST MILL
V VACANT
TH■ TOWN HALL
H■ HALL
RR■ RAILROAD
⊞ CEMETERY

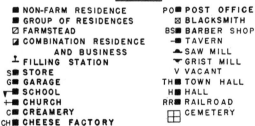

HAMLETS. The most embryonic form of clustered settlement, hamlets
assumed an astonishing variety of forms. This composite of drawings shows
Wisconsin hamlets. [Glenn Trewartha, "The Unincorporated Hamlet,"
*Annals of the Association of American Geographers*]

In towns across the continent through the nineteenth century, increasing uniformity characterized the styles of the buildings that were constructed. Residential, public, and commercial areas of towns became more demarcated and separated. Vernacular styles jostled with imported European styles as builders sought to incorporate local building materials and local designs with the latest architectural influences from Europe. Buildings in all sections of towns—commercial, public, residential—displayed the influence of a succession of European styles: Georgian, Federal, Greek Revival, Neo-Gothic, French Second Empire, Italianate, Queen Anne Revival, Victorian Renaissance, Victorian Functional, Chicago Commercial, Beaux Arts Classical.[60]

Builders came to rely on pattern books, which contained scaled-down versions of the major architectural styles. "Pattern book" buildings gradually displaced vernacular styles. Andrew Jackson Downing, the first influential landscape and building architect, wrote a pattern book that became highly popular during the middle of the century. Downing drew upon the English cottage, but other authors popularized styles from other parts of Europe, adaptable to residential, commercial, or public uses.[61]

Towns founded and developed during the nineteenth century usually had a main business and public street, often named Main Street. Even towns founded earlier, in the East, sometimes later designated their principal street by the same name. Main Street came to stand for the center of town, the place where commercial, industrial, political, and social activity occurred, the public core of the community, connected to but often physically set off from residential areas—though where one ended and the other began often was not precisely demarcated, and indeed changed over time. Horses and wagons and stagecoaches moved riders over roadways that typically intersected in town centers, with inns and hotels often at the center of the town. Railroads brought passengers to rail stations, which also often occupied a central location. Town halls and county courthouses were sites for political and governmental activities, and were usually at a town's center as well.

Hermon W. De Long remembered that Main Street in Dansville, New York, in the 1850s and 1860s was muddy and dusty (depending on the season), "oftentimes perilous and always inconvenient."[62]

But Anne Dodge remembered that the Main Street in late-nineteenth-century Stonington, Connecticut, was filled with horses and carriages "clop clopping up and down the street." To her the "most nostalgic sound in the world . . . [was] the sound of horse's hoofs on a dirt road." Main Street in

MAIN STREETS. By the late nineteenth century, wide-angle photographs of entire towns, or at least of their Main Streets, were fairly common. Most towns across the continent exhibited a clear division between commercial and residential areas, as in Fountain City, Wisconsin, top. A major street, Main Street, was the commercial center, as in Atchison, Kansas, below. [Top, Gerhard Gesell Collection; below, Library of Congress]

summer, she remembered, "was as much an outdoor living room as a street."[63]

Main Streets typically went through several stages of physical development, linked to the growth of a town. For example, in northeast Oregon, towns in the earliest stage had Main Streets that were areas of one-story buildings, widely spaced, with gable-ended false fronts, made of wood with frame construction, and situated on alternate lots. Stage two was a mixture of one- and two-story buildings, with a few bricks structures, and most lots filled in. Stage three was a mixture of one- and two-story structures in close proximity, with some made of brick and stone. Stage four consisted of uniformly two-story, tightly packed buildings, mostly of brick and stone. Stage one towns were small, pioneer towns. Stage two towns were distant from industry and railroads, with economies based upon the surrounding districts. Stage three towns had economies with both industry and services for the surrounding area and were linked to the regional economy, perhaps even to the national economy. Stage four towns were rapidly growing and sometimes evolved into cities. No matter which stage (short of stage four), such towns usually had two-block Main Street business districts, with a nearby but separate ancillary zone containing public or institutional buildings, such as schools and churches.[64]

Around these edifices were arrayed the commercial and professional firms located in town. Craft shops no longer typically fused commercial and residential space, as more and more products were mass produced by machine power in buildings separate from the retail shops where such products were sold. But the commercial edifices that were built in the business districts of nineteenth-century towns continued typically to be multi-use buildings, with upper floors containing spaces for purposes different from those of the street-level floors—as offices or even as apartments, thus continuing to some extent to merge residential and commercial functions in a single building. As public education became virtually universal during the course of the century, and as a variety of Christian denominations and sects typically gained adherents in most towns, churches and schools came to define particular sections of town, with the more substantial towns divided into several school districts and parishes.

Commercial and public buildings were usually made of wood in the early years of a town's existence. Brick and stone edifices (more durable) were an indication of growth and maturity. Unpaved streets for transportation by horse and buggy and wooden platforms for pedestrians were standard until late in the century, with dust and mud and animal urine and dung ever-present aspects of town life. Occupants and users of all commercial and pub-

THE SURFACE OF MAIN STREET. In the nineteenth century Main Streets were unpaved and often had wooden platforms for pedestrians, as in this town near La Crosse, Wisconsin, top. By the turn of the century, some towns had modernized by paving their Main Streets, usually with cobblestones, as in Watertown, Wisconsin, below. [State Historical Society of Wisconsin]

lic buildings relied on well water and oil or gas lanterns and wood-burning stoves and outdoor privies.[65]

By the late nineteenth century, technological innovation brought revolutionary change to the physical appearance of Main Street. Electricity became the energy and lighting source; indoor plumbing was introduced, along with water and sewer systems; the street was paved, first with cobblestone or brick and then with tar-based substances; cement sidewalks were laid; motor vehicles replaced horses as the favored means of transporting people, and interurban trolley systems filled in the older rail network, providing rail connections among neighboring towns.[66]

Residential streets outside the business district were typically unpaved, weed-choked, and grooved by wagon and carriage wheels. The better-traveled streets were periodically smoothed by horse-drawn road graders or, in the winter, by heavy rollers to tamp down snow. But, as with their Main Streets, more affluent towns began to construct cement sidewalks in their residential areas too. The favored material for street paving was at first either brick or cobblestone. Streets were sometimes named in a systematic fashion, often after presidents or trees. But sometimes streets were left unmarked, and houses were better known as a basis for establishing directions. The introduction of house-to-house mail delivery forced towns to erect street signs, at which point they followed post office regulations. When electrical and telephone lines were installed at the turn of the century, they dominated streetscapes, as trees were often cut down. But by the 1920s power companies were emphasizing the placement of poles along "easements" to the rear of homes.[67]

Building styles varied greatly in the residential areas of towns during the nineteenth century, owing in part to the residual presence of local vernacular styles and in part to the socioeconomic makeup of a town. For instance, in eastern Beekmantown, New York, log cabins remained until well into the nineteenth century the most common form of residence, comprising nearly two-thirds of all homes in 1798, and still almost one-third as late as 1855. The original proprietors continued for decades to urge settlers to build "blockhouses" of simple timber or log construction which could be easily clapboarded or added to. The persistence of inexpensive log houses and blockhouses indicates that a town like Beekmantown contained a significant number of inhabitants of a comparatively low socioeconomic status.[68]

Middle-class homes in Waverly, Kansas, during the 1850s and 1860s, Eliza Wiggin remembered, "were set back from the street in large grounds, which added greatly to their beauty and charm, especially when the trees which the first settlers had diligently planted had grown large enough to cast

HOUSES. By the nineteenth century, houses of the middle class, top, in towns across the continent featured architectural details and were photographed in all seasons as an indication of the owner's pride and status in the community. By contrast, in special communities such as company towns, below, housing was monotonously uniform and cheaply designed, an indication that the purpose of such communities was narrowly economic. [Top, Melvin Adelglass Collection; below, James B. Allen, *The Company Town in the American West*]

a delightful shade." She also recalled that "[the] more pretentious homes had white 'picket' fences all around their grounds."[69]

By the late nineteenth century, Rose Wilder Lane remembered that in her town typical houses "had no more architecture than boxes. Usually a gable faced the street, displaying in its window white machine-lace curtains looped back on either side of the many small panes. Between these curtains the glass shone as dark as deep water. . . . [It] was the parlor, if the family could set aside one room solely for receiving callers. If not, it was the front room, and there would be a bed or two in it. . . ."[70]

In a steadily developing Midwestern town such as Jacksonville, Illinois, the wealthy lived in custom-built homes to display their newly acquired wealth, not only for their own generation but for those that followed. Yet even in Jacksonville, many more lived transiently in nondescript frame cottages or four-flat tenements, or in the homes of the wealthy—in attics or basements or in small rooms up steep stairways from the kitchen.[71]

The most unusual housing among nineteenth-century towns, housing that anticipated the large-scale developments of the twentieth century, was that of the Western company towns. The lumber and mining corporations that took over or built these towns constructed houses all at once, usually with a drab, uniform appearance. Building materials were usually the most readily available and the least expensive. Coal camps were constructed of wood, cement block, or crude brick. Lumber towns were without exception built of wood. Mining towns were more varied. Most companies tried to provide comfortable houses for their employees, but for economic considerations they provided no more than basic necessities. A standard floor plan included a kitchen, a living room, two bedrooms, a bath, and sometimes a porch. When companies painted their houses, they typically painted them all the same color.[72]

In a more general sense, what is clear is that during the nineteenth century the homes of town dwellers provided a refuge for the family who lived but no longer worked in them. Homes also proclaimed the status of their owners and did so with increasingly elaborate design. Writers of architectural plan books provided several styles from which a home-builder might express his own taste: Gothic Revival (signifying that the owner was of old English stock); Italianate villa (proclaiming a cultured and artistic household); the French style (indicating a stylish and fashionable home). Style and status meant embellishment with useless ornamentation. The less affluent middle class lived in simple, functional frame houses. Workingmen sometimes occupied shacks, either of their own devising or company houses, single-story sheds with three or four rooms, without garden and front porch, with thin walls and cramped rooms.

The very poor lived in "shacktowns" or "shantytowns," as squatters in makeshift dwellings. The wealthy lived on "the Hill" or "Elm Street," in neighborhoods that were as much as reference to social class as they were a geographical location.[73] In towns with an ethnically or racially mixed population, the neighborhoods containing particular groups sometimes had popular labels. In Jacksonville, Illinois, for example, Portuguese, Irish, and black migrants lived in areas called, respectively, Madeira, the Patch, and Africa.[74]

In contrast to the flexible and varied use of space within seventeenth- and eighteenth-century homes, during the course of the nineteenth century such spaces became increasingly differentiated: rooms began to have particular uses. The extent to which a home displayed this development depended very much on the status and wealth of its inhabitants. In a well-designed middle-class home, on the first floor was the parlor (for formal intercourse with the outside world) and/or a sitting room (where the family engaged in leisure, culture, and recreation), a dining room (where the family gathered for meals), and a kitchen (where the woman of the house prepared food, cleaned clothes and bodies, made supplies, and served meals, if the house had no dining room). On the second floor were three or four bedchambers. As the century progressed, these spaces became increasingly shut off from the outside (or public) world. Furniture became heavier, more "immovable" and "permanent"; windows became shrouded by heavy drapes. For those to whom status was of concern, rooms became increasingly crowded with small accessories. Household furnishings—both furniture and utensils—became more specialized in their use and function.[75]

The only part of a well-ordered middle-class home where private and public space became ambivalent or confused was the porch. Here, in a area protecting them from the weather, family members could view the passing public and were themselves on display yet still in private space. Willis F. Dunbar remembered that in turn-of-the-century Hartford, Michigan, almost everyone had a front porch: "A house would have looked naked to us without one of some sort." Sitting on a front porch provided a "vantage point from which people observed the passing scene."[76] Rose Wilder Lane recalled that "across the front of the house there was invariably a porch. At least one hickory rocker stayed on it in all weathers; on summer afternoons other chairs would be brought from the house and children sat on the steep porch steps. . . ."[77]

The porch developed during the nineteenth century in rural settings

when farmers extended their doorway ledges to protect their guests from in-
clement weather. This in turn expanded into a square porch with a low roof
and several posts. During the mid- to late nineteenth century, the porch grew
to cover much of the front of a house. Its floors were slanted to allow rain-
water to drain. Rocking chairs were added as porch furniture in a still narrow, enclosed area. By the late nineteenth century the porch had grown to
enclose entire homes and had become wider, with more elaborate porch furniture.[78]

The whole question of private versus public reached a pitch of complexity among the communitarian groups that founded towns as utopian experiments. The inhabitants of these communities emphasized the communal
nature of their undertakings. Every such community required space for its
collective activities: churches for community worship; dining halls for feasts;
assembly halls for decision-making; dance halls for social activity. But should
the inhabitants also share domestic space? The various groups responded in
different ways. The groups who inhabited communal dwellings tended to
break up over issues of sex or personal privacy, whereas the groups who built
private dwellings often quarreled over private versus public ownership.[79] For
instance, the followers of Fourier tried to construct the physical arrangements of their phalanxes (or "compact bodies of troops") according to
Fourier's own detailed plans. The main building of each phalanx was called
the phalanstery. All parts of the building were to be connected by interior
streets, called street galleries.[80] In another instance, the True Inspiration
Congregation of Amana, Iowa, avoided the large, communal dwellings of the
Shakers and decided to have families occupy suites within communal houses
grouped in neighborhoods served by communal kitchens, a pattern repeated
throughout their seven villages in Iowa.[81]

The homes of most town dwellers in the nineteenth century continued
to be quite similar to farmsteads in the countryside, except that they were on
contiguous street lots in towns. Like farmsteads, homes in towns contained
other elements. Town houses were embedded in lots filled with service buildings and different kinds of activities. There were gardens and outbuildings
for sanitation, the limited production of food, and trash disposal. Each
household had to grow some of its own food, feed and care for its own animals, acquire its own water through wells, dispose of its own organic and in-
organic waste, store its own fuel for cooking and heating. In various
combinations on town house lots could be found outside kitchens, wash
houses, privies, well-houses, spring-houses, wood or coal sheds, equipment
sheds, poultry sheds, carriage houses and wagon sheds, harness rooms, gra-
naries, potato houses, hay barns, general storage sheds, livestock barns, cel-

lars and pits for storage, a back yard for a garden and animals, woodpiles, clothes-washing apparatus, arbors, trash piles, fences, and walls, along with elements of ornamental display, such as flower beds, improved pathways, and gazebos.[82] Rose Wilder Lane remembered that in the late nineteenth century in her town, "behind the house was the vegetable garden, the woodshed, the chopping block and the well. A path . . . led to a privy near the henhouses and the barn. Every family kept a cow and everyone wanted fine horses and a buggy. . . . Fenced lawns were mowed with scythes or with mowing machines. . . . Vines were trained on strings to shade sunny windows and ends of porches. . . ."[83]

That townhouses were little more than farmhouses in town was a standard situation until late in the nineteenth century, when technological change greatly reduced the need for townspeople to provide for their own sustenance on their house lots. The development of commercial food preparation meant that processing firms who canned or froze foods were able to distribute them over wide areas of the continent. The adaptation of refrigeration to the transport of meat and fish and produce also greatly extended the reach of large-scale vegetable and livestock farmers in the plains, California, Florida, and in truck-farming areas along the Atlantic and Gulf coasts. The installation of water, sewer, and electrical lines speeded the adoption of indoor plumbing, the electrification of lighting, and the introduction of refrigerators, stoves, and a growing number of household appliances.

During the nineteenth century, town dwellers became far more organized in their use of space than they had been during the seventeenth and eighteenth centuries. In the clearer, more orderly layout of their streets, of their residential, commercial, and public areas, and of their domestic space with its variety of rooms, each with a particular use—in all the ways that nineteenth-century town dwellers occupied space, they became more specialized, more functional, more obvious in defining the public and the private. Theirs was a spatial world with sharper borders, with clearer demarcations, with particular activities more often confined to particular areas.

## · III ·

AS WITH TOWN FOUNDINGS, so too with town sites: the design and laying out of towns followed the movement of settlement across the continent. Both processes effectively ended at the close of the nineteenth century, as the frontier closed. During the twentieth century, real estate developers added to already settled areas with "tract" or large-scale developments at the edges of already formed towns.

Such "go-getter" promoters first flourished with the real estate booms of the 1880s in southern California and of the 1920s in southern Florida. "Boomers" were not usually directly involved in the development of a particular locality; they were speculators at a distance who sought a quick profit before the bubble burst. Sheer optimism veered into hoax and fraud as promoters advertised the unsurpassed attractiveness of these coastal areas.[84]

During these same years more conventional real estate developers began to subdivide and develop tracts of land at the edges of settlements. Americans after World War II revealed a pent-up demand for housing after the restrictions of fifteen years of prolonged depression and a world war. It was partly satisfied by tract housing, pioneered by Abraham Levitt, who drew on his experience in building houses for the military during the war. In the late 1940s and early 1950s Levitt built three Levittowns, in New York, Pennsylvania, and New Jersey. Although located in already settled areas, these were whole new towns, complete with commercial and public facilities.[85] Under the New Communities Act of 1968 the federal government guaranteed bonds issued by new community developers to help finance such large-scale development and established grants to state and local governments for the building of needed utilities for such projects.[86]

Whether involved with tract developments on the edges of towns or with entire new communities, real estate developers introduced the first revolutionary design in town layouts of the entire modern era: curvilinear street patterns, that is, streets that followed the contours of the land and not an imposed grid, and allowed a variety of vistas for homeowners. In 1873, Frederick Law Olmsted had designed Tacoma, Washington, as a railroad town for the Northern Pacific Railroad's Tacoma Land Company, in this fashion, to take account of the steep topography of the area. Not surprisingly, Tacoma's town promoters rejected such a revolutionary scheme.[87] But the emergence in the mid-twentieth century of a suburban ideal—of homeowners who lived in clustered communities but on large lots in settings that "flowed" with the natural topography—and of the mass ownership of automobiles made this kind of town layout desirable. Suburban developments were not crowded, had spacious house lots, yet were connected to older, established settlements: those who lived in such developments could partake of town life but in a rural-like setting.[88]

In town after town across the continent after World War II, newer de-

velopments were often laid out in curvilinear fashion. It was jarringly different from the older grid pattern of the streets in the older parts of town, creating a kind of fault line in a town's design. In Mattapoisett, Massachusetts, in
the late twentieth century, curvilinear streets with large lots were laid out
along the highway leading out of town. In Cazenovia, New York,
post–World War II subdivisions were similarly designed to the north of town
in hilly, heavily wooded terrain. In Hudson, Michigan, which experienced
little growth late in the century, only one very small subdivision of curvilinear
streets lay on the town's northeast periphery. But in Millersburg, Pennsylvania, new sections located east on the heights above the town contained spacious lots on curving streets. In Mount Gilead, Ohio, a looser grid was
added to its northwest section. In Rockville, Indiana, curvilinear streets in
various subdivisions were added incongruously to an older grid pattern. In
Hermann, Missouri, a grid coexisted with several subdivisions of "curvilinear grids" dating from the 1960s and 1970s, a kind of cross between the two
types of layout. In Southern towns, major crossroads were often filled in with
streets platted between the interstices, but curvilinear street developments
extended beyond the early grids, as was the case elsewhere.[89]

The widespread ownership of automobiles in the twentieth century profoundly affected the layout of towns. Not only did the privately owned automobile facilitate the development of suburban tracts at the edges of towns by
making them conveniently accessible, but motor transportation had the effect
of dispersing the overall pattern of settlement in towns. As state and federal
road systems developed during the first half of the century, roadways passed
through the centers of towns, as they had during the era of horse transportation during the nineteenth century. But when automobile traffic greatly increased because of mass ownership in the years after World War II, state and
federal officials began bypassing towns to avoid traffic congestion and to ease
the movement of travelers whose destination lay beyond. Hotels that had occupied central locations in the age of horse and rail transport gave way to motels (easily accessible to automobiles) on roadways leading out of towns. As
rail transport declined, railroad stations were sometimes rebuilt in open areas
outside of town.

Secondary schools became consolidated to serve more efficiently as educational centers, which meant that the schools with defined neighborhoods
were sometimes moved outside their established neighborhoods altogether.
Churches that similarly demarcated their settings were sometimes consolidated, and newer churches were built along roadways on the edge of town,
not at the center of anything. Even municipal buildings and town halls were
sometimes relocated to uncluttered settings, away from the center of town.

Stores and shops and offices were often located not in the old business district, with its congestion, but along "strips," that is, roads leading out of town, providing easy access to those with motor transport—though not to pedestrians, as in the old business district. Small drive-in shopping centers were built here and there in towns, dotting neighborhoods the way schools and churches had done. If a community was large enough, full-fledged malls were built at the edge of town, with large parking lots and indoor "streets."[90]

In all these ways motor transport had the effect of dispersing town dwellers, spreading them out, with commercial and public activities and structures widely spaced but still easily accessible. At the same time the rural population was leaving the countryside. The percentage of Americans who lived in rural areas and farmed declined steadily throughout the twentieth century. As the farm population moved into clustered settlements, town dwellers themselves spread out, shredding apart the services that during the nineteenth century had become typically centralized. Easy access to motor transportation made both movements possible.

During the twentieth century, commercial and public buildings continued to mirror prevailing architectural styles, influencing builders everywhere. Local and regional traditions had steadily less impact. The functional style of the modernist movement decreed that many nonresidential buildings until the 1960s were shorn of decorative detail, though after that such buildings often displayed the influence of the postmodernist outlook and contain bits of features of earlier styles.

In the twentieth century, domestic architecture continued to mirror prevailing architectural styles, at least for the specially designed homes of the well-to-do. But as development became typically a large-scale enterprise, developers mass-produced certain types of buildings in styles that could be built relatively cheaply and quickly for many buyers of limited means. Through World War II, the prevailing type of home was the bungalow, a low-slung structure, often built on a high basement, with wide projecting eaves, exposed brackets, a large front porch, a prominent chimney, and many windows. Porch and house were under one large, simple roof. At first built in England as a vacation dwelling or a cottage, bungalows attracted developers who sought to promote images of recreation and health. They were intended to blend indoor and outdoor spaces, and prominent porches were meant to be outdoor living space. The emphasis was on a minimal house that blended with nature. With the cost of construction labor and building materials soaring, middle-class town dwellers could no longer afford elaborate houses. Home-building guides provided bungalow-style houses in abundance.[91]

After World War II the prevailing mass-produced house became the

FIRES AND FLOODS. Most towns experienced major fires and, if they were near waterways, occasional flooding before the installation of fire-prevention equipment and flood-control devices in the twentieth century. Top, a fire in Cooperstown, New York. Below, a flood in Paducah, Kentucky. [Top, New York State Historical Association; below, David R. Phillips Collection]

"ranch" house, a single-story dwelling with garage and usable basement. Ranches differed from bungalows in their low, sprawling appearance. The elevated basement disappeared, and roof slopes were of a much lower pitch. The ranch-style house was spread across its wide lot. This one-story house was efficient and cheaper to build and to maintain, with shorter utility lines and easier repairs. Popular in house-building guides, the ranch became widely prefabricated. Its contour-fitting form mirrored the curvilinear streets it typically was built along. Indoor and outdoor spaces continued to blend as picture windows and sliding glass doors faced a more private rear patio instead of a front porch, which had gradually disappeared after moving to the side, in order to be more private, and then being screened in. After World War II, when air-conditioning became a feasible alternative, many homeowners chose backyard terraces and patios over porches.[92]

Suburban developments, with their large houses, large lots, and large lawns and vistas, represented an effort to combine the farmer's rural setting with the clustered settlement of a town dweller. But the suburban house did not have the array of necessary outbuildings that typified town houses during the nineteenth century. Earlier town dwellers worked outdoors on their house lots to do what was necessary for their survival. Their well-off twentieth-century successors strove to create a rural-like setting, but outdoor activity was for them a recreational, leisure-time undertaking. Twentieth-century town dwellers retained their predecessors' concern for domestic privacy, however, even moving away from the porch, that most ambiguous of spaces, when technology allowed them to do so. Only in such relatively rare open-space dwellings as A-frame houses and reconditioned studio apartments in reused commercial and industrial structures have town dwellers opened up their private domestic spaces.

The physical appearance of towns—their street layout and the structures built along those streets—changed markedly from the seventeenth to the twentieth century. In colonial America an absence of clearly demarcated domestic and commercial or public spaces within towns, and a similar lack of division as to the use and function of space and furnishings within homes, gave way during the nineteenth century to much more clearly organized residential, commercial, and public areas within towns, and to much more clearly defined spaces and furnishings within homes. But in the twentieth century these trends promoted dispersion, even if town dwellers retained, indeed enhanced, a well-developed division between the public and the private. In the physical appearances of their communities, town-dwelling Americans thus revealed much about the character of their lives.

Although intended to be "permanent" by their builders, towns were routinely ravaged by natural disasters—fire, flood, hurricane, and tornado. It was a rare town that escaped such forms of destruction altogether. Quite apart from natural destruction, towns were regularly rebuilt as homes and buildings aged or deteriorated. Builders generally moved from wood to more durable brick or stone. When the economic basis for a town collapsed, the settlement might simply be abandoned by its inhabitants, turned into a "ghost town." By contrast, when a town's economy burgeoned, it became either a city in itself or part of an advancing urban development.

# THREE

# Political Life

THE NATIVE POPULATION of America whom the white colonists encountered did not lay claim to fixed, permanent territories. Land was used by families, bands, and tribes for various purposes, and boundaries shifted, depending upon the use of an area. Hunting and fishing grounds varied according to the animals being sought. In the case of agricultural tribes, villages were mobile, occupying one site—adjacent to cultivated fields—in the growing season and another—with access to hunting and fishing grounds—in the winter.[1]

Political authority among the North American bands and tribes inhered in a sachem or sagamore (or other names) but was not rigid or fixed or abstract, involving as it did a relatively fluid set of personal relationships. Kinship and personality, not ongoing institutional mechanisms, were the bases for determining who exercised power in the tribes. A sachem (or his equivalent) derived his power from such things as personal assertiveness, marrying (if male) several wives to proliferate wealth and kin obligations, the reciprocal exchange of gifts with followers, and inheriting the title from close kin.[2] Sachems—either male or female—asserted authority only in consultation with advisers or counselors, often of shamanistic or religious authority; sometimes paid tribute to other sachems, acknowledging some sort of band or tribal hierarchy; and grouped together into a larger confederacy during a major conflict or external threat. Sachems were principally coordinators, responsible for the supervision of all those activities and functions of concern to the group as a whole—hunting, interband trade and diplomacy, the administration of intraband justice.[3]

Leaders and followers were bound together reciprocally closer in character to the lords and vassals of medieval Europe than to emergent modern forms of government. Sachems sometimes entered into sharecropping arrangements, assigning garden plots to the families of bands and tribes, and receiving a portion of each harvest in return. Sachems and their counselors enjoyed high social status and lived quite ostentatiously off the tribute collected from their followers. Yet chiefs and counselors were careful to present gifts regularly to those followers upon whose support they depended.[4]

Native Americans were thus bound together politically in a hierarchy of communities, from bands to tribes to confederacies, that were of inverted importance—the smallest and nearest (bands) were most important; the largest and most distant (confederacies) were least important. Overall there was significantly more flexibility and movement in the bands' and tribes' personalized and medieval-like political arrangements than could be found in the more modern, institutionalized forms of local government developed by the white colonists during the seventeenth and eighteenth centuries.[5]

From the beginning of white settlement, colonial assemblies and, after political independence, state governments assumed the authority to grant a legal existence to towns through acts of incorporation. Unlike native Americans, the Europeans who settled in North America delegated to a higher level of community (provinces and states) the power to grant a legal, political existence to more local forms of community. Such towns were established, like the colonies and states that created them, with fixed territories, though these territories were sometimes either divided or augmented as time passed. By the nineteenth century, state governments also commonly distinguished between towns and cities, establishing a minimal level of population that a politically defined community had to attain before it could be reincorporated as a city—in much the same way as the inhabitants of new Western territories could petition Congress for admission as states only when a certain population level had been reached. This fixed territoriality—for towns or cities—contrasted sharply with the fluid, mobile manner with which the native population organized itself politically in relationship to territory.

But the essential nature of local government for both groups was similar. Although in theory the colonists subscribed to forms and practices evolved in England, the actual functioning of political life was infused with the same kinds of personalized relationships that characterized the political life of the native population. The English had institutionalized local government by developing various local and county offices whose holders performed certain functions or duties. But the comparatively small population within townships and counties in British North America meant that local officeholders were personally known and involved in reciprocal duties with the people they served in much the same way that sachems and sagamores were with their fellow tribesmen. In neither case was there a modern bureaucracy filled with technically trained people and characterized by its impersonality. It was well into the nineteenth century before town dwellers in the United States began to develop forms of local government that took on such attributes.

Natives and white settlers were also similar in their mutual creation of inverted hierarchies of political communities. Just as native Americans joined together in bands, tribes, and confederacies, so too did European migrants create towns and cities, counties, provinces (and later states), and belong to an empire (and later a nation). And just as bands or tribes were the most significant politically defined community for the native population and confederacies the weakest, so too for white colonists, and later Americans, were towns and cities and counties the most important communities with a political definition, and provinces (and later states) and the empire (and later the nation) the least significant communities of a political kind. Not until the domestic economic crisis produced by the decade-long Great Depression of the 1930s did this pattern shift. Only then did the federal and state governments clearly gain primacy in the political authority they exercised over the lives of Americans.

Both town and city governments were "representative" in the sense that local electorates chose municipal officials to govern in their behalf. The chief overall distinction between the various forms of town and city government that emerged during the four centuries of white settlement was that town (and county) governments were elected by all the voters within their territory whereas city governments were usually elected by voters in the "wards" or districts into which cities were typically divided. This distinction was a function of size. Cities were such large entities that colonial and state authorities believed they should be subdivided as political entities, just as the provinces and, later, the states and the nation themselves were.

During the nineteenth century, city governments also initiated the professionalization of services they provided for their communities, as urban electorates demanded an ever-expanding variety of public services for themselves as large but concentrated populations. By contrast, in the towns during the seventeenth, eighteenth, and well into the nineteenth centuries, widespread popular participation in officeholding and community-wide public activity gave town governments an informal, amateur quality. By the mid-nineteenth century, however, the towns began to imitate the cities and also introduced professionalized services, usually in piecemeal fashion. During the twentieth century all levels of local government—town, city, and country—

were eclipsed by state and federal governments. Under the spur of the economic crisis of the 1930s and the demands of World War II in the 1940s, these broader governments greatly enlarged their scope of operations and introduced, under their greater taxing authority, a great complex of programs which they financed and regulated but allowed local authorities to administer.

## · I ·

DURING THE seventeenth and eighteenth centuries, the loose, decentralized character of British colonization was exhibited in the varied ways that individual colonial assemblies made arrangements for local government, even while drawing on English forms and practices. Only in New England—where the Puritans consciously sought to create a village-centered society—did those assemblies grant the town primary local political authority. In New England the entire colony was divided into townships. Counties were reduced to little more than judicial entities, as locations for the court system.[6] In all other regions—in the mid-Atlantic as well as in the Southern colonies—county government was made the chief political instrumentality. Colonial New England's township-centered system was not copied in the mid-Atlantic and Southern colonies. Other assemblies refused to allow towns to become the most important political units, basically because of the dispersed, rural character of settlement and the sporadic location of towns.

The colonial South's county system (in which towns, boroughs, villages, and cities were incorporated, surrounded by rural territories placed directly under county government) provided the most feasible means for organizing political authority at the local level, given the dispersed character of settlement in North America. It was copied throughout the mid-Atlantic area, where the assemblies were also influenced by New England's township system. As a result, the middle colonies created a dual arrangement: contiguous *townships* throughout the colony, but with primary political authority vested in *county* governments.

In colonial New England, during the early phases of settlement in the seventeenth century, the Massachusetts and Connecticut assemblies tightly regulated the founding and settling of towns, enacting much detailed legislation regarding specific townships. In stark contrast, towns in Rhode Island assumed wide autonomy; indeed, the colony itself was formed out of four preexisting towns, early havens for religious dissenters. By the late seventeenth century the geographic dispersion of settlement and demographic growth made close supervision by magistrates in colonial capitals infeasible, and the Massachusetts and Connecticut assemblies allowed the towns considerable autonomy in governing themselves.[7] By the eighteenth century, in all the New England colonies, local autonomy had become a significant feature of political life.

The towns founded during the seventeenth century were quasi-public, quasi-private entities—private enterprises sponsored by land corporations, whose members were shareholders. They owned the common land given to them by the assembly as their new town's territory. These land corporations sponsored settlement and shared the cost of organizing the town—raising revenues among themselves, spending funds on public ways and on the surveying of lots, gaining profit as they divided and sold the land to other settlers. Not until the late seventeenth and early eighteenth centuries did these "proprietors" typically become clearly distinguishable from the town and its inhabitants (or voters). Early New England towns were comprised of circles within circles of people: the town residents (whether voters or not), the politically empowered voters (whether proprietors or not), and proprietors (whether residents or not). Individuals could be members of one or more of these groups, but the three groups had distinctive identities and an ascending scale of authority over the town's life: from residents to voters to proprietors. In both their founding and their early political life, there was a pervasive ambivalence as to whether the early New England towns were public or private undertakings. With political maturity, proprietors and town governments took on separate identities.[8]

The civic life of early New England towns was reserved, as everywhere else in the European world, for males. Although they were accepted as church members, women were barred from participation in public or municipal activity. Voters were at first adult male inhabitants, who were usually church members during the early years of a town's settlement. When the Puritan congregations were no longer coterminous with the town itself or no longer claimed the allegiance of most adult males, the suffrage was shifted by colonial law to include adult males with a certain level of property, a level that was low enough not to bar significant numbers of adult males.[9]

The basic form of government developed in each of the region's colonies was the town meeting, in which all voters directly decided on a course of public action in all matters placed on the agenda. Just as church members assumed a wide authority over the religious life of the community, so too did voters directly make decisions on matters that affected their civic life. Nowhere else in the Europeanized world was there such a clear example of direct democracy in a political context.

Although the Puritans rarely commented on why they chose this form of government, it seems clear that the democratic character of their political life mirrored the democratic character of their religious life. The evidence is physical: the meetinghouses that were built at the edge of the commons and that constituted the centers of otherwise typically dispersed settlements were used as both churches and town halls, for both religious and civic purposes. The fact that voters were at first (male) church members also indicates that the early town settlers made basic connections between their spiritual and secular lives.

But this was a profoundly conservative democracy, limited to those who subscribed to a particular kind of reformed Anglicanism. Puritan towns were meant to contain a cohesive population, both English and Congregational in character. Those who were ethnically or religiously different were not usually welcome. New residents needed affidavits from outside officials or oral testimonials from those already resident.[10] Political democracy functioned in townships whose inhabitants shared a common European background and a common faith. The Puritans' emphasis on local autonomy and on mass decision-making and officeholding was unique in the Western world during the seventeenth and eighteenth centuries and was a direct consequence of their religious beliefs and goals. Nowhere else did propertied adult males act, en masse, in an ongoing public and political capacity.

Yet the Puritans did not create a liberal, democratic polity in their local communities. The Puritan village was profoundly anti-liberal and emphatically conservative because it was based on intolerance and a uniform adherence to a single, religiously based orthodoxy. Puritans made strenuous efforts to keep the peace, to maintain harmony and unity, to avoid controversy, division, and strife—and a plurality of views and ways of acting.

Such efforts did not always produce unity and peace, however. As settlement dispersed through the arable portions of the townships, those who were far from the meetinghouse often petitioned the colonial assemblies for the creation of a new township, split off from the original one. The petitioners believed that they lived too far from the meetinghouse, from the center of political and religious life, to attend services and meetings easily. As tensions grew between those with access to the original town center and those who believed they were too far away, the colonial assemblies often acted in favor of the petitioners, incorporating new towns out of portions of old ones. In other instances, when coastal townships divided into commercially oriented seaside and agriculturally oriented interior portions, similar tensions arose, sometimes leading to petitions and assembly-ordered divisions.[11]

In Massachusetts, for instance, Walpole split off from Dedham in 1724, its inhabitants having long felt separated from the town center.[12] Springfield divided into often divisive communities, separate settlements that later became Longmeadow and Chicopee.[13] In Connecticut between 1767 and 1789, twenty-nine new towns were carved out of old ones. The chief reason the petitioners gave for seeking separation was their distance from the meetinghouse.[14]

Town meetings also produced dissension and divisions, but at least they contained a built-in mechanism for the resolution of differences: the vote. Typically the participants failed to keep a tally of the votes, thus hiding the identity of those who disagreed or the numerical extent of the division.[15] Unrecorded votes often reflected little more than a sense of the meeting.

A great variation among the colonial New England towns was whether the voters as a whole wielded decisive political power at their town meetings or whether the officials they elected were the primary managers of the town's public life (especially the "selectmen," who varied in number as a multiheaded town executive). In Connecticut the inhabitants of newly formed towns generally held frequent town meetings. But as the towns matured and created various offices, more and more of the town's business was managed by those agencies and offices, and town meetings were called less frequently.[16] But in Massachusetts, in Dedham, a self-perpetuating elite of selectmen dominated the town's affairs throughout its early years. With political maturity, voters at town meetings reasserted their political authority.[17] In at least a few towns, elite families dominated from the start. William and John Pynchon of Springfield became political chieftains with patriarchal authority akin to tribal sachems, holding office by virtue of prowess and skill in every area of community life, creating patterns of reciprocity and dependency that made them as much like medieval lords as modern magistrates.[18]

In general, the larger the town, the more likely it was to have an ongoing elite of oft-elected officeholders.[19] But this was tendency only, and there were many exceptions, like Dedham. And the question as to whether the voters at their town meetings or their elected officials functioning between meetings was the more important political force is an especially complicated one, with great variation, even within the political history of a particular town. What is not in question is the fact that town meetings everywhere in the region created a great array of offices whose occupants performed widely varied, publicly defined functions. They were filled (apart from selectmen in some situations) usually on a short-term basis by many different adult male villagers. The direct decision-making of all voters at town meetings and the wide variety of popularly filled offices are both indications that the Puritans believed in an exceptionally wide definition of public or political life for their local communities, even if an elite of officeholders sometimes emerged to dominate a town's civic life.

Selectmen constituted a kind of executive or administrative group, and the extent of their authority varied according to the colony, the century, and the age or phase of development of a given town. But in most towns these officials were not self-perpetuating elites. A regular turnover of selectmen was usual, and of other important offices as well, such as assessors, treasurers (or "raters" or "listers"), clerks, and moderators of town meetings.[20] Lesser offices revealed the wide ambit of public life: constables (to keep public order), tithingmen or grand jurymen (to supervise moral or social behavior), branders, key keepers, sealers, animal watchers, fence viewers, highway supervisors.[21] In Connecticut, for example, the towns averaged fifty to sixty officers in 1725, sixty to seventy in 1750, seventy-five to one hundred in 1775.[22]

In sharp contrast to the New England colonial assemblies, those in the mid-Atlantic provinces, responsive to the widely dispersed character of settlement, granted most of the authority exercised by local government to county officials, which by the eighteenth century in New York were appointed by the provincial government[23] but in Pennsylvania counties were elected by the propertied adult male voters.[24] The entire territory of the mid-Atlantic colonies was divided into townships, as in New England, but they were of less political consequence.

In New York, towns in the seventeenth century, often settled by New Englanders moving westward, also had rules for admission and expulsion, but there was not a high incidence of litigation in the courts or evidence of paralysis by dissension. As in New England, town governments valued peace and harmony but learned to tolerate dissenters amidst the more varied population of the region. Because of the New England origins of many of the original settlers, town meetings again became the primary source of local authority, even though they were not usually mentioned in town charters and only briefly in the Duke's Laws (the colony's overall frame of government). Town meetings were especially active in the early years of settlement (as in Connecticut), but such a mass democratic device proved to be not very efficient. It became easier to let regularly elected officials handle the town's day-to-day affairs, though the town meeting retained control over the process of distributing unsold lands within the township. But this town-centered system of local government lost its vitality by the late seventeenth century as the colonial government reasserted its authority over local affairs.[25]

In Pennsylvania, at least, elected county officials—assessors, sheriffs, especially commissioners—became the most important local officeholders. Townships at first were without elected officials: the county commissioners appointed what few there were—constables and overseers of roads and of the poor.[26] Political townships became little more than units of assessment for the counties, and, indeed, county officials even had the authority to create new townships.[27] Such a political system meant that those eligible to vote had far less opportunity than existed in New England to become officeholders as well.[28] In Germantown, for example, sporadic community action was taken by an ill-defined "inhabitants of Germantown," because there were no voters empowered to elect local officials and no mechanism (like the town meeting) for the popular resolution of local issues.[29]

In the Southern colonies, also exhibiting characteristically widely dispersed settlement patterns, the county and county government were even more important. Assemblies placed large portions of each colony's territory directed under county governance, incorporating towns only at actual settlements. County governments operated at regular intervals in the crossroads courthouses. Their work was at least *witnessed* by the community at large in a way similar to the New England colonies' town meetings with their popular decision-making. Although county officials—judges, clerks, sheriffs—were usually planters who constituted a local (and provincial) political elite, the wide-ranging activities of empaneled juries consisting of ordinary freeholders meant that local government in the colonial South had a popular dimension too. Juries translated the community's sense of wrongdoings into recorded indictments[30] and determined causes and assessed damages. The county courts, though operating in a judicial mode, were involved in considerable policymaking, administering their territories and acting as assessors and arbitrators on a great many issues.[31]

In all of British North America, local government—whether at the town or county level—acted on behalf of the community in a great variety of ways: the public sphere was notably large.

In New England, elected town officials performed a wide range of tasks that directly affected the lives of their fellow townspeople. In Rhode Island, town councils issued licenses to taverns or public houses; granted certificates to people who were moving to another town with the commitment that the town would assume their support if they went on relief; warned people out of town who could not support themselves; established guardianship for orphans and bound out children as apprentices; established quarantines during epidemics and greatly limited freedom of action and movement of the inhabitants; and became involved in many matters involving either the assistance or regulation of particular town dwellers with unusual problems.[32]

In Connecticut, at least in its earliest phases of settlement, townsmen themselves were charged with an array of responsibilities that involved the self-regulation of their behavior: searching (without a warrant) any home if they suspected the inhabitants were breaking the law; watching taverns to prevent tippling (i.e., drinking more than a half-pint of wine and staying in the tavern for more than half an hour); teaching all children how to read as well as how to develop the skills for an occupation—on pain of forfeiture of the children if others noticed that they had not been so trained.[33]

The authority of the towns was determined by colonial assemblies at first, but as settlement burgeoned and towns multiplied, town meetings and their elected officials assumed the responsibility of determining their own tasks. For example, in New London, Connecticut, town officials were to maintain the town's boundaries, supervise the fence viewers (functionaries who ensured that fences dividing properties were maintained and accurate), deal with complaints regarding land grants, maintain the streets and common lands and appoint individuals to work on them, maintain the ferries, regulate the felling and sawing and transport of timber, maintain the town's and colony's laws, provide the town magistrate with arms and ammunition, regulate matters involving the native population, assure that children were educated and servants well ordered, be vigilant that people did not live in idleness, maintain the meetinghouse, control the agenda of town meetings and prevent needless discussion, hold regular officials' meetings, and keep good town records.[34]

During the early activist phase of town government in New York, male voters took turns devoting time to communal work, building roads, bridges, animal pounds, and even mills and meetinghouses.[35] In Germantown, the Philadelphia County government "attended to the opening and maintenance of roads, the building of bridges, the licensing of taverns and peddlers, the capture and punishment of criminals, the settlement of local quarrels and disputes, the assessment of property, and the collection of taxes for these chores. The poor and orphaned had to be provided for, and the orderly passage of property from one generation to another through the registration of wills and the administration of estates had to be accomplished."[36]

And in Virginia, county magistrates "issued the licenses for the establishment of water mills in the country, they licensed and supervised the conduct of ordinaries [taverns], they arranged for the construction of bridges, jails, and other public works, and they submitted recommendations for the governor's annual appointment of the inspectors in charge of the tobacco warehouses, where all tobacco had to be certified as of standard for the market."[37]

Throughout the colonies, and later the states, one kind of politically oriented town became the center of government at the local level: the county seat or "shire town." The designation of such special towns by provincial and state governments gave local political activity a natural focal point for a dispersed and rural population. Colonial assemblies assumed this responsibility soon after the earliest settlements. In Georgia, as we have seen, the legislature regularly founded or designated existing settlements as county seats, as the largest of the English mainland colonies became progressively settled and populated.[38] In Pennsylvania, as noted earlier, the Penns as proprietors designated and planned many county seats as settlement spread westward across the colony.[39]

Everywhere—even in New England, where county seats were simply locations for the court system—shire towns often became the largest towns in their counties, sometimes significant market towns or trade centers as well. In the most rural parts of the Southern colonies, courthouses located at crossroads were sometimes later designated as county seats and became significant settlements as political activity attracted both residents and visitors.

Elsewhere in North America during the colonial period, in areas of Spanish settlement, in what later became the American Southwest, local government in the towns founded under Spanish auspices took the form of a *cabildo* or town council elected by the citizens of the municipality. But it governed territory beyond the confines of the actual settlement. The *regidores* or councilmen in turn chose two *alcaldes ordinarios* or municipal magistrates who exercised judicial authority at the town level. A significant part of municipal administration in the Spanish borderlands was the adjudication of judicial disputes. The senior magistrate ordinarily presided over meetings of the town council and issued ordinances enacted by it. The junior magistrate usually restricted his activities to judicial matters. A *fiel executor* was chosen by the council as the official who enforced the ordinances dealing with trade and commerce, the ownership of municipal and private property, and all the other aspects of economic life within the community. The *alquacil mayor* was the appointed police official charged with keeping peace and order and executing the orders of the court magistrates.[40]

On the whole, the municipal governments of the Spanish borderlands functioned as viable institutions during the eighteenth century at such towns as Villa de San Fernando and Laredo. Spanish colonists in areas that later became part of the United States thus shared with the English colonists along

A SOUTHERN COURTHOUSE. Courthouses in the rural South were a one-stop government center, with all the operations of local (county) government centralized in a building that was itself centrally located in a predominantly rural county—as here in Hanover, Virginia, ca. 1735. [Virginia State Library]

the Atlantic seaboard long experience with a form of local government that was popularly elected, actively regulated municipal life, and performed a wide array of functions for the well-being of the town dwellers it governed.

· II ·

DURING THE American Revolution (1775–1781), the erstwhile colonial governments arranged for constitutional conventions to draw up new state constitutions. Later, during the nineteenth century, these new frames of government (and successive revisions) for states in the "middle"—

the mid-Atlantic, Midwest, the Plains—divided local authority between counties and towns, avoiding the extremes established in the colonial South and New England. Outside of New York and Pennsylvania, only Ohio and Illinois, Wisconsin and Minnesota, Missouri and Arkansas developed New England's township system in which incorporated towns made up the entire territory of a state. It was far more common for the new states to follow the system first developed in the colonial South of having rural territory outside incorporated towns placed directly under the jurisdiction of county governments.[41]

Although given their legal and political existence by state governments, local governments in rural areas—that is, town and county governments—remained the level of government that most affected the lives of those who lived in and around towns. The hierarchy of political communities remained inverted: the activities of still-distant state and national governments remained less important to town dwellers than the many ongoing ways in which local governments interacted with their lives. During the nineteenth century, towns and counties enlarged their electorates, thereby significantly expanding the parameters of local political communities, but only in response to the enlargement of the franchise at state and national levels. As state constitutions approved during the 1820s and thereafter adopted white male suffrage, ending traditional property-holding qualifications, so too did towns and counties as local governments were established with settlement across the continent.

In New York the Constitution of 1787 provided that towns had the right to elect all their own officials, though the state retained the power to prescribe their manner of election, their powers and duties, the fees for their duties, and the fines for their failure to perform them. But not until the 1840s did the New York legislature cease to deal in detailed ways with problems that arose in the governance of particular towns—the sort of thing that the New England provincial and state governments had abandoned as early as the eighteenth century.[42]

County officials—justices of the peace, sheriffs, district attorneys—performed law enforcement duties. Revenue raising, spending, and accounting functions were shared by county and local officials: county supervisors determined the tax rate and audited local accounts, and county treasurers disbursed the revenues assessed and collected by locally elected officers. The most important functions from the 1770s through the 1850s involved the regulation of roads, schools, poor relief, and the fencing of livestock.[43]

As time went on, the townships of Pennsylvania played a more active role in their own governance. From the beginning, townships kept the peace, maintained highways, cared for the poor, levied and collected taxes, and implemented other programs as directed by law. Voters had to serve as constables, highway supervisors, and overseers of the poor. Gradually the number of township officials increased, and voters began to elect certain officials, though others continued to be appointed by justices of the peace, a county-level official. Township officials not only collected provincial and county taxes, but taxes came to be levied at the township level as well, with regular local taxes designated for support of the poor and special levies earmarked for road maintenance. Local government gradually grew in size. Voters were typically involved either as officials or as road crews several times in a lifetime.[44]

In Wisconsin the mix differed somewhat. Counties had no court system of their own but possessed considerable legislative and administrative autonomy.[45] Wisconsin statutes created and defined such county offices as a board of supervisors (a kind of county "legislature" comprised of delegates from each township), sheriffs, treasurers, clerks, and district attorneys—all of whom operated out of county courthouses in county seats. As incorporated entities, counties could own property, enter into contracts, sue, and be sued. The state gave counties authority to fix county seats, create new townships, name geographical features, construct public works, build and maintain roads, confer charters on ferries and toll roads or bridges, encourage agriculture, promote the conservation of wildlife, care for paupers and the insane, educate children, and exercise during the course of the nineteenth century "ordinance powers of indefinite scope to protect the property, safety, and health of its citizens."[46]

Townships in Wisconsin retained the New England–based town meeting, which provided the basis for mass political democracy for adult males. A high proportion of eligible citizens attended annual meetings, which were sometimes characterized by vigorous debates. Town officials—chairmen, supervisors, assessors, treasurers, clerks—usually obtained an early unanimous vote, and the offices were typically "passed around." Towns were particularly active in road and bridge construction and maintenance and in the care of the indigent. Roads were built entirely by the men of particular neighborhoods, men who selected one of their number to serve as overseer of roads for a year. Voluntary road crews provided most of the road labor. Town boards advertised their need for new bridges, and firms were invited to bid. The resulting contract contained a date by which construction was to be completed. The care of indigent neighbors was a major responsibility of town governments, though such persons did not usually become a town charge unless they were mortally ill or friendless. Very few names appeared on town relief rolls;

neighbors and friends gave temporary help as it was required. Short-term aid to those who became town charges included medical attention, drugs, nursing care, and funeral expenses.[47] Overall, Wisconsin established a complicated mix of state-county-township revenue raising and spending.

In many towns during the course of the nineteenth century, local governments increased the range of their authority over the lives of the inhabitants within their jurisdictions. In Jacksonville, Illinois, for example, the town charter of 1830 provided for an annually elected board of trustees with the power to tax, enforce the laws, improve the streets, and regulate public nuisances. This was a local government that involved few citizens and intruded very little into the daily lives of Jacksonville's inhabitants. The large brick market house, built at public expense shortly after incorporation, was an apt symbol of newly created local governments during the nineteenth century: such governments maintained a minimal framework within which individualistically oriented capitalistic economic activity could flourish.

But as Jacksonville grew, the state's assembly broadened the board of trustees' powers, encouraging the expansion of municipal services.[48] Local officials responded by dealing with dangers to the physical, social, and moral order. Ordinances were passed requiring healthy, safe, clean, and beautiful public squares and streets in order to prevent strange animals, refuse, and rowdy humans from disturbing peace and order; a fire department and fire regulations were imposed in an effort to prevent disastrous fires and the ruination of property; a public health inspector was appointed to investigate unhealthy conditions among the population, even the privies and cellars of residents; a public school was created to provide a disciplined environment for students, who were taught basic literacy and numeracy as well as being exposed to moral training; a police force was established to enforce public order; crimes were more strictly defined; and laws were passed to prohibit the sale and consumption of alcoholic beverages, thus preventing intemperance, the greatest of all threats to public order.[49]

Those most involved in Jacksonville's government were persisting (that is, they stayed in town and did not move out), property-owning, upwardly mobile, middle-class men in their thirties and forties who supported an ethos of respectability, hard work, and self-improvement and favored the expansion of public authority over the moral behavior of the community.[50]

During the nineteenth century, town governments in communities where there were serious divisions among the politically involved public became forums for the discussion and sometimes the resolution of issues. In the well-documented case of the cattle towns in Kansas after the Civil War, political life registered the factionalism of the politically active elements of these communities, whether on the basis of old timers and newcomers, ins and outs, rival real estate cliques, or reformers and defenders of the status quo. Such factionalism was healthy for the development of democracy because it kept voters politically alert and allowed those with differing perceptions of the public good a common basis for debate and political action. As in Jacksonville and other towns, reformers in the cattle towns were those who sought to widen the ambit of government by extending its coercive power over public morality. In particular, the prostitution, gambling, and drinking that so permeated social behavior in frontier towns, reformers argued, should be regulated or even eradicated by the exercise of public authority.[51]

Local government also became more professional, its personnel specially trained, its functions more varied. In this way towns followed what was initially an urban phenomenon. Temporary road crews comprised of taxpayers, volunteer fire fighters, and constables—citizen participants of all kinds were gradually replaced by those trained for the job. Town governments also became more democratic as elected officials were chosen by all adult male voters. But in the process of becoming electorally more democratic, town and county governments became less democratic in another sense. As direct, popular participation in the functioning of local government—so common in the colonial period and into the nineteenth century—gave way to the practice of appointing professional, trained officeholders, town dwellers and those in rural settings became less connected to municipal and county governments. Local government became more truly representational, as had always been the case with respect to higher levels of government, at the provincial and imperial, then the state and national levels.

Still, some town dwellers continued to feel that town officials had light duties. For instance, even in early-twentieth-century Hartford, Michigan, Willis F. Dunbar felt that the town marshal, though charged with the responsibility of enforcing village ordinances, in fact did little more than "[stow] the town drunks in jail when they got noisy or troublesome." The relationship between rural populations and town dwellers of particular townships were strained throughout the nineteenth and well into the twentieth centuries. Dunbar remembered that, from the farmers' point of view, "[all] the village government did was to provide a few services the farmers in the township did not want or need." Although town dwellers sometimes became highly partisan supporters of the national and state political parties, Dunbar remembered that in Hartford, at the turn of the nineteenth century, "[on] the whole, local elections attracted more interest and created more excitement than state or national elections."[52]

As in the Colonial period, so throughout the nineteenth century, certain

MUNICIPAL GOVERMENT. As local or municipal government expanded its
perimeters and became more and more professionalized during the nineteenth
century, its buildings—like the town hall of Winchester, Kentucky, above—
became more of a focal point for community life, often sporting towers, which
became landmarks, as church spires had. Municipal employees became
trained and wore uniforms. Opposite, top, the constabulary in Massillon,
Ohio; below, firemen in Mullan, Idaho. [Above, University of Louisville;
opposite, top, Massillon Museum; below, Library of Congress]

towns were designated as county seats or political capitals at the local level.
Midwestern state governments usually assigned this duty to the county commissioners.[53] In Missouri, as elsewhere, the prime consideration for the location of a county seat was that it be on a site roughly in the middle of the
county. But locations along navigable waterways and along railroad lines
were also major considerations because, even though county seats were
meant to be centers of local government, it was also hoped they would
emerge as trade centers.[54]

What differed from colonial times was the intense rivalry that broke out
among existing settlements for a much-sought-after designation. Towns

founded during the nineteenth century were much more overtly speculative enterprises than earlier towns had been, and town founders in the great mid-continent valleys and plains became convinced that to snare the business of government for their town was one of the surest ways to guarantee its future. As settlement moved across the continent, countless county seat "wars" flared.[55] Extended squabbles sometimes led county authorities to choose a new location rather than one of the nascent settlements, as was the case with Jacksonville, Illinois, when it was chosen as the shire town for Morgan County.[56] At other times the struggle to be named the shire town was quite protracted, with other towns contesting the appropriateness of the original choice, as the center of population shifted within the county, or as water or land transportation routes developed elsewhere. In Trempealeau County in Wisconsin, for instance, the originally designated county seat, Galesville, which was chosen because of the efforts of Judge Gale, was opposed by the inhabitants of, first, Trempealeau village, second, Arcadia, and third, White-hall. This opposition forced the county to agree to no fewer than four more elections on the location for the county seat, elections that resulted in the seat's being moved twice beyond its original location.[57]

Among the many different kinds of special towns founded during the nineteenth century, the inhabitants of some developed a basically different kind of local government; others created governments that did not differ in kind from those of ordinary towns. For example, black towns developed a standard type of political system, but only after evolving beyond the special circumstances that attended their foundings. In the case of Allensworth, California, since the promoters had not incorporated the town, residents and developers established an advisory council of administration, with elections for chairman, finance and public utilities, policy, fire, water and transportation, illumination, streets and parks, and female auxiliary departments, which governed until incorporation came. In Langston City, Oklahoma, settlers voted for incorporation and organized an elected town government with three trustees, by ward, and a town marshal, justices of the peace, a tax assessor, a treasurer, and a city clerk.[58]

In forestry- or mining-oriented towns owned by companies in isolated mountainous or desertlike areas, there was no government at all. The companies themselves provided public services. Residents paid no taxes and had no elected government.[59]

At the other extreme, in utopian, communitarian towns, the usual arrangement was that all men and women participated in public decision-making and served on committees that dealt with the ongoing governance of the community.[60] In this the communitarians followed—and extended to women—the earlier practice of the Puritans. For example, the "Perfection-ists" had twenty-one standing committees to deal with such matters as fi-nance, roads and lawns, waterworks, fire, sanitation, water and steam power, heating, education, and amusements, further dividing the "duties of admin-istration" among forty-eight departments, including medical, dentistry, legal, publication, children's, science and art, dyeing, food preservation, laundry, furniture, housekeeping, repairs, traveling, hardware, carpentry, and real es-tate.[61] In other words, in the communitarian towns there was no important distinction between the private and the public. Political life was economic, so-cial, and cultural life.

## · III ·

DURING THE twentieth century the nature of town govern-ment changed dramatically. For centuries town governments had been the most significant level of government for a largely rural population. Begin-ning in the late nineteenth century, however, farmers began moving from rural settings into towns and cities as agriculture grew increasingly mecha-nized and enabled relatively fewer farmers to supply the remainder of the population. This depopulation of rural areas was accompanied by a simulta-neous migration of town dwellers to urban areas, where they believed they would find greater economic, social, and cultural opportunities.

These demographic movements in turn coincided with a vast increase in the speed of transportation and communications through such means as radio, television, and telecommunications as well as high-speed motor vehi-cles, trains, and airplanes—a process that had been under way in the nine-teenth century with the development of rail and telegraph systems. As a consequence of these developments, the isolation that had marked the lives of those who lived in and around towns was hugely diminished. Everywhere economic, social, and cultural activities and institutions of all kinds grew much larger: corporations assumed continental size; labor unions became na-tional, as did business organizations. Group after group, institution after in-stitution created organizations of national dimensions.

Local government in rural areas—in towns and counties—continued to follow the lead of higher levels of government on the question of voting rights, that is, on the very size of local political communities. When the states or the nation added women and Indians and blacks as citizens with voting rights, so too did the towns and counties. But the locus of political authority did not significantly shift to higher levels of government until the 1930s, under the impact of the depression. Only then did the scale of government enlarge to deal effectively with an expanded economy, society, and culture.

As for the towns themselves, by the 1920s retired farmers were a significant element in the politically active element in the service centers that had provided goods and services to their rural hinterlands. They had the leisure to discuss public policy issues, to form opinions on them, to hold office, and to have influence within these communities. Their objective was, typically, to keep municipal expenses low. The three most significant matters in the public life of such communities were the search for desirable candidates for public office, the consideration of expenditures for proposed improvements, and the recruitment of public officials who would enforce existing laws.[62] Town government still exercised the authority to levy taxes, pass legislation, and administer its own laws. Its heaviest expenditures were for streets and highways, physical improvements, and the protection of life and property.[63]

But by the onset of the Great Depression, town governments had failed to accommodate to drastically changed circumstances and much greater demands for public services. Such governments still operated as they had when the towns were first settled, when life went on in quite localized ways. Dissatisfaction rose during the 1930s with what appeared to be an outmoded entity. Two ways of dealing with this crisis in government were consolidation or joint action with neighboring communities. The depression years saw the increasing influence of state and federal governments, both of which enacted programs that sometimes involved town and county governments as administrators. A consensus grew that most local governments were simply too small to initiate major new public programs.[64]

New federal agencies were at first criticized for offering relief rather than genuine rehabilitation, for not reaching very deeply into local communities (to engage the less prominent inhabitants), for being too concerned with particular localities, and for ignoring the difficulties that children faced in moving from towns to urban areas in search of a better life.[65] The intrusion of federal agencies with their new nationwide programs divided townspeople into traditionalists and innovators—those who accepted change and those who resisted it, those who wanted local government to continue as preeminent and those who realized that conditions made such preeminence no longer possible. The fact was, whatever the attitudes of the local political leadership, the economic crisis of the depression led to a fundamental shift of political power from local government to the state and federal governments.

After World War II it was quite clear that by itself town government could not serve the needs of the people within its jurisdiction. Thus many of the functions of local governments were gradually assumed by county, state, and federal governments. In such major areas of governance as welfare, the construction and maintenance of bridges and roads, and social control (that is, policing and the administration of justice), administrative control moved to county, state, and federal levels.[66]

For example, during the 1950s in "Springdale," the researchers' pseudonym for a real town in the Finger Lakes area of upstate New York, both the village and township boards in every major area of jurisdiction adjusted their actions to take account of regulations imposed by outside state and federal agencies whose duties paralleled their own. The state police, regionally organized fire districts, state welfare agencies, state highway departments, state conservation agencies, state youth commissions—all evoked bitterness and resentment among local officials, but their services were grudgingly accepted by local governments because they were free or provided grants-in-aid for local communities. Because the acceptance of such aid required adherence to certain regulations and laws, local governments thus surrendered some of their legal jurisdiction to outside agencies. Police and welfare functions were performed by the county and the state. Licensing of all kinds was conducted by a clerk who performed his or her duties essentially as an agent of the state—as its administrative arm—rather than of the town government. Forms and legal requirements were derived from state agencies, which set procedures and required reports. Even in the case of town (as opposed to state and county) roads or public ways, the major cost of maintenance and development was borne by the state highway department, which set standards for town government and, through a state highway engineer, enforced state regulations and offered technical advice.[67]

Even though theoretically the village and town boards in Springdale had the authority to control and regulate a variety of community services and facilities—licensing, water supply, garbage disposal, fire protection, police protection, roads, street signs and lighting, parks, and social welfare—they surrendered jurisdiction to county and state agencies and sought to minimize the impact of their own decision-making by keeping taxes low and by avoiding divisive issues, seeking consensus and even unanimity on matters that came before them. The boards sometimes relied on extra-legal bodies to deal with problems that were too controversial or complicated for easy handling, problems that required nontraditional solutions or quick decisions and action. Local government in Springdale continued to reflect what was still the most politically active element in such rural settings: the better-off farmers

who actively farmed in the agricultural areas of the township or who were retired and lived in the village.[68]

By the 1960s, local governments in towns such as Benson, Minnesota,
were surrounded by translocal authority emanating from county, state, and
federal governments. County courthouses contained a much greater array of
officials than municipal halls: the county attorney, the county auditor, the
county clerk of court, the county supervisor of assessments, the county treasurer, the county health officer, the county nurse, the county superintendent
of schools, county welfare officials, the county sheriff, the county register of
deeds, the judge of probate. Many of these officials shared their duties with
their municipal counterparts. But in relation to state and federal governments, the county government too was being curtailed in a governmental system in which political power increasingly determined who performed and
paid for public tasks. More often, the inhabitants of Benson dealt directly
with the federal government through the branch offices of such federal agencies as the Department of Agricultural Stabilization and Conservation Commission, the Farmers Home Administration, the Federal Crop Insurance
Office, the U.S. Fish and Wildlife Service, the U.S. Forestry Service, the
National Armory, the Selective Service board, the Neighborhood Youth
Corps, and the U.S. Post Office.[69]

By the 1970s perhaps a quarter of the U.S. population lived in rural
areas and under local government whose jurisdictions covered towns and
counties. With the breakdown in rural isolation caused by revolutionary
changes in communications and transportation, rural and urban populations
grew much closer in their needs and expectations for public services. After
the 1970s the level of services provided by local government in towns and
counties rose steadily as a result of local demand or the imposition of programs from higher levels of government. But the funding ability of these
local governments did not rise as rapidly as service costs. Such governments
had highly restricted tax bases. They relied heavily on property taxes, which
while they were minimally sensitive to economic shifts were also less lucrative
than graduated income taxes favored by higher levels of government.

Rural local officials also faced problems of economy of scale: it was
much more expensive on a per capita basis to provide service over a widely
dispersed area for relatively few people. As in industrial production, costs
were high at low levels of production. When production levels rose, unit
costs fell to an optimum point, beyond which urbanlike congestion forced
costs up again. Thus isolated rural communities shared with very large urban
centers expensive public service costs. Maintenance and replacement were
costly.[70]

Local services had traditionally been funded by taxes, user fees, and intergovernmental transfers. The property tax had been the historic basis of local revenue. Even with sales taxes, income taxes, and intergovernmental transfers of funds, the property tax remained, in 1970, the source of over half of local revenues. Later, the most significant growth in local revenues came from intergovernmental transfer payments, both state and federal. Procedures for the expenditures of such funds, according to law, varied greatly among the states.

Assessments for property taxes were difficult and inexact, especially in times of inflation. Some states offered relief in the form of "use value" taxation (where the level of property taxation was set by the actual level of use of a governmental service by a municipality) or by the transferring of municipally owned land to the state in return for lower assessments. But real property was a very poor index of the ability to pay taxes. In a poor area it did not yield sufficient revenue to maintain services. Other local taxes were costly and difficult to collect. For such taxes as those on occupations and income, state or federal collection was a solution. Fees for service, especially at the county level, were an important and growing source of local revenue: people paid according to the level of their use (trash collection, for example). State and federal transfer payments also grew in significance. The State and Local Assistance Act of 1972 provided federal funds to supplement local revenues.[71]

The "planning and development" districts created by federal and state governments in the late twentieth century fostered confusion about the plans and objectives of local governments. A single village might be part of many special planning districts. Efforts by outside authorities to redraw local boundaries created fierce local resistance. Overlapping and duplication characterized the dual efforts of federal and state governments to organize programs at the local level. By the mid-1970s, though, states had begun to organize multi-county development districts that the federal government agreed to honor. Such districts provided area-wide planning for public services, provided a ready-made forum, and were stable enough to hire professional staff.[72]

During the course of the twentieth century, local governments in rural areas either developed or further professionalized an array of public services. Town and county governments followed the lead of cities in their provision of police and fire service (or public safety), education, welfare, health care, water/sewer/waste disposal, and transportation.

The crime rate rose slightly in rural areas late in the century but remained much lower than it was in urban areas. Still, local police forces were adequate only for traffic control. Modern law enforcement was a complicated enterprise, involving specialized training and expensive equipment. Crimes seldom involved only one jurisdiction. Federal assistance for local communities was available from the Federal Law Enforcement Assistance Administration.

Volunteer fire departments persisted in many towns, especially smaller ones. Such departments staged fund-raising events and continued to constitute a social organization as well as a public service. Among all the services provided by town governments, the emergency services provided by fire departments were the last to become professionalized. Losses from fire in rural areas were relatively greater than in urban ones. Personnel and equipment costs and the great distances to cover made it difficult for small communities to employ professional firefighters. And volunteer systems became weaker as fewer town dwellers worked where they lived, making an adequate number of firefighters questionable. Towns tried to improve this situation through fire-police communications networks that could direct equipment where it was needed; by training police to operate fire equipment; or by combining police and fire departments into a single force.[73]

A dispersed population was the key feature of rural school systems. Scale and distance had to be dealt with, yet rural people wanted schools that were comparable to those in cities. Economy of scale thus favored the establishment of consolidated schools. Income was generally lower in rural than in urban areas, and the total assumption of school costs by state governments was proposed as a solution—but with greater state control. Federal and state programs began to provide experts for local school systems. Modern telecommunications systems were introduced as standard equipment in some schools.[74]

Many welfare services were available to towns through state and federal programs. But town and county governments were not enthusiastic administrators of such programs. Being a welfare recipient was embarrassing for a town dweller.[75] Chronic physician shortages in rural areas made for a large disparity between urban and rural health care. Disproportionate numbers of older and lower-income people in towns and rural areas resulted in poorer access to services, and poorer facilities.[76]

Historically, local governments in rural areas did not develop water, sewer, and waste-disposal systems. The technology needed for them to work on a proper scale for small communities took a long time to develop. Federal programs to help towns build sewer systems so that they could promote economic development were overwhelmed by requests for aid. Federal assistance did help clean up pollution resulting from sewer and waste-disposal systems.[77]

A good road network for rural America was developed in the late twentieth century, but it was a system utterly dependent upon private motor vehicles. Public transportation was almost nonexistent in towns and rural areas. Expedient arrangements included the planned use of school buses for special occasions; informal access to nearby intercity bus lines; and the use of school buses, vans, and even postal vehicles in off-hours. The fact is that it was not economically feasible for private transport companies to serve towns and rural areas.[78]

By the late twentieth century, local governments in rural areas were commonly grappling with several major public policy issues. Such governments traditionally adopted minimal control of land use. But greater controls became necessary to protect prime agricultural land, to locate electric power plants, and to protect fragile environments. An ongoing question was whether public services districts and planning districts were becoming more efficient. Local finances often reached their limit. Other, nonproperty taxes had to be collected by higher levels of government, with an open-ended question of how much local governments would receive through the intergovernmental transfer of funds. Schools were consolidated, but how much of future costs would be paid for by state governments? Would telecommunications be adequately utilized? Would there be an increased use of special services districts to share the cost of specialized services and equipment? The planning of health care at the local level was an urgent matter, with a similar need for the development of an integrated health system. If energy costs increased, rural residents and town dwellers would need alternatives to the private automobile, alternatives that would undoubtedly be publicly funded. In general, town and county governments needed full-time local officials providing more public services, not part-timers responding to emergencies. Citizens in the towns and counties needed to be involved, to be engaged in planning and to find revenues that matched their expenditures.[79]

From the seventeenth to the twentieth centuries, the character of local government in the towns and counties of rural America changed enormously. Once it had most profoundly affected the lives of town dwellers and those who lived in the rural areas beyond; now it had become little more than a conduit for the administration of programs and services created and largely financed by state and federal governments. But this shift mirrored developments in every other aspect of the lives of town dwellers. As the scale of life enlarged, as transportation and communication grew ever faster, progressively breaking down rural isolation, the economic, social, and cultural aspects of town life were similarly changed. In every case the relatively restricted dimensions of local life gave way to enhanced opportunities. What connected individual town dwellers to activities and institutions far beyond their locality became more important than how they connected to local activities and institutions. One's local community was of less consequence than one's place in a mass society that had become organized along national, continental, and global lines.

# FOUR

# *Economic Life*

THE NATIVE BANDS AND TRIBES whom the white English colonists first confronted on the Atlantic coast of North America did not claim land in a proprietary sense. This was the case whether the natives were nomadic hunters or hunter/farmers who lived in villages. Natives *used* land according to the seasons and defined each hunting or fishing ground by referring to the habitats of particular animals. Sachems proclaimed their symbolic sovereignty over land that their tribes used for agriculture, hunting, or fishing, and sometimes negotiated with one another for the transfer of land. Using the swidden—slash and burn—agricultural techniques common to hunting and farming tribal groups around the world, North American natives periodically burned and cleared areas, whose soils were thus enriched, and planted crops, bunching seeds together in "hills." They used these lands until diminishing crop yields prompted them to move on to other, undepleted or suitable areas. The only things that "belonged" to native families were the tools and weapons they made with their own hands. Natives handcrafted nonmetallic objects to be used in their domestic and work lives or to be given as gifts in social rituals. Wealth—whether in the form of group fishing, hunting, or farming, or in the form of family tools and weapons—was not accumulated and passed on from one generation to another.[1]

By contrast, the European settlers sought to possess or own in a fixed or permanent sense their land and the property on it. Some groups, such as the proprietors of New England towns, held land in common at the outset of settlement, but everywhere in the colonies, settlers wanted to own land and property as individuals. Farm lands—fields for crops and pasturage for livestock—were fenced in or "bounded," and mills and craft shops were constructed, all as "permanent" sites for the generation of wealth claimed by their "owners." These individuals also sought to "improve" their land or property and accumulated wealth in order (1) to spend it as cash or credit transactions in the exchange of products or services, (2) to invest it as capital in profitable economic activity, (3) to loan it with interest to generate further wealth, and (4) to pass it on to the next generation as an inheritance. A huge gulf thus existed between the natives' conception of how they related to the land and the white European colonists' conception of land and property as commodities, as things of increasing or declining monetary value that could be owned or possessed, bought and sold, and passed on through inheritance.[2]

Although the hunting tribes of eastern North America were nomadic, the agricultural ones clustered into villages according to the season: one settlement was situated close to their fields during the growing season; after a hunting season, another settlement was located in a protected woodland site, where produce could be stored in cellars.[3] So while agricultural activity among the tribes was connected to settled village life, as was the case with the English colonists, village life among the natives was seasonal in character, without the sense of permanence that characterized the settlements of the white European migrants.

As the white settlers and their descendants developed economic activity across the North American continent over the seventeenth, eighteenth, and nineteenth centuries, their clustered settlements became trade depots and service centers for a rural population that engaged in various forms of agriculture as well as fishing, lumbering, and mining. No important distinction, other than scale and size, was apparent between towns and cities. Both types of local communities became commercial centers for a wider population in their hinterlands. With respect to economic life, all towns and cities were located along an unbroken continuum or hierarchy of settlements.

The one major exception to this was the swift emergence in the early nineteenth century of the factory mill town, which was located where water could be harnessed as the energy source for the machine production of goods. Since cities were either situated along the coasts at good harbors (and thus became ports for international trade) or, if inland, at natural focal points in road, canal, or rail systems (and thus became commercial centers for large, internal regions of the nation), they were not at favorable sites for early factory complexes. For much of the nineteenth century, therefore, towns, not cities, ordinarily became the first industrial centers.

When first steam power and then electricity became new sources of energy during the course of the century—sources not tied to water power—

cities increasingly absorbed industrial production, taking advantage of far-reaching transportation linkages, large labor pools, more accessible investment capital, and more concentrated managerial talent to create factory complexes. By the late nineteenth century, towns had typically failed in their efforts to develop further or remain as industrial centers.

By the mid-twentieth century, however, the cities' preeminence was itself challenged when widely available motorized transport allowed employees to live in varied settings while commuting to work, and when widespread electrical networks made possible the location of plants wherever a favorable combination of capital, management, labor, transportation, and markets existed. By the late twentieth century, both towns and cities might be locations for industrial enterprise, just as they had always shared the capacity to be commercial centers. By then the distinction between towns and cities was similar with respect to commerce *and* industry. Cities exhibited greater size and scale, but both kinds of local communities were situated along a continuum, along a common hierarchy of activity.

· I ·

FOR THE COLONISTS, during the seventeenth and eighteenth centuries, the enterprise of founding towns was always to some extent an economic enterprise. As already noted, the land corporations that founded New England towns were limited-liability corporations whose shareholders sought profits in a "wilderness." These land corporations developed colonization schemes that were expected to make a profit. After the shareholders had incurred the expense of surveying and constructing public ways, non-shareholding settlers would be lured into establishing residence and purchasing lots from the remaining common land or from the shareholders themselves.[4]

Elsewhere in the colonies, the original proprietors of town lots also bought and sold property with the aim of enhancing their wealth. Those who founded towns in the mid-Atlantic and Southern colonies had to pay the previous owners for the land they surveyed and sold to others willing to become town dwellers. And such town founders as Daniel Francis Pastorius and others in the German-based Frankfort Company, when they surveyed Germantown in Pennsylvania, became interested in buying and selling lots, in treating land as a salable commodity, as something to be used for its profitability.[5]

The English colonists shared with the North American native population a range of economic activity involving agricultural, extractive, and craft endeavors. What differed was not so much *what* the two groups did but *how* they did it. Both raised crops, killed animals, caught fish, used forest products, and handcrafted utensils. But where the natives hunted in the forests, cleared some areas for farming, and used the bark of some trees as a building material, the colonists by contrast used great numbers of trees for construction and for fuel, and in the process denuded huge forested areas. While the natives hoed and hilled the parcels of land they cleared in order to cultivate plants, the colonists deep-plowed the land they farmed, turning it into "permanent" agricultural acreage. While the natives hunted wild animals, the colonists fenced in the livestock they raised, thereby creating a more dependable supply of meat. In crafting objects, the native tribes lacked the more durable metal tools of the colonists, as the tribes had not developed the metallurgic skills of the European immigrants. Waterpowered milling enabled larger numbers of English settlers to live together in village settings, for unlike the native tribesmen they were able to turn such basic commodities as grain and logs into mass-produced flour and boards. In all their economic activity, the English colonists employed a technological sophistication that was far beyond that of the native population.[6]

Some of the colonists' economic activity did not directly result in clustered settlements of a kind that became towns. For example, during the seventeenth and eighteenth centuries, numerous fishing camps emerged along much of the Atlantic coast,[7] but fishing by itself was not usually a sufficient magnet to attract and sustain sufficient numbers of people to produce a town. Similarly, in lumber camps through much of the forested regions of eastern North America during this period, logging was typically a seasonal activity, confined to winter, when loggers created camps for their operation and used horses to drag logs out of snow-covered woodlands. Searching for iron ore wherever it could be found, colonists usually brought the mineral to blacksmith forges located in established villages. In areas where there were sizable veins, iron works were founded during the Colonial period, where mining and forging were combined and where crews were employed. But even ironworks did not require a clustering of people large enough to constitute a town. Tanneries, where leather products were crafted out of animal hides, were also operations that were usually located in established villages.[8]

Among the range of "extractive" activities, only milling sometimes led directly to the creation of towns. The presence of a grist- or sawmill in some

THE VILLAGE MILL. The photograph of this mill in Rumford, Rhode Island, built in 1690, was taken more than two hundred years later. Its plain wooden structure indicates that mills were sometimes very ordinary buildings that happened to house the water wheel and the grindstones that ground the grain produced in the area. [William F. Robinson, *Abandoned New England*]

cases attracted craftspeople to sites in sufficient numbers to produce substantial settlements. For example, within the river valleys of southeast Pennsylvania there were multiple mill sites in virtually all the early townships, though there is no indication that all these sites were the basis for clustered settlements.[9] Similarly in the broad river plains of the Southern colonies there were mills all along the fall lines, and many of the early towns in the tidewater and piedmont regions grew around such locations.[10]

Craftsmen were attracted to mill sites because virtually the entire farming population regularly came there to have their own (or a merchant's) grain and a sawyer's logs turned into edible and usable products, the most basic food and building materials: flour and boards. Thus mill towns developed as a direct consequence of the location of first milling and then craft activity. Even so, neither milling nor craft activity could have prospered by itself. It was the presence of a large, rural farming population, for whom these towns provided basic services, that made their existence possible.

Only in the largest craft centers, in towns near the port cities along the Atlantic coast, was craft or milling activity truly the defining feature of particular communities. In Germantown, in the Pennsylvania area, for example, the array of crafts was astonishing. Germantown was in effect a suburban craft center supplying the largest urban area in the English colonies. There one could find fabric crafts (weavers, tailors, hatters, dyers, fullers, breeches makers, glovers, collar makers), leather crafts (skinners, tanners, cordwainers, harness makers, saddle makers), woodworking and building crafts (turners, coopers, carpenters, masons, joiners, nailers, chair makers), general crafts (clock makers, printers, bookbinders, type makers, painters, limners, basket makers, rope makers, starch makers, powder makers), metal crafts (blacksmiths, coppersmiths, miners, tinmen), food production (millers, millwrights, millstone cutters, bakers, butchers), and transportation crafts and services (coach makers, chair makers, chair trimmers, wheelwrights, curriers, carters, drovers, coachmen).[11] But such a concentration of craft activity was quite rare, especially outside the port cities.

Most English colonists were farmers, overwhelmingly so. But instead of living in villages and working in fields outside the settlements, as had been the case in peasant villages everywhere in the world, most colonists moved directly to their farm property and lived on it, creating a dispersed, rural form of settlement, that is, a huge rural population throughout the English Atlantic coastal colonies, a population that lived outside of settled communities altogether. A typical farm property in North America was larger than its European counterpart. In the dispersed character of their settlement, the English colonists followed the lead of those in their homeland who had "enclosed" small, peasant farm properties and thereby created large-scale, commercialized farming operations.

Although farmers typically *lived* in separate farmsteads during the seventeenth and eighteenth centuries, they nonetheless needed all the products and services that such families could not provide for themselves. At the most basic level, these needed products and services were provided by itinerant craftsmen who often used their customers' raw materials to make finished, customized goods.[12] But a range of services could most effectively be provided in a clustered settlement which farmers could periodically visit in order to deal with a variety of needs at once. Thus throughout the English colonies during the seventeenth and eighteenth centuries there emerged service centers for the surrounding rural population, located at points of optimal accessibility for buyers and sellers. The larger the settlement, the greater the array

Occupations Listed by Germantown Taxpayers, 1773 and 1793

| | | No. Workers | | | | | No. Workers | |
|---|---|---|---|---|---|---|---|---|
| | Category | 1773 | 1793 | | | Category | 1773 | 1793 |
| I | *Fabric Crafts* | | | VI | | *Food Production* | | |
| | Stocking weaver | 20 | 19 | | | Miller | 6 | 14 |
| | Weaver | 11 | 22 | | | Millwright | - | 2 |
| | Tailor | 12 | 20 | | | Millstone cutter | - | 3 |
| | Hatter | 6 | 13 | | | Baker | 4 | 2 |
| | Dyer | 4 | 3 | | | Butcher | 10 | 21 |
| | Fuller | 1 | 1 | | Total | | 20 | 42 |
| | Breeches maker | 1 | 2 | VII | | *Transportation* | | |
| | Glover | - | 1 | | | *Crafts and Services* | | |
| | Collarmaker | - | 1 | | | Coachmaker | 8 | 1 |
| Total | | 55 | 82 | | | Chairmaker | 1 | 23 |
| II | *Leather Crafts* | | | | | Chair trimmer | - | 2 |
| | Skinner | 7 | 8 | | | Wheelwright | 6 | 9 |
| | Cordwainer | 17 | 22 | | | Currier | 1 | 2 |
| | Saddlemaker | 8 | 4 | | | Carter | 8 | 17 |
| | Saddletree maker | 1 | 9 | | | Drover | - | 3 |
| | Harness maker | 2 | 4 | | | Coachman | - | 1 |
| | Tanner | 10 | 18 | | Total | | 24 | 58 |
| Total | | 45 | 65 | VIII | | *Tradesmen* | | |
| III | *Woodworking and* | | | | | Innkeeper | 4 | 8 |
| | *Building Crafts* | | | | | Shopkeeper | 8 | 9 |
| | Turner | 2 | 5 | | | Tobacconist | 1 | 1 |
| | Cooper | 26 | 43 | | | Merchant | 1 | - |
| | Cedar cooper | - | 13 | | | Lumber dealer | - | 1 |
| | Carpenter | 9 | 30 | | Total | | 14 | 19 |
| | Mason | 10 | 11 | IX | | *Professionals* | | |
| | Joiner | 8 | - | | | Doctor | 3 | 7 |
| | Nailer | - | 1 | | | Pastor | 1 | 2 |
| | Windsor-chair- | | | | | Schoolmaster | 4 | 4 |
| | maker | - | 1 | | | Barber | - | 1 |
| Total | | 55 | 104 | | Total | | 8 | 14 |
| IV | *General Crafts* | | | X | | *Other* | | |
| | *and Industries* | | | | | Farmer | 28 | 68 |
| | Clockmaker | 5 | 6 | | | Gardener | 1 | 1 |
| | Printer | 2 | 10 | | | Laborer | 52 | 78 |
| | Bookbinder | 3 | 3 | | | Head tax (no | | |
| | Typemaker | - | 1 | | | occ. given) | 83 | - |
| | Painter | 3 | 3 | | | Occ. not given | 42 | 11 |
| | Limner | - | 1 | | Total | | 206 | 158 |
| | Basketmaker | - | 1 | | | | | |
| | Rope maker | 1 | - | | Total all occupations | | 455 | 597 |
| | Starchmaker | 1 | 1 | | | | | |
| | Powdermaker | 1 | 1 | | | | | |
| Total | | 16 | 27 | | | | | |
| V | *Metal Crafts* | | | | | | | |
| | Blacksmith | 11 | 26 | | | | | |
| | Coppersmith | - | 1 | | | | | |
| | Miner | 1 | - | | | | | |
| | Tinman | - | 1 | | | | | |
| Total | | 12 | 28 | | | | | |

CRAFTS. This chart shows the astonishing variety of crafts that were practiced in a well-developed crafts center—in this case, Germantown, Pennsylvania, in 1773 and 1793. Although itinerant craftsmen were present throughout the colonies, it was more common for those with such skills to cluster in villages. [Stephanie Wolf, *Urban Village*] of available products and services and the larger the area such towns served.[13] The more substantial of these towns served both as collection depots for agricultural produce on its way to coastal urban areas or for export, and as retail centers in which farmers could buy goods brought in from afar. Smaller centers featured products made by local craftsmen and markets where produce from the rural farmsteads could be sold to town dwellers.

Through many of the English colonies there emerged a hierarchy of service-center towns. For example, in New England and especially in Connecticut, by the late eighteenth century there were five urban river ports or seaports, major trade depots that were important to many towns in the surrounding region and were heavily involved in the export trade. Twenty-five secondary centers served as inland markets whether directly involved in the export trade or not—for several surrounding towns. And forty-three country towns were service centers for only their own hinterlands.[14]

In the mid-Atlantic colonies, notably in Pennsylvania, one could find the same sort of hierarchy, ranging from the coastal urban center of Philadelphia, through a succession of county seats, market towns (often a given town was both a county seat *and* a market town), transportation points, and processing centers (either craft or mill villages).[15] In the county seats, political activity generated economic activity as such towns became both the political and economic centers of entire counties. But there were many small villages as well, separated only by short distances. Some developed at crossroads or at points where traders, wagoners, and drovers met. Others emerged as a result of an ambitious merchant or craftsman who sought a location for trade or industry. When a mill was established, it sometimes attracted craftsmen and storekeepers.[16]

The Southern colonies boasted port cities, most notably Baltimore and Charleston, but also planned port towns in North Carolina and somewhat upriver trader depots in Virginia. What Maryland, Virginia, and North Carolina lacked, though, was the tiered hierarchy of towns that was so obvious in colonies to the north. Many hamlets and villages in the Southern colonies performed economic functions, but in their size and range of services they were "flat." They constituted a linear rather than a hierarchical network of small clustered settlements, spreading through the vast plains and piedmont regions of the South but not growing in the tiered way of settlements elsewhere in the English colonies. The Southern colonists' desire to settle in a dispersed, rural manner across the largest continuous coastal lowland anywhere in the English mainland colonies was deeply ingrained and worked against the easy emergence of a hierarchy of settlements.[17] Throughout the colonial period, the Southern colonial assemblies tried to induce settlers to found towns that would serve as ports or processing centers, an effort continued by Georgia's activist government during the late eighteenth century, when the state planned five towns at the inland fall line of the state's rivers, recognizing that there was still little interest in providing services at centralized facilities for a largely rural population.[18]

The economic activities of the English colonists ranged from near self-sufficiency to almost total involvement in the commercial, market, money economy, and ranged in scale from very localized to vast transoceanic. Towns became involved in the commercial and international end of the spectrum when they were outlets for the export trade. In New England this took the form of shipbuilding for the empire and the shipping of goods from New England's agricultural, forestry, and fishery surplus.[19] Similarly in the mid-Atlantic region, particularly in Pennsylvania, the commercial development of grain farming spearheaded the growth of a large export trade in agricultural and forest products, funneled through Philadelphia and Baltimore. Both the New England and mid-Atlantic transoceanic trade were characterized by their varied destinations: not only the empire and Britain but also the Caribbean and European worlds beyond.[20]

In the South, the colonial assemblies tried to funnel staple crops, whether tobacco or wheat or rice, through port depots. To promote this objective Virginia, at least, established a tobacco inspection system in 1730, creating forty public warehouses located at sites along major rivers throughout the state. Producers sent their tobacco to these warehouses where county inspectors certified it as "merchantable" or not. The certificates, or "tobacco notes," circulated like money, with the crop as collateral.[21]

The three Southern staples differed in bulk, weight, and perishability. Each produced different commodity flows and processing demands which in turn affected packaging, transportation, and the provisioning and repair of freight shipments. The result was that each staple, at least in the area in which it dominated, affected the size and spatial pattern of regional ports and hinterland towns. The movement of wheat from the Great Valley of Virginia, of tobacco from much of the tidewater and piedmont in Maryland, Virginia, and North Carolina, and of rice from the coastal plain and sea islands of South Carolina and Georgia, all stimulated the growth of inland towns. They served as integrators between the backcountry or tidewater and coastal ports—Baltimore in Maryland; Alexandria, Fredericksburg, Petersburg, and Richmond in Virginia; the port towns (particularly Wilmington) of North Carolina; Charleston in South Carolina.[22]

But, unlike the emerging transatlantic market economies of New England and the mid-Atlantic colonies, the staple-crop economy of the Southern colonies depended increasingly upon the British, who restricted trade in these commodities to the empire itself, thus allowing the English and Scottish mercantile houses to manage the financing and shipping and marketing, if not the actual production, of the staples.

Towns that were heavily involved in the transoceanic market economy tended to grow into urban centers, whether along the coast or on inland rivers. A good example of this commerce-driven urbanization dominated by a mercantile elite was Springfield, Massachusetts, founded in 1636, in the usual manner, as an inland town. But Springfield quickly became dominated in every aspect of its economic life by the Puritan entrepreneurs William and John Pynchon (father and son). The Pynchons were involved in the fur trade, developed a commercial livestock operation, raised commercial crops on extensive fields, owned a general store, and ran the village's mills. With vast labor needs, they forged "patron-client" relationships as the employers of many of the community's earliest settlers. They were merchant-entrepreneurs whose beneficial personal relationships with employees and debtors tempered the growing judicial sanctity of contractual relationships and made them figures positioned somewhere between the manor house and the marketplace, between a feudal lord and an industrial owner. Springfield, as an early commercial center, quickly became urbanized and was later a city, though not on the scale of the region's chief urban center, Boston.[23]

In nearby Connecticut, merchants herded into the colony's five major towns—Hartford, New Haven, New London, Middletown, and Norwich—where they imported an array of goods from Britain, Holland, France, and other European sources, received produce from a variety of points in the rural hinterland, and served as wholesalers for merchants and shopkeepers in smaller surrounding towns.[24] Similarly, in Pennsylvania, a hierarchical mercantile community stretched from London, through Philadelphia, to a network of inland towns and on to their rural hinterlands, connecting all to a transoceanic system of trade and exchange and credit.[25] Only in the Southern colonies, with its British-sponsored staple-crop economy, did British merchants deal directly with colonial producers, without a significant local mercantile community emerging to assume its place in the hierarchy.

While the British North American colonies became an important part of a growing transoceanic, commercial, market economy, there were major obstacles to the rapid growth of a similar kind of economy *within* the colonies. Transportation was limited to wagons over a primitive road system or to boats along the coastal waterways of widely varying navigability. Horse-drawn wagons were slow and costly, capable of traveling only thirty miles per day in the most favorable weather conditions. Agricultural tools were rudimentary, with the horse-drawn plow the only major technological advancement over the farming techniques of the native population. Milling operations were limited largely to the traditional processing of grain and logs. Farmers crafted many of their own tools, even with the presence of local craftsmen. And though merchants served as creditors and bankers, their activities reflected only the beginnings of a financial or banking system.[26]

Among farmers, who constituted the vast majority of the colonists, "extensive" rather "intensive" agricultural practices prevailed; that is, general mixed farming, not specialized, commercial agriculture, was typical, and for a variety of reasons. A lack of crop and field rotation and fertilizers, superficial tillage, an indifference to labor-saving and technological improvements, the high cost and short supply of labor, the availability of land to the west, the presence of a wider market that made specialized products available from afar, and a general lack of interest in highly commercialized agricultural production—all these factors inhibited the large rural population from rushing toward specialization and commercialization.[27]

The exception to this pattern was the staple-crop agriculture of the Southern colonies, which was both specialized and commercial in character. Rice was most profitably grown on plantations in the sea islands and tidewater area of South Carolina and Georgia. By contrast, tobacco was profitably grown in Maryland, Virginia, and North Carolina on both large plantation complexes and small farming operations. In either case, the staple-crop agricultural process became connected by the eighteenth century to a network of ports and inland towns, as was the case with agricultural producers elsewhere.

The largest producers, the planters, created plantations, which were themselves embryonic communities. Indeed, contemporaries saw plantations as communities. A French traveler in 1686 thought of one he visited as "a rather large village." An English visitor in 1732 called such complexes "little" villages. Another French traveler in 1782 thought that William Byrd's Westover, when seen from across the river, "with its different annexes, has the appearance of a small town. . . ."[28] In sharp contrast to the urban centers along both sides of the Atlantic Ocean, dominated by British and Northern colonial merchants, the agricultural elite of the Southern colonies established a small kind of "rural community" with economic and social, if not political, dimensions. As powerful an elite in their rural settings as the merchants were in their urban contexts, the planters strove to develop communities that would be as nearly economically self-sufficient as they could make them. In addition to fields for the production of the staple crop, plantations also typically contained craft shops and additional fields for food crops. Enslaved laborers lived in their own quarters on the plantation or in the master's house itself, depending on their tasks. Field hands produced the tobacco or rice; craftsmen made many of the goods needed by the master for domestic and agricultural purposes; domestic servants served the master's family in the main house. All were forced to be members of a close-knit economic community that was wholly owned by the master.[29]

Ironically, the most commercialized and market-oriented of agricultural producers sought to become as self-sufficient in production for their own households as the smallest, simplest farm operators, those largely outside the market economy altogether. The planter "owned" his rural community in a way that no merchant could own the urban community he dominated, but like the merchant, the planter established patron-client relationships, personalized steeply hierarchical relationships with a variety of workers who produced the goods he traded, and represented a mixture of earlier and later economic characteristics. Both planters and merchants developed enterprises with a commercial, market orientation at the same time they retained the mentality of earlier feudalistic elites steeped in traditions of personalized relations with the lower orders.[30]

But ordinary towns in the English colonies contained neither a mercantile nor an agricultural elite. Most settlements were neither urban centers with merchants nor plantations with planters; they provided economic services for a farming population that was still closer to self-sufficiency than it was to commerce and market. Agricultural service centers such as Dedham, Massachusetts, were far more typical than commercially oriented towns liked Springfield, Massachusetts. Dedham did not, at least before the Revolution, develop a significant amount of commercial agricultural, though the number of craftsmen who had shops there increased somewhat during the eighteenth century. Although it was not far from Boston, Dedham was basically a village that served as a center for subsistence farmers, and as such it was largely outside the wider commercialized economy that emerged in the English colonies.[31]

Like farmsteads in the country, family households in towns produced as much as they could for their own use. Wives and mothers managed household-centered economic operations involving farmyard animals and outdoor crops eaten as food as well as indoor craft work worn as clothing. Men and women shared a preindustrial work rhythm. In the agricultural work process, men procured the raw materials, and women processed them into finished goods. Grains were milled into flour and then made into bread. Sheep were sheared, and the wool was then spun into cloth. Cattle were milked, and the milk was churned into butter or processed into cheese. Textile production was totally women's work: the carding and breaking of fibers, then spinning, weaving, sewing, knitting, quilting. Women's work was constantly interrupted by the needs of the family. Preindustrial domestic work was sporadic and uneven in tempo but meshed with the natural cycle of a family's evolution through time.

Domestic space was divided by gender. The house was female space: the living area, the cooking hearth, the dairy, the vegetable garden adjacent to the kitchen doorway. Women's space took in the kitchen and its appendages—cellars, pantries, brewhouses, milkhouses, butteries—and outdoors to the pigpen, the garden, the milkyard, the well, the henhouse, the orchard. Men's space was more open and wide-ranging: the outlying fields to plow and to mow, the wood lots to cut wood on, the mill, the market. Certain shared spaces united male and female work areas: the barnyard (an intermediate area between the house and barn), the barn itself to some extent (the storage area for produce and the stables for the family's livestock). Both men and women milked cows, though fowls were identified with women.[32]

Farm or craft-oriented families needed those products or services they were unable or unwilling to provide for themselves. The range of services that ordinary inland towns provided their own inhabitants as well as the farmers who lived in the surrounding countryside varied considerably. Among Connecticut's country towns, for example, Sharon had (in 1776) a local merchant and shop, a blacksmith, a brickyard, and a tannery.[33] Whatever the mix of craft shops and stores, the two were involved with different kinds of retail activity. In the shops, craftsmen not only made but sold their goods. General retail stores were involved in the sale of goods not produced by the storekeeper, who served as a broker between farmers or craftsmen and merchants. Storekeepers sometimes brought local farm and craft goods to larger towns for sale there and brought back goods from merchants involved in the export trade. In an inventory of Connecticut general stores, the stock consisted of over 60 percent cloth and clothing, 10 percent hardware, 10 percent leather goods and condiments, 6 percent stationery and books, and a variety of goods with smaller percentages.[34] Similarly, inventories of stores in Urbanna, Virginia, revealed that cloth, thread, buttons, buckles, combs, mirrors, window glass, oils and paint colors, locks and hinges, nails, pots and pans, and household and farm tools were prominent items that local craftsmen did not produce.[35]

But these craft and retail services also existed throughout the English colonies in locations by themselves, outside of any clustered settlements. And numerous itinerant craftsmen and peddlers lacked an ongoing location of any kind. Stores and craft shops were sometimes located alone at crossroads or at favored spots along shorelines or at river mouths. Mill sites were always at fall lines along waterways, sometimes alone, sometimes at the center of settlement.

Still, the larger the town, the wider the array of economic services for the populations of ever larger hinterlands. Connecticut's five urban towns were home to most of the colony's merchants, who were general importers and exporters but also wholesalers for surrounding, secondary market-center towns located along the coast or major rivers. One of these secondary towns, Fairfield, had thirty stores and shops during the 1770s, and all the towns had merchants who dealt with the export trade. Even store- and shopkeepers in country towns sometimes owned shares in ships involved in oceanic trade. Secondary market towns also were trade depots for the country towns surrounding them.[36]

Throughout the colonies, in the seventeenth and eighteenth centuries, a hierarchy of settlement emerged from the economic activity of the European settlers and their progeny, everything from individually located mills and stores and shops, to country towns serving rural agricultural hinterlands, to larger market towns that were important trade depots of regional significance, to early urban centers whose populations were heavily involved in transoceanic trade. Although most colonists were farmers living on their own farmstead, outside any community, they nonetheless needed services that were usually, though not always, provided in clustered settlements. The need was so great that the largest agriculturalists, the planters, tried to create their own communities, and though plantations were too small to constitute a clustered settlement of any significance, these plantation communities represented serious efforts on the part of the planters to reach toward economic self-sufficiency.

Crucial to a town's emergence as a service center in the hierarchy was its location. Those settlements that were situated at good harbors or navigable points on inland waterways were most likely to grow. During the seventeenth and eighteenth centuries, trade of all kinds was most effectively and cheaply linked to water transportation. The movement of goods overland was hampered by roads that were a bewildering variety of private and public ways, often poorly maintained and thus prey to changing climate and weather and seasons. Few roads extended for long distances among the seaboard settlements, or connected sizable market towns and port cities, and could therefore emerge as major arteries of commerce.

Regardless of its size, the economic success of a community had nothing to do with its physical shape or political boundaries. Trading areas involved hinterlands, which linked those who identified with Dedham, Massachusetts, for example, with farmers in the surrounding rural area and to people in other, larger, distant towns or even urban centers. Craftsmen and storekeepers and mill operators who lived in particular villages were involved in economic transactions with people who lived in places far beyond the village, thus creating an economically defined territory with its own dimensions.

As settlements expanded throughout the English colonies in the seventeenth and eighteenth centuries, the extent to which people stayed and became part of a town's core citizenry for generations, or migrated and became part of a town's transient element, varied considerably. In New England, at least, the Puritans sought to keep together families of those who had settled in particular towns. In an early town such as Andover, Massachusetts, the progeny of the original settlers did try to remain in the immediate vicinity for as long as land could reasonably be divided into additional farmsteads. But continuous land division pressed sons in the third or fourth generation of settlers to seek land elsewhere—to the West—or to pursue occupations outside of farming.[37] Throughout New England, land became a highly sought commodity and, by the late colonial period, prompted rampant speculation.

In colonial Pennsylvania the relentless buying and selling and dividing of land produced similar pressures for sons to move westward for land or to become farm tenants or to change occupations. But unlike the New Englanders, who at least made an effort to stay together as long as land divisions permitted, Pennsylvanians seem to have perceived land as a salable commodity from the very beginning of settlement in the late seventeenth century. In many townships in the early-settled southeastern counties of Lancaster and Chester, as many as 40 to 80 percent of township dwellers moved beyond township boundaries over a ten-year period in the 1770s and 1780s.[38] In Germantown, children of the founding settlers often quickly sold the family homestead to the highest bidder and moved on.[39]

The Southern colonies too saw a constant movement westward to clear new areas for tobacco and wheat, if not rice, cultivation. As in New England, families in eastern coastal areas tried to stay together through the generations in kin-related, planter-dominated neighborhoods, and indeed the Southern colonists did succeed in building up communities of interlocking families. But, as elsewhere, such families also had members, or entire branches, who were forced to settle farther west, compelled to abandon holdings reduced in size by repeated divisions among heirs. Southern colonists were not only dispersed in their coastal settlement pattern, but even these households were further dispersed as members constantly came and went between old settlements and new frontiers.[40]

During these same centuries along the Spanish frontier, in what later became the American Southwest, Spanish authorities so organized settlement in the semi-arid region of northern New Mexico, for example, that the economic life of the settlers was preordained. As in New England, where the proprietors held common lands they progressively sold off, so too in these Spanish colonial towns, ranching (the most significant economic activity) was carried on in communal pastures and grazing lands located outside the villages. These were lands held collectively for an indefinite period by the town dwellers.[41] The economic life of the Spanish colonists who settled in towns was very much like that of the classic peasant community. Farmers lived in the village and went out to their fields to farm. But there was also a distinction: in Spanish America the land holdings were communal; in the classic peasant village individual peasants could own their own strips of land. To Europe's frontier in the Americas the Spanish colonists brought their Catholicism in the form of a vibrant communalism. Its only echo among the English colonists could be found among the Puritan proprietors, whose common land holdings reflected the Puritans' emphasis on community as they launched a major experiment on that same frontier.

· II ·

DURING THE nineteenth century the economic world of town dwellers became more complicated. As settlement moved westward, vast new areas of arable land came under cultivation in the great mid-continent river valleys and plains and in the Pacific coastal valleys; and great mountain ranges were found to contain extensive mineral and timber areas. In settling a continent, Americans greatly enlarged the scale of territory on which they worked to develop resources and amass wealth.

In the process they became technologically innovative, spurred on by nonagricultural labor shortages caused by the relative ease with which family farming could continue to be pursued in some form almost everywhere. American inventiveness transformed energy sources, transportation, communications, the making of finished products, mining, forestry, fishing, and even agriculture itself. With dizzying rapidity waterpower was replaced by steam power, which in turn was overwhelmed by electrical power—all in the course of a single century. Power-driven machinery transformed agriculture and extractive activity of all kinds and became the basis for the mass production of hitherto handcrafted goods. Technology enormously quickened the speed and reach of transportation and communications, as first steam and then electrical power fueled ships and trains, and as the telegraph delivered messages instantly.

In the nineteenth century, extractive activity dominated the economic life of some towns. Fishing villages continued along the coasts. In forested areas, logging operations often involved (as in earlier times) a lone sawmill near a village center or, at most, lumber camps for larger, longer efforts. But on occasion the extraction of forest products dominated the life of new towns, to the point that small economic elites exploited a plentiful resource for which there was a great demand. For example, after the Revolution, Beekmantown, a frontier settlement near Lake Champlain in New York, became the locus for a profitable trade in forest products taken from the rich timberlands that surrounded the lake. In Britain and elsewhere there was a market for the plentiful white oak, which was used for barrel staves and ship construction. The proprietors and their agents were enriched by the timber trade. They hired the farmers who had begun to settle in the township, putting them to work in the lumber business and as provisioners for other workers, and created relatively large-scale trading enterprises involving distant markets. At first they shipped through Montreal and Quebec City via water and land transport, and then through New York City, when a canal connecting Lake Champlain and the Hudson River opened in the 1820s. But the forest resources of frontier towns were finite as a sudden, major source of wealth (though eventually replaceable), and by the mid-nineteenth century Beekmantown became an ordinary, agriculturally based community.[42]

Later, from the 1870s to the 1890s, for as long as it took to deforest the area, lumber towns in Michigan flourished. Preexisting settlements—Bay City, Muskegon, and Saginaw—all developed swiftly when entrepreneurs created large-scale lumbering operations and brought in significant numbers of wage laborers. As in Beekmantown, an elite relatively briefly dominated a resource-based community; the lumber town phase passed after a generation of logging had depleted the forests; and the timber was sent via water transport not to Montreal or New York City but to Buffalo and Albany or to Chicago. But the subsequent economic history of the Michigan lumber towns varied considerably. In Bay City, absentee lumber barons crushed strikes; brought in scab labor; did little to deal with the ethnic tensions among a mixed labor force of Poles, French Canadians, and Germans; and failed to invest in a postlogging era. Instead they moved farther west to look for other investment opportunities. In Muskegon and Saginaw, by contrast, resident entrepreneurs took advantage of ethnic homogeneity and invested in a varied but lumber-related economic future.[43]

As settlement moved west across the continent and as logging became technologically more sophisticated, lumber corporations built company towns in isolated areas in the forested mountains of the Pacific coast. In the 1850s and 1860s the Puget Mill Company developed Port Gamble, and in the 1880s Port Ludlow, both located along the shores of Puget Sound. In the 1860s the Washington Mill Company built another company town, Seabeck. In the 1880s the Pacific Lumber Company developed Scotia, California.[44]

Mining followed a similar course of development. The gold rushes of the 1850s and 1860s attracted throngs of individual prospectors from the East and from abroad, who swarmed various spots in the Rocky Mountains where this most valuable of minerals was discovered. Their placer mining was technologically primitive, consisting of a simple screening process, and at first failed to attract the interest of groups of investors who could develop large-scale mechanized operations. The mining camps that grew up around every strike were usually short-term communities that did not outlast a particular rush. But the supply towns for mining districts, such as Central City, Colorado, sometimes became durable communities.[45]

In the case of copper mining, corporations developed some of the largest and most stable company towns. The Phelps Dodge Corporation built Morenci and Ajo in Arizona. The Kennecott Copper Corporation built company towns in Arizona, New Mexico, Nevada, and Utah. The Anaconda Copper Mining Company's town was near Butte, Montana. By the turn of the century, open-pit mining for copper became common as smelting techniques made possible the recovery of copper even if it constituted only 1 or 2 percent of the ore. This low-grade mining demanded large-scale operations, once again in isolated areas.[46]

When coal replaced charcoal as a fuel, coal-mining corporations in isolated areas of Wyoming, Colorado, Utah, and New Mexico established company towns in order to supply railroad companies or metal mining companies with a supply of fuel. To ensure supply, many of the rail and mining companies owned their own coal-mining company towns, such as the Union Pacific Coal Company and the Phelps Dodge Company. The Colorado Fuel and Iron Corporation controlled more company towns than any other corporation in the West.[47]

In company towns that concentrated on extractive activity, corporations sought to lure workers to isolated areas that had poor transportation connec-

COMPANY STORE SCRIP. This scrip from the Simpson Timber Company is typical of what was issued by the owners of company towns as a credit against the earnings of those who worked in the towns. Workers could use the scrip anywhere in town but were confined as customers to company-owned facilities. [Allen, *The Company Town in the American West*]

tions, areas apart from existing settlements. These corporations usually built the workers' housing all at once in a uniform style. Houses were simple in design and were rented to those who worked for the corporation. Because workers were being enticed into a new, still isolated community, the corporations usually provided a recreation hall or other community facilities and a company store where workers could buy food and provisions of all kinds with scrip—company money issued as credit against actual earnings. No municipal government existed, only a company administrator. And the corporations resisted the unionization of their employees, often prohibiting union organizers on their property. When workers had grievances—most often in the coalmining towns, which were the least attractive—unionization drives became quite frenzied and labor-management relations turned sour.

On the whole, however, workers seemed content, rents were generally fair, company stores did not overcharge even though they were the only source, the recreation halls were busy community centers, and many who worked in the towns did so quite temporarily, leaving when they had saved enough money to move on.[48]

Extractive activity involving forest products and minerals had been confined to lumber camps and iron forges in the East in a time of primitive organizational and productive capacities. But when settlement moved west, such activity became mechanized and could be pursued on a large scale with wage laborers. Milling activity, by contrast, was already mechanized, with waterpower as its energy source. Mills had long been sites for the mechanized production of flour from grain and of board from logs. Mills had already become the focal point for the emergence of craft-oriented villages.

But in the nineteenth century, milling operations were turned to a new use. The waterpower that had turned the gears and shafts, which in turn had moved the grist stones to grind grain into flour and saw blades to cut logs into boards, was now utilized to power more sophisticated spinners and weavers. Thus basic foodstuffs and basic building materials were joined by basic clothing materials, mass produced in a mechanized operation that for the first time involved the use of substantial numbers of wage laborers. This new, mechanized way of making cloth not only replaced the domestic, hand-crafted method but also replaced the family mode of production with wage labor. The producers of cloth no longer owned what they produced, the mill or factory owner did.

Cloth-making at mills vastly enlarged the scale of production of a basic commodity. Milling activity up to that point had not done so: millers and their assistants typically processed the grain and logs brought to them; they were processors of other people's materials. Thus the enlargement of milling activity to include cloth-making had a profound effect on the entire economy. If cloth could be mass produced on machines by wage laborers, why couldn't many other products?

During the first half of the nineteenth century, dozens of factory towns emerged from preexisting or newly constructed mill villages situated at sites for waterpower—along rivers flowing into the Atlantic Ocean throughout the northeastern and, to a far lesser extent, the southeastern parts of the United States. The British had already developed power looms for the mechanical production of cotton cloth, and two English mechanics, the brothers Samuel and John Slater, emigrated to the United States and introduced the new machinery at the turn of the century. American millwrights had no problem erecting wooden or stone buildings suitable for textile manufacture, as the physical space needed fit within an enlarged version of the traditional mill buildings.[49] There was no economic reason why Southern millwrights could not have created mill factories close to the cotton they needed for cloth manufacture. But Northern millers seemed more open to innovation, to the conversion of milling to a new kind of industrial production, just as the existing mercantile community of the Atlantic port cities took over from the British the task of financing, shipping, and marketing cotton, which became after 1800 the preeminent staple crop of Southern agriculture.

The new factory villages were small and typically operated by former millers, with existing nearby grist- and sawmills. Such factories were financed by coastal merchants and local millwrights, often in partnerships. A miller was usually the active manager, having the technical skills necessary to maintain and repair textile machinery. With relatively small capital needed to start such an operation, many textile mills were established in dozens of villages. The great number made competition fierce, and many failed.[50] Lowell, Massachusetts, became the first truly industrial city in the United States because a number of different corporations (whose investors usually were Boston merchants) designed large-scale textile mill factories there, factories that dwarfed in size those in a typical mill village.[51] But Lowell was exceptional. Most factories were located in villages: the birthplace of modern industry was the town, not the city.

These early factory towns were not usually company towns like the logging and mining towns of the Rocky Mountain and Pacific coast regions. They were not built for a sole purpose. Mill villages were typically industrial centers whose cotton mills were surrounded by the attributes of a company town, even though the new factory operation did not embrace the entire village. Even Lowell, as the first industrialized urban center, attracted manufacturing corporations that built a great deal of tenement housing for their wage labor forces. For the women who comprised their initial labor force, these corporations provided residence halls and planned all recreational, religious, and social activity, acting as a kind of chaperone.[52]

Far more typical was the Rockdale manufacturing district near the Delaware River, between Wilmington, Delaware, and Philadelphia, where seven textile mills were built at sites that had waterpower, in the vicinity of existing settlements. Owned by millers, most of whom lived nearby, these factory villages contained tenements for the mill workers as well as housing for the supervisory personnel, all built by the mill owners on their own land.[53] By contrast, in Ware, Massachusetts, Boston capitalists constructed three large textile factories in the late 1820s at the site of an already-developed village. When factory owners were absentee, little economic benefit (other than for wage-earning machine operatives) accrued to established communities, as profits were siphoned off to the faraway proprietors.[54]

Mill villages typically had about a hundred workers. The company usually used any housing that had already been built on the owners' land, then built whatever additional housing was needed. Tenements for one, two, or four families were common. Nearby taverns sometimes doubled as boardinghouses for single employees. Some companies provided garden plots and pasture land that village employees could rent to raise at least part of their food. In other villages, company-owned farms supplied fuel and meat and produce. Some of the early employees kept their farms as well, shuttling between both types of work. Nearly all villages had company stores where goods could be purchased on credit against future wages. New villages were often too far from established stores for convenience or were too small to entice a prosperous storekeeper located elsewhere to open another store.[55]

Outside of the experiment with unmarried female labor at the great factory center at Lowell, the labor force in the smaller mill villages typically consisted of whole families of agricultural laborers, farmers, or even craftsmen, all of whom sometimes worked in the mills while continuing with their work on farms and in shops. Their children too (those in their teens) were often hired to perform tasks in the mills. At first, native-born Americans of British origin predominated among those hired, but by the 1840s and 1850s both Irish and French-Canadian immigrants transformed the nature of the workforce.

Workers in the smaller mill villages tried to unionize, but the organizations they sometimes created under the spur of a workplace crisis were fragile, often temporary. Yet such workers were involved in work stoppages or strikes from the 1830s on, chiefly caused by the efforts of mill owners to reduce wages in periods of declining demand. As dependent wage earners, early mill workers were concerned that they would lose their independence and become enslaved to the mill owners. Their dependence was tied to a wage payment that fluctuated with the market. Early factory workers came from other kinds of work, and though farm laborers were already familiar with wage labor, farmers and craftsmen (and their daughters and sons) were not. To those who had had independent work lives, wage dependency and the ownership of production by an elite, especially when their wages were threatened, felt like a kind of enslavement, a loss of independence.[56]

As the nineteenth century progressed and settlement moved across the mid-continent valleys and plains, milling operations became textile factories. In the South too, textile mill towns emerged as Southerners began to manufacture cloth near its cotton source and to finance, store, ship, and market the finished product under the direct control of their own producers, rather than continuing to depend upon Northern mercantile operations. In the Midwest as well, milling operations typically developed into processing centers for the agricultural products that were grown and raised there on an increasingly commercial basis. Gristmills became grain processing centers as local merchants assumed the task of shipping, processing, and marketing grain crops. Similarly, mechanized meatpacking plants processed the livestock that farmers shipped to marketing centers under the aegis of other local merchants.[57] By the late nineteenth century, industrialization in the large-scale commercial farming districts of mid-continental valleys and plains, as well as of Pacific coast valleys, increasingly took the form of processing plants in which canned food products were prepared for market.[58]

In areas where mineral deposits or forests were the raw material, processing took on other forms. For example, in Bellefonte, Pennsylvania, situated near a vein of iron ore, an array of industrial firms that used this material arose: a machine shop and foundry (1879), a glass works (1867), a railroad car manufacturer (1873), a planing mill (1879), and a nail works (1881).[59]

Throughout the nineteenth century the mass production of machine-made goods made by wage labor spread from cloth to other products, such as shoes, clocks, and rifles, and then to a growing list. The process was the same: first one part of a product and then other parts came to be machine made, until all parts were. Although handcrafted versions of the product continued to be made, they were usually in a losing competition to the cheaper (both in price and in quality) version. A by-product of mass production was the manufacture of interchangeable parts, which became (for a time) a distinctively American contribution to industrial production. The process was pioneered at the beginning of the nineteenth century by Eli Whitney in the manufacture of rifles for the U.S. government at a waterpowered site at Mill Rock, Connecticut. Whitney devised a procedure in which each piece of the rifle was made independently and in large quantities, with the numerous copies so identical they would fit into any rifle of the kind being made, interchangeably. This simple procedure transformed the mass production of machine-made products.[60]

As first steam power (important by the mid-century) and then electrical power (beginning late in the century) released industrial production from its dependence on waterpower, the factory system spread wherever there was an effective combination of capital, management, labor, raw materials, transportation, and markets. People at the time recognized the revolutionary importance of electricity as a power source. Roderick Turnbull, who reminisced about his youth in a town at the turn of the nineteenth century, remembered that "electricity almost by itself is the difference between the modern way of living and the old horse and buggy days."[61] People with entrepreneurial skills and access to capital in towns all over the continent attempted to start factory enterprises during the mid- and late nineteenth century, but the failure rate was very high. Willis F. Dunbar remembered industry after industry failing in turn-of-the-century Hartford, Michigan: "Few other small towns were any more successful in attracting manufacturing industries in this period than Hartford was." For Dunbar, successful industries in towns were "small-scale processors of locally produced raw materials and provided only seasonal employment."[62] Towns, the site for the earliest waterpowered factories, were no longer the obvious place for such operations, as labor, capital, and power sources all became concentrated in urbanized areas. Frenzied efforts to establish local industries led townspeople to adopt subscription bond rallies and tax-relief schemes. But the combination of managerial talent, skilled labor, sufficient capital, and adequate transportation and markets was difficult for towns to bring together.[63]

As a result, from the mid-nineteenth to the early twentieth century, many of the industries that were started in towns eventually died. In an economic sense, many towns became "failed cities," wanting industrial growth but lacking the capacity to attain it.[64] Industrial production more and more came to be located in urban centers, which for the first time combined commercial with industrial preeminence. People with entrepreneurial skills and access to large amounts of capital gravitated toward cities, with their greater labor supply and more developed transportation networks and markets, their more varied financial resources and storage facilities.

Even though many towns across the continent became early extractive and industrial centers during the nineteenth century—a distinctive moment in the history of American towns—most towns continued to be service centers for agricultural hinterlands, not factory towns or even processing centers. But the nature of agriculture too changed significantly during the nineteenth century. Everywhere it became either more mechanized or more commercialized, or both. Only Southern producers of cotton were able, through slave labor, to avoid the mechanization that producers of livestock and grain in the great valleys and plains of the mid-continent felt compelled to adopt. In all parts of the nation, fewer and fewer farming areas remained outside the market economy. Fewer and fewer farm families were willing or able to lead largely self-sufficient economic lives.

In the longest-settled areas along the northern and central regions of the Atlantic coast, farmers involved in the production of grain and livestock could not directly and successfully compete with those who managed similar but much larger operations in the mid-continent valleys and plains. Agriculture in the East became increasingly commercialized as farmers supplied ever larger urban markets, but only in the case of the livestock and crops that Midwesterners failed to produce for wider markets.

Farmers around New Gloucester, Maine, for example, grew more commercialized during the first half of the nineteenth century, concentrating on particular commodities as Midwestern competition drove some products from the area off the market. Farmers became suppliers of raw materials for processing centers and markets elsewhere and developed specialized operations involving dairying, orchards, and poultry. They dealt with the agents of dealers in such products as milk, cheese, fruit, and corn who either processed the raw products or sold them at large urban markets (such as the Quincy Market in Boston) that were capable of handling huge amounts of animals or crops each year.[65]

In this same period, in Lincoln, Massachusetts, farmers became substantially more productive by adopting systematic crop rotation, new methods of planting and stock breeding, and improved farm equipment, enabling them to supply nearby urban markets with a mixture of livestock and crops.[66] Farmers outside of towns everywhere along the East Coast were forced to raise agricultural products that were profitable and without direct competition from large Midwestern farms: sheep farming, dairying, and cheese making instead of beef cattle; fruit and garden vegetables instead of grains. During the nineteenth century the farmers of Chelsea, Vermont, remained attached to sheep farming rather than switching to the more profitable dairy farming because sheep farming was far less labor intensive, less mechanized, and less demanding of feed supplies.[67] Chelsea's farmers found a commodity for which there was a steady market, a commodity they could afford to produce. In this they were typical of farmers up and down the East Coast for whom successful farming during the industrial era meant finding a crop or a kind of livestock for which there was sufficient demand and not too much competition from farmers in other locations.

In the South, as staple-crop agricultural production moved from the coasts and major rivers to inland areas, slave-owning cotton growers still needed to get their crops to the seaports. Richmond, Charleston, Savannah, Mobile, New Orleans, and Natchez served as entrepots for the export of the United States' most valuable commodity. The wealthiest masters who owned the best lands along major waterways shipped their crops directly to factors or purchasing agents at major port cities. Smaller slaveholders who lived near a river or major port brought their cotton directly to market or hauled their crops overland to small inland centers, such as Vicksburg, Mississippi, if there was no town close by. They did so over a poor road system. If smaller growers were in the vicinity of large plantations, they sometimes sold their produce directly to the planters, who in effect acted as middlemen by ginning cotton for their neighbors. Other small slaveowners sold their crops to itinerant merchants who traveled through the more unsettled areas of the South.

But the usual pattern for the smaller cotton growers was to become involved with nearby small settlements where gin operators, store owners, and small merchants were located. The town store was the most readily available agency of credit, and it supplied the farmers with groceries and tools, accepting crops in payment at the end of each growing season. Those growers who did not own their own cotton gin frequently went to the local gin house or country store, where ginning was offered. Store owners often marketed the crops of small slaveholders, selling them to their own factors. Small clustered settlements—places like Raymond, Clinton, Washington, and Port Gibson in Mississippi alone—thus served important economic functions for the all but the largest cotton-growing operations in the South.[68] For instance, in Grayson, Louisiana, Albert Mixon, Sr., took over the village store in 1896 and served as a cotton buyer and creditor to many farmers.[69]

In the post–Civil War decades this system continued as planters and smaller cotton growers became landlords and former slaves became tenant farmers or sharecroppers on their former master's estates. In a chain of economic dependency, sharecroppers remained indebted to landowners, who in turn were indebted to storekeepers, who in turn were indebted to merchants, who in turn were sometimes indebted to Northeastern financial interests.

As the great mid-continent valleys and plains were settled from the early to the late nineteenth century, hundreds of settlements became service centers for the thousands of farmers who created farmsteads from the Appalachians to the Rocky Mountains. In the Ohio River valley, agriculture was pursued as it was in the eastern valleys and hillsides: farmers settled on forested land, cleared the timber, and uncovered the sought-after forest-bottom soil. In a rural neighborhood such as Sugar Creek, Illinois, at the edge of the prairie, the original settlers tilled the timber land, using the prairie grassland for grazing livestock. Farmers did not know how to use grassland for crops until the invention of steel plows, which came into common use in the 1840s and 1850s.[70] Once the highly productive prairie soil was utilized for the raising of crops as well as for the grazing of livestock, the plains—both the eastern tall grasslands and, beyond the 98th meridian, the more westerly semi-arid short grasslands—became the site for large-scale commercial farming, which, beginning in the 1850s, became increasingly mechanized as well, as planters, mowers, reapers, and threshers were invented and widely adopted.[71]

Family farmsteads continued to produce a variety of crops and livestock for domestic use as well as for wider markets—marketable garden vegetables, dairy products, and meat. Corn was not a market crop because of its bulk. It was distilled into whiskey, which was marketable in kegs, or fed to pigs, which were often driven to markets in hog drives. Those who owned small farms often had to supplement their income by selling such additional products as rails, furs, and whiskey, or they labored for better-off farmers elsewhere.[72] Rose Wilder Lane, in her memoir of town life at the turn of the nineteenth century, succinctly summed up the economic relationship of family farmers everywhere on the continent to the towns in their vicinity: "On Saturdays [farmers] came to town, dressed for the occasion and bringing the week's surplus of butter, eggs, vegetables, and fruits. They came to the stores, to trade."[73]

By contrast, owners of large-scale, increasingly mechanized farms hired wage laborers, rented land to tenants, and specialized in the production of corn, wheat, or livestock. A variant of these huge farming operations was the cattle drive from the southern plains to cattle trading centers in Kansas during the 1870s and 1880s. Abeline, Ellsworth, Witchita, Dodge City, and Caldwell—ever farther to the west—competed to become the terminus of choice for cattle drovers, who raised cattle in Texas and drove them through open, unfenced range to railroad termini, from which they could be moved by rail to meatpacking firms in Chicago.

Cattle drovers quickly came to dominate towns that otherwise would have been ordinary agricultural service centers, just as other economic elites sometimes emerged to dominate extractive activity by exploiting valuable resources. The presence of the cattle drovers created tensions with the farming populations that surrounded these towns, because merchants developed services that catered to the drovers and their cowboys, to the neglect of the farmers themselves. Ordinary farmers charged that the cattle enterprises caused expensive law enforcement efforts because the unruly behavior of the drovers and their employees led to high crime rates; that drovers were favored by local banks; and that revenues were spent on public improvements that unfairly assisted drovers.[74] In semi-arid plateaus farther west, in places like "Starchey," California (a fictitious name for a real town), open-range sheep and cattle ranching also flourished during the late nineteenth century, competing with dry farming for grain crops.[75]

As the plains and plateaus were fenced in, open-range ranching gave way to operations confined to farmsteads. Towns like those in the East McLean area of central Illinois—Ellsworth, Arrowsmith, Saybrook, Cooksville, Anchor, Cropsey, Colfax—became collecting points for farm produce en route to urban markets and distribution points for surrounding agricultural populations.[76] Similarly, on the high plains to the west of the Mississippi River, "plains towns," often founded by railroad companies, in the 1880s, served a similar function for the farmers in their hinterlands.[77] Wherever these agricultural service centers were founded on the plains or more westerly plateaus, their economic activities centered on the grain elevator or the livestock pen, as rail connections replaced drives across open plains or plateaus or along roadways to river ports. Refrigerated trains prolonged the life of commercial fruit and vegetable crops grown in Florida or the central valley of California and protected produce and meat of whatever source over long distances. By the end of the nineteenth century, crops and livestock raised anywhere on a large scale could, through refrigerated rail transport, reach national markets.[78]

Whatever their economic orientation, towns were typically founded as real estate ventures during the nineteenth century, just as they had been during the seventeenth and eighteenth centuries. But now there was a difference in emphasis. Town founders typically "boosted" their towns, deliberately publicizing them to lure ever greater numbers of migrants, hoping from the outset that "their" towns would mushroom into cities, even naming them "cities" at the outset.[79] Such founders believed that whatever enriched themselves, as civic leaders, was good for community growth: private enrichment and the commonweal were inextricably mixed.[80] Just as towns competed to become county seats and state capitals, so too did they compete to become ever larger trade centers for ever larger hinterlands.

But very few towns became urban centers. A rare combination of factors—a favorable location at a waterway or at a natural break along inland transportation lines, a talented business elite with exceptional entrepreneurial skill, an ample labor pool, large amounts of investment capital, good transportation connections, a well-developed market—all were essential in conjunction before a town could grow into a great city.

The one feature that allowed a great many towns to grow into significant service centers or trade depots was their connection to a transportation system. Early in the century this meant enticing a canal corporation to build a canal to the community. For example, the Delaware and Hudson Canal, which connected the Delaware River at the New Jersey border to the Hudson River at Kingston, New York, greatly augmented the scale and variety of goods traded at Kingston for reshipment elsewhere, particularly coal and the produce of Kingston's rural hinterland.[81]

But later, for most of the century, transportation meant luring railroad

RAILROAD STATIONS. During the nineteenth century the railroad station, like this one in Jackson, Mississippi, along with the livery stable, was one of the transportation centers of the town. It was thus a focal point of community life—though, unlike the livery stable, both men and women were comfortable using this public space. [Fred Daniel Collection]

corporations to lay track right through an established town, as was often the case east of the Mississippi River by the 1840s and 1850s, or in connection with a new town, as was often the case west of the Mississippi River after the 1850s. From the middle of the century to its end, the most crucial determinant of a town's capacity to grow and flourish, if not burgeon into a city, was its rail connections.[82]

Jacksonville, Illinois, became a rail center as its trade in grains and meat expanded, each enhancing and enlarging the other. Although local promoters were among the town's elite, many town dwellers got involved in petitioning rail companies to build track through the town. Local capital was invested as subscription drives for railroad stock won the support of businessmen and farmers, all of whom were anxious to profit from Jacksonville's likely development as a commercial center. Boards of directors for each of the local railroads were drawn from prominent citizens of the town and from other towns along each line. Local voters usually approved large bond issues for railroad investment, bonds which were sold in the East in order to provide further support for these ventures.[83]

If towns were county seats *and* had connections to rail transport, their stability seemed assured, especially if they were service centers for rural produce of any kind. The following county seats, with the date at which rail connections were made, amply illustrate this point: Cazenovia, New York (1870s), Chilton, Wisconsin (1870s), Grundy Center, Iowa (1870s), Petersburg, Illinois (1870s), Hermann, Missouri (1850s), Woodstock, Virginia (1850s), Sanford, Kentucky (1860s), Centerville, Tennessee (1880s), Berryville, Arkansas (1900), Southport, North Carolina (1910), Mocksville, North Carolina (1890), Louisville, Georgia (1880s), and Apalachicola, Florida (1850s).[84]

Throughout the nineteenth century, boosters everywhere on the continent continuously publicized their towns in an effort to lure others to settle there. Of those who came, many soon left. The rate of migration in and out of towns, already in evidence during the seventeenth and eighteenth centuries, was quite high during the nineteenth. Many names that appeared in one census were gone by the time of the next census. This massive geographical mobility divided a town's population into a core, persisting group and a transient, temporary one. The core population tended to be middle-aged, of relatively high socioeconomic circumstances and occupations, and of some prominence in the community. The transients tended to be young, with low income, and of unsettled occupation. In a setting of economic change and impermanency, the unskilled and propertyless were buffeted about in search of work. The core and the transient, the stable and the mobile elements of a town's population occupied the same geographic space, but they were two separate populations. Even so, the mobile element usually did not disrupt the continuity of the stable folk.

Everywhere the overall pattern seems to have been the same, but there were infinite variations. For instance, in Massachusetts, in towns such as Pelham and Ware, half of those who moved were young men under the age of thirty. Highly mobile, with a tendency to enter developing towns in large numbers, this age group expected to move frequently during this phase of their lives, a phase in which they were concerned to achieve security and find a place for themselves. Young men moved when they needed work. The least skilled became floaters or permanent transients; others acquired skills and moved among relatives and friends to more advantageous places.[85] In Jacksonville, Illinois, only a minority remained in the town from one census to another. A small, stable core croup was surrounded by immigrants and emigrants. The core persisted to build businesses, homes, and careers, and to raise families. Those in less-skilled jobs—construction and other kinds of laborers, as well as servants—moved often, whereas those with professions and

HOUSEWORK. The work of most women involved both the interior and exterior of the home. In the nineteenth century, women's domestic labor was still notably varied and demanding. [Top, Brown Brothers; below, Culver Pictures]

skilled crafts tended to stay. The wealthier an individual, the more likely he was to stay. The core population was suffused with the booster spirit.[86] In Trempealeau County, Wisconsin, transients were those who were not prospering, who were young, unmarried, had little property, and were foreign-born.[87]

In rural areas such as Sugar Creek, Illinois, at the boundary line between the forested land of the Ohio River valley and the prairies or grassland of the trans-Mississippi West, typical farm families were largely self-sufficient well into the nineteenth century. Children continued to be an economic necessity and contribute much to the domestic economy of a farmstead. There were rails to make, fences to build, grubbing to do, lands to clear and prepare for crops. Boys mucked out barns, made hay, cleared and gleaned fields, hoed, husked, and plowed. Girls learned how to prepare yarn and cloth and do needlework. By the time they reached puberty, boys had assumed most of the tasks of full-grown men, and girls followed their mother's endless round of chores, quickly learning women's work. Women bore and cared for a large family of children, prepared three meals every day, and cleaned, washed, ironed, and mended clothes. In the garden they raised vegetables and herbs. In the evenings they carded, spun, wove, and tailored cloth. In the henhouse or farmyard they tended flocks of chickens and geese, collected eggs, set hens, plucked down, and strangled roosters. In the dairy they fed and milked cows, and on the porch or in the pantry they churned butter and sometimes made cheese. They produced towels and blankets and quilts, as well as pickles, cider, dried fruit, soap, and candles, and frequently helped the men in the fields as well. And when illness or accident disabled a farmer, farm women did the work that could not wait.[88]

During the nineteenth century, however, households *in towns* gradually abandoned the activities that had made them largely indistinguishable from farmsteads outside of settlements. This was a long and messy process, and in many towns households that operated much like farmsteads continued to coexist with those whose owners gradually abandoned efforts to be as self-sufficient as possible. It was largely a matter of wealth: the better off a family was, the more it could purchase products and services provided by others, the more it could make the interior of the house more comfortable by purchasing technologically innovative gas jets, wood and then coal stoves and furnaces, and iceboxes.[89] But it remained typical for homemakers to have summer gardens for housewives to "can" or preserve fruits for winter use, for husbands to stock cellars with vegetables and apples, and for households to have cow barns, pigpens, smokehouses, and chicken houses.[90]

WHEELWRIGHTS. The largest craft shop in most towns was the carriage shop, like this one in Winchester, Kentucky, a work site for craftsmen with a variety of skills. Craft-dominated carriage and buggy shops were the preindustrial precursors of the later mass-assembly and then automated production facilities for motor vehicles. [University of Louisville]

Towns continued throughout the nineteenth century to be centers for those who handcrafted goods. In some cases such craft work was quite complex and involved a number of craftsmen assembled in a large shop, with each one making a part of the finished product. The most typical of these large craft centers was the carriage or wagon shop, but furniture shops, particularly for chairs, were also of large scale. The operations of these shops mirrored the processes that characterized the making of machine-made products in factories: in both cases the product was put together with many parts, made by hand or machine, by a craftsman or machine operator. Like the wage laborers of a factory, the craftsmen in a carriage or furniture shop were paid for their labor; neither craftsman nor machine operator "owned" the finished product any more than they "made" all of it. Yet most crafts still involved a lone craftsman, or a craftsman with a journeyman or an apprentice.

In another kind of craft operation, raw materials, such as animal flesh and skin, were transmuted into material that *others* would make into usable products, such as the slaughterhouse, which supplied butcher shops, and the tannery, which provided leather for craftsmen specializing in the use of that material. Milling was in a category of its own. Although it involved the skill of a miller in the processing of grain and logs and wool, the material purchased by customers, whether flour or boards or woolen yarn, was created by machines, not by hand power.[91]

Towns that served as service centers in productive farming areas, exporting crops and livestock to wider markets, sometimes also became processing centers for agricultural products. Machine-made tin cans were used to preserve produce and meat at processing plants that were largely unmechanized until electricity became a common power source at the end of the century. But large numbers of relatively unskilled laborers were required for the boiling and packaging of the produce.[92] Agricultural service centers such as Chilton, Wisconsin; Grundy Center, Iowa; and Hermann, Missouri, were among many that became processing centers of this kind.[93]

In the early nineteenth century, craftsmen were as much in evidence in towns as they had been during the seventeenth and eighteenth centuries. In a town like Kingston, New York, in 1820, there were twenty-five or so artisans: among them seven blacksmiths, two saddlers and harness makers, a wagon maker, and a cider miller. Over half the craftsmen still combined their homes and their shops; for others, homes and shops were close to each other. Some of the crafts were still itinerant, with work performed in the home of the customer rather than in a shop. This was the case with such crafts as shoemaking, tailoring, and butchering.[94] By the mid-nineteenth century in Chelsea, Vermont, a town where there was still no large-scale machine production, village artisans provided services for the farmers of the area. Blacksmiths shod horses and made agricultural machinery while the shoemakers and tailors crafted clothes and footwear.[95] As settlement moved into the valleys of mid-continent, the early river towns remained craft centers for the making of wagons, furniture, guns, leather goods, and tin, iron, or sheet-metal products.[96]

But between the middle and the end of the nineteenth century, the traditional crafts were gradually displaced by the marketing of machine-made products over an increasingly dense network of rail transport. These products were sold at prices that undercut handcrafted items. In Chelsea, Ver-

BLACKSMITHS. One of the most visible and typical of village craftsmen, the blacksmith was essential for the forging of all metal products before the emergence of foundries. But as much as any other craft, blacksmiths were victimized by industrialization. This shop did business in Boylston, Massachusetts. [Henry E. Huntington Library]

mont, from 1850 to 1900, the number of crafts declined from twenty-four to ten, and the number of craftsmen fell eighty-eight to thirty (even as the population of the settlement remained stable). Among the displaced crafts, the decline was steep during these years: shoemakers (from fourteen to two), tailors (from five to none), chairmakers (from five to none), tanners (from three to none), cabinetmakers (from two to none). There were marked declines in the numbers pursuing even the more durable crafts: carpenters (from seventeen to five) and blacksmiths (from nine to four). In Chelsea, local craftsmen adopted several survival strategies to compensate for the decline in demand for their products. Several relied increasingly on custom work and repair jobs. Others diversified their business: shoemakers became shoe repairers and makers of leather goods generally; carpenters became undertakers and coffin makers as well; wheelwrights also made shingles; others added part-time farming to their craft.[97]

But the extent to which the crafts declined varied greatly in towns

*Trades and tradesmen in Chelsea, 1850–1900*

| Year | No. of trades | No. of tradesmen |
|------|:---:|:---:|
| 1850 | 24 | 88 |
| 1860 | 20 | 69 |
| 1870 | 16 | 60 |
| 1880 | 18 | 67 |
| 1887 | 12 | 52 |
| 1900 | 10 | 30 |

*Occupational groups in Chelsea, 1850–1900*

| | 1850 | 1860 | 1870 | 1880 | 1887 | 1900 |
|------|:---:|:---:|:---:|:---:|:---:|:---:|
| Merchant | 15 | 18 | 22 | 23 | 22 | 25 |
| Professional | 17 | 13 | 13 | 17 | 15 | 12 |
| *Displaced crafts* | | | | | | |
| Shoemaker/cordwainer | 14 | 8 | 7 | 7 | 3 | 2 |
| Tailor | 5 | 5 | 1 | 3 | 2 | 0 |
| Chair maker | 5 | 2 | 0 | 0 | 0 | 0 |
| Tanner | 3 | 1 | 1 | 1 | 0 | 0 |
| Cabinetmaker | 2 | 0 | 0 | 1 | 0 | 0 |
| Gunsmith | 1 | 0 | 0 | 0 | 0 | 0 |
| Machinist | 1 | 0 | 0 | 0 | 0 | 0 |
| *Stable crafts* | | | | | | |
| Wheelwright/carriage maker | 4 | 5 | 6 | 2 | 2 | 3 |
| Saddler/harness maker | 3 | 2 | 2 | 7 | 5 | 2 |
| Tinsmith | 2 | 2 | 4 | 3 | 2 | 1 |
| *Service trades* | | | | | | |
| Blacksmith | 9 | 9 | 8 | 9 | 9 | 4 |
| Teamster | 5 | 2 | 3 | 2 | 3 | 4 |
| Miller (saw & grist) | 5 | 3 | 2 | 2 | 3 | 4 |
| *Construction trades* | | | | | | |
| Carpenter | 17 | 22 | 18 | 18 | 18 | 5 |
| Painter/plasterer | 3 | 2 | 4 | 6 | 4 | 5 |
| Mason (stone & brick) | 0 | 2 | 1 | 1 | 1 | 0 |

THE DECLINE OF CRAFTSMEN. These figures from nineteenth-century Chelsea, Vermont, provide graphic evidence of the precipitous decline of many crafts as a consequence of industrialization. The first chart indicates the diminishing number of crafts; the second plots the decline in numbers of those who worked in the crafts. [U.S. Census, with 1887 data from Hamilton Child, *Child's Orange County Gazette, 1762–1888*] across the continent. The decline depended on the extent to which machine-made products were made available through rail transport but also on the willingness of customers to give up handcrafted goods for cheaper machine-made ones. Newly settled areas in the interior of the continent often relied on local craftsmen long after more easterly town dwellers with well-developed rail connections had shifted to machine-made goods. For example, in the towns of Trempealeau County, Wisconsin, the number of craftsmen continued to rise through the late decades of the nineteenth century. From 1860 to 1880, those engaged in the building trades (from 43 to 102), the metal/wood/leather trades (from 17 to 109), and all trades (from 111 to 388) rose markedly. Those in the building trades were especially needed to build houses, barns, and stores, but so were those who crafted products out of metal, wood, and leather. The work of the smiths and the wagon makers were essential to the farmers of the county. Only carpenters surpassed blacksmiths in number.[98] Similarly, in Clarence, Iowa, the number of craftsmen or artisans remained quite steady during the new town's early decades.[99]

Throughout the nineteenth century, storekeepers sold goods that neither town dwellers nor the farmers who lived outside of towns produced for themselves—items raised, crafted, or machine-made elsewhere. Storekeepers played a complex economic role in towns throughout the continent. They not only provided goods and services for town dwellers and nearby farmers, they also served as an outlet for farm surpluses. In highly rural areas, storekeepers and their store buildings were sometimes the kernels of settlements that later developed around them. This was the case in the inland South, where stores were miniature trading centers that served nearby cotton growers, and on the high plains beyond the Mississippi River, where stores were often the beginning of "inland" towns (settlements that started apart from rail routes).

In the early nineteenth century, Kingston, New York, as an agricultural service center without canal or rail connections, contained general retail stores whose owners sold a variety of merchandise and bartered with customers, accepting grain as payment.[100] In the case of the general store in Saint George's, Delaware (in 1810–1811), the owner, William Polk, was a middleman who was caught between the agrarian seasonal calendar and the fiscal calendar of international trade. He extended credit, bartered, and absorbed the costs of fluctuating wholesale prices until his debtors could repay him. He sold textiles for home sewing, enhancements of diet (molasses, rice, raisins, chocolate, coffee, sugar), convenience items supplied locally (lard and bacon), and some household or farmstead items (ceramic, glass, decanters, nails, gimlets, scythes, hunting supplies, tools). Transactions were debited to the customer's account, with payments to be made later—which encouraged consumer spending. Polk gave credit for work done for him that supported his business, such as shoeing horses, hauling goods, or making casks and barrels. He instituted three types of debt assumption: (1) individuals assumed the responsibility for paying off another's account to satisfy private transactions; (2) a customer took out a loan; and (3) a customer deposited a sum of money and the assigned recipient was entitled to purchase goods. Polk also loaned money directly and got into "merchant" milling—buying grain and logs from people in the area and selling the milled flour and boards elsewhere. The key to his success was his versatility: he provided a variety of services and established a variety of payment schemes.[101]

In the late nineteenth century, Willis F. Dunbar remembered of his father, the village butcher in Hartford, Michigan, that "[there] were certain people to whom my father was glad to extend credit, for they were 'good pay.' Occasionally, he would 'trust' others, even though he was aware that they might not pay up."[102]

Typically merchants in general stores put seasonal merchandise on front platforms, but display goods in the narrow windows flanking the front door remained unchanged for some time, a practice that illustrated the range of stock. Both sides of the interior were flanked with shelves, making the store dark and unventilated. A screened off desk and chair on a platform was the location for the owner's accounting. Groceries were located along one side of the store, with hardware items toward the rear. Shelves on the other side contained dry goods, clothing, and shoes. Cellars and second stories were for storage, supplies, and surplus stock. Some merchandise arrived in bulk and was put in bins, kegs, barrels, and open tubs or kegs: tea, coffee, dried fruit, dried peas, beans, rice, oatmeal, spices, herbs, butter, vinegar, molasses, pickles, fish, kerosene. Mechanical devices were used for dispensing certain products: hinged cleavers for cheese; coffee mills for coffee; hinged blades for tobacco. Circular stools fastened to the floor enabled women to be seated while examining dry goods. Bolts of cloth were measured along a special section of the counter. Spool cases with many narrow drawers contained thread by size. General stores stocked a great conglomeration of goods produced both locally and shipped from far away.[103]

By midcentury, retail merchandising was becoming more varied and complicated. Established, stable Eastern towns such as Chelsea, Vermont, still had general stores,[104] but inland, in young, fast-growing towns such as Jacksonville, Illinois, both general stores and bartering were disappearing. In Jacksonville numerous "dry goods" merchants still handled a wide range of merchandise, but more specialized stores were also opening, stores devoted to agricultural implements, or musical instruments and books, or hair dress-

THE GENERAL STORE. As in this general store in Arkalon, Kansas, everything could be sold—from near and far, in bulk and bolt, with machine-made brand items jostling with craft-made products: an emporium of groceries, clothing, and dry goods. Such stores were also social centers where women chatted at the clothing counter and men sat around the potbellied stove. [Kansas State Historical Society]

ing, or jewelry, or furniture. Most merchants hedged and carried more than one line of goods, but these stores were far from the old general store. Merchants in Jacksonville traveled by rail to purchase wholesale goods directly and advertised a wide selection of stock. Salesmen were often called "traveling men," whom C. W. Goodlander, reminiscing about Fort Scott, Kansas, during the 1860s, remembered as coming to town "to educate . . . merchants in the new departure of buying goods. . . ." With the advent of the railroad, they became "quite plentiful and were heartily welcomed by the hotels. . . . The commercial traveler, like the railroad, was a civilizer on the frontier."[105] Advertising became elaborate notices in the local newspapers, with detailed descriptions of merchandise. And merchants in Jacksonville moved from credit systems to cash.[106] In another example, early Mississippi River towns such as Galena, Illinois, contained stores featuring clothing and hardware but also grocery stores and bakeries.[107]

In new settlements in Trempealeau County, Wisconsin, one could find few specialists in merchandising, half the businessmen in 1860 being "general merchants." But by 1870 there were drug, grocery, hardware, and lumber stores. Retailing was a volatile undertaking, however, and produced many failures, regroupings, and new combinations as merchants often became involved in several enterprises at once. The most profitable mercantile activity was that of purchasing and reselling grain, the great export item of the area.[108]

If a town grew into a more sophisticated and varied retailing center during the course of the nineteenth century, its merchants did not simply rely on walk-in customers. Most stores owned single-horse spring wagons, with advertisements painted on the sides, which made morning and afternoon deliveries to residential areas. The town's inhabitants, and perhaps rural shoppers too, had the choice of shopping in person or waiting for deliveries of such perishable or bulky items as ice, fuel, milk, bread, and meat.[109] Dairy farms, butchers, and bakers all developed delivery routes to ensure freshness. Fuel (especially coal) and ice firms sponsored home deliveries for bulky items that were not for sale in stores but were distributed from both distant (in the case of fuel) and local sites (in the case of ice, which was sawed in chunks from nearby ice ponds and stored in straw-filled, insulated icehouses before delivery).

Everyone involved in the economic life of the towns and the surrounding rural areas during the nineteenth century depended upon either horse-drawn or rail transportation. Most town dwellers and farmers in the surrounding area could afford horses and wagons or carriages as well as barns in which to shelter their driving equipment. Rural residents used horse-drawn transportation to shop and sell goods in town. In cold and snowy or rainy weather, farmers paid to stable their teams in commercially operated feed barns. Everyone hitched horses and wagons to posts, usually connected to iron chains, near town pumps and watering troughs. Livery stables served those, in town or out, who could not afford to own their own rigs. Commercial drays hauled freight to and from train depots, connecting the movement of goods to wider markets. Produce and livestock had to be concentrated at local shipping points because they could not be moved great distances over existing road systems. Economic activity, whether it involved the production, selling, or buying of goods, was restricted to unpaved road systems, both inside and outside of towns. Roads were muddy or rutty or dusty,

SPECIALIZED STORES. Specialized retail stores did not suddenly narrow to one specialty, like a craft shop, but rather sold related groups of products. Top, a hardware store in Monroe, New York; bottom, a leather goods store, also in Monroe. Such shops also continued to sell both craft-made and mass-produced goods. [Melvin Adelglass Collection]

depending on the season, and smelled of horse urine and dung, which in the warmer months attracted swarms of flies.[110]

Livery stables had small offices near the door for the use of an attendant who was on duty twenty-four hours a day to wait for customers and to guard against the threat of fire. A slate listed the names of the horses that had been rented out. Harnesses for each horse hung in front of the building. Toward the rear were a great variety of vehicles, with stalls behind them. A second floor stored hay. Somewhere in the building was a washroom for keeping the equipment and the horses clean.[111]

The economic activities of the towns produced some "gendered" spaces, places that were exclusively for women or for men. Livery stables were preeminently places for men and boys, but so were tobacco shops, saloons, and barber shops. Women claimed as sanctuaries millinery and dress shops. But most shops and stores, beginning with the general stores, attracted both men and women.[112]

As in the seventeenth and eighteenth centuries, so in the nineteenth century, the economic activities of those who identified with particular towns created trading areas that bore little relationship to the towns' political boundaries. Millers, store merchants, shopkeepers, craftsmen, and farmers were linked in an intricate pattern of exchange that plunged into the open countryside, extending far beyond a particular settlement. "Catchment areas," within which farmers traded with a village, were determined by how far horses and wagons could travel and return on a single day, perhaps a radius of six to twelve miles. As rail networks expanded during the nineteenth century, those who lived in rural settings might use rail transport, but such trips seemed to be confined to transactions of exceptional importance. Most farmers everywhere used horse-drawn transport both to bring produce to market or to rail depots and to shop in nearby towns. Towns that were regularly spaced competed for their business, however—both their produce and their shopping, and advertising campaigns designed to lure the rural population to a particular service center became a common feature of weekly journals or newspapers as the century wore on.[113]

Many towns with a special purpose were founded during the nineteenth century, but only those founded by radical reform groups—whose communities were based upon the communal ownership of property—developed an economic life that was clearly and basically different from that of ordinary towns. The towns founded by black settlers in the decades after the Civil War, for instance, were economically indistinguishable from ordinary towns.[114] So were towns founded by particular European ethnic groups, such as the Germans who founded New Braunfels, Texas.[115]

DELIVERY SERVICES. Delivery via horse and wagon from door to door was confined to products whose freshness was vital or whose weight made it impractical for householders to supply themselves. Top left, bread and pastry; top right, ice; below, teas and coffees. With the arrival of the motor vehicle after the turn of the century, such products were delivered by trucks. [Edith La Francis Collection]

Even among the utopian communitarians, there was wide variation in the extent to which particular groups adhered to the communal ownership of property. Such groups hoped to extricate themselves from the complexities of modern capitalist society. Repulsed by the consequences of the profit motive, shocked by the extremes of wealth and poverty, utopians sought to establish communities apart from the emerging capitalist society that had overwhelmed them. Some formed co-ops, otherwise retaining private property; others became communistic in varying degrees and for varying lengths of time.[116]

But the actual economic *activities* of the inhabitants of even these often short-lived experiments in communal living were quite typical of townspeople everywhere in the United States during the nineteenth century. There may have been no economic classes, but someone had to organize the work that needed to be done. For example, in the Amana community there were foremen or superintendents who arranged each day's labors. The inhabitants had an excellent reputation for both farm and craft work, with many farmsteads, four sawmills, two gristmills, two woolen mills, a tannery, and a print factory.[117] The communitarians hoped to create a new economic system that featured cooperation and harmony and an absence of classes based upon work, but the actual work they did was quite ordinary, as common in agricultural service centers as it was in utopian villages.

## · III ·

FROM THE BEGINNING of European settlement in the territory that became the United States, most towns were agricultural service centers. This was less true of the nineteenth century than it had been of the seventeenth and eighteenth centuries, but still the case. One of the most fundamental changes during the twentieth century was that towns gradually ended their economic function as trading depots for a farming population. This was because farming ceased to be the preeminent occupation of Americans. In 1790 more than 90 percent of the population listed agriculture as its occupation. By 1880 that percentage had declined to 42. By the twentieth century the decline became much steeper: 27 percent of the population in 1920, 14 percent in 1945, 4 percent in 1975, and less than 2 percent in the 1990s.[118] By the 1970s virtually all farming was commercial.[119]

HORSE TRANSPORT. Most town dwellers relied on horse transportation until the mass production of motorized vehicles in the 1920s. Top, a woman in horse and buggy in New Portland, Maine. Below, the livery stable, like this one in Merna, Nebraska, was a male-dominated public space, unlike the railroad station. The livery stable's successor, the gas station, has largely remained a haven for men. [Top, Culver Pictures; below, Nebraska State Historical Society]

GENDERED SPACES. All three of the shops on these pages are examples of public places that by common consent were the preserve of either men or women. All three functioned as economic services but were also social centers for the one gender that frequented them. Opposite page, a barber shop in Stillwater, Minnesota; top, a tobacco shop, also in Stillwater; below, a millinery shop in Watertown, Wisconsin. [Opposite and top, Minnesota Historical Society; below, State Historical Society of Wisconsin]

Another fundamental change during the twentieth century was the enlarged scale of economic life, as continent-girdling corporations operated in many areas of the nation and, after World War II, in other areas of the globe. This greater scale was made possible by faster means of communication and transportation, which together served to undermine the relative isolation that marked the economic life of towns even when transportation consisted of an emerging system of roads, canals, and railroads, and when communication was via the postal service, newspapers, and the telegraph.

These two simultaneous developments—the huge decline in the rural population that towns had served, and the greater scale in economic activity—had vast effects on the nature of economic life in the towns. But these effects were felt gradually during the course of the twentieth century.

In the 1920s there continued to be service centers in areas where agriculture still dominated. In terms of crops, the nation was divided into corn, wheat, cotton, and fruit and vegetable "belts." In towns in dairying areas one could find creameries and condenseries or milk and cream stations for receiving and shipping. In wheat-growing areas, towns provided storage and loading facilities. In cotton-growing areas, farmers either had their own gins and arranged to take their ginned cotton to market, or store merchants continued to provide ginning and storage facilities as well as advancing credit to farm tenants, sharecroppers, and owners alike. In areas where the raising of livestock prevailed, co-ops became the dominant marketing mechanism. Co-ops were favored in fruit-growing areas too, typically with county- and statewide affiliations.

One in three manufacturing firms in the towns were food-producing, that is, such enterprises as creameries, canneries, drying plants, and flour and gristmills. Such industries increasingly relied on electrical power. When Clarence Birdseye developed a process for the quick-freezing of food, such processing plants could by the 1920s begin to freeze as well as can meat and fish and vegetables and fruits.[120] They flourished more typically in the dairy, fruit, and vegetable areas than in the wheat, corn, and livestock regions, and represented a conversion of raw agricultural materials into a more easily transported form. Grain- and livestock-centered towns continued to serve as shipping points to other markets.

Town factories usually used local capital and raw materials. Only the textile villages, which manufactured cloth in the cotton belt, used outside capital. Chambers of commerce in America's towns continued to make frenzied efforts to attract industry, offering bonuses, free sites, and local capital, but even the established factories frequently failed because of poor management, insufficient capital, and an overall inability to compete with cities

FARMERS IN TOWN. Nothing more dramatically illustrated the fact that most towns were service centers for farmers than the occasions when farmers came to town—to shop or to sell or ship their goods. The major farmers' day was usually Saturday. Top left, bringing livestock to town in Black River Falls, Wisconsin; top right, bringing feed to Cooperstown, New York; below, a shopping day in Princeton, Wisconsin. [Top left and below, State Historical Society of Wisconsin; top right, New York Historical Society]

whenever the towns ventured beyond manufacturing processes distinctly related to farm produce or facilitating the transportation of a farm product.[121]

By the 1930s, when the Great Depression coincided with the long-term, relentless expansion of machine production, the crafts shops that for centuries had been such a prominent feature of the economic life of towns dramatically declined. Many craft factories, where such products as wagons and furniture and baskets and brooms and cigars and cheese were hand-crafted, and a variety of craft shops, for example blacksmiths and shoemakers and tailors, as well as feed mills and gristmills, rapidly disappeared.[122]

By the post–World War II decades, electrical power became so widely available that manufacturing plants could theoretically be located almost anywhere. This meant that urban areas, which since the late nineteenth century had absorbed most of the industrial or machine production, began to lose their natural advantage as sites where entrepreneurs, managers, investment capital, laborers, and markets came together. New plants began to be built not only on urban fringes, in industrial "parks," but on the edges of towns as well—indeed anywhere that more mobile laborers could be enticed to live and work. With nearly universally available electrical power, plants were located with greater flexibility but also with greater exactitude, as managers carefully calculated costs and profitability with respect to raw materials, production, transportation, and marketing. Astonishingly, by the 1970s the percentage of the workforce in manufacturing was as high in rural areas as it was in large urban centers.[123] By the 1980s manufacturing was the driving force in the towns' economy.[124]

Such fundamental change did not mean that older types of economic communities suddenly ended. For example, company towns were still being built in the Rocky Mountains and southern Appalachians well into the twentieth century. As long as transportation systems failed to connect resource-rich but remote mountainous areas, corporations continued to build such towns in an effort to lure workers to otherwise uninhabitable sites.[125] Nor did communitarian utopians suddenly cease to create settlements whose inhabitants tried to organize their economic lives along communal rather than capitalistic lines. In California up to 1950, at least seventeen groups were involved in idealistic community experiments.[126]

The century began with regional variations of continued importance, especially in the lagging South. But as the century wore on, Southern mill towns flourished as cotton processing centers, or industrial mill villages continued the process begun by Northeasterners of using mills to produce cloth from cotton, still the South's most important raw material.[127] In a sense, Southern towns "caught up" with the industrial activity started in the Northeast a century before. They now processed their own raw materials in the same way that Midwestern towns were processing their own grains and livestock. Indeed, after World War II, Southern towns became the fastest-growing industrial centers in the nation as electrification made it attractive to locate plants in heretofore nonindustrialized areas with nonunion labor. In Southern towns as scattered as Columbiana, Alabama; Centerville, Tennessee; Berryville, Arkansas; Mocksville, North Carolina; and Louisville, Georgia, the pattern was the same.[128] In an amazing reversal, the towns that had been most resistant to industrial activity came, during the course of the twentieth century, to embrace it more than anywhere else in the nation.

What gave increasing uniformity to industrial activity across the United States during the twentieth century was the proliferation of "branch plants" at many different locations, some of which were in or around towns. Local industrial firms coexisted uneasily with these branches of regional or continental corporations. Another form of this kind of coexistence occurred when industries owned by absentee investors from faraway urban centers located next to locally owned and managed companies. For example, in Benson, Minnesota, in 1960 the two largest manufacturing firms, Tyler Manufacturing and Wiman Manufacturing, were absentee owned. Both manufactured products linked to the farm economy, but the great majority of Benson's manufacturing firms were tiny operations, locally owned and serving the town and surrounding countryside.[129]

Economic life in all its aspects grew more uniform during the twentieth century, in both rural and urban areas. Technological developments made possible this growing uniformity, especially the electrification of power and vastly enhanced transportation and communications. The material basis for life in the towns changed dramatically, and the isolation that had characterized towns in rural settings for three centuries swiftly and progressively diminished.

Towns were electrified beginning in the 1880s, usually by means of a local dynamo powered by water or steam at local mills. As electrical firms consolidated and amalgamated, electricity was made available in rural areas as well, a process advanced by the work of the Rural Electrification Administration under the New Deal, which provided funds for rural cooperatives. In towns of all sizes, public spaces were illuminated at night, and home connections followed. Along with electrification came water and sewer systems and indoor plumbing. There often followed the paving of streets, at first in brick or cobblestone, then in tar-based substances. Home electrification led to the development of electrically powered housekeeping appliances such as vacuum cleaners, refrigerators, electric stoves, and oil furnaces. The self-sufficiency that had characterized town dwellers for centuries swiftly gave way to a residual vegetable garden or a few fruit trees.[130]

Technological developments in transportation and communication progressively broke down the towns' relative isolation. Gas-fueled motor vehicles were at first luxury items for wealthy town dwellers in the early years of the century, but with the introduction of mass-produced, assembly-line models in the 1920s, automobiles became the major personal means of transportation for everyone except low-income people, replacing a centuries-old reliance on horses and wagons or carriages.

Burns Fuller remembered that the earliest motor vehicle in Fenton, Michigan, created "the blamedest amount of chugging and snorting ever to be heard on the streets of this horse and buggy village. . . . [The owner drove through the village] in a cloud of smoke from the exhaust. . . . [Barking] dogs and a bevy of kids followed them all the way to the owner's barn. The whole neighborhood turned out. . . . In the year 1901, to climb into that rig and feel it take off without being pulled by a horse was 'Simply out of this world.'"[131]

Willis F. Dunbar remembered that in Hartford, Michigan, his parents' Model T Ford "got mired in the black prairie mud and a farmer had to be persuaded to pull us out. We made frequent stops to put water in the radiator."[132] Willis added that "[no] one dreamed that eventually these new gasoline buggies would put the blacksmiths out of business. Nor could anyone have had the faintest conception of the extent to which the automobile would ultimately transform the life of the people in the village."[133]

The shift from one mode of transportation to another was noted by the *Republican* of Oregon, Illinois, in 1928: "The sale of the brick livery barn on N. 3rd St. to be used as an automobile laundry and a salesroom for farm machinery and tractors puts one more nail in the coffin of the horse and buggy. Time was when Bert Fouch first built the barn that has housed as fine a lot of carriage horses and rubber-tired buggies and surreys as was to be found in the state, but along came Henry Ford and a few more men with visions of horseless carriages, with the result that the automobile put the skids under the livery business."[134]

Telephone service, like electrical firms, was at first quite local in character, with purely local exchanges managed by local companies. But, again like electrical grid systems, phone companies began expanding in the 1920s and 1930s, with firms combining smaller exchanges in a spiraling pattern that involved ever-greater territories.[135]

Motor vehicles and telephones had a profound impact on the economic life of towns. Telephone communication promoted economic activity on a

THE COMING OF THE AUTOMOBILE. Motor vehicles, like the carriages and buggies they gradually replaced, not only became the dominant form of transportation but also were linked to class and status. Just as the quality of an individual's carriage indicated the owner's social position, so too did his car—as here, in Corning, New York—especially when motor vehicles were a new and expensive technological advance. [American Heritage Collection]

vast scale, linking firms in towns to other elements of their economic world—suppliers and buyers, financiers and wholesalers, salesmen and customers, producers and marketers. The impact of the motor vehicle was even more dramatic and far-reaching, both on the production and retail sale of goods in towns. State governments raced to develop surfaced road systems as the ownership of personal and commercial motor vehicles burgeoned in the early decades of the twentieth century, and in the 1920s the federal government created a national road system, enlarging it in the 1950s to an interstate, divided highway system. Trucks gradually reduced the importance of towns as trade depots or assembly points for farm produce, as farmers in the vicinity of cities began to haul their own produce and livestock to urban markets in their own trucks, thus eliminating their reliance on rail transport. In towns, horse-drawn delivery wagons were replaced by delivery trucks from the 1920s through the 1940s.[136] After World War II the almost universal access to private or public motor vehicle transportation led to the near elimination of all but fuel and specialized food delivery services. In those same years trucking firms came to transport much of the product of rural areas, though rail freight was still needed for bulky and heavy items. In the later years of the century, package delivery services such as United Parcel Service and Federal Express revived the door-to-door delivery of smaller items.

The rather swift replacement of horses and wagons with automobiles during the early decades of the twentieth century had an enormous impact on the nature of retailing in towns. Cars allowed consumers in towns or in the countryside to range much farther for goods than they could have in their horses and wagons. This greater flexibility allowed for comparison shopping within greater retail areas. Horse-drawn vehicles could comfortably travel six miles an hour, and drivers were forced to shop within a relatively short circumference from their residences. Train travel was restricted to a few locations along the rail lines. But the highway systems that emerged in the 1920s allowed shoppers from towns and rural areas to drive over a wide area to shop for goods that towns now vigorously competed to sell to them. The interstate highway system furthered such shopping expeditions.

As early as the 1920s it was clear that shoppers did not need as many trading centers as they had when horse and rail transport prevailed.[137]

During the late nineteenth century, advertising mediums such as newspapers sanctioned the support of stores in trading areas well beyond the confines of their own towns. As the *Republican* in Oregon, Illinois, put it in 1902: "In our judgment a newspaper man that refuses to sell space to a legitimate business establishment simply because it happens to be located in another town makes a mistake. . . . The *Republican* covers territory beyond . . . Oregon [and is] a good advertising medium for Rochelle, Creston, Ashton, Dixon and Rochford merchants. We don't refuse business from these people and our merchants don't expect us to." But by the 1920s the *Republican* had become alarmed at the growing threat to local merchants signaled by the shift in transport from horse and buggy to motor vehicles: "Money earned at home should be spent at home. Money spent away from home is gone—ultimately to help develop some other town. Those who earn in Oregon and spend it elsewhere are undermining their own earning powers, their jobs, and their local investments. Money earned at and spent at home divides itself into every avenue of community activity." Along such lines, the *Republican* tried to evoke efforts by local merchants to expand their trade territory: "The trade territory of a town is not all dependent upon the distance to neighboring trading points, but upon the enterprise of the merchants and the residents of the town. If the town does not reach after the trade it will come only as fast as it has to, and it will grow only as it is forced to."[138]

By the 1930s it was quite common for town dwellers and their rural neighbors to shop at several centers. In these circumstances the towns that adjusted to changing circumstances in retailing, and that offered as full a range of stores as towns of comparable size elsewhere, were relatively stable as retail centers. Women were shopping more often, driving the family car, judging quality and value, and knowing what they wanted.[139] By the 1940s farmers and town dwellers had clearly broadened their trading or shopping area because of their access to motor vehicles and well-developed highway systems. Such shoppers had a choice of trading centers, some of which had started to specialize in the retail services they provided.[140] By the 1960s larger towns had become centralized trade and service centers, but smaller towns were becoming centers for "convenience" goods and services, like neighborhood variety stores in cities. Whether larger towns would remain stable as retail centers depended on the proximity and size of competing centers.[141]

Towns that were well established as retail trade centers could remain stable in the age of the automobile *if* the number of former shoppers who moved on to larger, urban centers roughly equaled the number of new customers who would shop at smaller centers. This is what happened in Oregon, Illinois, at least between 1900 and 1930. This medium-sized town saw no significant decline in the number of stores that sold groceries, meat, dairy products, baked goods, candy, drugs, stationery and books, music, jewelry, flowers, furniture, hardware, clothing, lumber and building materials, and flour and feed and grain.[142]

But over a longer term, from the early to the late decades of the twentieth century, the commercial landscape of the towns did in fact change. For example, four relatively small towns (under 2,500 in population) in Oklahoma—Bromide, Wapanucka, Caddo, and Calera—contained in 1920 groceries and general stores, restaurants, cotton gins, livery stables and auto repair shops, hotels and motels, feed and farm implement centers, drug stores, furniture stores, dry goods and hardware stores, banks, lumber yards, meat markets, confectioneries, clothing stories, and still some mill and craft shops (blacksmiths, tinsmiths, tailors). By 1990 these same towns featured convenience and grocery stores, beauty salons, auto repair shops, restaurants, banks, antiques shops, and lodge halls, but many specialized retail stores had vanished.[143]

As shoppers drove to the largest towns or cities they could conveniently reach, retailing in smaller towns was often reduced to general or convenience stores—a return to the kind of retailing that had prevailed in the early nineteenth century and before. Even fairly substantial towns could boast far fewer specialized stores and shops. Shoppers favored special trips to larger centers for the items that were needed only occasionally.

Retailing in towns was subject to the same translocal influences as town industry. From the mid- to late nineteenth century, national corporations introduced brand names as they competed with one another to make and sell the same consumer products.[144] In the 1890s Sears, Roebuck pioneered the mail-order catalog, which allowed customers in towns as well as in the countryside—with the introduction of rural free postal delivery during the same decade—to buy mass-produced products directly, through the mail, thus eliminating the retailer altogether.[145]

The Great Atlantic and Pacific Tea Company (the A & P) introduced the chain grocery store, the counterpart to the branch plant, in the early years of the twentieth century, opening locally managed but not locally owned "cash and carry" stores, without frills but with discount prices. Each local store—there were more than 4,300 by 1971—was stocked with a variety of goods that the national corporation had purchased in large quantities at lower prices.[146]

In the early twentieth century, national oil companies and automobile makers introduced "franchising," that is, gas stations and car dealerships that sold nationally produced gasoline and automobiles through locally managed and owned outlets. Under these arrangements the local manager/owners agreed to sell a particular product for a national producer and distributor under an exclusive right to do so, paying a wholesale price for the item but gaining the benefit of national advertising and brand recognition. The franchising idea soon spread to other kinds of products, such as mufflers (Midas), drugs (Rexall), desserts (Mister Donut, Dairy Queen), and lunches (McDonald's).[147]

Brand names, mail-order catalogs, chain stores, franchising—in all these ways retailing in the towns was subjected to the same homogenizing influences that branch plants of national producers brought to industrial production in the towns. In both cases, economic activity was made more uniform and standardized. In both cases, local and translocal firms coexisted uneasily.

The "gendered spaces" that so obviously characterized the economic life of the towns during the industrial era gradually became obliterated in the twentieth century. As women and sympathetic men exerted social and political pressure to enlarge the parameters within which women could operate openly and in concert with men, heretofore separate economic spheres became blurred. By the late twentieth century, men and women shared most oc-cupations, and old gender-specific work spaces gradually became open spaces. Male-only gas stations became auto repair centers with lounges. Bar-ber shops and hair salons became "unisex" hair styling centers. Most cloth-ing and shoe stores developed departments for men and women. Saloons and taverns appealed to both sexes. Smoke shops became anachronistic as pack-aged tobacco came to be sold in a variety of outlets.

As a proportion of the national census, the rural population steadily shrank from the late nineteenth century on, as farming became increasingly mechanized, commercial, and large-scaled. Towns most vulnerable to a de-cline in their hinterland populations were those located too close together for the movement of people and goods in the era of motor vehicle travel. The vast number of towns founded in the interior valleys and plains of the conti-nent were often spaced just eight to ten miles apart, both to accommodate horse-drawn vehicular travel and in recognition of the frequency with which rail steam engines required water.[148] Farmers wanted towns close together during the nineteenth century, and town promoters and operators of grain el-evators and stockyards all responded to that desire. No one anticipated how antiquated the onset of motor vehicle transport would make this geographical pattern. The most extreme consequence was the creation of ghost towns, of abandoned communities that ceased to exist as service centers.[149]

The farm population that moved out of rural areas usually moved into towns where, for the first time in the three centuries since Europeans first settled in North America, they became a significant element among town dwellers. For example, in Eben, Michigan, in 1933, three-fourths of the population in the township lived in open countryside outside the settled vil-lage. By 1964 that figure had declined to two-thirds. The number of house-holds in the village had doubled while the number of farmhouses outside the village had significantly declined.[150]

This rural migration continued until the 1970s, when, for the first time in a century, migrants to rural areas outnumbered those to urban areas. A back-to-the-land movement started in reaction to urban pollution and social tension at a time of racial disharmony. Urbanites of means bought second homes in towns or in the open countryside. People who had been raised in towns but who had moved to urban areas to work returned to spend their re-tirement in their hometowns.[151]

In the last decades of the twentieth century the rural population stabi-lized, but, starting even before the shift of the 1970s, *within* rural areas those near urban centers grew and offset continued declines in those far from such centers.[152] Towns in rural areas in the vicinity of cities in effect became commuter towns—for example Hudson, Michigan; Mount Gilead, Ohio; Rockville, Illinois; Woodstock, Virginia; Stanford, Kentucky. More specifically: Columbiana, Alabama, for Birmingham; Centerville, Tennessee, for Nashville; Cazenovia, New York, for Syracuse.[153]

Most towns ceased to be agricultural service centers in the course of the twentieth century. Wider economic developments had a great impact upon the towns, good and bad. In those areas where the consolidation of family farms into corporate farms was far advanced, nearby towns did not greatly benefit. They became hosts to armies of transient, low-income farm laborers. Even new firms created by outsiders—various kinds of stores and plants and offices—were mixed in their effects. They usually hired younger workers, often from outside the community rather than from within it, and demanded tax holidays, land acquisition, site preparation, increased police and fire protection, expanded school, health, and recreation services—all of which offset the added revenues and increased employment that resulted from their location. Beginning in the 1920s, towns increasingly attracted retired persons, often on fixed incomes, and commuters, who lived in town but worked elsewhere—persons who performed no service within the town itself.[154]

Throughout the seventeenth, eighteenth, and nineteenth centuries, most towns were service or trade centers for a largely rural, chiefly agricultural population. They were gathering places for agricultural products and funnels for goods needed but not produced by a farming population. Urban centers, before the late nineteenth century, were focal points of commerce and craft production for huge regional hinterlands and stood at the apex of a great hierarchy of trade depots that linked the movement of goods between rural settings and towns to urban and foreign markets.

During the nineteenth century, towns also assumed other functions that made them economic production centers for both their rural surroundings and for markets far beyond. Some towns, those already located—or occasionally planned (as company towns)—at waterpowered mill sites, became the first industrial centers. Gradually, at midcentury, with the growth of steam power, and then, with great velocity in the late nineteenth and early twentieth centuries, with the development of electrical systems, cities became the typical location for industrial firms, superseding the earlier preeminence of towns. Other towns became or were planned (as company towns) as extractive centers for mining and forestry products. Still other towns became processing centers for crops and livestock raised in their surrounding rural areas. In all these ways, towns were the *primary* economic production centers for a largely rural population.

The central role of the towns as production centers dissipated during the twentieth century. It did so for three basic, interrelated reasons. First, the vast enlargement in the scale of economic production caused the towns that *remained* viable production centers to depend more and more upon the existence of branch plants of national corporations. While such firms typically coexisted uneasily with locally owned enterprises, their presence created both economic stability and growth.

Second, industrialization became an urban phenomenon, as the American population itself became increasingly urbanized. This was so even though electrical power made the location of industry anywhere a theoretical possibility. Towns that remained production centers tended to be located beyond the fringes of urban areas, in locations near where people wanted to live or commute from. Towns in rural areas far from urban centers generally declined as economic production centers.

This is because of a third factor that influenced the decline of towns as primary centers: the collapse of agriculture as the basis for a large rural population. The swift and steep decline of the farm population meant that during the twentieth century the towns lost their traditional rural hinterlands. As agriculture became ever more commercial, technological, and large scale, towns that had been service centers or processing centers for the crop and livestock production of the vast Southern and Midwestern plains often became retirement communities for former farmers and elderly retired exurbanites. Other towns, nearer to urban areas, became mainly commuter or "bedroom" communities.

As retail centers, as depots for the distribution and sale of crafted and machine-made goods, towns became far less distinctive than they had been as gathering places for agricultural produce or as production centers. The evolution of retailing, whether in rural or urban settings, followed the same path. General stores in towns became, by the nineteenth century, department stores in cities. Specialized craft shops gave way to specialized stores as machine production replaced handcrafting in the course of the same century. During the twentieth century, the automobile greatly enlarged the ambit of shopping for those who lived in and around towns, significantly reducing the variety and quantity of stores and services that had typically been available during the nineteenth century. Retailing in smaller towns was sometimes reduced to what it had been during the agricultural era of the seventeenth and eighteenth centuries, to that of the general store.

# FIVE

# *Social Life*

Nᴀᴛɪᴠᴇ ᴛʀɪʙᴀʟ ꜱᴏᴄɪᴇᴛʏ during the seventeenth and eighteen centuries differed in basic ways from the society that the English colonists established during that same period. But both societies were hierarchical, divided vertically into social groups or classes that had distinctive positions and varying amounts of status and power.

Tribal chiefs gained their positions through inheritance and surrounded themselves with elite corps of counselors, that is, with shamans or religious figures. Chiefs and their counselors lived ostentatiously off the tribute collected from their bands and tribes. But their leadership depended upon the consent of the group, and chiefs were careful to present gifts regularly to their people. Reciprocity was maintained through a complex sequence of rituals and ceremonial games at which wealth was redistributed among the tribesmen or sacrificed to the deities, thus preventing an increasingly wider gap between the elite and the rest of the tribe. Chiefs ritualistically played and lost at games, reminding everyone that they were, after all, only members of the band or tribe. Rituals also reinforced the essential interdependence of band or tribal members. At council meetings the men sat and smoked their pipes in silence so as to concentrate on each speaker's words. A collective emotional commitment from all members was required. Tribal society was hierarchical in a fixed way, but through the mechanism of various rituals that involved the principle of reciprocity, that society cohered and functioned and endured, at least until contact with the white settlers led to its evisceration everywhere on the North American continent.[1]

A relatively fluid set of personal relationships in a context of elaborate kin networks (or bands) made the hierarchical social structure of the tribes quite like Europe's medieval feudal system. But native society exhibited a rigidity, a static character, that was not to be found in white colonial society. The society that the English colonists established during the seventeenth and eighteenth centuries was also hierarchical, but it was characterized by a different kind of fluidity: social and geographic mobility for the white men who dominated it. This mobility was a novel feature of white settler society on the frontier of European civilization. In Europe, men typically were ascribed a status or position in society at birth, with the *expectation* they would remain there throughout their lives, though in reality some individuals and families did change their standing, either upward or downward.

In North America the English colonists chose not to replicate this kind of hierarchical system. The English nobility was not inclined to emigrate, with the result that colonial society lacked the "top" of European society and, with it, the model for a social structure based upon ascribed status. To complicate matters, the colonists added at the "bottom" of the American social hierarchy a slave caste, as enslaved Africans became the labor force for the production of the staple-crop agriculture that emerged in the Southern colonies. The colonists displaced the rigidity that characterized the European system as a whole onto this slave caste and introduced a novel mobility for a white society whose members sought to improve their status through the accumulation of wealth. One's position in society, rather than being ascribed, was earned. In North America, social *expectations* changed. White men had the opportunity, because of a resource-rich continent, to improve their status. In the absence of the ascription that characterized European society, they did so on the basis of wealth accumulation. Wealth, not birth, determined a white man's position in this frontier society.

Yet social hierarchy remained and was as much a feature of life among the colonists as it was among the English and European societies they had emigrated from. Town dwellers along the Atlantic coast were divided into classes or groupings typically called the "better sort," the "middling sort," and the "meaner" or "poorer sort." As settlement moved across the continent during the nineteenth century, towns continued to exhibit these same divisions, which came increasingly to be called the upper, middle, and lower (or "poor") classes. Throughout these centuries, the less developed economically a town and its rural hinterland was, the less steeply socially hierarchical was its population. By contrast, areas rich in resources that small entrepreneurial groups could exploit commercially were far more likely to contain an elite who towered socially over other elements in the population.

In this regard, towns were indistinguishable from cities. Size did not matter: how big or small a settlement was did not predetermine whether its social hierarchy would be steep or truncated, bunched toward the center or exhibiting a vast gulf between the richest and poorest of its inhabitants. In the seventeenth and eighteenth centuries, all the port cities had merchant elites who dominated urban life in all its dimensions—but so did plantations, which were embryonic rural communities or settlements, with a planter elite that was even more dominant than the merchants who stood astride complex urban societies. Similarly, in the nineteenth century, commercial and industrial elites in coastal and inland cities dominated urban communities, but so did contemporaneous lumber, cattle, grain, and mining elites in towns of varying sizes. Common to such towns and cities was the presence of an entrepreneurial elite that swiftly exploited the economic resources of the area.

By the nineteenth century, town society had become increasingly imitative of an emergent urban society, as cities grew with astonishing swiftness. The whole complex of factors that made town dwellers into members of the upper, middle, or lower classes—questions of status, position, respectability—were derived from prevailing urban norms or innovations. Town dwellers looked to the cities for standards relating to class. In the twentieth century such imitative behavior became the norm as the urban population dominated American society to an ever-greater extent.

Indeed, towns and cities were largely indistinguishable through the whole spectrum of social life. Town and city dwellers were alike in their adherence to Christian morality; in their most common forms of misbehavior (inebriation, prostitution, and gambling); in the ways they sustained social coherence in the midst of ethnic, racial, and class division; in their efforts to reform and improve their lives; in their social and leisure-time activities; and in the manner by which they celebrated the important "passages of life."

Although it had little effect on social structure, the most enduring distinction between cities and towns was their size. Town dwellers lived in small communities where everyone knew or knew of everyone else (or thought he did). In such communities the core population (distinguished by its longevity of residence) emphasized its community's neighborliness, loyalty, and overall equality. Such town dwellers looked upon the city as a huge, impersonal community filled with strangers and festering social problems that derived from extremes of wealth and poverty, from the stressful living together of large numbers of immigrants and transients, and from the ongoing anxiety produced by ethnic, racial, and class division. But these same town dwellers also tried in many ways to emulate the way urban society functioned and ignored the extent to which towns shared problems with cities. This profound ambivalence produced among town dwellers a deeply schizophrenic attitude toward the city.

The small size of towns did in fact distinguish the way town dwellers engaged in social and leisure-time activities and celebrated the passages of life, but not in the sense that their activities and celebrations were different. Town and city dwellers joined the same kinds of clubs and social organizations and engaged in the same kinds of leisure-time activities, but the inhabitants of towns could make them community-wide events, something urban populations could never do. Similarly, both town and city dwellers celebrated the same life passages, but only the inhabitants of towns could involve the entire community in a celebration of the life of one among them.

## · I ·

MOST SMALL SETTLEMENTS, most towns, were characterized by a social profile that was relatively flat, lacking depth and height. For example, Dedham, Massachusetts, was typical of craft-oriented villages in not highly developed agricultural settings. The top 10 percent of the people in terms of assessed property owned perhaps one-quarter of the wealth, whereas the bottom 20 percent claimed 8 percent in 1690, and 5 percent in 1730. This meant that the middle 70 percent owned the remaining 70 percent of the wealth.[2] In Connecticut the most egalitarian social structure appeared in those towns that were located in rural settings somewhat removed from the flow of commerce.[3]

The distribution of wealth in a town related both to its age and to the stage of its economic development as a service center. Whether or not a town became a growing trading depot and craft center, repeated land subdivisions as well as natural soil depletion meant that the numbers of rural, agriculturally oriented residents without landed property increased in various townships, and poor people began to receive relief, along with widows, orphans, the insane, and the handicapped.[4]

The situation was similar in the mid-Atlantic colonies, where town dwellers of middling wealth were easily the most numerous. There too, growth and increasing commercialization led to widening gaps between the richest and the poorest. In the 1690s in Chester County in southeastern Pennsylvania, in the area of the earliest settlements, the wealthiest 10 percent paid 24 percent of the taxes, and the poorest 30 percent paid 17.5 percent. By 1800 the wealthiest 10 percent paid 38 percent of the taxes while the poorest

30 percent paid only 4 percent.[5] In Germantown, the craft center outside Philadelphia, by the 1770s the top 10 percent owned 36.5 percent of the wealth, and the bottom 10 percent had just 4.5 percent, with later divisions revealing even larger gaps.[6]

In some of the towns with agricultural hinterlands, mercantile elites appeared and exploited whatever resources could be profitably traded with port cities and beyond. The larger the town, the more likely that such a merchant group would emerge.[7] But in some cases such entrepreneurs were among the earliest settlers. The best-known example is that of Springfield, Massachusetts, where a single family—the Pynchons—dominated every aspect of the community's life as proprietors, magistrates, mediators, military commanders, legislative representatives, mill owners, storekeepers, fur traders, landowners, and commercial agriculturalists. The Pynchons were a one-family merchant-entrepreneurial elite. In wealth, power, and status, they towered above everyone else in Springfield, even when it was young and small.[8] They constituted an extreme example of the mercantile domination that affected many towns as they took on a commercial orientation and became substantial trading centers. Indeed, one-family domination of the kind the Pynchons managed was possible only in a small settlement. The larger a town, the more varied and numerous its elite.[9]

Similarly, in the Southern colonies, in those areas where staple-crop agriculture flourished during the seventeenth and eighteenth centuries, the planters who amassed land and slaves completely dominated the plantation communities they created as well as the rural neighborhoods beyond. Such planters not only owned and managed their agricultural estates but were typically vestrymen in the local churches, justices of the peace, colonial legislators, and captains of the local militia.[10]

In towns located in areas whose resources went beyond farmland to include substantial inland forests or coastal fishing grounds, where extractive activity rather than agricultural pursuits could attract merchant entrepreneurs, similar elites emerged. In Gloucester and Marblehead, Massachusetts, for example, these two coastal towns fell under the domination of merchant elites who concentrated on fishing. As was the case with towns in predominantly agricultural areas, the inhabitants of these fishing ports became more steeply hierarchical in their distribution of wealth as they grew in size.[11]

Thus colonial towns were divided into hierarchical groupings based upon differing levels of wealth accumulation. Usually the hierarchical structure contained a large middling level of wealth, but it became steeply hierarchical if an entrepreneurial elite emerged. These towns were also sometimes divided ethnically. Migrants from Britain—England, Scotland, Wales, Ireland—dominated almost everywhere in the English colonies, especially in New England and the Southern colonies. The Puritans tried to restrict immigration to their own kind of dissenters within the Church of England.[12] The model for the Southern colonists remained the replication of English society in North America. Only in the mid-Atlantic colonies did proprietors such as William Penn encourage immigrants from areas outside the British Isles. In response, significant numbers of settlers from the German states moved to Pennsylvania after its founding in the late seventeenth century,[13] and were prominent in towns such as Germantown.[14] During the eighteenth century, German settlers moved through Pennsylvania to the backcountry, both to the north and to the south along the valleys in the foothills of the Appalachian Mountains.

In the Southern colonies the plantations, that is, the communities created by planters, were divided racially between the planter's family and the white overseer (or estate manager), who operated out of the plantation house, and the slaves, who lived in separate quarters. The slaves had their own hierarchical social structure, with house servants and occasional black overseers constituting a black elite, and craftsmen and field workers below.[15]

The town society developed by the dominant white English colonists during the seventeenth and eighteenth centuries contained social groupings consisting of, in descending order, merchants or planters or large landowners; professionals (lawyers, doctors, clergymen); craftsmen and farmers who owned and managed their own farms; laborers of various kinds; apprentices to craftsmen; domestic servants; and the poor. Outsiders in this society were non-English-speaking immigrants (mainly from the Germanic states but also the Dutch colonists that the English incorporated in the 1660s) and black slaves, most of whom labored for planters and other farmers who produce staple crops. The status of each group was clearly demarcated and clearly recognized by others.[16]

Elites were defined by their mansions, designed to reflect the latest styles in English architecture, by their specially crafted home furnishings, by their hand-sewn gentleman's or gentlewoman's dress, by their own horses and carriages, by their assured use of spoken and written language, by their libraries, by their interest in the arts, by their exclusive leisure-time activities, and above all by the gentility and refinement that characterized their behavior, activities, and settings.[17] The planters in the Southern colonies were set apart as a class in many aspects of their lives, by what they wore and ate, even how they danced. "A periwig was a distinguishing badge of gentle folk," the Reverend Mr. Devereux Jarrett remembered of his childhood during the

### Proportions of National Groups in Two Counties

| National | Chester Co. | | | Lancaster Co. | | |
|---|---|---|---|---|---|---|
| Group | 1730 | 1759 | 1782 | 1722 | 1758–59 | 1782 |
| German-speaking | 2% | 5% | 8% | 65% | 58% | 68% |
| English | 67 | 59 | 63 | | 15 | 10 |
| Scotch-Irish, etc. | 12 | 23 | 19 | } 35% | 19 | 13 |
| Welsh | 17 | 8 | 7 | | 1 | 1 |
| Other and unassigned | 2% | 5% | 4% | | 7% | 9% |
| Approximate total population | 10,800 | 27,000 | 34,450 | 1,400 | 26,000 | 47,000 |

Note: Some columns do not add to 100 because of rounding.

ETHNIC GROUPS. **Early evidence of ethnic variety in colonial Pennsylvania was a harbinger of what later developed in large areas of the United States as its population was swelled by immigrants from many parts of Europe. These figures are from eighteenth-century Chester and Lancaster counties. [James Lemon, *The Best Poor Man's Country*]**

1730s.[18] Those in the professions clearly saw the elites as their social models and sought to exhibit many of the same indications of status, but they were often without the means to maintain such a style of living.

By contrast, farmers and craftsmen made their own homes and furnishings and clothing, owned their own horses and wagons, if not carriages, indulged in popular leisure-time activity associated with the more popular arts and entertainment, and were literate in rudimentary ways. Within the artisan community could be found a hierarchy within a hierarchy. Millers had the most prestige, followed by extractive processors such as blacksmiths, tanners, and resin/tar/turpentine manufacturers, and then by the "light" artisans: tailors, shoemakers, and weavers, with the building trades presided over by carpenters and stone masons and "trading" crafts led by coopers.[19] Only the poor lacked status, because they lacked an occupation. Slaves were in a separate racial caste.

In addition to divisions based upon status, ethnicity, and race, town society was also divided between a core population consisting of families that remained in a given community across several generations, and a transient population whose members did not remain as town dwellers for as long as a single generation, typically far less. In New England, in towns such as Andover, Massachusetts, families stayed in place over considerable periods of time, creating extended kinship neighborhoods, until land holdings could no longer sensibly be divided as workable farms.[20] A major Puritan goal was for families to remain together in order to live proper Christian lives in an ideal community setting. But even in New England the founding of new towns went on through much of the seventeenth and eighteenth centuries, and many migrants came from already-settled areas.[21]

Similarly, in the Southern colonies, planters and their relatives often clustered into rural areas around plantations, but such groupings did not remain stable for long as individuals moved to find fertile new land and extend the plantation system beyond its seaboard confines.[22] In the mid-Atlantic colonies, geographic mobility was quite pronounced. In southeastern Pennsylvania by the late eighteenth century, from 40 to 80 percent of the inhabitants of Chester and Lancaster counties moved in the period between censuses.[23] In various assessments of the residents of Germantown, Pennsylvania, from the late seventeenth to the late eighteenth centuries, fewer than half, sometimes considerably fewer, of the names on one list reappeared on later lists.[24]

In spite of divisions based upon status, ethnicity, race, and longevity of residence, colonial towns cohered and were relatively peaceful and harmonious. Their inhabitants were usually law-abiding, their behavior acceptable from the perspective of the churches that practically all attended. This did not mean, however, that town dwellers were invariably united and well behaved.

Many of the towns founded by Puritans, for example, were wracked by religious and political disputes. There was not always agreement on where to locate the meetinghouse, the central location for all religious and political activity. As settlement spread away from the original building, groups petitioned the colonial assembly for permission to build their own meetinghouse and to incorporate as a new town.[25] Parishioners sometimes divided over rival ministerial candidates, and ministers sometimes feuded with their parishioners.[26] Religious phenomena such as witchcraft and evangelism deeply divided some communities in New England.[27]

In Springfield, Massachusetts, a steeply hierarchical town where an economically based individualism overran a religiously induced communalism, there was much evidence of criminal activity. The court records are besmirched with cases of verbal and physical assaults, slander, family feuds, ethnic antagonisms (directed against the Scots), and disputes between ministers and parishioners.[28] When the lofty elites were outsiders, as in Marblehead, Massachusetts, where many of the merchants were either from Boston or had ties to the mercantile community there, the native population expressed its resentment in various ways.[29] Sometimes the geographical fault lines in communities divided into two factions, one residing in dispersed homesteads in outlying areas and adhering to a traditional agricultural life, the other living in commercially built-up settlements and welcoming the development of trade and a market economy.[30]

In the Southern colonies the biracial plantation communities that emerged with the development of staple-crop agriculture were disrupted when the slaves engaged in arson, work slowdowns, feigned illnesses, and escapes, and occasionally either planned or executed insurrections.[31]

Several religious groups who founded towns in the English colonies, among them the Mennonites and more notably the Puritans, were imbued with a great commitment to peace and harmony and unity, to forms of communalism that were at odds with the prevailing individualism that induced most colonists along the Atlantic coast to migrate directly to farm lands and live in farmsteads outside of community. Mennonite and Puritan towns were meant to be closed societies, excluding those with other ethnic and religious identities. The Mennonite religious communities did retain their exclusivity and apartness from the rest of the population, but it was an isolation sustained by the enforced insularity of a German-speaking group.

Similarly, in many seventeenth-century New England towns, everything that town dwellers aspired to and tried to practice reflected their adherence to a communalistic outlook: religious and civic life were combined in a single physical setting; both church and town were founded with covenants, solemn agreements that all who lived in the town would sustain a model community whose principles and practices would reflect the best Puritan ideals; both church and town were democratically governed by the voters and the parishioners, initially the same groups (except that the women parishioners could not also be voters); others, those who did not subscribe to the covenant, who were different in belief and behavior, were warned out of town.[32]

But the Puritan experiment in communalism was not sustainable. Settlement in most New England townships was dispersed. Only those towns that developed trade and craft and mill-centered villages, which were often located in the vicinity of the old meetinghouses and commons, achieved the kind of *physical* clustering that communalism implied. By the eighteenth century, when proprietors turned town founding into a wholly speculative enterprise, communalism became rarer still. The pattern of life among Springfield's residents, with its emphasis on the economic dimension rather than the religious, with its ethos of individualism rather than communalism, was at first unusual but became increasingly common among the town dwellers of New England. Even the early religious unity of seventeenth-century towns was shattered by the growing presence of other sects, something that received official imperial sanction in 1691 with the passage of the English Toleration Act. Both the outbreak of witchcraft, which occurred sporadically during the seventeenth century, and evangelism, starting in the 1740s, also had divisive effects.

The purest form of communalism, other than that based upon the initial linguistic exclusivity of the Mennonites, was based upon race. The biracial plantation communities contained a racial caste whose work life was meshed with the larger white society but whose social life centered on the physically separate slave quarters. There the tribal in-gathering of African-American slaves produced Gullah, a linguistic amalgam of English and African languages, which in turn made possible verbal communication and the creation of a slave community. It was a society infused with the remembered forms of communalism that had permeated an earlier village society that all slaves had shared in West Africa. This communalism shaped every aspect of life in the slave quarters, from social behavior to leisure to popular culture.[33] Forced into a separate social caste, herded when present in significant numbers into separate slave quarters, black slaves practiced heightened forms of communalism that the dominant white population failed to achieve, unless in a linguistic prison, as the Mennonites initially were.

Absent from the rather ample evidence of social disharmony among white European settlers in the English colonies is any clear indication of serious class antagonisms. Town dwellers were usually able to live together peacefully in small community settings even though divided in obvious ways. One factor in this social cohesion was the social mobility that marked community life everywhere in the English colonies. There may have been a social hierarchy, but it was not a static one: most town dwellers moved around in it within their lifetimes; only the elites seemed fairly stationary. Groups did not solidify and remain unchanging in their makeup generation after generation. Indeed, it was the other end of the hierarchy, the poor, who were most likely to move in search of greater opportunity.[34]

In towns throughout New England, selectmen (town officials) warned outsiders without means of support out of town. Many towns passed vagrancy ordinances and sometimes quarreled with each other over the responsibility for a particular pauper. Towns provided "outdoor relief" for their own poor, never very numerous. Overseers of the poor provided direct aid—medical or nutritional—or managed a vendue system whereby paupers were auctioned off to the lowest bidder, whom the town would pay to look after the indigent for a period of time. Children of the poor were often "put out" or indentured to families of steady means until they reached a certain age. "Indoor relief," or the maintenance of poorhouses was, outside the largest urban centers, a nineteenth-century phenomenon, and many towns like Otisfield, Maine, retained an "outdoor relief" system until well into that century.[35]

The poor were provided for in the mid-Atlantic colonies too, but, town dwellers in Germantown, for example, unlike those in New England's public system, did not regard poverty as a community responsibility. Instead Germantowners left money in their wills for the poor, and some of the churches set aside funds to aid those who were destitute. But those in poverty did not remain in town for long periods; no continuing group could be classified as poor.[36]

Similarly, linguistic minorities, the Dutch and the German colonists, especially if they settled amidst the English-speaking majority, as the Germanic settlers did in Germantown, rather quickly learned English in order to end their isolation and enhance their opportunity for linguistic as well as geographic and social mobility.[37]

Both social and geographic mobility were indications that town dwellers aspired to higher status, that they considered elites to be social models and not oppressors—unless the elites came from afar, were outsiders, or were using the town for larger, foreign interests. A great array of craftsmen could aspire to enter the ranks of the mercantile elite. And many farmers in the Southern colonies could dream of attaining the commercial complexity that a plantation represented. Or farmers in the mid-Atlantic or New England colonies could at least imagine a more commercialized and market-oriented version of their own operation.

So the new emphasis on social and geographic mobility enhanced rather than damaged social cohesion because it harmonized with another, older, European-derived emphasis that the English colonists adhered to throughout the seventeenth and eighteenth centuries: deference. Town dwellers routinely deferred to social "betters" and often elected members of prominent families to leading local public offices and as militia officers and church authorities, everywhere providing them with the best pews in those churches. Nothing revealed the hold of deference more baldly than when the proprietors of the New England towns, holding land in common, parceled out house and farm lots to individuals based upon their prominence (as well as the size of their families and their usefulness to the community).[38]

But deference toward elites did not mean that these groups, in maintaining their hegemony or patriarchy, generated widespread hostility among their inferiors. Both merchants and planters in the village and plantation societies of the seventeenth and eighteenth centuries related to laborers and slaves in a manner that stood somewhere between feudalism and modern industrial capitalism, in a "patron-client" relationship. Planters like the Byrds, the Carters, and the Washingtons, and merchants like the Pynchons, developed personal relations with those whom they dominated economically and socially, whether they were white farmers or craftsmen who created a financial indebtedness to these elites, or whether they were tenants and sharecroppers, or hired laborers, or slaves. The merchant/planter elites dominated a highly personal world, treating their social inferiors as known individuals with whom they were obliged to deal individually. Such relationships could lead to delays in the repayment of debt and to customized work agreements.[39]

Slave labor was fundamentally different because of its coercive character. Planters had to master the art of labor control in order to make enslaved men and women work. But even in the case of slave labor, the planters were quite varied in the way they dealt with individual slaves, deploying a complex array of rewards and punishments, effective and ineffective, kindly or brutal.[40]

Social cohesion in town society along the Atlantic coast was also fostered by a churchgoing population whose behavior could be censured by other parishioners, formally or informally, depending upon the practices of the particular Christian denomination. If individuals misbehaved or broke God's laws, the widespread religious faith of this colonial population became a powerful instrument for the confinement of social behavior within acceptable Christian bounds. Individuals often sinned, but they often repented as well. Parishioners were also called to account on a weekly basis in ministerial sermons, which were regular judgments on the extent to which church members as a group were living up to God's commandments.

Civil governments, through their detailed legal codes, further enforced acceptable behavior by punishing those who committed illegal acts. The court system was an instrument of county government throughout the colonies, and judges regularly meted out punishment in forms common to Europe as well as the colonial frontier: the stocks for lesser crimes, whippings for more serious crimes, public hangings for the most serious crimes. The police or constabulatory force in the towns was usually a single man who was responsible for keeping the peace and apprehending those charged with criminal offenses, though in many of the more rural areas the county sheriff was the official designated for this task.

Such rudimentary instruments for law enforcement are vivid evidence that town society relied on internal mechanisms, agreed-upon rules of behavior that most subscribed to, as the chief way to maintain law and order. The punishments handed out by civil governments certainly had repentance as their goal, which was also the goal of town dwellers as parishioners. In other words, even though government had assumed the secular authority to decide through its legal codes what were society's rules and punishments, the aim of government was the same as that of the Christian churches: to induce towns-people to behave as good Christians, and when they did not, to punish them in ways that would induce rule-breaking Christians to repent and sin no more. Thus did religion and politics, church and state, work together to make town society cohere and its members behave.

But it was the inhabitants of Spanish colonial towns in the area that later became the Southwestern United States who produced a society that was the most socially cohesive of all the European colonial settlements anywhere in the Americas. Steeply hierarchical and patriarchal, Spanish town society was characterized by strong communal traditions that suffused every dimension of village life—familial, political, economic, social, and cultural. It was most visibly demonstrated in its patron/peon system, in which the patriarchs of the wealthiest families formed an even more pervasive counterpart to the patron-client relations between early merchants and planters and their dependents in the English towns and plantations. Nowhere else in the Americas was there a closer bond between social hierarchy and social cohesion.[41]

After the Revolution, during the nineteenth century, towns continued to ex-hibit a socially stratified society, one made more complex with the explosion of occupational specialization that accompanied the industrialization and commercialization of economic life.

The commercialization of an area's economy and the growth that ac-companied that shift had a major impact on the towns' social structure. In Massachusetts, hill towns such as Ware and Pelham, market and administra-tive centers such as Northampton and Worcester, and seaports such as Salem, to the extent that they grew and became more commercially oriented, saw their social structures become more hierarchical the larger they became, chiefly because larger centers attracted people with professional and manage-rial skills who could command higher incomes. Hill towns were on the in-land plateau of New England, on the more marginal lands for agricultural if not extractive purposes, and so towns such as Ware and Pelham did not grow much. But towns in the valleys and along the coasts, such as Northampton, Worcester, and Salem, burgeoned as political and economic centers, and their social structures revealed the mobility of a large, enduring middling element, and a high degree of transiency among the young and those who failed eco-nomically. When all five of these different sizes of towns are averaged together, half the adult men over thirty gained moderate holdings of property as members of a substantial and relatively prosperous middle stratum.[42]

Similarly, in Kingston, New York, during the pre-canal era before the 1830s, the town's society consisted, in ascending order, of a few slaves, then white laborers, farmers, craftsmen, storekeepers, professionals, and officials.[43] But with the canal (which connected the Delaware and Hudson rivers), Kingston became a trade center, moving coal from the Appalachians, cement and lime from its own limestone, and agricultural produce from the Hudson Valley—all to wider markets. A growing commerce brought ethnic, religious, and occupational diversity, as an agriculturally based community of native-born Protestants of Dutch origin gave way to a society of much greater complexity. By the 1840s and 1850s, Irish and German immigrants came to comprise half the population. This immigration brought religious variety as well as a large transient population, physically separated into its riverside village within the township. Commercialization in turn produced a much steeper social structure. By 1860 the wealthiest 10 percent of Kingston's inhabitants owned three-fourths of the assessed wealth.[44]

Farther west, in Jacksonville, Illinois, by 1850 the wealthiest 10 percent of property owners held half the assessed wealth. The larger Jacksonville grew, the steeper the hierarchy became. But, once again, a large middling element improved its economic position and comprised the "core," stable population in a community with large numbers of transients.[45] The unskilled experienced significant upward social mobility between 1850 and 1870 (they comprised nearly 50 percent of the population during the first decade but less than 30 percent during the second decade), and so did the skilled (from nearly 60 percent to less than 50 percent for those who were not proprietors; from over 30 percent to just under 20 percent for those who were proprietors).[46] Jacksonville was further divided by migrants from both the Northeast and the Southeast—by Yankees and Southerners; by immigrants from Portugal, the German states, and Ireland; and by a small nonslave black community. Except for the Yankees and the Southerners, these groups hived into their own sections of town.[47]

In the villages of Trempealeau County, Wisconsin, from 1850 to 1880, transience was prominent at all income and age levels, but especially among the young and propertyless and immigrants from abroad. A hierarchical social structure was led in descending order by businessmen, bankers, manufacturers, millers, and craftsmen; foreign immigrants gradually improved their standing.[48] In the villages and rural areas of Trempealeau County in 1860, the wealthiest 10 percent owned nearly 40 percent of all property, whereas the poorest 10 percent had but 1.5 percent. But the middle 60 percent claimed about 40 percent, which demonstrated that there was a large middling element in the population.[49]

In the Rocky Mountains, late-nineteenth-century trade centers such as Grand Junction, Colorado, also experienced a high incidence of transiency. Businessmen and professionals were less likely to move than those who were unskilled or propertyless; younger and single men were more likely to leave than older and married ones. But, above all else, wealth distinguished those who stayed from those who left.[50]

As in the earlier agricultural era, elites dominated some settlements from the very beginning, and, as before, this happened when those with entrepreneurial skill exploited a resource that could be produced on a large, commercial scale. In areas where agriculture remained the predominant economic activity, planters continued to produce a staple crop. They shifted to cotton from tobacco, rice, and sugar as settlement spread inland from the coasts and river valleys. The owning of slaves and involvement in staple-crop production became the supreme status symbols of Southern society, and during the antebellum era slaveowning drew a greater variety of Southerners into what became an attenuated version of the planter elite of the colonial period: those of French, Germanic, Scottish and other non-English origin, women (usually as widows), natives, even other blacks (usually mulattoes). A new middle class of slaveowners emerged, with many professionals dabbling in the South's premier economic activity, periodically climbing into or falling out of the bottom of the slaveowning class.[51]

Those slaveowners who migrated westward and inland typically failed to develop stable, full-fledged plantations. In their focus on profit and growth, they became indistinguishable from entrepreneurs elsewhere. The slave system lost its quasi-feudalistic attributes just as commercial and industrial (machine production) enterprises were losing theirs. The newer plantations in the cotton districts were much like those in the older tobacco, rice, and sugar districts. The planters created biracial communities with a one-family elite, possibly white overseers or managers, and a steeply hierarchical black community (within a community) whose members, while working as field hands and craftsmen and domestic servants on the plantation, nonetheless existed as a community in their separate slave quarters.[52]

In the years after the 1863 emancipation of the slaves, many freedmen stayed on former planters' lands and became tenants or sharecroppers, mired in a system of work peonage, unable either to pay off their accumulated indebtedness to their new landowners or to buy the land on which they were tenants. Although the staple-crop system, which continued to focus on cotton growing, was sustained until the twentieth century, the embryonic plantation communities that had been a prominent feature of Southern life since the seventeenth century ended with emancipation. Former planters could go on managing a staple-crop economy with their black tenants and sharecroppers, but they lacked the authority they had had as slaveowners to create and sustain self-sufficient, economically oriented plantation communities.

On the treeless plains and prairies from the Mississippi River to the Rocky Mountains, when farmers developed the mechanical capacity to farm prairie land beginning in the 1850s, agriculture became large-scale, commercial, and machine-operated, employing large numbers of farm laborers who did not own their own farms. Squatting gave way to well-demarcated farm operations. In such a setting, the distribution of wealth became significantly steeper, and a commercial farming elite who grew grain crops and raised livestock quickly emerged. In a rural neighborhood such as Sugar Creek, Illinois, located at the very edge of the prairie land, in 1838 (before farmers learned how to plow the prairies), the wealthiest 10 percent of the households owned 25 percent of the land, while the poorest 20 percent owned 10 percent. By 1858 (after agriculture had spilled over onto the plains), the same 10 percent owned 35 percent and the poorest 20 percent only 5 percent.[53] But even as the social hierarchy became steeper, there continued to be a large middling element: the middle 60 percent continued to own approximately 45 percent of the landed property.[54] Like the post-Civil War staple-crop agriculture of the South, large-scale commercial farming on the Western plains produced widely spaced farms, with facilities for hired hands, not clustered communities.

By the 1870s and 1880s the open-range raising of livestock involved the movement of cattle from Texas across the Southern plains to towns in Kansas that served as terminals for rail transport to the slaughterhouses of Chicago. Cattle drivers managed large commercial operations that were centered on the rail terminal or "cattle" towns, and they became elites in towns that were founded to be forts and trade centers for agriculture as well as rail terminals for the cattle drivers. The drivers skewed the social hierarchy, making it much steeper than it would have been had their cattle business not been present. In the cattle towns, "proprietors, managers, and officials" controlled as much as 75 to 80 percent of real and personal property, even though they comprised at most 15 to 20 percent of the population.[55]

In extractive centers, elites frequently dominated town society. At its founding in the late eighteenth century, Beekmantown, New York, was on the northern forest frontier. The Platts and the Mooers and other original proprietors constituted an elite for as long as the forest products of the area provided them with unusual wealth. Those who were farmers supplied those who worked in the forestry operations, and by the 1820s and beyond, the settlement at Beekmantown became a rather ordinary center for a middling farm population, which nonetheless included, by the 1840s and 1850s, significant numbers of Irish and French-Canadian immigrants from abroad, via Canada, who brought ethnic diversity to the town.[56]

Similarly, the company towns that mining and forestry corporations founded in the Rocky and Pacific coastal mountains between the mid-nineteenth and mid-twentieth centuries were corporate versions of plantations and merchant-dominated towns like early Springfield, Massachusetts. In place of family domination came corporate control. Absentee corporate owners were represented by company supervisors, store owners, and recreation hall managers.[57]

The new industrial towns of the nineteenth century also contained elites who dominated steeply hierarchical social structures. Sometimes these elites were homegrown, entrepreneurially oriented core families, even former millers of grain and logs, as waterpowered mills became, with architectural alterations, the early sites for machine production and the assemblage of wage laborers. Other factory towns were beholden to absentee elites, the owners of industrial corporations who resided elsewhere. Slowly, during the course of the nineteenth century, factories became more impersonal, more efficient, more tightly organized, as the modern industrial corporation became the major source of employment in some towns, replacing the older, quasi-feudal, patron-client relationship that had existed between merchants and planters and even early factory owners, especially if they were local families, on the one side, and various kinds of dependents, on the other.

In the Rockdale manufacturing district south of Philadelphia, for example, by the 1850s there existed a hierarchical social structure that was perfectly mirrored by the physical layout of the factory villages of the area. The resident owners lived in mansions on the top of the hill; in descending order, as the topography sloped downward toward the mill streams, were the residences of the managers, sometimes in rented supervisors' houses, mingled with hired service and craft providers, with the mill laborers living in rented tenements built alongside the mill itself.[58]

As settlement spread across the continent during the nineteenth century, the social structure of towns everywhere continued to exhibit the same kind of hierarchical shape that had been obvious during the seventeenth and eighteenth centuries. In areas where small elites exploited valuable resources, that hierarchy continued to be very steep. But in towns serving large numbers of family farmers or loggers or fishermen or miners, what was striking about the social profile, about the distribution of wealth in such ordinary communities, was its middling character. *Even with* an elite, a large middling element continued to own a significant portion of the wealth.

With the industrialization and commercialization of economic activity, specialization and training for particular occupations became more evident, though some town dwellers continued to derive income from several kinds of work, or shifted from one occupation to another during the course of their work lives. Whether the total range of occupations grew is difficult to determine, as there were a large number of crafts that were gradually absorbed into machine production at the same time commercialization and industrialization were creating many new positions. What is quite clear is that social status continued to be associated with work. The planter elite divided by the 1860s into various kinds of large landowners and agriculturalists; merchants gave way to industrialists and "businessmen" of many kinds.

In ordinary towns, at the apex of the elite group were typically the bankers, those who were trained to handle other people's money, one facet of the many-sided activities of the earlier town merchants. Money symbolized the materialistic emphasis of American society, and bankers manipulated the deepest symbol of social status in town society: an individual's wealth. Bankers were expected to be conservative, close-mouthed, wise, and dignified. Bank buildings were often seen as temples of wealth, the most impressive buildings on Main Street. Burns Fuller remembered banks as "awesome places," which, with their tiled floors and high cages with little windows and serious people, were "nearly like being in jail."[59] Everyone who worked in the banks dressed conservatively. Banking cards (little advertisements) in newspapers were as sedate and professional as those submitted by doctors and lawyers. Some bankers became wealthy through real estate ventures; others started out as storekeepers. All were acquainted with real estate loans and investments, which were the major source of village banking wealth during the nineteenth century. All had opportunities to buy town lots, buildings, and farms in the surrounding countryside at bargain rates. Bankers were highly respected because of their power, but they were seldom popular. Town dwellers saw them as standing in the very center of the community's elite, with families that moved in the best social circles, and at death bankers received long, laudatory obituary notices.[60]

Below bankers in the towns' social hierarchy were the professionals: lawyers and doctors. Both became better trained during the course of the nineteenth century, though the apprenticeship system continued to coexist with formal training at schools. Lawyers were prominent members of town society, advertising their name and location in chaste business cards on which were listed additional functions, such as their acting as land agents or legal representatives of particular firms. Lawyers were better educated than most town dwellers, had opportunities to make profitable investments, and typically sought political office, whether at the municipal or higher levels, as the practice of law and a political career became strongly linked.[61]

Doctors served not only the town dwellers but the rural population that lived in the vicinity. In an age of horse transport, people "rode for the doctor." Doctors were priests, confidants, and friends rather than skilled specialists, and in the absence of nurses they remained with patients until a crisis passed, so that their services required long hours at the bedside. Country practitioners were usually willing to accept payment in barter from those who could not afford monetary payment: provisions for services rendered. Their irregular hours often excused them from participating in community organizations, but because of their standing, their wives often dominated the organized social life of the community. Successful practitioners eventually prospered and did so without arousing criticism. In nineteenth-century towns, bankers were respected but feared; lawyers were commonly thought to be ambitious and shrewd; but medicine was perhaps the most personally satisfying of all the professions.[62]

Other "professional" people in the towns lacked the status of doctors and lawyers but provided services that town dwellers considered important. Printers were often among the early settlers in the new towns of westward expansion. They sought contracts with municipal and county governments to publish tax lists, land sales, and other legal notices, but many also became newspaper owners/editors and, as such, great boosters of their towns. These newspaper editors made a low financial investment to start their journals and had the freedom to engage in a kind of personal journalism without feeling the need to please advertisers on whose revenue they did not rely. Editors were fierce partisans with respect to state and local politics, but at the community level they endorsed those activities that pleased town dwellers, favoring schools and churches, suggesting improvements to a town's physical appearance, crusading for rail and other forms of transportation, endorsing local manufactures, and generally boosting their town so that it could continue to grow. By the 1860s, town newspapers began printing local news, and in so doing they became community journals, adding printed versions to the oral gossip that had always sufficed as a mechanism for disseminating information in small communities.[63]

Town dwellers reserved their highest praise for churches and schools and believed that preaching and teaching were of paramount importance. Yet teachers and clergymen were in the poorest paid and generally the least distinguished of all the professions. Even though more and more teachers re-

BANKS. This bank building in Independence, Kansas, like similar structures, mirrored the high social status of the banker himself. The bank building was usually the most impressive architectural construction along Main Street. [Charles Phelps Cushing Collection]

ceived normal school training during the nineteenth century, and even though clergymen of mainline Protestant sects were highly educated before their ordination, town dwellers continued to believe that just about anyone could teach or preach. Lay preachers were common among the newer sects, and untrained teachers continued to be hired in significant numbers in the school system.

Because of low salaries, town dwellers did not expect either ministers or teachers to stay very long, and they typically did not, which further weakened their influence. Apart from religious activities, a minister's social life was limited. He was not expected in gatherings that involved dancing, drinking, or gambling, but he was a frequent public speaker at lodge meetings. Congregations were often behind in paying a preacher's salary, and ministers commonly received at least one donation party a year to supplement their income. Christmas baskets, funerals, marriages, gifts from local monument companies (in return for names of prospective customers!), substitute teaching in local schools—all were means of supplementing ministerial incomes.

Similarly, low prestige and inadequate salaries encouraged teachers to think of their profession as only a stepping-stone to something better. Men usually taught just long enough to save money to enter the professions or business. Women generally married after a few years of teaching. It was relatively easy to enter the profession and relatively easy to leave it. Towns preferred to hire teachers from elsewhere and to change them every few years. Like preaching, teaching was a nomadic occupation. Teachers were expected to board at the home of the school director or with one of his relatives. Since the county officials who administered examinations for the renewal of teaching certificates also taught refresher institutes before the examination, teachers usually felt it was wise to pay the annual attendance fee.[64]

Below the professions were storekeepers and their clerks, as retailing became increasingly specialized. A new division opened between those who worked with their hands and those who did not, between those who made products and those who sold them. The crafts gradually shrank as machine production steadily made inroads on products or parts of products that had been handmade. But even within crafts there was a hierarchy, as masters hired both journeymen and apprentices. Craftsmen who hired others had a higher standing in the community than those who had their own shops. When crafts disappeared as the dominant way of making a particular product, what sometimes remained was the craftsman as repair man, as in the case of shoe repair shops or tailor/restorers. Millers had the highest status among craftsmen and sometimes became early industrialists.

With industrialization and commercialization came wage labor wherever machines produced goods. Although machine operators ranged from skilled to unskilled, the manual character of their task brought them low status. Only the poor and the destitute were below them—indeed, were without status of any kind. Elijah J. Wiggin remembered that in early Waverly, Kansas, during the 1850s and 1860s, an "illiterate Irish girl" worked at the City Hotel, having "drifted into Waverly from some unknown place and worked in nearly every house in town. This poor creature was the object of much ridicule, possessed an insane temper and was sadly abducted to the use of bad language."[65] Willis F. Dunbar recalled that in turn-of-the-century Hartford, Michigan, "[the] chronically poor lived in filth and squalor. . . . When they faced starvation, the township supervisor would see they got something to eat."[66] Dunbar added that "respectable people . . . took a fierce pride in being self-sustaining and regarded any reliance on public aid as a great disgrace. . . . [The prevailing belief was that] no one needed to be in want. . . . [The common assumption was that] poverty was the result of laziness or indulgence, chiefly in alcohol. The idea that poverty might be the consequence of a maladjusted economic system was unheard of. . . ."[67]

The social structure of the towns was further complicated by the presence of large numbers of transients who surrounded a stable, core population, and by the emergence of ethnic, religious, and racial variety, as foreign immigrants, Catholics, and freed blacks (both before and after the Civil War) moved into towns. In Waverly during the mid-nineteenth century, Elijah Wiggin recalled a "negro settlement of little white-washed cabins." This settlement was "away down in the lower part of town, which was by common consent given over almost exclusively to the negroes." Wiggin recalled that "[our] good colored people had their own corners in the churches, and all the older ones were, as a rule, found in their places on Sunday." Wiggin also found that "[our] better class of Waverly negroes had many fine qualities, and nearly all of them retained an abiding pride in the name and fame of their former masters, which was very touching. They had no desire to break down the barriers between the races, for no self-respecting negro wished to associate with white people on terms of equality. In humble fashion, as hewers of wood and drawers of water, they lived their quiet, useful lives among us, respected and befriended by all. . . ."[68]

Promoters of black towns were anxious to indicate that the inhabitants lived exemplary lives. The editor of the *Western Cyclone*, in May 1886, wrote that in Nicodemus, Kansas, the black inhabitants had "no whiskey shop; no billiard hall or other gambling hole . . . [and] no drunkenness or rowdying, no cursing and whooping disturbs the peace of the place."[69]

During the nineteenth century, status continued to be an ever-present feature of a town dweller's social life—in the style of his or her home, mode of transportation, dress, food, language, and social behavior. Such indications were even more nuanced and precise than had been the case in previous centuries. For instance, Roderick Turnbull thought that in turn-of-the-century Maple Hill, Kansas, horses were "a mark of the kind of farmer and citizen a man was."[70] Those who sought to improve their status tried to emulate their social betters by copying their manner of living. Writers, typically clergymen, catalogued what a "proper" home and family life consisted of in a proliferation of "manuals" and guides.

During the nineteenth century the refinement and gentility that had formerly been hallmarks of elite living became qualities that the middle class attempted to emulate in order to gain status and social position. The standard physical setting for such efforts to adopt elite traits of behavior was the parlor. By these means, middle-class town dwellers turned the "gentility" of the earlier elites into nineteenth-century "respectability," that is, from a mode of social behavior that had been instilled in a colonial gentry from birth to one that was learned. Only the poor remained irremediably mired in behavior characterized by others as rude and crude, and brought shame and humiliation to those who lacked respectability.[71]

As was the case during the seventeenth and eighteenth centuries, so too in the nineteenth century, a hierarchical and varied social structure in the towns did not ordinarily produce deep, ongoing divisions. Once again this did not mean that town dwellers saw eye to eye on every aspect of their lives. In many towns there were issues that occasionally divided the community: the proper nature of private and public morality; how a variety of Christian denominations should coexist; the appropriate reaction to influxes of strangers, whether transients or foreign immigrants; the opportunities and dangers of physical and economic growth or stability; the desirability of new modes of transportation and communication and technology; the division of political allegiances between competing municipal factions or between the two major parties on the state and national levels; how coercive local government should be, that is, what services should be public services, what activities should be regulated or forbidden by law, what should be left to choice or to voluntary efforts. But, as before, ongoing, persistent divisions based upon class or ethnicity were absent, though there were racial divisions, given the universal character of white racism.

Although it was awash in social divisions based upon status, ethnicity, race, and longevity of residence, town society cohered during the nineteenth century, just as it had earlier. And for the same reasons. Geographic and social mobility worked against the hardening of class and ethnic, though not racial, divisions. In low-growth hill towns on marginal land, such as Ware and Pelham in Massachusetts; or in growing service centers, such as Northampton and Worcester in Massachusetts, or Kingston in New York, or Jacksonville in Illinois; or in seaports, such as Salem, Massachusetts; or in factory towns, such as the Rockdale manufacturing district in Pennsylvania—the kind of town didn't matter: everywhere on the continent, dissatisfaction with one's lot could and often did lead to either a social or a geographic change of place.

The newest and most important form of labor that emerged during the nineteenth century was wage labor. In town settings at least, this took the form of machine operators in waterpowered factory villages or farm laborers who went out of town to work on large, mechanized farms. But while they had low status, such workers were quite mobile, if not socially, then geographically. Indeed, as before, the most geographically mobile of all the social groups in towns were those with the lowest status: the poor and destitute, but also wage laborers. In factory districts such as Rockdale one could find not an undifferentiated mass of exhausted, sick, and starving wage-laboring families pushed around by cruel factory managers, but rather a wide range of ages, degrees of skill, and income. This group was extraordinarily mobile, with the financial ability to escape unfavorable circumstances, given wage levels and the expectation that the factory village would provide only a temporary residence for either the immigrants who flocked to such locations or, in the case of the first factory city, Lowell, the daughters of rural farm families who were attracted by an independent income.[72]

Social values, the basis for proper personal and social behavior, were instilled in individual town dwellers in a variety of ways, more extensive than in earlier centuries. Those who lived in towns certainly knew, at all phases of their lives, how they were supposed to behave, even if they did not always do so. Churches continued to be a focal point of discussion for what constituted a good, moral, Christian life. Ministers continued to sermonize, even if congregations typically no longer disciplined wayward members. But periodic waves of revival meetings, at which evangelical preachers sought to convert sinners, indicated that many Christians still yearned for a way to end their misbehavior through redemptive acts.

Of even greater importance to the maintenance of social order and cohesion were the court systems that defined society's rules and adjudicated those instances when individuals were charged by law enforcement agencies with committing crimes, with breaking those rules. During the nineteenth century, states and counties built jails that were meant to incarcerate but then rehabilitate criminals. Confining and isolating and disciplining them in institutions built for the purpose, rather than publicly humiliating and embarrassing them through whippings and stocks, was thought to be the correct path to repentance.[73]

Indoor trials of serious crimes replaced outdoor public hangings as theatres for morality tales. The lives of town dwellers were refracted through a particular crime, were lifted to the level of high drama (was the accused innocent or guilty?), and were examined for reasons why such a serious form of misbehavior had occurred. Alma W. Swinton remembered that trials served an important social function in early twentieth-century Ontonagon, Michigan. A murder trial "created a great deal of excitement. [The town's housewives] thronged to the court and listened with avidity, taking along knittings and luncheons."[74] Local lawyers usually cited the principles of the law as refined by a succession of commentators, whose words were frequently cited. The law was presented as a body of great moral principles, which all town dwellers could understand. The putative crime was shown to be a violation of those great principles.[75]

While most mechanisms of social control were familiar, new vehicles for social cohesion emerged during the nineteenth century. One of them was the newspapers, whose editors with increasing explicitness endorsed their community's deepest values, warning the younger generation of improprieties, reprimanding those who misbehaved, opposing those institutions for which there was popular hostility, such as saloons and gambling dens and houses of prostitution. But editors were careful to avoid unpopular crusades. They were above all boosters and had no desire to challenge the fundamental arrangements of local society. Rather, they perceived themselves to be moral watchdogs, ready to pounce on activities and developments that might undermine a proper, Christian-oriented society.[76]

By mid-century, editors of rural newspapers sought to emulate the penny press of the big-city dailies by including local news in their columns. They tried to entice town dwellers with leisure to serve as contributors of local news, so that what had been a matter of oral gossip could be printed and thus attract subscribers. Quite successful in their efforts, local news columns rather suddenly became a regular feature of the country press.[77] Although Willis F. Dunbar remembered that in turn-of-the-century Hartford, Michigan, "few farmers took a daily newspaper and many villagers did not," he admitted that "[people] read local news avidly. They usually turned to the inside pages and read the local news items first."[78]

In Lacon, Illinois, the *Home Journal* ran an article in 1884 urging town dwellers—in addition to its dozen regular contributors—to "Write for the

Journal:" "Tell us who died, got married or sold out. Tell us who is building a new house, who is going to move West, who had bought a farm, begun to plow, or had a runaway. Tell us when schools begin, about the plays, the parties, and the church and political meetings. Don't forget to tell us who is engaged to teach your schools, who has an extra large crop, who can't take a country paper, and give us notes of your literary societies, balls, institutes and shows. Give us the news. . . . We furnish stationery and stamps free to all who contribute regularly."[79]

Another nineteenth-century innovation was the explicit use of the schools to instill Christian values in succeeding generations of town dwellers. The "readers" and "spellers" of William Holmes McGuffey, professor of moral philosophy at the University of Virginia from 1845 to 1873, were vastly popular in school systems, public or private, in towns throughout the nation, with sales of perhaps 122 million copies. The book was adopted by the public school systems of 37 states.

McGuffey presented simple stories that reflected his belief that town life was, at its most proper, a manifestation of Christian virtues. The town society he idealized existed in a world overseen by a God who rewarded town dwellers who were virtuous—that is, truthful, honest, courageous, content, modest, and kind; who opposed greed, revenge, and selfishness; who worked hard but whose lives were not consumed by material ambition alone; who believed in private property but also in the obligation of the rich to aid the unfortunate; who avoided poverty, idleness, and vagrancy through labor and frugality; and who shunned liquor, tobacco, gambling, and sex outside of marriage.[80]

Popular crusades against these forms of misbehavior became moral battlegrounds in the nineteenth century. They divided town dwellers over the question of whether such misbehavior should be made illegal, even if immoral. It was widely agreed that serious sins and crimes—murder, physical assault, theft—deserved condemnation by the sinner's church as well as punishment and rehabilitation by secular authorities. Far less clear was whether inebriation, prostitution, or gambling should be regulated, controlled, banned by ministerial or editorial condemnation or by the force of law, or permitted.

Before the development of rail systems during the middle decades of the century, the cheapest way to transport grains was to distill them into liquor. Whiskey became the most common alcoholic beverage of the nineteenth century, just as rum, distilled from imported molasses, had been the eighteenth-century favorite. Even after grain could be transported by rail at reasonable cost, much grain continued to be distilled. The effects of drunkenness on the stability of family and community life could be devastating at a time when a sudden loss of income could not be easily remedied, when charity consisted largely of the compassion of committed Christians. Above all, drunkenness represented an un-Christian loss of control, a failure to regulate one's behavior. Similarly, gambling could lead to a sudden loss of wealth needed for the maintenance of the family. In a society that emphasized wealth accumulation, the impulse to gamble, to get rich quick, was quite widespread. Prostitution also represented a loss of control, a violation of the sanctity of Christian marriage and the commitment that bound a husband and father to his wife and children.

Drinking, gambling, and prostitution at their most developed occurred in places especially designed for them: the saloon, the gambling den, and houses of prostitution. But they were often carried on together or in some combination. They were most prevalent in frontier towns, which had a high ratio of men to women. In Michigan's lumber towns, for example, loggers frequented saloons, brothels, and gambling dens every weekend, especially in the spring, after the winter logging. At first there was little civic effort to end this vice. The economic benefits of the lumber trade encouraged the inhabitants to adjust to an unusually high incidence of fighting, brawling, gambling, drinking, and whoring.[81] In the well-documented case of the cattle towns in Kansas, the cowboys who drove the cattle from the Southern plains to the rail terminals in Kansas during the warm-weather months created a seasonal invasion of unattached men seeking amusement. Gamblers, prostitutes, and saloon managers arrived to set up facilities and provide wanted services that remained immune from serious criticism during the peak years of the cattle trade.[82]

Few tried to suppress prostitution when most of the town's inhabitants were young, single, transient men engaged in the cattle trade. The police arrested and fined prostitutes on schedule to raise funds for their law enforcement efforts. But far from a moral outcry, newspapers, churches, and the public displayed an amused tolerance until the cattle trade declined and the cattle towns returned to being agricultural service centers.[83] Similarly, Charles L. Sonnichsen thought the presence of prostitutes in "parlor houses" added refinement to raw mining camps in the late nineteenth century. The best of these parlor houses "offered a combination home, club, amusement center, and confessional for the lonely males of the place."[84]

Gambling was a way of life, a business occupation for its practitioners. In a setting in which acquisitiveness dominated, gamblers internalized their society's goals, concluding that wagering was worth the risk, offering change, escape, and a life of self-indulgence, excitement, and success without

SALOONS. By the nineteenth century, the more inclusive tavern had transformed itself into the male-only saloon, a place avoided by all who favored temperance or female respectability. Saloons occupied a great variety of settings, from hotels to very plain wooden structures—like this one in Wisconsin—but their windows were invariably covered so that drinkers could be well separated from those who denigrated the consumption of alcoholic beverages. [State Historical Society of Wisconsin]

struggle or sacrifice. Gamblers were men of property, respected leaders of local society, self-made men who exuded style, dignity, and respectability. In the 1880s in Tombstone, Arizona, according to one report, gamblers presented an appearance that was a cross between "Adonis and Beau Brummel with a dash of Captain Kidd thrown in for color."[85] Gambling was as highly regarded as other successful local business endeavors. Gamblers with the proper appearance and demeanor became leaders of society, sometimes even politicians, sheriffs, marshals, and mayors. They remained essentially businessmen, though their ultimate status symbol was a lot of money, all at once, without effort. As with prostitutes, politicians fined them as a source of revenue during the period the cattle trade flourished. But gambling, though it could start as a respectable occupation, could quickly degenerate when gamblers lost a great deal of money or when they ruined others financially. When the cattle trade declined and the cattle towns resumed their roles as ordinary service centers, the people began to shift their perception of gambling, which moved behind closed doors and became increasingly seen as something sordid and sinful. The professionals moved on.[86]

"Whiskey towns" in the Oklahoma Territory in the years before statehood in 1907 emerged as supply centers for white settlers and for native tribes on nearby reservations where liquor was prohibited. Several dozen in number, the whiskey towns flourished with multiple saloons dispensing liquor to native tribesmen as well as white settlers.[87]

In all these cases—prostitution, gambling, drinking—popular reform movements arose in reaction. They were especially effective in regulating or even prohibiting the offensive activity. In both kinds of frontier towns (in Kansas and in Oklahoma), wide-based temperance crusades led to a sharp decline in drinking.[88]

But prostitution, gambling, and drinking were not confined to frontier towns, with their skewed gender ratios. In the perception of many town dwellers, they continued to be problems long after their towns had matured. The anti-vice crusades that emerged during the nineteenth century were immensely popular in the towns, for they became a means of ordinary town dwellers to take an active role in the suppression of activities and behavior that, if left unchecked, they believed would undermine the social cohesion of their communities.[89] Immorality might create chaos as individuals spun out of control, living selfish, un-Christian lives. Popular reform crusades supplemented the efforts of town officials, editors, and preachers to maintain a peaceful, harmonious, and virtuous society. They enjoyed a broad appeal among the inhabitants of towns, for those who became caught up in such crusades were not dissatisfied with life in their communities. They wanted to *preserve* it—at least their idealized version of it—not *change* it.

Although each form of misbehavior spawned its own moral crusade, drunkenness evoked the greatest response. No other vice had the same potential for family and community disruption; no other form of misbehavior created such controversy as to whether it should be left alone, regulated, or prohibited. The arguments over temperance helped the movement grow. As the century wore on, the temperance crusade, especially its women's branch (the Women's Christian Temperance Union), became a kind of all-purpose anti-vice crusade. Local chapters had started by pressuring politicians for legislation, or asking parishioners to take no-drink pledges; but later in the century they formed a many-sided movement as WCTU adherents emphasized the importance of sexual purity and agitated against the use of tobacco, even providing charity to the orphaned, the sick, and the poor.[90]

Eliza J. Wiggin remembered that in early Waverly, Kansas, in the mid-nineteenth century, "citizens in all stages of intoxication were often seen in the streets and alleys. Many of these unfortunates were men of intelligence and education, college graduates, doctors, and more especially lawyers—for some reason the members of the legal profession seemed sadly addicted to drink. . . . [Women and girls] never appeared on the streets on convention and election days, when many of the best citizens had a habit of drinking in excess, though sober at other times."[91]

Alma W. Swinton recalled that in early-twentieth-century Ontonagon, Michigan, the saloon was located "in a disreputable shack. . . . Little boys frequented the place and reported all sort of things 'not nice' which went on in the secret back room and over the bar."[92] Willis F. Dunbar remembered that in Hartford, Michigan, in the 1900s and 1910s "churches and schools continuously expounded upon the evil consequences of liquor."[93]

In early-twentieth-century Esperance, New York, a resident recalled, the main support for the town's hotel "came from the saloon and the two pool tables in the saloon. The smell of beer came from the saloon door, and often on the porch the more disreputable loungers of the village would be sitting, smoking and spitting toward the sidewalk. . . . For those in the village and the countryside who were already on the road to hell there were two saloons, one in each of the old hotels and a pool room in each. Here the lost souls congregated, and against them the righteous fulminated. The saloon of Chapman House particularly incurred wrath, because being in the very middle of the village it set a bad example to any youth who passed by it. I was warned never to go into the Chapman House. When I walked past, I could always smell the odor of beer from the saloon door, and if it was late in the day old Doc Marsh would be sitting on the veranda, tipped back in his chair, feet in the air, head against the wall, dead drunk and snoring."[94]

Anti-vice crusades were devices to further social cohesion in the towns when they united town dwellers behind the cause. But sometimes they seriously divided the town's inhabitants and became a source of social unrest. In towns such as Chelsea, Vermont, temperance began in the 1830s and 1840s as a divisive force in community life, but by the 1870s it had become a major factor in the stability and consensus that came to characterize life in the town.[95] Thus moral crusades were dual-edged phenomena.

Another innovative nineteenth-century mechanism for the fostering of social cohesion in the towns was the town dwellers' widespread belief that they lived in a classless society.[96] Roderick Turnbull remembered that "if anyone had done anything just to suggest that he was little higher up on the social scale than other people, he would have been spotted a mile away."[97] Other, more discerning observers, were nonetheless aware of the existence of a class system in the towns. Mark Twain remembered that, as a boy growing up in a Missouri town in the mid-nineteenth century, "[there] were grades of society—people of good family, people of unclassified family, people of no family. Everybody knew everybody, and nobody put on any visible airs, yet the class lines were clearly drawn and the familiar social life of each class was restricted to that class."[98] That there were no classes was a myth, of course, but a powerful one. This belief was a distinctive adaptation by town dwellers of the wider American belief—emergent by the 1830s—in an egalitarian society, that all white men are born equal, without ascribed social status.

The inhabitants of towns frequently asserted that in their small community there were no strangers, that everyone knew one another, that no one was really better than another, that no one really belonged to an elite or was poor, that everyone in a town must contribute as his or her talents allowed to the welfare of the community as a whole—in short, that their towns were characterized by their "togetherness." John M. Gorman remembered his town, Manzanar, California, at the turn of the century as being "a nice place to live. We were all like one big family. Everyone was friendly. . . ."[99] Willis F. Dunbar recalled that early-twentieth-century Hartford, Michigan, gave him a "feeling of security. . . . You had a sense of belonging to a community, and a feeling that you could count on help if trouble came. There always were neighbors and kinfolk to lend a hand in case of sickness or other distress. There was a considerable amount of sharing in the neighborhoods of the town. Everyone knew you by your first name or your nickname. There were plenty of cantankerous people along with those who were kindly and helpful, but you were never alone as you can be in the city, or in the open country."[100] These assertions were all meant to be a denial of the centrality of class and the preeminence of a fixed social hierarchy. The *belief* in a classless town society when simple observation indicated otherwise was schizophrenic, but it was as deeply held as the *desire*, through the work of moral crusades, to rid the towns of particular forms of misbehavior. Neither reflected reality, but both helped to create consensus and were often mighty forces making for social cohesion.

Some of the groups who founded special towns during the nineteenth century did not seek to create a society whose basic structure differed from that of the larger society. For example, the towns that blacks founded in the decades after the Civil War in no significant way varied from towns in which the population was predominantly or solely white. Black towns too had a highly unequal distribution of income in settings dominated by a small group of investors who were involved in the multiple ownership of businesses.[101]

The communalistic groups who created their own, exclusive towns shared the common goal of creating a classless society based upon principles of cooperation and unity, not competition and division. Even in these towns, however, social distinctions appeared, though usually they were based upon degrees of commitment to the ways of the group, not on kinds of work or occupation. For example, the constitution of the German pietistic sect at Zoar, Ohio, divided its members into two classes: the novitiates and the full associates.[102] But these experiments in communalism were usually short-lived or quite schismatic; so, with a few exceptions, the effort to create a village society without a social hierarchy was not successful. The small groups of like-minded people who founded towns based upon the principles of cooperation and communal ownership did not ordinarily endure. Adherents disagreed about the best way to sustain their alternate way of life. Schisms were often followed by emigration and abandonment.[103]

It is ironic that so many ordinary, durable towns contained social hierarchies while special towns, whose founders sought communities without class distinctions, so often did not last long. Perhaps the reason is that durable towns with social hierarchies represented a *balance* between individualistic endeavor and communal needs, between the irreducible duality of the human species: its awareness that though each individual is unique, he or she is nonetheless required to live not in isolation but in community. *Both* individualistic and communalistic impulses must be satisfied for a human community to endure.

During the twentieth century, town society was profoundly influenced by the vast acceleration in communications and transportation and the huge increase in the scale by which people organized themselves everywhere that modern technology prevailed. Rural isolation was effectively ended as town dwellers became immediately aware of how life was lived in the urban settings that became the primary community for a steadily increasing majority of those who lived in modern, mass society. But as porous and as open as town society became to urban innovations, and as much as town dwellers' notions of status and class reflected those that prevailed in urban areas, the rationale for the town's class system remained distinctive and more traditional—if less so as the century wore on.[104]

The social hierarchy itself changed its complexion. African Americans moved in large numbers from the rural South to urban centers in the North and Midwest, and, as in the nineteenth century, only a minority settled in towns, where racially segregated districts gave way, with the institution of legal racial equality during the 1960s, to black neighborhoods based on poverty or low income. Similarly, among foreign immigrants, Hispanic or Latino migrants became the largest group during the course of the century, but outside of the older Spanish-settled areas of the Southwest, where large numbers lived in small communities, Hispanic Americans bypassed the towns, either as migrant workers in the commercial farming areas of California, Florida, and the Atlantic coast, or as migrants to urban centers in the East. Native Americans too tended to move from rural reservations into cities.[105]

The occupational hierarchy shifted during the century as the number of machine operators declined and "service" jobs mushroomed, then shifted again as industrial production gave way to "knowledge-based" endeavor. Regional distinctions disintegrated as the planter/slave and then the landowner/ tenant/sharecropper biracial social structure that had brought a distinctiveness to Southern rural and town life for three centuries gave way to social hierarchy like that of town society elsewhere. During the course of the century, the earlier belief that white men lived in an egalitarian society was extended to women and to nonwhites. Governments sporadically responded to popular pressure and legislated political and legal equality for all adults, even though social and economic inequality based upon class continued.

The distinctive attitude of twentieth-century town dwellers toward class was their overt *recognition* of it: everyone seemed to know that classes existed, knew how to recognize status, and could "place" people with exactitude. Such town dwellers also denied the existence of class, at least of class in a way that really mattered. In this they continued to exhibit the schizophrenic attitude that had emerged during the previous century. At the same time the prevailing moral code shifted from overtly Christian to vaguely secular humanistic in a setting of increasing ethnic, racial, and religious variety. The code was transmitted to new generations of town dwellers through a school system and media that reflected this variety. These "instructors" placed less emphasis upon the forms of misbehavior that had so dominated the efforts of their nineteenth-century predecessors.[106]

At times, particular towns provided snapshots of class and its justification. In the 1920s, "Mineville" in the Rocky Mountains contained a social hierarchy that was clearly evident, as everyone was "rated" by everyone else. Immigrants (in this case Italians, Swedes, and Finns) were seen as foreigners for several generations. Classes were based largely upon occupations. The elite had great influence over those beneath them and served as social models for the introduction of new ways and things.[107]

By the 1930s, in "Plainville," located in the Midwestern plains, class was based upon various criteria, wealth being one of them. But people in Plainville also made something of lineage, praising the longevity and prominence of certain families and criticizing "no-account," "trashy" ones. They also stressed a person's morality, admiring honesty, hard work, and sobriety, and denigrating dishonesty, idleness or laziness, family cruelty or neglect, gambling, drunkenness, and any serious "lawbreaking"—all traits associated with the lower class. People in Plainville also rated their neighbors by their manners, social behavior, knowledge, and lack of crudity and violence, which were also thought to be lower-class characteristics.[108] In Plainville, gossip and social opprobrium were stronger mechanisms of social control than either censure by the churches or punishment by the formal law enforcement agencies. Indeed, the formal code of laws seemed less important than what the townspeople thought was allowable or worthy of censure in the case of every form of behavior except obviously serious crimes.[109]

In the 1950s in "Springdale," an agricultural service center in upstate New York, the inhabitants valued equality but also industriousness, improvement, and optimism. The town's society was divided into a hierarchy of groups, from a vestigial commercial elite of a few families; to entrepreneur businessmen; to professionals; to skilled industrial workers; to semi-skilled and unskilled labor of various kinds—factory work, service occupations, manual labor, white-collar clerical work; to "shack" people, the poor, the residual scrapheap of a competitive economy. Only the last group, the lower class, rejected prevailing values.[110]

But the people of Springdale divided in other ways, not based upon class. While some individuals in all these groups expressed a willingness to buy and spend in order to *appear* better off, others preferred to save and be productive, and to live frugally.[111] This duality revealed an even deeper division that by the 1950s separated town dwellers everywhere: accepting or rejecting outside influences on town society. Those "modernists" who worked for translocal institutions—in branch plants, chain stores, or franchised operations—tended to have more status and influence than those "traditionalists" who maintained their allegiance to local organizations, just as those with a consumerist bent were more modern than those who emphasized savings and production.[112] These divisions were even more pronounced by the 1960s in a town like Benson, Minnesota, where "new-style" employees of translocal firms were younger and better educated, though less residentially stable, than "old-style" Bensonites, who were older, long-term residents of the community and resisted the incursions of national corporations.[113]

But such divisions were no match for older forms of social hierarchy. During the 1970s "Starckey," California, still contained such a hierarchy. The town's elite had to work at maintaining social cohesion in the face of the ever-present potential for disharmony that such a social structure presented. Five leading families exerted pressure on the town's inhabitants through the exercise not of economic or political but of social power: the fear of gossip or scandal, the pressure of public opinion. Their task became one of managing and molding public opinion as they discovered where discontent and dissent lay.[114] In Starckey two contradictory impulses were manifest: the importance of community participation and cohesion *and* individual economic achievement, that is, communalism and individualism. Community leaders tried to balance the two. Community-wide organizations welcomed everyone, and participation in community affairs was linked to social standing. But the economic/social hierarchy that everyone recognized did not harden into distinct classes. The towns' "n'er-do-wells" were usually young, unmarried farmers' sons working as farm laborers before they settled down and became respectable. In Starckey, social cohesion and individual achievement were not in conflict.[115]

But towns in the twentieth century differed widely in their cohesion or communality. For example, two fishing villages along the Chesapeake shore, "Crab Reef" and "Fish Neck," were a study in contrasts between a "tight" and a "loose" community. Crab Reef was "tight," that is, it featured a rigorous Methodist Church that emphasized hard work and both material and educational attainment; town dwellers also exhibited strong community-wide institutions and a commitment to a moral, Christian life. Neighboring Fish Neck, by contrast, was "loose," without a religious "center"; its inhabitants lacked community identification, focused their lives on extended family groupings, and failed to develop an ethic of hard work, material and educational attainment, and moral, Christian living, free of misbehavior and violence.[116] Crab Reef and Fish Neck are instructive examples of how widely ranging twentieth-century towns were—even neighboring towns—in the extent of their cohesiveness as communities.

Over four centuries from 1600 to 2000, town society was always hierarchical. Hierarchy has never been a function of size. During the seventeenth and eighteenth centuries, elites dominated that society, as others depended upon them, deferred to them, or sought to emulate them, even though the richest and poorest town dwellers were comparatively few in number in comparison to the many who were typically of middling status. During the nineteenth century this large middling element usually dominated town society and defined its values, punishing miscreants. In the twentieth century this task continued, with even greater awareness of class and even more reliance on social conformity, with an added division between those who accepted the domination of translocal institutions and those who clung to older, local ways.

Even though it has been awash in class, ethnic, racial, and core/transient divisions, town society has usually cohered. More stable, enduring elements in the population have employed a variety of mechanisms—censure by parishioners, punishment by secular authority, criticism from the media and the pulpit, public ridicule or hostility—to ensure that such diverse, small, local communities remain socially cohesive. Continuous geographic and social mobility have helped maintain social cohesion in town society, as class and ethnic, if not racial, divisions have never hardened into an entrenched, unchanging social hierarchy.

## · II ·

THE LEISURE OR SOCIAL ACTIVITIES of colonial town dwellers scarcely resembled those of the native society they encountered. Among the native tribes, this kind of activity was markedly ritualistic, as festivals and ceremonies consisting of games, gifts, and religious invocations punctuated the work rhythms of the four seasons.[117]

By contrast, among the rural farming population that typically surrounded the towns during the seventeenth and eighteenth centuries, the distinction between work and leisure was blurred. People routinely combined work and play in all those instances when tasks required more than the labor of a single man or woman or even a family, tasks that required a group of people, usually neighbors. Called "bees" or "frolics," these work exchanges infused sociability into daily work and involved such activities as house and barn "raisings," when neighbors helped to frame and board a family's needed home and outbuildings; sheep shearing in the spring; quilting parties, when women gathered to sew pieces onto what became bed covers that were stretched over large frames while being made; and husking or apple bees, when neighbors assembled to peel apples from the orchards or husk fields of corn for family and livestock feed. Other work parties were put together for enjoyment, not out of necessity; that is, the work might be done alone, but it was done more pleasurably in company—such tasks as spinning cloth or clearing stones from farm fields.[118]

These work exchanges among the colonial settlers extended to public or political group activity. Militia training days in the spring and fall were social events as well—as sham battles mixed with real fights and boozing. Work on the roads and snow plowing were group tasks that also evoked socializing. Many of these male-only gatherings involved heavy drinking, which was bound up with work, especially in group-related tasks, for the prevalent belief was that men would perish from their exertions without the restorative effects of alcoholic beverages. Those who complained about the licentiousness and anti-Christian character of work parties withdrew and became involved with private and sober recreational activities within their own family settings.[119]

During the nineteenth century, bees and frolics continued to blur work and leisure, even if the professionalization of public services gradually eliminated local militia units and road crews. Whole neighborhoods came out for collective labor at these events, which continued to feature drinking and competitive sport. Male frolics celebrated physical strength, with wrestling and racing as time consuming as the work. Wives prepared meals for the hungry workers but also engaged in productive frolics of their own. House and barn raisings involved preparation of the logs, clapboards, shingles, and joists by the family seeking help. Neighbors put the log structure together, leaving the family to chop out doors and windows and fireplace openings, to fit door and window frames, and to put on the roof.[120]

When mechanized, large-scale commercial farming developed on the prairies or grasslands of the mid-continent valleys and plains from the middle of the century, work exchanges continued, even if in altered form. As a setting, the prairies created a physical need for such gatherings. Neighboring ranchers cooperated in the grazing of livestock and in driving cattle to stockyards. Grain farming operations required more men, horses, and equipment than a single farmer could provide. Haying, for example, had to be done at certain times. As machinery (hay loaders) became available, its expense often led to joint ownership by groups of neighboring farmers. "Threshing rings" of eight to twelve farmers were common, or a "thresherman" himself owned and tended the machine that he operated on first one farm and then another. No other farm operation united a rural neighborhood like threshing. Social activities bound such neighborhoods into leisure-time communities at annual

POST OFFICES. People looking for a post office could find a great variety of spaces in towns. Many were located in plain structures like this one in Lake Clear Junction, New York. In the nineteenth century the U.S. postmaster general attempted to locate post offices in every settlement worthy of the name. Post offices continued to be social and communications centers of first importance for town dwellers. [Adirondack Museum]

threshers' picnics, weddings, farewell receptions, coffee after church, and to-bogganing or skating parties.[121]

How commonly town dwellers shared with their rural neighbors this blurring of work and leisure is a difficult question to answer. The inhabitants of towns, like the rural population that surrounded them, typically needed group labor to build their in-town houses and outbuildings, as most people built their own homes until late in the nineteenth century. But the bees and frolics associated with large-scale farming activity would not have generated a corresponding blurring of work and leisure among town dwellers.

In the towns during the seventeenth and eighteenth centuries, social and leisure activities occurred in particular spaces at particular times, though not as ritualistically as in native society. Some of these activities were inclusive and open to the community; they took place in spaces that were public in a broad sense. Religious services in churches were attended by whole families, and despite their place in a community's social hierarchy, churches were public spaces, at least for their parishioners. The Puritan settlers in New England and the Mennonites elsewhere tried to sustain religiously united, single-church communities, but in most colonial towns there were several churches, which collectively provided public spaces for adults and children to affirm their Christian faith.

Town dwellers used other, nonreligious public spaces for social and leisure activities. Post offices—at least during the course of the eighteenth century, as the imperial government developed a postal system in the colonies—became places for daily socializing. Town dwellers, while receiving mail at these designated sites, could also gossip and visit with others. The earliest "correspondents" were letter writers from afar; individuals would read aloud letters they had received from friends and relatives who sent news from their distant locations.

Taverns were very common "publick houses," places that were usually located in the center of settlements, where inhabitants of the towns and visitors could eat, drink, sleep, socialize, and play games involving dice, billiard tables, and cards. Those who traveled either left or entered town in their own horse and buggy or carriage or paid a fare to a coach line, privately owned firms that transported the public over rudimentary road systems (often on the post roads) that by the eighteenth century at least connected the larger towns. Other taverns along roadways served as stopping places for travelers.

But taverns also had limitations as public spaces. While they sometimes served as gathering places for informal political assemblies, women were not present because they could not vote or participate in political life.[122] In any case, respectable women avoided the "ordinaries" or common taverns altogether, as they sometimes became settings for male rowdiness and violence. Manly prowess pervaded these social interactions, filled with emulation, rivalry, and boasting. Affronted pride led to bouts of boxing and wrestling as bystanders formed rings and contestants kicked, scratched, throttled, gouged eyes, and dismembered genitals.[123]

Recreation too was male-dominated and reflected the crudity, rudeness, violence, and fierce competition that greatly characterized society in the seventeenth and eighteenth centuries. Animals were surrogates for common forms of human behavior: cockfighting and horse racing especially, which were sponsored or witnessed by individuals from all ranks of society.[124] Elkanah Watson, a Northerner, who was traveling through the Southern colonies in the eighteenth century, witnessed a cockfight in Southampton County, Virginia: Into a large cockpit, surrounded by people from all ranks of society, "exceedingly beautiful cocks were produced, armed with long, sharp, steel-pointed gaffs, which were firmly attached to their natural spurs. The moment the birds were dropped, bets ran high. . . . Advancing nearer and nearer, they flew upon each other, the cruel and fatal gaffs being driven directly into their bodies, and, at times, directly into their heads. . . . They often fought after being repeatedly pierced, as long as they were able to crawl, and in the agonies of death would often make abortive efforts to raise their heads and strike their antagonists."[125]

Elites in the communities served by taverns abhorred such misbehavior. By the eighteenth century, in taverns located near plantations and in larger towns, elites could at least hope to emulate their urban counterparts and establish separate "assembly rooms" where the genteel behavior of elite society would prevail and the more refined members of town society could meet, separate from others.[126] In Connecticut, for example, in the larger towns by the eighteenth century, taverns became numerous enough to attract specialized clienteles.[127]

Women were generally confined to certain social, leisure-time spaces, barred as they were from participation in public life. Their only public presence was in church. Even there, the prevailing practice in the established Protestant denominations was to separate men and women into their own sections. A woman's social space was mainly domestic, managing the family household. But she did visit with neighbors. And she hung a latchstring on the door when company was sought. Visiting providing women with a means for sharing mutual concerns and news of the community. Relations among female neighbors could be both vertical and horizontal, that is, between servants and mistresses in the better-off households, or among women of comparable position in society. In this role, women could show a neighborly concern and find out what was going on in the vicinity of their houses.[128]

Thus, though town dwellers shared public spaces for social and leisure-time activity during the seventeenth and eighteenth centuries, those spaces also reflected divisions in town society based upon class and gender. No single *social* occasion found all the inhabitants of a town assembled, just as they occupied separate work spaces, typically attended several different churches, and had a political role or did not.

The ways of town dwellers' socializing did not change their basic character during the nineteenth century. Indeed, class and gender divisions deepened.

Aspiring middle-class households sought the respectability that colonial elites had earlier developed as gentility, turning their parlors into formal "visiting" rooms where a family's best possessions were on display for friends who came by for tea and gossip.[129] Elites continued to keep domestic servants and became quite formal about the proprieties of visiting; visitors were formally received by servants and were expected to present their calling cards. Travel became more class-bound, as hotels, taverns, steamboats, and then steam-driven trains were divided into rooms or compartments based upon cost and therefore upon wealth and class. On some boat and train lines, compartments were even labeled "first class," "second class," "economy class."

Travel itself became a badge of class. One's prominence in town was linked to how far and how long and where one could journey for a holiday or vacation. By the late nineteenth century, with the development of a dense rail network throughout the continent, resort towns emerged, places where middle-class vacationers might visit, as vacation time became more and more a part of the contractual arrangements between industrial and commercial firms and their employees. But even these resort towns were class defined: some were cheaper or more expensive and thus more exclusive than others.

Gender distinctions also deepened. With notable exceptions, women continued to be missing from public life. They were still not members of the political community, and there were many public spaces that respectable women would not go to or be seen in. As work and home became increasingly separated during the nineteenth century, respectable women were supposed to remain at home, managing the domestic setting—the work that needed to be done but also the raising of children. Women were expected to serve as moral paragons who inculcated proper Christian values in their family as the home became a refuge from the stresses and strains of the outside work world.[130]

In this context, the proper woman's sphere was still domestic. She avoided social spaces where misbehavior prevailed or where men alone would gather. Male bastions were the barber shop, the tobacco shop, and the livery stable. In one of these bastions, the barber shop, Fred Lape remembered that in the early twentieth century his "hair, like that of most farm boys, was cut at home, but my father went every so often to have his hair cut and his beard trimmed. On the shelf in front of the barber chair was an open wall rack, on the shelves of which stood the individual shaving mugs of the principal men in town, usually with the name in gold letters on the mug and a private brush inside."[131] Other spaces were off limits to respectable women because of male misbehavior. The tavern of seventeenth and the eighteenth centuries was transformed into the saloon, a place where men drank but that women avoided, whether or not the town had an active temperance movement. Also beyond the woman's sphere were gambling dens or houses of prostitution. The favored women's places in town were dress and millinery shops. A setting where all those who avoided saloons could gather and socialize was the ice cream "parlor" or confectionery.[132]

Rose Wilder Lane remembered "a feeling that [the] center of town was masculine. Ladies went there. But with a certain circumspection. Usually they went in couples. . . . Ladies went uptown only for some definite purpose. They might pass through those business streets on their way to call on a lady who lived on the other side of town. They might enter the general store, the post office, the grocery store and the drug store, but they did not linger in these places, and on the streets they passed the livery stable, the barber shop, the poolroom and above all the saloon with a manner so haughtily oblivious that it all but denied the existence of these places. . . . Men got the mail at the post office and bought the groceries; there was no reason when a decent woman, with her housework, her sewing and mending and gardening and preserving to do, should go uptown. . . . When necessity or some definite pleasure dictated such an excursion into public places, a lady prepared herself for it."[133]

Yet in other public spaces, gender and class divisions were becoming more flexible, less fixed, though there continued to be no social occasions where the *entire* community was present. Popular dissenting Protestant sects (such as the Baptists and the Methodists) and evangelical groups avoided the class-bound church layouts of the established denominations. They built simple meetinghouses or temporary revival camps where there were no fixed gender or class divisions, even though the more established denominations persisted in having separate seating for women and men.[134] Women and girls were unwelcome at livery stables and blacksmith shops and locomotive works, where horse and rail transport was maintained and repaired, but all were welcome at the rail depot and the town's hotel or hotels, places where visitors and travelers could meet. These hotels were often two or three stories tall, with long porches filled with lounge chairs. Inside, "saloon parlors" with pianos and a dining room, often containing a single long table, were com-

RECREATION. By the nineteenth century, groups of adults became involved in organized recreational activity. Even eating took on a recreational coloration, as families planned picnics—which, at large public events, became mass barbecues, like the one above in Menomonie, Wisconsin. Bobsledding and cycling were also popular—opposite, top, in Saranac Lake, New York, and below, in Keeseville, New York. [Above, State Historical Society of Wisconsin; opposite top, David R. Phillips Collection; below, Adirondack Museum]

mon. Guest rooms on the second floor were furnished with a bed, chairs, pitcher and basin, and chamber pot, and were lighted by coal-oil lamps.[135]

Bees and frolics, the mixing of group tasks and socializing, continued throughout the nineteenth century in rural areas. Even in towns, work and play were not always sharply demarcated. But as families became less self-sufficient, as craft work and farming gave way to salaried and wage labor, town dwellers gradually separated their labor from their leisure and recreation and socializing, which became more organized and distinct as the century progressed.[136] Willis F. Dunbar remembered that in early-twentieth-century Hartford, Michigan, "whenever you were not working, going to school, attending church, eating, or sleeping, you were wasting your time."[137]

For instance, in the cattle towns, by the 1870s and 1880s local newspapers often listed events in columns titled "Society Gossip," "Social Circle," or simply "Society." "Partying" of many kinds was reported: surprise parties, box suppers, basket socials, and necktie socials, some of which were designed to raise funds. To the extent that such partying was involved with fund-

raising, it remained socializing but with an economic dimension. Fund-raising suppers were entertainment, fellowship, participation, courtship, sporting events, charities, and food—all in a single ceremony! In the necktie socials, the woman who prepared a box supper was matched with a man who bought the privilege of sharing the contents. The man's tie found inside the box had to match the dress of the woman who prepared the meal.[138]

Picnics were inexpensive and informal and took people out of their daily routines. They involved families, young adults, or organized groups of people. Sunset picnics were popular with young couples, though they were usually chaperoned by married couples. Young men sometimes called drinking bouts "picnics," and young couples sought excuses to escape the chaperoning of adults. Picnics might also be outings with rented buggies, and some towns boasted riding party associations. Also popular was serenading, spontaneous or organized (with or without musical accompaniment), for honored visitors, special occasions, or just for pretty girls. Card parties were tolerated, especially to play euchre, during which couples moved from table to table.[139]

Recreation became more organized as groups set aside time for particular sports. Sporting events that were violent in nature continued well into the century, with wrestling, boxing, and cockfighting popular whenever men played at a social occasion. "Shootings" were common as individuals and clubs competed to shoot live pigeons or glass bulbs. Hunting, less necessary now for survival, continued as recreation, as men hunted ducks, geese, deer, and wolves. Roderick Turnbull, reminiscing about his boyhood in a town, called hunting the preferred sport in winter: ". . . Our parents were worried about our wandering too far away in the countryside. After all, we grew up as a part of it, hunting with dogs."[140] Some games were played at places whose very legitimacy was often contested: for example, billiards in saloons.[141]

Recreation continued to be highly competitive in nature, but some of it became more refined as the century progressed. Croquet became quite popular beginning in the 1870s. Women liked to be fashionable while playing outdoors and being mildly active. Roller-skating parties were popular, and many rinks opened as formal rules were adopted and clubs organized. Fred Lape remembered that in his town "bobsledding . . . daring and dangerous, attracted a few of the old, but mostly the young. In the days before autos and snow plowing, a group could drag a bobsled to the top of the hills . . . and then go careening down the packed snow to the road at a tremendous speed. It was an exciting sport. The dangers were making the curves of the road successfully or meeting a team of horses on the road and having to swerve off the road into a snowbank when going full speed. Much depended upon the skill of the man steering the bobsled, but there were often tumbles and occa-

THE OPERA HOUSE. As general entertainment halls, these structures showed that a town valued cultural activity involving local organizations or visiting troupes. The euphemistic title, Opera House, revealed a lingering reluctance to associate one's community too openly with forms of entertainment that some Protestant denominations still looked upon as immoral. Strawn's Opera House in Jacksonville, Illinois, shown here, was built in 1861. [*Morgan County Atlas*]

sionally serious injuries.[142] Baseball became a popular amateur sport, and organized teams with uniforms were active, sometimes representing their towns in competition with teams from other towns. Spectator sports, particularly horse racing, were even more popular and became increasingly so throughout the century.[143]

Leisure-time activity also became organized by private firms whose operations traveled to innumerable towns, especially with the development of a rail system in mid-century. Minstrel shows were immensely popular as variety entertainment programs that featured actors, comedians, singers, dancers, and musicians who conveyed racial and ethnic stereotypes, thus reinforcing prevailing prejudices. Burlesques began as entertainment but gradually declined to a "parade" of fully clothed women disrobing to a drumbeat as they moved across the stage. At this point they lost their respectability and were thereafter restricted to the "sporting crowd."

Circuses included exotic animal shows with freaks and various forms of entertainment, all introduced to a town with a large parade down Main Street. Unlike burlesque, these highly popular entertainments were perceived as morally sound and preeminently family-oriented, and the cost of tickets was within the reach of most households. The circus's strange and wondrous sights could even be educational. Unlike the minstrel show, it offered no stereotypical depictions of contemporary society.[144] Hamlin Garland, in his autobiography, indicated the special place that circuses had for town dwellers: "It was a compendium of biologic research but more important still, it brought to our ears the latest band pieces and taught us the most popular songs. It furnished us with jokes. It relieved our dullness. It gave us something to talk about."[145]

Such forms of entertainment moved by road and canal and waterway until mid-century, after which the railroads became the choice. Rail travel made itineraries easier to manage but restricted performance to the larger towns, those favored with rail connections.

Unlike the circuses with their portable tents, indoor entertainment needed a venue, and organizers used churches, schools, lodges, courthouses, and town halls. By the mid-nineteenth century many towns built "opera houses," community halls especially designed for homegrown or itinerant entertainment. "Opera" was in better repute than "theatre" among town dwellers, and, though it was a misnomer (and reflected aspirations of respectability), late in the century "operettas" became part of the mix of what was performed. Built by private benefactor or municipal government, or by public subscription, opera houses were often two stories. In smaller towns they sometimes had a ground floor rented out to various stores and shops. In larger towns, opera houses could be architecturally elaborate, somewhat like a genuine opera house in their refinement of detail. Towns competed to have impressive community halls, and town dwellers tried to lure itinerant groups to present theatrical plays, musical concerts, lectures, dances, political rallies, graduations, minstrel shows, and operettas. Community groups often held meetings there or put on contests or performances. The churches approved of "educational" gatherings, such as singing schools, spelling bees, lyceum lectures, temperance meetings, and circuses.[146]

By the eighteenth century county fairs were an annual event for farmers (in a sense, a farmers' convention) and were chiefly educational. Farmers gathered at county seats to observe new techniques, new products, and new machinery. Prizes were awarded for the best animals and crops. Farm wives examined kitchen equipment, exchanged recipes, learned new sewing techniques, and competed for the best homemade foods, floral displays, needlework, clothing, and household articles. Fairs were also social events, meant to

FAIRS. As annual events, fairs beckoned to the rural population surrounding
the towns that held them (usually the county seats). Their main function was
to focus attention on the best that was grown and produced in the area, and to
bring to visitors' attention the latest technological innovations. Top, livestock
in Kentucky. Below, produce in New Mexico. [Top, University of Louisville;
below, Southeastern New Mexico Historical Society]

entertain farmers, not town dwellers, whether from the county seats or from other settlements in the county. But fairs also bound farmers to the county seats that provided the setting for the event, and town dwellers attended the fairs in any case. This mingling of people from the towns and their rural hinterlands reinforced the standards and values of the respectable elements in town society. Fairs represented the best that was produced as well as the best of what was new, mirroring state and national expositions.

A mingling of another kind at fairs was the educational with the social. As the century progressed, many fair boards built grandstands and half-mile racing tracks, exhibition halls, dining halls, stock pens, display and commercial stalls. Church suppers, foot races, wheelbarrow and greased pig contests, baseball games, horse racing, and gambling were all scheduled at these annual events.[147] By the late nineteenth century, carnivals and midways with games and freak shows were added, greatly extending the social dimension of fairs that had always been primarily educational in nature. This development aroused considerable hostility, even as it increased the fairs' popularity.[148]

As town dwellers separated their work lives from their leisure or social activity, they were much more apt to join voluntary organizations or clubs, and they did so exponentially as the nineteenth century progressed. The inhabitants of towns such as Kingston, New York, became noticeably involved with this type of association when the community was sizeable enough.[149] But though size was a factor (small towns simply did not have enough people to form a variety of such organizations), equally important was the extent to which work had become separated from leisure for the inhabitants of a particular town, that is, how many had moved beyond all-encompassing craft work and farm work to positions with fixed hours and wages and salaries. And some resisted the trend. C. W. Goodlander, reminiscing about Fort Scott, Kansas, during the 1860s, "found that I had enough business to attend to both day and night without wasting any of my time with lodge affairs."[150]

Fraternal organizations had existed since the eighteenth century. The largest was the Masons, but other secret societies established close bonds among members who were sworn to secrecy about the rituals of the brotherhood. Such secrecy evoked a feeling of exclusivity and at first attracted an elite membership, a manifestation of the gentility that elites had tried to create during the eighteenth century. While fraternal orders had grown out of earlier European guilds of craftsmen, by the eighteenth century some had lost their economic definition.

By the early nineteenth century, a popular hostility had developed toward the secrecy and exclusivity of associations like the Masons, a hostility that even found political expression during the 1820s and 1830s with the

FRATERNAL LODGES. The Masons were the earliest of the large and growing number of fraternal lodges that developed during the eighteenth and nineteenth centuries. If a particular lodge flourished, invariably its goal was to occupy its own hall. This is the Masonic Temple in Jacksonville, Illinois. [*Morgan County Atlas*]

emergence of the Anti-Masonic party.[151] Secret societies spread to embrace nativism in the 1840s and 1850s as groups organized to oppose immigration; in the 1860s and 1870s, and thereafter, white supremacy groups organized to oppose black equality in the South. But during the course of the nineteenth century, fraternal societies became popular among ordinary laborers and farmers as well. Both the Knights of Labor (for laborers) and the Grange (for farmers) recruited enormous memberships in the decades following the Civil War.

In the nineteenth century, every town of substantial size contained a profusion of local chapters of fraternal organizations, or lodges, as well as variety of one-of-a-kind local clubs. Foreign observers like de Tocqueville noticed in the 1830s that Americans had a proclivity for forming voluntary associations; the habit deepened throughout the century as work and leisure time became separated. Such organizations were typically for either men or women. For men, clubs and lodges were simply a social extension of an organizational proclivity that already characterized their political and economic activity. But social clubs were a major enlargement of the women's sphere, which had been largely confined to the domestic setting.

In Beekmantown, New York, for instance, an early domination by the masons gave way to more popular forms of clubs, and the 1830s witnessed an orgy of club-making.[152] In Jacksonville, Illinois, during the 1850s and 1860s, the Masons and the Odd Fellows stood out as lodges.[153] And in the cattle towns of Kansas during the 1870s and 1880s, added to those two organizations were the Rebeccas, the Knights of the Pythias, and the Good Templars.[154]

While they were more open and popularly oriented than earlier societies such as the Masons, fraternal lodges were quite middle class in their makeup. They appealed to respectable, upwardly mobile elements in town. Members of lodges subscribed to the Protestant moral code, benefited from the business contacts and credit references that the fellowship provided for them as well as mutual aid in the form of sickness and death benefits, and hoped their membership would give their lives the appearance of industriousness and sobriety but also charitability and good works. Although social in character, such organizations supplemented the work of municipal governments and economic firms of all kinds.[155]

The glitter and sham opulence of the regalia and ceremony of the lodges contrasted with their members' mundane lives of work, respectability, and mediocrity. This illusion of romantic grandeur reflected the controlled yearnings for an adventurous life. Much was made of funerals, when whole brotherhoods marched en masse to the cemetery, displaying in public their solidarity and faith in God, their community, and their country. The deceased was surrounded by an aura of religiosity and social concern and was referred to eulogistically as a man of sound character who did good works. Most lodges met on the second floor of commercial buildings in the towns. If successful they built separate halls as their membership grew and they could afford the upkeep of such quarters. By the late nineteenth century some added auxiliary lodges for women. Most of the lodges' sponsored activities were of a social nature, sometimes for fund-raising purposes: musical entertainments, dances, balls, specialty suppers, parades, lectures, educational excursions. The often stuffy and pompous appearance of lodge members revealed a self-confidence in their mission: to improve the social and personal behavior as well as the appearance of their communities.[156]

Even though special towns were strikingly different in their exclusiveness, their social and leisure-time activities were scarcely novel. In all-black towns after the Civil War, the mix of social and recreational activity—picnics, baseball games, dances, parties—and fraternal lodges and social clubs mirrored the mix that existed in white communities, though blacks who lived in racially mixed towns in Northern and Western regions typically had separate facilities and organizations.[157] The isolated company towns usually had recreation halls that had been built by the company for social activities, such as dances. These towns most often could boast baseball teams, and company authorities encouraged the development of lodges, sometimes even building the lodge halls.[158]

During the twentieth century the social and leisure-time activities of town dwellers became better organized, linked to a leisure/travel/vacation/recreation industry that itself became one of the most significant economic activities in all the advanced, mass societies. Branches or franchises of large corporations competed with local firms to plan travel and vacations and the visiting of relatives and friends elsewhere. First automobile[159] and then air transport greatly extended the ambit of those who sought socializing and recreation beyond the confines of their local communities.

The amusement parks created by short-distance trolley line companies early in the century were vastly extended as leisure-time destinations by the popularization of motor and air travel, which made contact with faraway resorts and vacation attractions of all kinds feasible for middle-class town dwellers. By the 1920s, with the mass ownership of cars, even families with modest incomes could at least go camping. Because of the automobile, leisure-time activity for those who lived in towns was not confined to their communities, for new amusements were accessible at night, on weekends, and during short motor vacations. Town hotels that had served travelers and visitors during the age of horse and rail transportation became more typically places for dining, as speedier transport allowed travelers to shorten their stays in towns.[160]

Amateur local sports teams that involved town dwellers of all ages as active players were enormously popular during the early decades of the century.[161] But such recreational activity vied for attention with the broadcast (beginning in the 1930s) or the telecast (from the 1950s onward) of professional sporting events. Once-active town dwellers were turned into passive spectators of distant "pro" teams.[162]

Public space gradually became less formal, less defined by gender. The Women's Club movement had developed a national organization out of innumerable local chapters in the 1890s and retained its vitality well into the twentieth century.[163] The League of Women Voters and many women's clubs attached at all levels to the major political parties grew out of existing female organizations, as the leaders to these political units used existing social networks in the towns as the basis for recruitment. To build up the new organizations, the strategy was to combine familiar social activities with partisan politics.[164] Through the century, women gained equal rights by stages—politically, legally, socially, economically. As a consequence, gender-separate spaces of social and leisure activities faded away.

Class separations, however, continued in altered forms. Town elites were the first to own cars, and when such ownership was extended to the middle class during the 1920s, these same elites were the first to travel by airplane. When air travel became affordable for the middle class by the 1960s, the elites typically restricted their travel to first-class compartments. Elites continued to indulge in their own "exclusive" social activities and continued to travel to expensive resorts that were beyond the means of others.

In numbers and size, purely local clubs and social activities steadily lost out to organizations and activities with county, state, national, and international reach. By the 1920s, clubs or lodges became immensely popular in town society, surpassed in number, membership, and influence only by schools and churches.[165] By the 1930s, though, in a time of economic crisis, such organizations appeared to lack the durability and stability of churches and schools.[166] Still, when the crises of depression and war had passed, these voluntary associations endured.

Shorn of their function as mutual aid societies (with the development of private insurance firms beginning in the nineteenth century), lodges and clubs remained vehicles for those who sought status and position in town society. Their exclusive character attracted those seeking to get ahead.[167] A twentieth-century "joinerism" replaced a nineteenth-century "boosterism" as the clubs helped town dwellers define their position in society. Far more clubs were founded during the twentieth than during the preceding century. The founders of new organizations emphasized the kind of togetherness that was being lost in an increasingly urbanized society. Outwardly the emphasis of the Rotary, the Kiwanis, and the Lions was on "service" to their communities; inwardly they continued the tradition of fellowship.[168] Those who sought to rise socially reached for social organizations that were "exclusive" (expensive) rather than "respectable," which had been the prevailing goal during the nineteenth century.

## · III ·

TOWNS PROVIDED a communal context for each of their dwellers, touching their lives at various stages of the life cycle. The English colonists focused upon themselves as individuals—on their salvation, their capacity for wealth accumulation through dependable and skilled labor, their rights as autonomous citizens—and in doing so placed relatively less emphasis on the community than was the case among the native tribes the colonists encountered. But no human group, however organized, has ever escaped the irreducible human dilemma of having to balance its members' individual self-awareness and imperishable separation from one another with their need for community, as social animals. For town dwellers, the task has always been somehow to find a balance between individualism and communalism, to further their interests both as individuals and as members of a community.

During the seventeenth century at least, lives that were threatened by illness or accidents were aided not by trained physicians, who were clustered mainly in the largest population centers, but by certain men who acquired a reputation for, if not training in, medical knowledge. These men received sick persons into their homes for treatment.[169] By the eighteenth century, physicians who received training through an apprenticeship system were fairly typically located in the larger towns, as was the case in Connecticut, for example.[170] But however available or unavailable a physician was, it was customary for someone to stay up all night and watch over anyone who was seriously ill. This was a task often assigned to young women who were called to the homes of relatives or neighbors to observe any changes in the person who was ill and to help in any way that was needed.[171]

Birth during this era was almost exclusively under the control of women. Groups of women, and sometimes midwives, would gather in an expectant mother's home as she labored and delivered, typically not in a bed but supported on a chair, on someone's lap, or on a "birthing stool." The women who gathered provided physical as well as emotional intimacy and support. In no other life experience were women so completely in control or so firmly bonded. In the childbearing years, life for women was bound by personal "seasons" of pregnancy and lactation, twenty- to thirty-month cycles that stretched from one birth to the next.

Daily life continued with little interruption for pregnancy. Mothers nursed in public as well as in private. They had little time to dote on their children. Seventeenth- and eighteenth-century households were busy and cluttered places, with open fires, wash kettles, unfenced streams and ponds

—places of danger vying with childhood illnesses as potential killers. Large numbers of children could typically be found in the homes of young parents, even though some died of contagious childhood diseases, and individuals in such households lived in crowded settings. Some parents dealt with the uncertainty and fragility of life through emotional disengagement, which might lead to indifference or neglect. Others became concerned about the salvation of their growing children.[172]

Typical households contained not only fathers and mothers and their children but also "servants," in the more prominent families, and sometimes grandparents as well. "Servants" was a loose term, referring to both adults and children who were apprenticed to a professional or craft person; poor or orphaned children; children who were "put out" by one family to be educated by another, and actual domestic servants who, if black or native, were property of the household that could be passed from one generation to another.[173]

Children were expected to obey their parents and could by law be punished under the criminal justice system for any sort of habitual disobedience—unless they were under sixteen, at which time they could be informally punished by their parents, who themselves could be charged for "extreme or cruel corrections" that maimed or killed the child. Children owed their parents unceasing obedience and respect, but parents accepted responsibility for their children's physical health and welfare, their education, and their material well-being when they became young adults.[174]

The English colonists, or Westerners anywhere else during the seventeenth and eighteenth centuries, had no conception of childhood. Children were not perceived as beings with distinctive needs and desires and were accorded no special places or roles or separate spheres of work or recreation. Children learned the behavior appropriate to their gender and station by sharing the activities of their parents, in their work life, leisure life, and even their religious life. Boys and girls were depicted in paintings and drawings as miniatures of their mothers or fathers. After wearing long robes that opened to the front until the age of six or seven, boys and girls began dressing as adults dressed. After that a child's development toward maturity came gradually and in piecemeal fashion, until the age when by law the child became an adult.[175]

Most marriages occurred when young adults were in their twenties. Courtship involved no formal social events. Sexual offenses involving single persons—fornication—became known and prosecuted when pregnancy resulted. The punishment was a fine and a public whipping. Such behavior met with strong community disapproval. Parental consent was required for a courtship to turn into betrothal and marriage. The betrothal was a contract, like the modern practice of being engaged, and failure to fulfill the contract could lead to legal action. Sexual intimacies between the contracted parties were treated far less seriously if a pregnancy revealed premarital sexual activity. A public announcement, or banns, of a betrothed couple was published. Parents transferred a substantial portion of their property, typically land and housing for the groom and domestic furnishings or money for the bride. Weddings were performed in a variety of services, usually in the home of the bride or groom, not in a church.[176]

Families were patriarchal, that is, the father or husband was head of the household. But though married women were largely subsumed under the legal existence of their husbands (without rights to own property, make contracts, or sue for damages), widows had to be left with adequate means from their deceased husband's estates. Sometimes husbands and wives made agreements before marriage that dealt with the future disposition of the properties each brought into the union. Husbands and wives also shared duties and responsibilities to each other. They were obliged regularly and exclusively to cohabit, to maintain a relatively peaceful and harmonious relationship, and to practice a normal and exclusive sexual union. Women were also managers of the household and sometimes made mutual decisions with their husbands regarding the transfer of property, the joint management of business enterprises, and the putting out of children to foster families.[177]

As men and women aged, there was no sense of a middle age followed by retirement or a life free of work. The elderly man or woman was called upon for counsel, especially to the young, and was to be treated more respectfully and even reverentially. In reality, old people faced the same problems and difficulties as those who were younger, as well as the nagging fear of being ignored or abandoned by family and relatives.[178]

When a person died it was customary for someone to stay with him and "watch" until the burial. Shortly after a death, the corpse was usually laid out and dressed in a shroud or other "grave clothes." As soon as the coffin was ready, the body was placed inside, and the coffin usually remained open until the time of the funeral. Most coffins were displayed on tables or sawhorses in the parlor, where mourners from the community assembled to listen to those who offered words of sympathy.

At the time of the funeral, the principal mourners put on black garments, veils, and ribbons. People of the town were summoned by the ringing of a church bell to mark the time of the funeral service and assembled at the house of the deceased, making their last farewells before the coffin lid was closed and fastened. The minister offered prayers, and the procession made its way to the cemetery. The coffin was carried by strong, young bearers, and the pall, a black cloth, was supported over the coffin by pallbearers, who were usually the most socially prominent people on hand. After burial the mourners usually returned to the home of the deceased for refreshments. Even in death, social hierarchy was on display. A distinguished person's coffin was left outside the house so that people could pay their respects without having to intrude on the bereaved family. Having carriages in the procession to the grave was a sign of gentility.[179]

During the seventeenth and eighteenth centuries the life of an individual town dweller thus intersected with his or her community at various points and phases of the life cycle, most emphatically during the beginning and end of life, less significantly at the time of marriage. All of these great turning points of life occurred in a person's home, not in a public setting such as a church or, later, a hospital. When the community participated in a person's life, it was directly in his or her domestic space. Through much of an individual town dweller's life, the community hovered in the background, aware of what was happening through gossip, anxious to uphold community standards as articulated by secular law or religious codes, but not directly involved in an ongoing way except for shared work sites and centers for social, religious, and leisure activity.

By contrast, the life of the individual in the Spanish colonial towns (in what became in the 1840s the Southwest in the United States) was less isolated and private, more encased in the community. From birth to death, the inhabitants of these towns lived in the midst of people, with births, marriages, and deaths celebrated as community events. Communal life was more continuous, more vital than in the towns of the English colonists. Families were typically extended and strongly patriarchal, with males dominant in every age grouping. Wives were expected to be tolerant, obedient, and faithful, even though husbands had considerable freedom outside the home. Family discipline was based upon scolding and shaming rather than upon physical punishment, which was under the mother's control. Children were taught to respect all adults in the village. Older brothers and sisters played an important role in socializing younger siblings. Close relationships between family members were based upon forms of mutual assistance.[180]

During the nineteenth century the life and health of individual town dwellers continued to be affected or ended by contagious diseases and accidents. For example, in Plattsburg and Beekmantown, New York, in the early and mid-nineteenth century, epidemics struck from time to time: spotted fever in 1813, smallpox in 1814, cholera in 1832.[181] In rural Sugar Creek, Illinois, in the same period, people froze to death in winter blizzards, drowned in mill ponds or in swollen creeks, were struck by lightning as they plowed open fields, were crushed by falling timber, were gored by enraged bulls, and were dragged to death by runaway teams of horses. Cholera epidemics struck in 1832–1834 and 1849–1850; deaths from typhoid steadily increased; and malaria was transmitted by mosquitoes indigenous to the Mississippi valley, producing chronic anemia.[182]

In rural central Wisconsin in 1880, in an area that included the towns of Wausau, Stevens Point, Grand Rapids, Centralia, Neillsville, and Marshfield, communicable diseases were brought on by crowded living conditions, poor sanitation, and a disregard for quarantines. Boardinghouses as well as work camps for lumbering and railroad construction suffered from crowded conditions and strained sanitary facilities. Farmhouses too were crowded. Barnyards and cesspools from privies sometimes contaminated wells. Sick and healthy children shared classrooms, and sick and healthy family members usually mingled. Serious accidents from logging, farm chores, railroad construction, and drinking occurred quite frequently.[183] In general, life was still in constant peril of being interrupted or ended by serious illness or accident.

Towns were more likely to have a physician during the nineteenth century than had been the case earlier. Doctors continued to be trained as apprentices, though American medical schools steadily increased the number of formally trained physicians as the century lengthened. Doctors continued to believe in a theory of disease that dated from medieval times: imbalances of the body's "humors" or fluids. Not until the late nineteenth century did medical scientists develop the "germ theory" of disease caused by microorganisms. For most of the century, physicians prescribed bleeding and the administration of cathartic and emetic drugs for many ailments, to restore "balance." The patient was bled with a lancet until he fainted, vomiting was induced with ipecac, or the bowels were cleared out with calomel, or opium was used to calm internal irritation. Sometimes these treatments produced scars from frequent bleedings, or toothless gums and uncontrolled drool from mercury poisoning, a consequence of a patient's taking calomel or mercurous chloride.[184] Camphor was a stimulant used for fevers, eruptions, and spasmodic diseases; mercury was used for venereal diseases, sore throats, and ailing digestion; bark was a stimulant and anti-spasmodic; and laudanum, opium dissolved in wine, was a painkiller.[185]

Doctors were general practitioners, prescribing medicines, bleeding patients, pulling teeth, and delivering babies. Drs. Cornelius, Miller, and Mooers in Somers and Plattsburg, New York, served many patients in town and in the countryside in a variety of ways. Cornelius, for example, in the decade from 1794 to 1803, was the physician to 839 households. Half his patients came from Somers or neighboring Carmel, and he probably served one-third of all the residents in those towns and their surrounding countryside—an estimated 3,310 in all.[186] "Riding for the doctor" was a common occurrence for patients in the countryside, and valuable time was lost before medical attention could be paid. Neither fever thermometers nor stethoscopes were in common use before the 1880s, so doctors were confined to taking a patient's pulse, looking at his tongue, administering drugs to kill the pain, and strengthening the courage of family members from his presence at the bedside.

Kitchen surgery and home nursing prevailed in an era when hospitals could be found only in larger population centers. During the century, patent-medicine companies ran large advertisements in country newspapers, making fantastic claims for their products. Traveling doctors also made extravagant claims of unusual skills and miraculous cures. More specialized medical practitioners, such as pharmacists and dentists, developed slowly through the century. Not until the last decades were dentists typically practicing in towns, extracting decayed and aching teeth, competing with doctors or even blacksmiths, barbers, and pharmacists.[187]

The life of an individual town dweller in the nineteenth century continued to intersect with the community at important moments, but those connections became more formalized, more subject to notions of what was proper or respectable. Of all of life's turning points, birth was the least exposed to public ritual, being basically a family matter. It was a time of apprehension, for the dangers of birth were a constant worry for a pregnant woman, who risked her own life each time. The death of a mother or child or both was a haunting specter for a family; a successful birth was an occasion of joy and wonderment. As before, women brought close friends and female relatives into the planning and the confinement that followed. Relatives usually arrived before the birth for a visit. At the turn of the nineteenth century, Willis F. Dunbar remembered that in Hartford, Michigan, "women had babies at home. . . . [A neighboring woman] came in, prepared the meals, and took care of my mother and me."[188] Midwives and physicians were sometimes involved, and doctor-assisted births became increasingly common as the century progressed.

Baptism and christening were not universally practiced. There was little publicity or socializing attendant upon a birth. It was the father's duty to bring the community into the event, spreading the news, handing out cigars, placing anonymous birth notices in local newspapers that frequently were

CHILDREN AT PLAY. Even childhood play, as an element of respectability, became organized and formalized. Here a four-year-old child celebrates his birthday with all the formality of a party. [University of Louisville]

clever or humorous, though thoroughly chauvinistic. By printing these personal birth notices, newspapers performed a collective emotional catharsis, releasing the tensions that a birth created with a collective titter after the danger to the mother and child had passed.[189]

Families gradually declined in size through the nineteenth century, as the need for children for purposes of labor and old-age security in farms and craft shops, where home and family and work overlaid each other, gave way to settings in which family and home were separated from work. By the late decades of the century, psychologists defined "adolescence," a teenage phase of life. There the child achieved biological and social maturity, typically while attending school in one of the primary and secondary school systems that during the century became universal. Throughout the century, children (and their parents) were instructed by authors of assorted guides and manuals on the rudiments of proper behavior. Children were to obey their parents in return for love and care, be seen and not heard, eat apart from adults when company was in the home, and always address elders as "Mr." or "Mrs." Burns Fuller recalled that children recognized that their families exerted "a good influence unobserved, [but] greatly appreciated."[190]

Children were to avoid all forms of misbehavior—alcohol, tobacco, gambling, and sexual activity of all kinds, including masturbation, which was portrayed as a cause of a great variety of debilities and illnesses.[191] Boys and girls inhabited different adolescent sexual worlds. Willis F. Dunbar never heard the word "sex" as a boy in early-twentieth-century Hartford, Michigan. Women were "in a family way," if pregnant. Sex education for the young "was supposed to come through intuition."[192] Without formal sex education, girls had to avoid error if they were to be respectable, since error might ruin a girl's reputation through gossip or the deep stigma of unwedded motherhood. Boys grew up believing there were two kinds of women: "bad girls," with whom secret sex was permitted, and "good girls," who were pure and inviolable and with whom sex was to be avoided until marriage. Boys married the latter after conducting their youthful experiments with the former. For boys, sex and romantic love occupied two separate spheres that would be fused only in marriage.[193]

Courtship and marriage were also encased in propriety and respectability. An individual's status in town depended upon doing what was proper. Among other things, this meant having a chaperone during courtship, and having a wedding that followed social prescriptions: invitations printed on plain or satin-finished paper; an inquiry by the father of the bride into the groom's health and financial state; a church service with extensive floral decorations or a civil service with a justice of the peace; a reception at a hotel or the bride's or groom's family home; gifts from those invited; and train-station parties for departing "honeymooners" (among the better-off couples).[194] But in the rural countryside a simpler way prevailed. There was no engagement period, elopements were common, church weddings were rare, and most weddings were not followed by special gatherings. Occasionally a couple was "serenaded," the bride was carried around in a zinc tub, and the groom was taken for a ride on a rail and thrown into a creek. Shivarees (banging pots outside the couple's room all through their wedding night) were still a custom.[195]

Divorce rates rose rapidly during the last half of the century as various states enacted legislation specifying the grounds for divorce. Most common were abandonment, gross neglect of marital duty, extreme cruelty, and habitual drunkenness. Divorce was a denial of marriage and family as social norms, but it provided a mechanism for dealing with abusive relationships.

COURTSHIP AND MARRIAGE. Both courtship and marriage became more formalized and more public during the nineteenth century, especially for those who wished to be respectable. Top, courting with a chaperone in Queens, New York. Below, a wedding party in Junction City, Kansas. [Top, Culver Pictures; below, University of Kansas]

Women saw it as an act of desperation or defiance. Abandoned or abused wives were treated with public sympathy, but if they had children their prospects of successfully fending for themselves were poor.[196]

During marriage, men and women continued to occupy separate spheres, just as boys and girls had. Women managed households while more and more men went out of the home to work. Respectability and status demanded that a household have a domestic servant. The cult of domesticity or of true womanhood was grafted onto an older tradition of female inferiority and subordination and was considered to be an enhancement of status and privilege. Women were meant to keep the home as a peaceful refuge in which children were raised to be morally sound and husbands were respected. This "cult" was observed only by upper- and middle-class town dwellers, but they set standards for lower-class women as well.[197] Eliza Wiggin remembered that in mid-nineteenth-century Waverly, Kansas, "there was a little coterie of choice friends in the neighborhood and they often met to compare notes as to their housekeeping and their gardens, and many a hearty laugh they enjoyed over various mistakes and failures." But Wiggin also found "so many women who lived in strict seclusion and were so seldom seen abroad, that it would be no stretch of the imagination to say that the place was unusually rich in genuine recluses."[198]

When individual town dwellers aged, as Willis F. Dunbar remembered from turn-of-the-century Hartford, Michigan, "the possibility of spending one's declining years in the county poorhouse was about the most awful prospect one could imagine. . . . [Those who abandoned their parents] were regarded as being utterly depraved, no matter what the circumstances might be."[199] Death continued to be the most elaborate and public of life's passages. During the nineteenth century, funerals as public events were among the most important social affairs of a community. Home-centered services continued to be arranged as they had been in earlier centuries, but now they were more stylized, more prescribed for respectability. Bodies were laid in parlors for viewing after the immediate family had received those who extended their condolence. Flowers (frequently homemade wreaths) sometimes banked metal caskets. Eliza Wiggin remembered that she and her schoolmates went into a "darkened parlor" where Lizzie, a girl of fourteen, "lay as if asleep in her dainty silken bed. . . . Hushed and awestruck, we remained only a few minutes, but for weeks the memory of that lovely, silent face haunted my thoughts."[200] Cards edged in black were placed in places of business, and newspaper notices announced both the time and place of the service. The dreaded letter edged in black was sent to distant relatives. Acquaintances of the family felt a duty to be seen and to "pay their last respects," so most fu-

DEATH. Like marriage, death became more formalized and more public as the nineteenth century progressed. Here, in Lancaster, Wisconsin, both coffin and mourners were carefully staged by the photographer. [State Historical Society of Wisconsin]

nerals were well attended. Sermons and prayers were long and solemn. Mournful hymns were chosen to encourage weeping. Everyone wore black. The slow procession to the graveyard included uniformed members of the various organizations to which the deceased belonged. Ornate hearses drawn by horses were used by those who could afford them. Gatherings after the burial were times of sorrow but also provided an opportunity to meet old acquaintances and renew old memories.[201]

In the countryside, funerals remained even simpler. The body of the deceased was kept at home. In the community, men built the coffin and women made a new outfit for the deceased. Neighbors continued to help with funeral preparations, washing and laying out the corpse on a table, placing a cloth with camphor on the deceased's face to keep his or her color. At a "wake" two days before the funeral, family and friends gathered. The family stayed with the body day and night. Finally the coffin was carried to the grave site.[202]

During the twentieth century, disease was limited by the development of vaccinations and antibiotics. The health of town dwellers was treated by a medical system that linked rural and urban settings. Even in the early decades of the century, the automobile speeded the work of doctors in the towns. Physicians could move much faster and care for more patients. By mid-century, however, with the wide availability of automobile and air transportation, town doctors moved toward larger centers to practice, and rural doctors shifted into towns. Many rural hospitals were founded in the earlier parts of the century for rural doctors, but these institutions declined as road conditions improved. Public health services, a novelty during the mid- and late nineteenth century, became standard during the twentieth century. They sometimes included mobile units, augmenting medical examinations in schools and home nursing.[203]

As late as the 1930s, the life cycle of the individual town dweller still intersected with the community in familiar ways, but older customs were blending with modern innovations. In "Plainville," in the Midwest, the family was still man-centered. The father or husband was supposed to be a good provider and faithful to his wife, who was supposed to be a good "helpmate" and to manage the household. Parents were supposed to take care of their children and to educate them. Children were meant to be obedient and hardworking. In better-off families births were planned, and the ideal size for a family was thought to be two children. Pregnant women were embarrassed to be seen in public, and most births occurred in the local hospital, not at home, and were attended by a doctor, not female friends, relatives, and midwives. The friends of better-off mothers instead planned baby "showers."

Plainville boys and girls were treated differently in order to bring out characteristics thought to be male or female. Children were instructed to be modest and not expose themselves to each other. They were taught obedience by whipping, spanking, slapping, shaming, teasing, scolding, nagging, threats, privations, rewards, encouragements, verbal approval, and physical affection. Youths learned behavior appropriate to their class: the higher the status of their parents, the more refined and the less aggressive and crude they were expected to be.[204] Girls were taught to be nice; boys learned not to be sissies, how to fight.

Sex education was left up to nature, and boys learned from other boys, who sometimes indulged in group masturbation. They frequently experimented with drinking and sex before marriage. But, under a double standard, they were not subject to the same moral disapproval from the community as the bad girls or prostitutes who were their sex partners. Chaperoning declined, but parents kept a close watch over formal dating and courtship and tried to limit their children to dating with members of their own social class. Engagements were short. Weddings were held either in a preacher's house or in a church, no longer in a home. Honeymoons were standard but brief. Marriages were regarded as permanent, and divorce was strongly disapproved of and fairly rare.

Old people were greatly aided by the institution of old-age pensions during the depression of the 1930s. At death, people were embalmed and mourned and buried under the supervision of an undertaking firm, so that funeral arrangements were no longer dealt with by families and friends. Funerals were as often in a church as in a home. Only kin followed the hearse to the cemetery for burial, but funerals were still unusually important events for the whole community.[205]

By the late twentieth century in most towns, the life cycle of an individual still connected him or her to the community, but the patterns of those connections—in birth, childhood, marriage, maturity, old age, and death—mirrored more clearly those of society as a whole. The inhabitants of towns increasingly absorbed the patterns of life that prevailed in the mass society that became ever more apparent.

# SIX

# *Cultural Life*

CULTURAL LIFE in a broad sense refers to all those institutions and activities that have to do with the intellectual, spiritual, and artistic dimensions of community life. Churches, schools, and entertainment or art venues were the central locations for religious, educational, and artistic endeavors that involved the European migrants and their descendants.

In both the towns and the cities, churches and schools formed cultural "neighborhoods," that is, they were focal points of parts of the larger community, places where town and city dwellers living within a relatively small area could direct their intellectual and spiritual energies. The only distinction between the role of churches and schools was that in the towns, which were smaller, simpler communities, religion and education had relatively greater authority than they did in the more complicated cultural context of the cities.

From their beginnings, cities were great cultural centers whose variegated populations were less susceptible to the influences of particular institutions. It was in the cities that art and entertainment flourished, especially during the seventeenth and eighteenth centuries, when religious censure stifled such activity in the towns. By the nineteenth century, when various Christian denominations became less censorious, urban-based traveling artists and entertainers performed in the towns, thus spreading a largely urban activity. By the twentieth century, town and city dwellers shared a common art and entertainment delivered by radio, television, feature films, and the Internet, as well as a growing array of recorded mechanisms for domestic viewing and listening.

Both town and city dwellers celebrated religious and national holidays, commemorated their own community's anniversaries, and tried to improve its physical appearance. But during the twentieth century, as town life became a slower, smaller, paler copy of the interests and activities of ever-larger urban populations, Americans became nostalgic for the intimacy and relative isolation they associated with towns in their past. In this context the towns began to be re-created as symbols of the kind of local community that Americans purported to want, whether in the form of the museum village or of the theme park, both of which were physical icons, manageable manifestations of the town, whose great historical importance was at an end.

· I ·

AMONG THE NATIVE POPULATION that the English colonists encountered, religion and secular life were intricately connected. In some Indian tribes, chiefs assumed shamanistic or religious powers. Other tribes relied on their shamans or holy men who served as advisers and conducted large-scale séances during which they invoked spirits whose counsel was desired for critical decisions.[1] The native population treated plants and animals and the land itself as gifts to be cared for in a reciprocal relationship, not something to be possessed by humans. Festivals commemorating the animal cycles acknowledged these gifts through the sacrifice of material possessions. Animals, such as crows, were sources of spiritual power that could withhold their benefits if not properly respected. Plants, such as corn, were inanimate and thus without spirituality, but they were the gifts of certain spirits who could withhold them if they too were not properly respected. "God" was any manifestation of spiritual power, occurring in varied forms and responsible for everything the tribes could not understand.[2]

Christians believed in one God, but in many ways. Their pluralism took the form not of endless kinds of spirituality but of many forms of worshiping one true God. Through the Christian churches, the European colonists expressed their beliefs in the ultimate nature of existence in general and of human life in particular. Religious faith was also the chief source for morality, the main basis for the tenets of a good life. The role of Christianity in the lives of the European colonists was of basic importance, affecting all other dimensions of life, just as the economic system that the colonists developed influenced everything else they did.

Ministers interpreted God for parishioners regularly at church services, indicating the extent to which local congregants had either succeeded or failed to live up to the imperatives of a Christian life. During the seventeenth and eighteenth centuries, most town dwellers attended church, though there were always those who didn't bother, were indifferent, or were even nonbelievers. For most, however, their church was one of the most important institutions in their community, a place for praising moral and castigating immoral behavior, and an important social center too.

In North America the splintering of Christianity into many sects was more advanced than in the Christian heartland of Europe, where in many countries there were state churches and restrictions on dissenting groups until well into the nineteenth century. By contrast, beginning in the late seventeenth century a growing stream of settlers of varied affiliations emigrated to North America. By the time of American political independence in the 1780s, this variety undermined the perpetuation of a state-supported religion as well as the continuation of towns with only one church or one denomination.

But the development of Christian pluralism was a gradual process in the North American colonies, and through much of the seventeenth century the Anglicans (the Church of England) or their reformist but nonseparatist fellow congregants, the Puritans, dominated settlement. In the early phases of English provincial life in North America they brought to the Northern and Southern flanks a religious unity that was later lost in a maelstrom of denominational variety and dissent. Although the Church of England never succeeded in its sporadic efforts to extend its hierarchy to the North American colonies, the Anglican and Congregational churches overwhelmingly dominated most colonies through most of the seventeenth century. By the mid-seventeenth century, adherents of various Christian denominations and sects were welcomed in Rhode Island, founded as a religious sanctuary, and by the late seventeenth century in Pennsylvania, founded by Quakers. But the arrival of dissenting and foreign sects was gradual and sporadic. Christian pluralism was established piecemeal over long stretches of time, and unevenly.

The Northern Puritans and the Southern Anglicans imposed a unitary church on early New England towns and Southern rural neighborhoods. The Puritans created democratically oriented Congregational parishes (with membership for adult males who demonstrated they were likely among the saved) while the Southern Anglicans formed hierarchically oriented Anglican parishes (dominated by self-perpetuating "vestries" whose members were usually planters). The result was the domination of particular areas or communities by churches to whom nearly everyone belonged or at which al-

CHURCHES IN NEW ENGLAND. The colonial New England meetinghouse, serving as both church and town hall, by the nineteenth century had evolved into a purely Congregational church as the early close ties between civic and religious life came apart. These churches, like this one in Avon, Connecticut, featured tall spires and belfries, indicating the central place that congregants still thought religion played in the life of town dwellers. [Peter Mallary, *New England Churches and Meetinghouses*]

most everyone worshiped. Thus Anglican and Congregational churches shared the same boundaries as the towns and rural neighborhoods they were located in. They were the sole religious institutions for their communities.

The Puritans in particular provided a public, communal, or community-wide setting for their local Congregational churches. When towns were incorporated, churches were "gathered"—that is, groups who convinced each other through public confession that they were visible saints (among God's preordained saved or elect) founded churches in new towns and entered into solemn agreements or church covenants.[3] Congregational churches were meetinghouses, which were also used for political activities and which were located in the center of the townships at a commons.

Puritan town dwellers in dozens of towns tried to sustain religious purity, unity, and exclusivity.[4] Much of the adult community gathered in a kind of public forum to debate and decide on congregational matters, to "call" a minister, to hear public confessions, to pass censures on wayward congregants, to readmit those who repented, or to excommunicate those who were unrepentant in their adherence to heretical views.[5] In Connecticut, Congregational churches formed ecclesiastical societies, embracing their entire townships, until a town's population grew so large that the society was then divided in two or more.[6] But though the Puritans' churches were communal, and though congregations as a whole exercised ultimate authority over the affairs of a parish, early New England religious life in certain respects reflected the hierarchical character of society. Ministers were usually figures of great spiritual authority in the towns (though they were barred from holding civil office), and church seating mirrored the social standing of members.

This Puritan experiment in religious unity did not last. With each new generation, relatively fewer town dwellers became church members, failing to satisfy the existing congregants that they were visible saints.[7] Adherents of other denominations moved into the New England towns. For example, in Connecticut, Anglican, Baptist, and Quaker groups founded their own churches, and in 1790 the new state government gave them the legal right to establish their own ecclesiastical societies.[8] Coastal towns, such as Marblehead, in Massachusetts, attracted Anglicans from the beginning of settlement, creating a more complicated, fractious religious life.[9]

In Southern rural areas, Anglican parishes contained several churches, their locations determined by their centrality and accessibility by roads, often standing—like the early courthouses—in a cleared area near a crossroads at the center of the parish precinct. Church structures, built of wood during the seventeenth century, later came to be made of brick in increasingly uniform styles. In Virginia, at least, church attendance was mandatory by law (once in every four-week period). Seating was by status, with the planters as vestrymen assigned the central pews. Ministers explicated Christian scripture from raised pulpits; below them at desks, lay assistants read scriptural lessons and "lined out" psalms for the musical intonation of the congregants. Above the altar were black tablets containing in gold lettering the words of the Ten Commandments and the Apostle's Creed, which together provided the cosmic framework within which the community was contained and the moral

CHURCHES IN THE SOUTH. Anglican churches in the colonial South were often located at crossroads or near plantations, natural gathering places for the same rural population that visited courthouses for their civic or political (and even economic or marketing) activities. Such buildings were plain, not very tall, and not impressive in the way that more religiously conscious New Englanders made their churches. This one is in Lancaster County, Virginia. [Isaac, *The Transformation of Virginia*]

absolutes to which it was subjected. The liturgical service was based upon the Book of Common Prayer, a mode alien to dissenting sects and Puritan reformers alike. In contrast to Congregational democratic governance, Anglican parishes were ruled by self-perpetuating vestries of twelve gentlemen, presided over by ministers.[10]

As in New England, this early religious uniformity did not last. By the 1760s Baptists had moved into the Southern colonies in significant numbers. They emphasized emotion and enjoyed a broad popular appeal, counting many members from among the poorer settlers. They built plain meeting-houses and gave each congregation wide authority to manage its own affairs. Ministers were often individuals of obscure origins. Instead of emphasizing hierarchy, ministerial authority, and a required liturgy, as the Anglicans did, the Baptists' main public ritual was adult baptism, by which candidates were sealed into fellowship, in closed circles for the laying on of hands. Preaching

*Estimated Numbers in Denominations,*
*Southeastern Pennsylvania, 1790*

| Denomination | Number | Percentage of Population |
|---|---|---|
| *"Sects"* | | |
| Quakers | 30,000 | 9 |
| Mennonites | 20,000 | 6 |
| German "Baptists" (Dunkers, etc.) | 5,000 | 2 |
| Moravians | 1,500 | < 1 |
| *"Churches"* | | |
| Presbyterians | 60,000 | 19 |
| German Lutherans | 45,000 | 14 |
| German Reformed (including some French Huguenots and Dutch) | 40,000 | 12 |
| Anglican | 7,500 | 2 |
| "English" Baptist | 5,000 | 2 |
| Roman Catholic | 8,000 | 2 |
| Other | 6,000 | 2 |
| Not assigned | 95,000? | 29? |
| Total | 323,000 | 100 |

RELIGIOUS DENOMINATIONS. The astonishing variety of religious denominations in colonial Pennsylvania, under the tolerant Penns, was a precursor of what gradually became a feature of most parts of the United States, in towns throughout the continent. These figures are from southeastern Pennsylvania in 1790. [Lemon, *The Best Poor Man's Country*]

itself became an incantatory ritual at mass assemblies, the object being to obtain ecstatic release among listeners.[11]

By the late seventeenth century the Penn family, adherents of the dissenting Quaker sect, founded a major colony which they opened to those with other Christian affiliations. By the eighteenth century, Pennsylvania swarmed with Anglicans, Presbyterians, Quakers, Lutherans, Dutch and German Reformed, German Pietistic sects, and even Catholics. In the presence of these pluralistic denominational patterns, in which several religious groups inhabited the same areas, a single parish system, like those established in the early Southern and New England colonies, had no chance.[12]

Religious pluralism diminished the authority enjoyed by single-parish churches in early New England towns and Southern rural neighborhoods. In Germantown, Pennsylvania, for example, settlers felt no pressure to conform, no persecution against which to dissent, and no common bond of belief to encourage religiosity. The growth of church attendance lagged behind the population growth of the town itself. More women than men were church members, indicating that religion had become more the province of women in a patriarchal society. Over time many families gradually fell away from formal religious practice. Members of the various Christian denominations in Germantown lived randomly throughout the settlement, not clustered around their church. Ministers were viewed by parishioners as objects of charity rather than authority, as congregants often had acrimonious debates over methods of raising money for their minister's salary. Marriages took place in homes; cemeteries were public and nonsectarian. The question of how town dwellers were to maintain their religious convictions when so many churches offered the true way and competed for public support was a vital one in Germantown.[13] It became an essential question wherever different kinds of Christian churches were located in one town.

The emergence of evangelism during the 1740s produced further splintering among the Christian sects. Sometimes the effect of evangelist preaching was to split existing congregations, creating New Light groups that established their own churches apart from their former fellow parishioners, the Old Lights. The Baptists became thoroughly evangelized.

The first visit of itinerant evangelist preachers to a neighborhood occurred when a group of penitents had already formed and had been actively meeting together, spreading alarm about the sinfulness of the world. This preceded the creation of a mass movement spurred on by evangelical preachers. Each sinner underwent radical individualization as each was "awakened" to a sense of sinfulness and alone faced the meaning of God's judgment. After having a "conviction" of sin, segregating themselves from the world, and experiencing the lone ecstasy of conversion, the initiates received the comfort of close fellowship.

But Baptist conversions were validated among church members only by a radical reform of conduct, and there was much concern for the proper disciplinary supervision of such changes. Censure, ritual excommunication, and moving experiences of penitence were invoked as means to deal with such persistent problems as drunkenness, quarreling, slander, and disputes over property. Evangelized Baptists emphasized self-control but also wanted to impose controls over a loose society. They were determined to be serious and disciplined and to abstain from frivolous pastimes. As converted individuals removed from a sinful society, Baptists sought to create among themselves a tight, supportive group of persons who lived together as brethren.[14]

As various Christian denominations and sects appeared together in the same communities with increasing frequency during the eighteenth century, towns came to be divided into parishes. Churches were at the center of culturally defined neighborhoods, whether in towns or in rural settings. And though parishioners of a particular church did not necessarily live near it, they came to it as the center of their religious community.

The Puritans were easily the most notable of the religious groups that founded towns and set out to keep them religiously pure and unified. During much of the seventeenth century they insisted that towns throughout New England have only one Congregational church for the entire town. This impulse moved certain of the German Pietistic sects, such as the Moravians and the Mennonites, to found their own towns as well.[15] Thus religious adherents either divided towns into neighborhood parishes or united towns into one parish, depending upon whether they wished to share a town with other congregants or whether they sought to maintain their unity and purity.

In the Spanish colonial towns in the area that later became the Southwestern United States, religious purity was successfully sustained far more durably and continuously than by the Puritans in New England. The Catholic church provided the only permissible form of Christian faith. In smaller villages, however, in places rarely visited by a priest, Catholicism was a folk religion, and its focus was on family worship. Each home had an altar where village and family saints were worshiped. In remote New Mexico one could find another dimension of Catholicism, beyond family worship. The Penitentes Brotherhood was a unique religious order, organized into local, independent village congregations headed by an Elder Brother. The brothers met in a chapter house and performed religious duties, took care of the sick, the wounded, and the orphaned, buried the dead, punished those who violated the village norms, and settled village disputes, thus blurring the line between religious and secular activity.[16] In general, Spanish colonial towns integrated the various dimensions of town life into a communal whole in a way that English colonial town dwellers avoided.

In the nineteenth century, religious unity was confined to towns that were, like those founded during the Spanish colonial era, wholly Catholic, or, among Protestants, founded by particular religious groups for their own exclusive use. The religious impulse to remain pure and unified that had guided the Puritans during the seventeenth century, and that had animated certain Pietistic groups in the seventeenth and eighteenth centuries, remained strong through the nineteenth century, especially among sects who were governed by the utopian dream of a communitarian town society shorn of class division and private property. The largest of these efforts were those involving the Shakers, an eighteenth-century English Quaker splinter sect ("shaking Quakers"), who sustained at their peak, during the nineteenth century, twenty-seven communities with five thousand inhabitants;[17] and the Mormons, a sect founded in America during the 1830s, who developed numerous towns in Utah territory during the 1850s, after the migration to that part of the frontier.

What unified many of these utopian religious enterprises and made them the spiritual descendants of the Puritans was their insistence on a unifying covenant or agreement and ongoing public confessions by those who misbehaved and broke the rules. For example, the followers of John Humphrey Noyes founded Oneida, New York, and Wallingford, Connecticut, where town life centered on mutual criticism, a form of public confession and repentance. This took place at weekly meetings, where individuals were subjected to close scrutiny and careful analysis. Similarly, Adin Ballou's Hopedale community in Massachusetts had monthly communications, whose aim was to publicize reprehensible conduct and thereby restore harmony. German Pietists in Amana, Iowa, had a regular *untersuchung*, a general examination of the spiritual condition of all the inhabitants, who were called upon personally to confess their faults or sins.[18]

In the vast majority of towns everywhere on the continent, settlers adhered to a variety of Christian denominations as dissenting sects of Europe's state-linked churches proliferated and spread to North America. This religious in-gathering of Christians was more widespread and common than anywhere else in the Western world. As Europeans retained their church-state linkages well into the nineteenth century, Americans shunned a state church altogether from the inception of their nation. Anglicans (renamed Episcopalians), Congregationalists, Presbyterians, Quakers, and Methodists were joined by Lutherans, Dutch Reformers, Baptists, and various splinter sects to produce the world's greatest variety of Christians in towns everywhere on the North American continent.

Although churches continued to define neighborhoods within towns, later parishioners were far more apt to live away from their church than was the case when a town was founded. Migrants from one town to another typically carried letters of transfer with them, so that they would be welcomed into the same church in their new community. But denominations also competed for members and sometimes engaged in theological debates in order to maintain the purity and definition of their respective doctrines. During the course of the century, as the churches attempted to expand their membership, they also lowered their standards of admission. Increasingly they stressed pietism over doctrinal orthodoxy and welcomed newcomers at revivals or readily accepted letters of transfer. The major Protestant churches gradually let go of their insistence on theological purity as they competed for new converts. Rather than screen members for religious orthodoxy, they required submission to a pietistic moral code.[19]

The many different kinds of Christians were unified in their common concern that Christian morality suffuse all aspects of town life. In town after town the presence of a great variety of Christian churches coexisted with their congregants' collective adherence to a form of morality that was identifiably Christian, even though its exact content might lack precision, especially in the contested forms of misbehavior that involved drinking, gambling, and prostitution. Christian preachers still used their pulpits to interpret the words of God to parishioners; still used their sermons as a means of judging how well and badly adherents were living good, Christian lives; still used the Bible as the ultimate source by which humans could understand life and existence.

The division of Christians into many churches in the towns was standard everywhere, even in New England, where the Puritans had founded one-church communities. In a town like Chelsea, Vermont, founded in 1781, the Congregationalists were never in the majority and were soon joined by Baptists and Methodists, among others.[20] In Beekmantown, New York, founded about the same time, Presbyterians predominated in the early years, but by the 1850s the Methodists were far ahead. In both Beekmantown and in neighboring Plattsburg, the early Presbyterian churches combined features of Presbyterianism and Congregationalism as both employed covenants and confessions of faith. Church discipline and orthodoxy were still important aspects of religious life. Nonattendance and various forms of misbehavior (drunkenness, lying, slander, even dancing) could lead to repentance, exoneration, or excommunication. Between the late eighteenth century and the mid-nineteenth century, early groups of Baptists gave way to a surging tide of Methodists. Poor Irish and French-Canadian settlers brought Catholicism to the area and made the Catholic church one of the largest in either town.[21]

As settlement moved west, an array of Christian churches appeared in every rural neighborhood and country town across the great valleys and plains of the mid-continent. In the countryside called Sugar Creek, in Illinois, families brought their faith with them, whether Catholic, Presbyterian, Baptist, or Methodist.[22] By the 1860s in Jacksonville, Illinois, a town with a population of about 5,500, about half belonged to eighteen different congregations spread among eight separate denominations—a good example of how varied and numerous the Christian churches were in a well-established town. Church discipline in the town's Presbyterian church shifted from a concern for doctrinal orthodoxy to dealings with moral offenses. Wayward belief was far less significant in the church's disciplinary proceedings than wayward behavior, such as drinking, gambling, attendance at theatrical productions, or disrespect for church elders or the congregation itself.[23] In the villages of Trempealeau County, Wisconsin, from the 1860s through the 1880s, Congregationalists, Presbyterians, Baptists, Methodists, Lutherans, and Catholics all lived together without evident tension or hostility.[24]

Even in special towns, such as those founded as exclusively black towns, a variety of Christian churches was the norm. Five churches welcomed parishioners in Mound Bayou, Mississippi (the oldest and largest being the Baptist church), and several existed in Boley, Oklahoma, and Nicodemus, Kansas. In all these towns, and in others, newspapers bragged about the variety of churches for promotional purposes.[25] When black migrants settled in the North after the Civil War, there were even instances in a thoroughly racist society of blacks and whites working together to construct a (Methodist) community church on land donated by an African American, in the Cheyenne Valley in rural Wisconsin.[26]

In their hierarchical structure, the Christian churches continued to vary considerably. Catholics, Episcopalians, and Presbyterians had well-defined and permanent levels of authority, whereas Congregationalists, Methodists, and Baptists gave primary authority to local parishes, reserving important matters for occasional synods. The churches also differed in their adherents' conceptions of what constituted a properly trained ministry. Episcopalian, Presbyterian, and Congregational ministers received formal training and degrees, but such dissenting sects as the Quakers, Baptists, and Methodists used lay or untrained preachers. Since the Baptists and the Methodists were the faster-growing denominations in nineteenth-century America, increasing numbers of town dwellers associated preaching with the efforts of ordinary believers who had a natural talent for explicating the Bible.

Whether trained or not, clergymen by the nineteenth century lost their position at the center of the towns' cultural and intellectual life. Ministers had always depended upon their congregations for a definition of doctrinal orthodoxy and for their appointment, salary, house, and continued employment. But in the seventeenth and eighteenth centuries they had been figures of authority and prestige, especially in communities confined to a single church. And though preachers and their congregations fairly often found themselves in disputes, a minister's overall authority in interpreting the word of God and in leading the parishioners in church services or at prayer was not in question.

In the nineteenth century, congregants came to believe that preaching was the least distinguished of professions, that anyone could preach, that special skills and training were unnecessary. Bible-reading parishioners insisted on individual interpretations of the scriptures. If individual believers felt the "call of God" to preach, the fast-growing denominations were inclined to let them preach. Towns served as testing grounds; those with promise moved to larger places. Congregations of all kinds expected preachers to remain only a few years and to accept better-paying jobs when they were offered, thus creating a highly unstable ministry. The congregations within the towns became smaller as the century progressed, meaning that they had to struggle with inadequate equipment and poorly paid ministers. Clergymen presided over as many as six Sunday services, spread out during the morning, afternoon, and evening. They also officiated at marriages and funerals; prayed with individuals, comforted the dying, and attended prayer services, meetings of reform-oriented and lodge organizations, sociables, and holiday celebrations.[27]

Protestant evangelism continued to be a force for unity as preachers of various denominations participated in revivals that generated new members, converts to Christianity who underwent an experience of conversion. Evangelism evoked emotional responses, was enormously popular among nominal Christians, and was largely responsible for whatever growth the Christian churches experienced in the numbers of active believers. The fastest-growing denominations—the Baptists and the Methodists—were thoroughly evangelical. Although revivals might be held indoors, in particular churches, the largest revivals in rural areas assumed the form of outdoor camp meetings that sometimes went on for days. These ecumenical assemblages took on the form of temporary communities, or tent towns, replete with "streets" and "houses" and public squares (preacher platforms and conversion pits, where penitents would writhe in agony induced by ministerial exhortations before suddenly growing limp and quiet with the awareness that they had been saved by Jesus Christ).[28]

Many towns across the continent were near the sites of these revival meetings. In Addison County, Vermont, towns such as Middlebury, Shoreham, and Cornwall experienced thirty-five revivals in three phases of activity from 1801 to 1850. In this case, evangelical religion found its most fertile soil in stable, prosperous, structured communities that were experiencing agricultural commercialization.[29] In Chelsea, Vermont, the Congregational church experienced widely scattered revivals—1809, 1819, 1831, and 1842.[30] Camp meetings were held in the Beekmantown/Plattsburg area of New York beginning in 1819 and continuing throughout the 1820s and 1830s, and became known as the most effective form of proselytizing available.[31]

In Sugar Creek, Illinois, for many years after the initial settlement, re-

EVANGELISM. Among the evangelically oriented denominations, the Baptists exhibited the added practice of public baptisms. Here near Richmond, Virginia, in the segregated turn-of-the-century South, blacks perform a baptism with white spectators as invited guests. [Valentine Museum]

vivals occurred annually in the "Sugar Creek Camp Ground" at Harlan's Grove, a location that suggests that settlers were still connected to the ancient tribal belief in the spiritual nature of sacred spaces or groves. Hundreds of farm families came from a radius of forty or fifty miles during the late summer, between "laying-by" and harvest, to worship but also to enjoy robust fellowship, male gaming and drinking, and female socializing and gossiping. A proper camp meeting grove was near pasture and water, allowing for a "lay-over" for several days. All felt they were participating in an extraordinary event as anxious crowds milled about, both sexes mingled in a public space, and campfires cast an eerie light through the forest at evening. Preachers guided the meeting through a number of phases that lasted for several days. In their exhortations the preachers affirmed that participants were mired in sin and guilt, a state that could lead to their fall into the bottomless pit of hell. After wearing down their resistance, preachers offered these sinners the redemptive power of salvation. Congregants sometimes responded to such harangues with uncontrolled, highly physical exhibitions of emotional release: singing, running, jerking, barking—often resulting in the experience of conversion, that is, a sudden awareness that they could be saved.[32]

In town, in Jacksonville, Illinois, the Protestant churches provided the sites for a series of revivals from the 1840s through the 1860s. The Methodists, whose itinerant preachers had perfected the technique of revivals, often took the lead, but other denominations in town sometimes followed, creating a general revival throughout the community. The level and character of enthusiasm varied from one denomination to another. Presbyterians and Congregationalists, for example, had restrained and educated ministers and were less open to spontaneous physical displays of religious enthusiasm than such congregants as Methodists and Baptists. But whoever was involved, revivals in town, like those in the countryside, were protracted meetings. Ministers exhorted, and those who felt moved came forward to mourners' benches to be readied for conversion, which could happen spontaneously. In the more emotional denominations, those who were converted stood and loudly proclaimed their newfound faith by howling like dogs or letting their bodies be convulsed by the jerks.[33]

The Christian churches, united in their emphasis on the importance of congregants' living moral lives, also shared an important connection to town society: respectability. No more cherished social distinction separated the respectable from the disrespectable than regular church attendance. The presence of the churches added a crucial element to the establishment of social status, of a hierarchical town society. It was not just wealth that determined one's position, or one's family background and reputation and longevity, or one's education or occupation: status was also a matter of religiosity, of church attendance, of whether one behaved well and was perceived to be a good person.[34]

The churches permeated the social life of town dwellers, who were overwhelmingly Christian. On Sunday morning, church bells from the various parishes could be heard all over town. Morning and evening and midweek services were common, as well as Sunday school. Although parents sometimes left infants at home with older children or the hired girl, church services stressed family worship. Churches became nongendered public spaces. All could participate in Sunday school. Babies were put to sleep on back benches during evening services. Young women attended Sunday evening and midweek services as a way of meeting their beaus, and, when services ended, young men gathered at the church door or along the walk to escort their favorite young woman home. As for Sunday school, the superintendent called the group together for opening exercises, usually a prayer and a song, and then the classes, sectioned in accordance with age or sex, adjourned to their assigned places in the main auditorium. All could memorize the Golden Text, and all could listen to someone comment verse by verse on the appropriate scriptural subject.

Individuals differed in their assessments of the importance of religion in their towns. Eliza Wiggin remembered with poetic intensity what her church in mid-nineteenth-century Waverly, Kansas, meant to her: "Many of my most precious childish memories are twined about this church. How I loved, from my favorite seat next to the window, to feast my eyes upon the exquisite, soul-satisfying beauty of gently waving grass and leafy trees; listening meanwhile almost unconsciously to the sonorous tones of the minister or the sacred songs of praise rising sweetly on the fresh morning air."[35]

Margaret L. Johnson was sure that when she was growing up in Woodstock, Vermont, in the 1880s, "I absorbed something of the atmosphere of reverence and worship."[36] Fred Lape remembered that his hometown of Esperance, New York, was a religious town in the early twentieth century, and that "both dancing and card games were prohibited by the disciplines of the Methodist church and of the Presbyterian church."[37] With a somewhat different emphasis, Burns Fuller remembered that in Fenton, Michigan, "daily life ran quite smoothly and peacefully, and then some exciting events such as religious revival meetings and occasionally a funeral at which human emotions really ran wild [would occur]."[38]

But some questioned how deeply felt religious belief was among town dwellers. Willis F. Dunbar thought that his mother had a "take it or leave it attitude toward religion," an attitude he thought was "shared by many Hartfordites." Dunbar felt that "everyone, if pressed, would have avowed that he believed in God, but you had the notion that his faith was neither deep nor profound in many cases."[39] Similarly, Burns Fuller recalled that as children he and his friends were amused at "sinners" "converting," only to relapse a short time later and go through the same stunt at another revival, just to get attention.[40]

With less emphasis on doctrinal rigor and purity, during the course of the nineteenth century, the churches became great social centers. Fundraising and social activities were popular everywhere. C. W. Goodlander remembered that in mid-nineteenth century Fort Scott, Kansas, "like all towns, the church people were hard up, and were giving entertainments to raise money."[41] And Willis F. Dunbar recalled how in turn-of-the-century Hartford, Michigan, "it was a constant struggle to raise enough money to pay all these preachers even a subsistence salary."[42] Donation parties for ministers vied with sociables where entire families met at a private home, at the parsonage, or in the church for entertainment and fellowship. Churches sponsored suppers, festivals, and fairs as fund-raisers, selling food, entertainment, and articles donated by members and friends, and even held lotteries if church policy allowed for such "good" gambling.[43] Increasingly, women parishioners held the congregations together. They raised the money for the minister's salary, brought children to the services, taught Sunday school, maintained church charities, sang in the chorus, and filled the pews. By contrast, men gave land for church buildings, helped plan and dedicate the church as a sanctuary, hired and fired the preacher, served as church elders, and gave public speeches.

In order to sustain the interest and commitment and financial support of members, church officials felt compelled to involve congregants in social or leisure activity. But by becoming social centers the churches diminished religion as a distinctive, transcendent endeavor, one whose purpose went beyond ordinary, secular life. Maintaining membership in a competitive environment also meant that the churches generally avoided controversial reform movements, unless they were so popular that ministerial support would not drive away congregants. This was the case with temperance, which some of the churches supported and others did not, depending upon whether adherents of a particular denomination had a strict or a loose definition of what constituted good and bad behavior. In general, the Christian churches boosted their towns, damned aberrant or immoral behavior wherever and whenever found, praised honest wealth accumulation, and admired successful private economic activity of all kinds.[44]

During the twentieth century, religion and the churches remained an important but less central aspect of town life. Technological changes in transportation and communications enlarged the scope and scale of town dwellers' religious activity. Until the end of the nineteenth century, horse transport meant that "going to church," at least for the rural population that town churches served, was a full day's event. Widespread ownership of the automobile by the 1920s made it possible for this rapidly diminishing population to engage in all the religious activities scheduled for a Sunday and still have time for recreation and leisure. Proper behavior for rural churchgoers had to be redefined.

They could also drive to churches in larger population centers rather than to the nearest village. As mobility increased, it became possible for the Christian churches to consolidate their parishes and centralize their activities regionally.[45] But though the trend toward consolidation was continuous throughout the twentieth century, churches in rural areas were typically the local institution that most resisted change. Consolidation came slowly and in various forms. A larger parish administration might be created, even with the retention of existing churches. Or one clergyman might serve several churches. Or several different denominations might share a particular church building. Or a community might settle on a single nondenominational church.[46]

Advances in communications also affected the practice of religion among town dwellers. The growth of mass audiences for radio, in the 1930s, and for television, in the 1950s, led to the creation of the "electronic church," that is, church services and preaching that were broadcast or televised and therefore experienced by individuals or families directly in their homes. The Reverend Charles Coughlin (on radio) in the 1930s, Bishop Fulton J. Sheen (on television) in the 1950s, Reverend Billy Graham in the 1970s, and the Reverends Pat Robinson, Jerry Falwell, Oral Roberts, and Jim Bakker in the 1980s—all created great followings with continent-wide religious services and messages that town dwellers everywhere could share simultaneously. By the 1980s cable television included channels devoted entirely to religious programming. TV preachers sought to build up their own religious organizations, not to encourage attendance at local churches.[47]

In the twentieth century, marked by its dramatic enlargements in the scale and speed of life, local clergymen were more easily made aware of church policy as it was determined by their national or even international organizations. But the Christian churches continued to vary considerably in their hierarchical characteristics. For instance, local Congregationalists and Baptists chose their own ministers; Catholics, Episcopalians, and Methodists did not. But ministers of all descriptions acted as mediators between higher authorities and local parishioners, distilling and interpreting church policies and pronouncements to fit local circumstances, usually avoiding contentious social, economic, or political issues that seriously divided the community.[48]

Through the twentieth century Christians continued to splinter, dividing into still more denominations and sects. The newer congregations built churches on the outskirts of towns, thus losing the physical centrality of the older parish neighborhoods where the more established denominations had built their churches. An ecumenical movement sought to unite Christians, but this impulse was weaker than the interest in maintaining distinctive religious identities, and the councils of churches both nationally and worldwide coexisted with thousands of local churches, each of which sought to expand its membership.[49]

Linkages between class and religion became much murkier during the twentieth century. To a considerable extent, the bond between social respectability and church attendance broke down as many middle- and upper-class individuals and families ceased to be churchgoers. Socially marginalized elements in the towns tended to join denominations and sects that emphasized the emotions in their services, avoided complex theological positions, and had a relatively uneducated ministry. But this was a tendency only, and many lower-class town dwellers were not religious at all.[50] What is more, all the well-established churches had members of varied family and social backgrounds.[51] Church membership gradually declined through the century (as a percentage of the total population), with increases in newer denominations and sects partially compensating for declines in older ones. Church attendance declined far more dramatically than membership, as greater numbers of Christian congregants reduced their churchgoing to special services for baptism, marriage, death, and holy days, even while they continued to proclaim their religious beliefs.

Evangelism continued throughout the century to be a strong force among Christians, with revivals periodically sweeping across towns and rural neighborhoods in all parts of America, moving from one location to another until television created electronic mass meetings that united believers across the continent. Fundamentalist sects emerged in the early years of the century, with congregants affirming their literal belief in the entire Bible. Evangelism and fundamentalism together generated growth in those denominations and sects that subscribed to them while the older, mainstream denominations lost active members.

The prevailing viewpoint among the older, nonevangelical, nonfundamentalist denominations was the "social gospel." It emphasized not divisive theological dogma but what its adherents insisted was Christians' overriding duty: to create a good society and to serve others. In the towns the social gospel movement invaded community and social clubs, the YMCA and the YWCA, the Boy Scouts and the Girl Scouts, as well as many organizations that helped children, the aged, and the underprivileged. Ministers sometimes became the mainstay of service organizations and community clubs.[52]

All Christian churches continued to provide social activities for their members. In "Springdale," New York, in the 1950s, for instance, church-related activities made up half of the community's organized social activities. Each church (except the Baptists) sponsored a broad range of social events and supported a variety of auxiliary organizations. Ladies aid societies, men's societies, youth groups, missionary societies, and choirs conducted their own social programs. These auxiliary groups sponsored church suppers, ice cream socials, bake sales, rummage sales, men's suppers, hayrides, and picnics. The churches were an important part of the community's social life be-

cause of the public nature of their activities, most of which were open to anyone who cared to attend. In practice, only those who were active church
members attended, and the churches divided the available dates on the calendar to avoid duplication. Of seventeen hundred adults in Springdale, three
hundred to four hundred active congregants attended.[53]

In the twentieth century the Christian churches continued to provide
moral standards and explanations for the meaning of life, even while churchgoers comprised a steadily diminishing portion of the population in general
and town dwellers in particular. Popular awareness of secular laws and of law
enforcement machinery became a more effective basis for the instillation of
morality, as did a school system that inculcated among the young a vague,
secular humanism in a society whose inhabitants chose more varied formal
religious affiliations. Town dwellers were as aware as anyone else of this
broader, vaguer, more secular morality, even those who lived in towns without ethnic or racial or religious variety. Another institution came to rival the
churches as a center for probing the nature of morality and truth, existence
and reality, an institution that more intelligent and usually better-off town
dwellers attended in increasing numbers through the century: the college or
university, whether public or private, secular or religious.

Christian churches in the towns continued to exhibit contradictory positions on society. They were variously liberal and conservative, reformist and
tradition-bound, proclaiming both exuberant patriotic rhetoric and stern
jeremiads. The Christian faith, which had permeated the lives of a largely
European-derived population, increasingly gave way to churches that provided religious support for good and moral living in an increasingly secular-
ized, multi-ethnic, and multi-racial society.

· II ·

UNLIKE THE NATIVE TRIBES they confronted, European
colonists developed schools as formal institutions for the education of their
young. This was a gradual process in both Europe and on its North American frontier. During the seventeenth and eighteenth centuries, town dwellers
lived with a mix of educational sites—those provided by individual schoolmasters and schoolmistresses, church-supported denominational schools,
and other schools supported by public funds.[54] Above all, education was a

family responsibility, a domestic activity that involved all parents. Children in the towns were thus exposed to influences from parents, schoolteachers, and schoolbooks (primers). The common task was to inculcate in the young the prevailing Christian values; to instruct them in the basic skills of reading, writing, and ciphering; and to instill in them the appropriate childhood traits of obedience, discipline, and correct behavior.[55]

Through much of the seventeenth century schools were widely scattered and sporadic. For instance, in early Plymouth colony (before its absorption into the Massachusetts Bay colony), one finds early efforts to hire schoolmasters, but evidence for the actual construction of schoolhouses is virtually nonexistent.[56] The Puritans who dominated the colonial assemblies of the New England colonies enacted legislation requiring towns to establish publicly funded schools, but the towns were slow to respond. Although the idea of a public school system was current in Europe during the seventeenth and eighteenth centuries,[57] Puritan legislators were attempting to create religiously unified towns, model communities whose purified congregants would also be educated in order to understand God as revealed in scripture. In the Puritan towns, what was religious was also public.

In Connecticut, for example, every town with more than thirty families was required to maintain a school. Early in the eighteenth century the colonial assembly devolved onto the "church societies" (the organizations that Congregational parishioners belonged to) responsibility for the management of the schools within their territories. The colonial government also provided a school fund (based upon the amount of assessed wealth in a particular town), funds augmented by the colony's revenues from the sale of western lands. These church societies met once a year to decide where the schools would be held, who the teachers would be, and how much of the cost would be borne by the society and by the students. In the early years, schools were rotated through the society's territory, with students attending school only when it was held in their area. But as the population of the towns grew, the societies stopped rotating schools. By the mid-eighteenth century the Congregational church societies averaged five to seven permanent school sites within their town territories. By then, the societies commonly elected a number of school committeemen equal to the number of their schools. School committees hired both schoolmasters and school mistresses and charged students only a fraction of the actual costs of operating the school, exempting the poor and indigent.[58]

Elsewhere in the colonies, in towns with more than one church, schools were typically and explicitly denominational. In Pennsylvania, for instance, Quakers, Presbyterians, Lutherans, and Reformed Germans all established

SCHOOL. Most schools were ungraded and located in a single room, as shown here in Indiana. The training of teachers and the grading of students came when a town's voters felt they had the interest and the means to introduce such forms of modernization. [Indiana Historical Society]

schools, often held in their own church buildings, with ministers sometimes serving as teachers. In some places, interdenominational schools were established to teach English to German settlers, to integrate them into the prevailing culture. Other denominations maintained "charity schools." But schools remained quite scattered, often on a corner of a farm or in or near a church.[59]

In Germantown, Pennsylvania, as elsewhere, education was essentially a family responsibility. Some town dwellers set aside specific sums of money or the interest therefrom in their wills to be used for their children's schooling. Others left money for poor children of any denomination.[60] But in multi-denominational Germantown, most of the churches took little direct responsibility for the education of the young. Only Mennonites (who soon left to found their own town at Bethlehem) and Lutherans were directly involved in the management of a school.

Congregants from all the major denominations were involved in the founding of Germantown's Union School, however, a very early example of a genuinely public school. In accordance with its charter from the colony, in 1701 the town appointed three men as supervisors of a community school.

Their duty was to collect contributions from local citizens and to hire a teacher. Such a school had in fact already been operating, with Pastorius, the principal founder of the town, as its teacher. When that school collapsed, inhabitants of the town met to found the Union School. But while congregants of the various denominations were involved, the new school had a nonsectarian admissions policy, and its teachers offered no courses in religion. Thus did denominational variety lead to public education.[61]

In the nineteenth century, school systems came to blanket the continent as state after state established requirements for the towns to institute publicly funded and managed education. These systems varied in their timing and organization, but those who managed them, funded them, taught in them, and attended them all shared in a common enterprise whose purpose continued to be the learning of Christian values and the mastery of certain basic mental skills, chiefly literacy and numeracy. Teachers, whose training expanded during the course of the century, taught students through the recitation method to understand "readers"—at first Noah Webster's and then William McGuffey's—and thereby exposed them to *both* Christian morality and language.[62]

As a result of their exposure to this educational system, the young were supposed to be capable of becoming responsible adults in a Christian, capitalist republic. The swift emergence of a universal public education system in a multi-ethnic, multi-racial society did not result in the obliteration of the existing array of private schools but rather their continued coexistence. Town dwellers typically attended compulsory primary schools beginning in the early and middle parts of the century, and by the later nineteenth century, ever larger numbers of them also attended secondary schools and colleges and universities, usually located elsewhere. Beyond the school systems, adult education became a popular activity as "lyceums" and itinerant camp "schools" flourished across the continent.

In Beekmantown and Plattsburg, New York, the two towns taxed their property owners to raise a sum equal to half the state's school fund, which was apportioned among the towns of their county. Under the 1795 state legislation each town, in order to receive state aid, was required to choose school commissioners who supervised the school districts that the assisted towns were required to establish. Voters in these districts then elected trustees to operate their schools and to hire necessary teachers. The New York state legislature enacted further school legislation from time to time and established a common school fund, essentially an endowment derived from lotteries, sales of public land, and investment. In 1812 school district voters were given the

ADULT EDUCATION. No form of adult education was more popular than the traveling "Chautauqua," a tent gathering at which a variety of cultural and educational activities took place. Here is one in Kearney, Nebraska. [Nebraska State Historical Society]

authority to choose the schoolhouse site and to impose a district tax on property to pay for the site and for the construction of a school, as well as for repairs, fuel, and "appendages." School trustees were authorized to hire, fire, and pay teachers. The towns' school commissioners were to examine and approve the teachers so chosen and visit them periodically.

Town or state funds covered only a small portion of the teachers' salaries, however. Parents of the students were charged "rate bills" or tuition payments, which proved to be an incentive for lower-income families to keep their children out of school. Keeping children at home also reduced the obligation to share in the cost of boarding the teachers, who stayed by turns with a number of different families. District families were also sometimes assessed the cost of the firewood for heating the schools. Because of low attendance, the state steadily increased the publicly funded portion of the costs of running the schools. Initially, men were hired to teach the older children for the winter sessions; women were hired to teach the younger children, at a lower wage, for the summer sessions. Most of the men and women were in their early twenties, and school district trustees fairly often found them to be poorly trained and incompetent. Low wages and youth led to high turnover. By the 1820s the New York legislature moved to provide teacher training by designating and financially assisting particular academies, requiring them to provide teacher training courses and subsidizing them in that effort.[63]

In Sugar Creek, a rural neighborhood on the edge of the prairies in Illinois, the most reliable support for education before the institution of a state mandated system in 1855 came from parent subscriptions, often in the form of produce. A prospective teacher went from household to household circulating a "subscription paper." Parents wrote down the number of students they wished to enroll for a set fee for a three-month period. Under the provisions of the Land Ordinance of 1787 (by which the Northwest Territory was settled), the proceeds from the sale of a section of each township surveyed had to be used for educational purposes, and the Illinois constitution of 1818 required citizens to form their own school trustee committees and to lease the school lands, using the income from the investment of the proceeds to support public education. These local education funds supplemented the subscription fees charged to parents. The system discriminated against settlers too poor to pay subscriptions and forced some children to walk for great distances.

The schoolhouse in Sugar Creek was also the meetinghouse and became a center of neighborhood activity, not only the place for children in class but for adults in political meetings or court sessions, even for congregants in religious services. For educational purposes the building was a one-room schoolhouse which included boys and girls as young as five and six and as old as young men. Teachers emphasized memorization and recitation. Students learned their lessons by rote, repeating them aloud to older classmates ("monitors"), so that one schoolmaster could deal with scores of students of widely different levels and abilities. Teachers typically had problems in disciplining such a motley group. Big boys often "turned out" the teacher at Christmas, locking him out of the schoolhouse, coatless and shivering, until he treated all to whiskey and sweets. In retaliation, teachers resorted to the use of the "rod" for discipline.[64]

Similarly, the town of Jacksonville, Illinois, relied on ad hoc subscription schools, and hired as teachers itinerant young men temporarily willing to instruct the young. Even so, some of the earliest settlers of Jacksonville wanted the town to become an educational center and so founded Illinois College, which they hoped would train teachers as soon as an adequate school system existed. Beginning in 1849 a series of state laws allowed towns to receive state educational funds and to levy their own school taxes. In 1850 Jacksonville organized its first graded public school in the Masonic Hall, and during the 1850s and 1860s several schoolhouses were constructed around town.

Reports in these years by county and state education commissioners repeatedly emphasized the benefits of graded schooling, which recognized different levels of learning among children of different ages and abilities. Reformers emphasized the importance of discipline and moral behavior among children, and by the late 1860s elaborate rules were introduced to regulate students' punctuality, absenteeism, and social behavior. Free graded public schools open to everyone were also supported as the way to prevent society from dividing into two classes and as a vehicle for socializing the children of foreign immigrants. But the Lutherans in town founded their own German-speaking school (which remained quite small), and in the 1860s Jacksonville's black population founded a publicly funded but separate school.[65]

In Wisconsin, in the towns of Trempealeau County, several levels of government addressed public education in the 1860s and 1870s, but primary responsibility lay with the local district boards, which built, equipped, and staffed their schools. The state granted aid after 1871 and loaned money for schoolhouse construction. The county board of education levied a school tax to match the state's grant-in-aid and supervised the work of the county superintendent of schools. Schoolhouses were often unattractive, physically uncomfortable, poorly planned, badly heated, inadequately equipped, and overcrowded, as taxpayers frequently complained about the cost of such a building. Teachers' salaries were low, turnover was high, and teacher training was still a novelty—"normal schools" for teacher education were inaugurated during these very years. County commissioners, responsible for the licensing of teachers, often refused to grant licenses to applicants.

"Galesville University" was the county's initial secondary school. It had an open admissions policy and was coeducational, a good example of the move late in the century across the continent toward a free, public secondary school system. For adult education, Trempealeau County had newspapers, a lyceum, and literary societies. The Galesville lyceum was well attended and provided a wide variety of programs but was eventually overshadowed by the literary societies at the "university" (the secondary school), whose "assemblies" were open to everyone.[66]

In the cattle towns in Kansas, early education took the usual form of temporary housing, untrained teachers, overcrowding, and badly maintained buildings. Early schools had no restrictions on age or attendance; both schools and parents sometimes ignored the state compulsory attendance laws (in Kansas, dating from 1874). The movement, in Kansas as elsewhere, toward compulsory attendance and the grading of students was hotly contested in the cattle towns, for such innovations involved more teachers, more money, and more school buildings. Local governments in the cattle towns capitulated only after strong public pressure, painfully apparent overcrowding, and the perceived benefits to local businesses from the needed construction.

School costs thereupon became the single greatest item in the local governments' budgets. Teachers had to be certified by appropriate state or county boards. County superintendents were required to hold a teachers' institute each year, at which certified teachers received formal instruction by faculty members of normal schools, who emphasized both content and methods and who administered exams that the teachers must pass before resuming their duties.[67]

The cattle towns were also active centers for adult educational activities. Literary societies were important organizations, formally constituted with constitutions, bylaws, and officers. Meetings consisted of recitations of various kinds: declamations, poems, essays, excerpts, plays, charades, with the main event a debate of a serious or humorous subject. A variation on the literary society was the library club, whose members were devoted to making books available either for a fee or for free. Such groups held benefits to raise money. Public libraries, on the other hand, generally lacked public support. Adult "spelling bees" were quite popular and took the form of team contests or "spell downs," individual competitions. The judges came equipped with unabridged dictionaries. Winners were given prizes in these church-sponsored social events, which reduced intellectual endeavor to correct spelling.[68]

In the late nineteenth century, schools in rural settings continued to be quite primitive. In the Rocky Mountains of Wyoming, schoolhouses were often log buildings, their walls covered with muslin and burlap. Schools were frequently moved to accommodate shifts in population. Teachers even did janitorial work—making curtains and sweeping floors with an oil and sawdust compound. If the school was without a nearby spring, students brought their own water in jars. If there was a spring, water was kept in a bucket. Ranchers' wives often served as teachers, and their teaching was done along with housework.[69]

In rural neighborhoods everywhere on the continent, schools continued to be important community centers. In Wyoming, schools typically functioned as places for leisure activity. Often a school was the first public building in an area and, as such, a natural setting for community meetings. Initially the teacher was sometimes the only paid public official and became for a time the unofficial director of his school district's affairs. Schools often preceded churches, and church services were sometimes held in them. Cattlemen associations, unions, local granges, the Red Cross, women's clubs, even water boards also met in the schools.

Rose Wilder Lane recalled that the schoolhouse in her town in the late nineteenth century was "two storied, with unshaded windows regularly spaced on all sides . . . it rose gaunt above an irregular space of trodden earth on which not a spear of grass survived. Its height was increased and seemed unbalanced by the cupola . . . rising from the eaves of the door. A large bell hung there, and when the Principal pulled the rope in the entry below, that bell clanged an iron imperative over the town. It was the voice of a place austerely devoted to toil, permitting no frivolity and righteously crushing any impulse toward merriment or play.

"In school hours, whispering, fidgeting or a moment's idleness were crimes. Release from book and desk was granted only to urgent need properly expressed. The water and dipper were on a bench by the door. The dictionary lay on its stand in a corner. In bright and lawless outdoors, the privies stood behind the schoolhouse, girls' and boys' separated by a short length of tight board fence and the whole overlooked by the schoolroom windows.

"Unsupervised play was unthought of, but play was strictly supervised. An indecorous outburst of energy in the schoolyard at recess was promptly stopped by a teacher's rapping on a window, or The Principal himself descended on the culprits. No pupil talked back to The Principal, nor indeed to any lesser teacher. Teachers were always right; there was no argument. A whipping at school meant that any proper father would administer a second sound thrashing at home."[70]

Schools were located in the centers of their districts, in order to equalize travel distances for students. This centralized location made the school a logical site for voting and for use as a town hall, a church, and a social center. Schools held card parties and a variety of other social functions to raise funds for schoolbooks and equipment. The schools put on Christmas programs, an event that was the highlight of the year at the schoolhouse. But there were also spelling bees, arithmetic contests, and debates. Graduation was a day-long event planned by the teacher, replete with a picnic and ceremonies. Dances for adults were also sometimes organized by teachers and were usually well attended in isolated rural areas. Teaching was a respectable job for women, who were attracted to a male-dominated area and in fact were often boarded on ranches, where ranchers and cowboys sought them out. School boards often added clauses to teachers' contracts forbidding them from marrying during the school year.[71]

Similarly, in rural Missouri at the turn of the century, schools served as community centers, with "literaries" on Friday evenings the most popular and common social event. People arrived by every available means of transportation. There was no admission charge or fund-raising; the prime purpose was entertainment and education. Debating was highly popular and covered a great range of subjects. "Kangaroo courts" brought a "defendant" to trial for an infraction of an imaginary law. The charge was based upon a defendant's real action but took the form of the antithesis of his act. (Thus if he contributed to charity, he was charged with robbery.) A fine was the usual punishment. Literaries also included spelling bees, ciphering matches (with contestants solving mathematical problems on a blackboard), and declamatory and dramatic programs.

A second major social use of the schools in rural Missouri was their "closing-of-school" program, an event for the whole community. The program had two parts. One was a display of the students ranked as to their ability. The second was a literary type of entertainment: recitations, dialogues, playets, declamations, music. The parents (or "patrons") usually made remarks and brought out picnic baskets at lunch time.[72]

Through the century, in established towns at least, schools became graded and used only for educational and attendant social purposes; that is, they ceased being general community centers, places for religious or political meetings. Teacher training became as standardized as the system of primary and secondary schools that also emerged during the century. By the end of the nineteenth century even the "boarding" system, whereby teachers "boarded around" in the homes of parents on a rotating basis, was gradually changing.

Teachers found that boarding afforded them little space to study, no room for guests, inadequate sleeping quarters, and poor meals. Hosts found it a financial burden to board teachers, and the teacher's presence brought a lack of privacy. Enid Bern remembered that in the early twentieth century, "as a rule, we teachers were held in high esteem and respected by the people of the area in which we worked, but on the other hand, we lived the proverbial life of a goldfish and were in a sense at the mercy of the whims of the community."[73] By the 1890s professional educators proposed that there be "teacherages" (the counterpart of ministers' parsonages), buildings for teachers and administrators located near the school. Stock companies or investment clubs were formed to finance them. When buildings were finished, rentals to teachers (in the form of payroll deductions) paid the interest on the construction loans. Sinking funds were created so that the buildings could later be given to school districts. By 1900 newer, more consolidated schools often included a teacherage, favored by school officials because it gave teachers dignity and independence and provided the district a social and visiting center. By the early 1920s there were three thousand teacherages in the United States, most of them in the remotest rural areas, in the Southern and Western plains.[74]

Among the groups who founded special towns during the nineteenth century, inhabitants of black towns developed mixes of educational institutions similar to those of their white counterparts. Mound Bayou, Mississippi, had a public school and a Baptist College, but it also boasted the Mound Bayou Normal and Industrial Institute, which the Baptist Women Workers Union found in response to Booker T. Washington's challenge that blacks must above all concentrate on gaining practical, industrial, and agricultural skills. Langston City, Oklahoma, became the educational center among black towns of that state when its school board established a public school and a boarding high school but also persuaded the territorial government to provide an annual allocation as well as an initial subsidy of free land to establish the Colored Agricultural and Normal School.[75] In rural Wisconsin, black and white settlers together built a completely integrated school on land donated by a white man.[76]

In the twentieth century, public educational systems involving both primary and secondary schools became universal in towns throughout the continent. The more intellectually gifted town dwellers also had access to a vast number of colleges and universities. Typically these schools involved the students' movement to other places, though a significant number of institutions were located in towns that became known as "college towns," where the college or university came to dominate the town in which it was located.

Education and the schools were deeply affected by the greater scale of all aspects of life. Most dramatically, schools physically consolidated. Their administrators responded to the greater speed and distance that motorized transport made possible and enlarged the catchment area of students for their consolidated operations. By the 1920s motorized school transport was widespread, and consolidation became common. District schools in the towns and in their surrounding countryside amalgamated, making them more efficient and bringing together students from town and country. Town dwellers and their rural neighbors sometimes resisted but never stopped consolidation, fearing the loss of neighborhood control to more distant authorities. In fact, state and federal educational authorities did gain greater control over the structure of what continued to be locally managed public school systems.[77]

In "Plainville," in the Midwest, consolidation began around 1920. Schools in the surrounding countryside were voted into the Plainville consolidated school system one by one after much resistance and divisiveness. Some mourned the loss of their neighborhood school and blamed consolidation for destroying the old neighborhood life. Others welcomed the modernizing aspects of consolidation that raised the level of education, dispelled the geographic isolation in which farm children had lived, and leveled social differences between town dwellers and those who lived in the countryside.[78] By the 1960s in Benson, Minnesota, with the exception of twelve ungraded rural schools scattered in the countryside and smaller villages close by, scores of one-room schools that had once dotted that countryside had closed, their students sent on to the consolidated schools of Benson.[79]

Adults found that even library services became consolidated. By the 1920s cars and buses allowed town dwellers to visit larger centers with greater libraries, but they also allowed librarians from more substantial towns to visit small villages and the open countryside regularly, bringing with them in their bookmobiles or bookwagons entire collections of magazines and books, vastly extending the reading material available to rural readers who had been used to relying on deposit stations or extension libraries (sparse bookshelves situated in country stores, post offices, toll gates, churches, or even private homes).[80]

Schoolteachers became unionized during the twentieth century, and their labor contracts brought them long-term employment. But this was a gradual development, and until at least mid-century, in more rural areas, teachers still had to have their contracts renewed annually, were forbidden to smoke or drink or marry, and were advised to stay in town over weekends and teach Sunday school classes. Teacher training came to be universal and increasingly standardized, however, and district school boards no longer had the task of dismissing untrained teachers or paying to have them trained.

Schoolbooks and teaching (which came increasingly to involve discussions, readings, and the writing of papers as much as rote and memorization through the recitation method) still inculcated moral values as well as mental skills. But the Christian-centered moralizing of the Webster and McGuffey readers gave way to the nonspecific, humanistic focus of such modern series as those provided by Scott, Foresman publishers, which educational authorities deemed more appropriate to a multi-ethnic, multi-racial, religiously varied population. Emphasized moral values were still recognizably Christian, even with the nondenominational or neutral language that characterized the modern readers. Education came under the influence of the "progressive" view, that school should be a full-scale preparation for life. The subjects that teachers offered students grew increasingly varied and more specialized, so that students might mature mentally, physically, and socially as well as become literate and numerate.

Schools also became much more complete social centers as extra-curricular activity rivaled academic subjects in educational importance. Organized recreation and athletic teams as well as a great variety of musical, theatrical, cinematic, artistic, literary, and journalism clubs greatly extended student life beyond the narrowly academic, as did social events such as dances and proms. At graduation ceremonies, achievement continued to be recognized in the midst of a strong communal and social emphasis, with the announcement of prizes and the speechmaking of valedictorians and salutatorians.[81]

Thus the schools, which during the seventeenth and eighteenth centuries had emerged in various forms to supplement the education of children by the family, became, over the course of the nineteenth and twentieth centuries, increasingly organized as parts of a universal public education system. By the late twentieth century that system, though still locally managed, was more standardized by state and federal authorities. While the public system has always coexisted with a great many private educational institutions, schools of all sorts have steadily usurped the educative role of the family. Local school districts, long a focus of neighborhood activity in the towns, were often consolidated in the twentieth century, when motorized transportation rendered the older, closely spaced schools obsolete.

## · III ·

AMONG THE NATIVE tribes on the North American continent in the seventeenth and eighteenth centuries, art was thoroughly spiritual in character. The artistic creations of the indigenous people were indivisible from their religious life. Such creations were themselves sacred in character and were filled with religious symbolism. This was as true of the ways the tribes decorated their temples, lodges, houses, tools, and clothes as it was as of their rituals and ceremonies.[82]

By contrast, the largely Protestant colonists who settled in North America during these centuries evidenced little connection between religious faith and artistic activity. Their faith was a simplified Christianity, shorn of most of the festivals and pageantry that marked the lives of Catholic Christians throughout Europe and beyond, in the overseas colonies of Spain, Portugal, and France. Arts in the English colonial towns thus lacked a religious foundation. Indeed, many of the dissenting and pietistic sects stressed plain living and opposed theatre, music, dance, and art, especially if it seemed in any sense immoral.

The most sophisticated forms of art in England, in London, were patronized by a court society. The colonial population did not include an equivalent elite who could serve as patrons, except for the merchants who clustered in the port cities, and their efforts to develop a cultural life of the kind that flourished in London were quite faltering. The "provincial" culture of the colonies lacked the infrastructure (the theatres and museums and halls and associations) that had developed in the more permissive atmosphere of an aristocratic culture that flourished under a tolerant Church of England.

Colonial town dwellers generally did not encourage artistic activity. Not only was there opposition on religious grounds, but work and leisure were not two distinct spheres of life for a population whose work life was so extensive that even socializing was blended with group tasks such as barn or house raising, corn husking, and quilt-making. Even the planters, though they dominated their embryonic plantation communities in the colonial countryside, had as their model not the court but the "provincial" English gentry. The only art forms that were popular and public were directly connected to the observance of religious faith: music and verbal recitations. Protestant congregations sang hymns at church services and recited passages from the Bible and prayers from the various liturgies that the denominations prescribed for their congregants.

Not until the nineteenth century did town dwellers gradually become more comfortable with artistic activity. But this was a slow, sporadic development. Protestant churches remained divided among themselves as to which forms of art and entertainment were morally correct. The more evangelically oriented sects—the Baptists and Methodists—remained opposed to theatrical, literary, or artistic activity that portrayed immoral behavior, and to musical events that included dancing. But other denominations tolerated artistic activity and indeed sometimes sponsored local or traveling groups.

The acceptance of artistic activity was aided by the ever more common division between work and leisure, as craft work gave way to industrial wage labor. Work "bees" gradually declined as an in-town activity during the century, though they continued to be important activities in the countryside. To town dwellers, art and entertainment came increasingly to be seen as leisure-time activities. But this did not mean that art was considered important to the life of the community or that artists ought to be highly rewarded or regarded. To many men in the towns, art was a "sissified" activity, one not fit for a true man, something women might safely attempt. Those who sought to live as artists, especially if they were men, often left the towns and moved to urban centers, which by the nineteenth century had developed the beginnings of a cultural infrastructure.

Art for town dwellers was popular art, not sophisticated, and though the construction of "opera houses" during the mid- and late nineteenth century indicated that towns were becoming more tolerant of artistic activity, it was art as entertainment that interested them. The traveling troupes of actors, musicians, artists, and readers that town dwellers invited to these catch-all entertainment halls were meant to entertain them and to avoid immorality as they were doing it.[83] Alma W. Swinton remembered the opera house in Hartford, Michigan, as a "huge barn of a structure," unkempt without, and painted a "hideous light blue" within.[84] By contrast, Willa Cather thought that the operas and dramatic productions presented at her home town's opera house gave her unforgettable experiences as a child. Live theatre, she believed, had a greater impact than books and paintings and movies on a child because theatre presented a story that was literally alive on the stage.[85] Town dwellers also sought to participate in the more popular, acceptable forms of artistic activity: they wanted to draw, paint, sculpt, sing, play musical instruments, dance, and act, and not just witness performing professionals. The result was a profusion of local organizations whose members were involved in the whole panoply of artistic activity.

The balance between relying on traveling professionals and banding together as local amateur groups varied according to the art form. Town dwellers were reluctant to hire architects to design new homes or buildings, and, throughout the century it remained typical that carpenters' handbooks and builders' manuals were used as the basis for construction. Only those who were prominent came to favor architecturally styled homes as a proper indication of their status.

Sculptors and painters received little encouragement from the inhabitants of towns. Statues of notable public figures were a common sight in the courthouse squares of county seats, but elsewhere in the towns art and sculpture were rarities. As the century wore on, prosperous families extended the visual signs of status to death itself, erecting elaborate gravestones in the family plots of town cemeteries. Very few town dwellers had the wealth or status to have portraits painted in oil, especially when, after mid-century, a local photographer could provide a satisfactory visual substitute. Starting fairly early in the century, the mass production of prints (lithographs) went far to satisfy a widespread fondness for pictures, that is, for visual depictions of various aspects of human life and the natural world around it. Painters seeking popularity and wealth had to do something striking to win the attention of the public. Itinerant artists rose to the challenge and often brought to the towns enormous "panoramas" several hundred feet in length. The scenes portrayed on these panoramas, usually of some spectacular spot somewhere on the continent, were unrolled panel by panel as the bases of illustrated lectures. These nomadic folk painters and lecturers turned art into geographical newsreels.[86]

Music was a far more popular artistic activity in the towns during the nineteenth century. Although town dwellers sometimes flocked to hear and see professional traveling musicians at local entertainment centers (usually singing and playing the more popular forms of music), their own local musical life was rich and varied. Christopher S. Crary remembered that in early-nineteenth-century Kirtland, Ohio, singing "was the one great source of pleasure and enjoyment."[87] Protestants still sang hymns at church services, but church choirs also became common, a recognition that services were improved with the presence of a trained or serious group of singers to augment the efforts of ordinary parishioners. Musical societies sprouted in every substantial town, and music was played at virtually all social activities. Except for the male singing masters who wandered from town to town, women and amateurs (people whose occupation was of a more "serious" kind) dominated the musical life of towns.

Local amateur orchestras furnished music for dancing parties, just as fiddlers and guitarists did for country square dances or "hoedowns." The local "band" (or outdoor orchestra) outranked all other musical organizations in popularity. The band in Burns Fuller's Fenton, Michigan, was composed of "good, well known, substantial citizens, interested in the worthy use of their leisure time."[88] Like volunteer fire departments and baseball teams, bands represented their towns in musical competitions with other towns. Bands were also fixtures at all manner of celebrations and commemorations and annual events. In their range of appearances, they furnished music for rallies, announcements, speeches, and parades; serenaded departing or returning residents on holiday excursions; performed at funeral services and athletic events; and even accompanied traveling artists who were performing in town. By the 1870s weekly concerts at local bandstands were popular. But even though the band was the most popular of all the musical organizations in towns during the nineteenth century, even though its brilliant uniforms, flashing instruments, and military movements created town pride and spirit, it was likely to be precariously financed, for voters balked when town governments tried to provide funding. Bands relied almost wholly on what they could earn at paid performances, and they were fortunate when they received enough to cover the costs of out-of-town trips. Members often had to pay for their own instruments and uniforms. Nothing more dramatically indicates the prevailing view of town dwellers on the importance of the arts: even the

BANDS. Bands were the most popular of all local cultural activities, and most towns had several. The larger and more trained ones, representing their towns, sometimes competed with other bands from other towns in parades and at other public events. Top, a small band from White Pine, Colorado. Below, a large band from Canal Fulton, Ohio. [Top, State Historical Society of Colorado; below, Massillon Museum]

most popular of all artistic organizations, the community's own band, had to struggle without public financial support.

Music was also a family-centered domestic activity. Musically trained members of families, sometimes with neighborhood friends, played and sang in the parlors of the more impressive homes in town. Musical instruments were prized possessions, and it was important for town dwellers to pass on their musical skills to their children. Sheet music and musical instruments were enormously popular and widely advertised; by mid-century one could find a constant supply of new songs composed by song writers—most of them melodramatic and sentimental in their treatment of ordinary lives.[89]

Through most of the nineteenth century, dancing was the most ubiquitous of all forms of entertainment, though it did not include ballet. While there were no professional traveling dance companies, dance in its popular forms was omnipresent. Young people, especially, patronized dance instructors. National magazines made dance fads and dancing costume fashions showcases for elegance and self-expression. Still, throughout the century dance was opposed as immoral by the evangelical denominations, so its popularity was always contested. Many of the Protestant churches crusaded against public dancing in the kinds of urban dance halls and saloons that hired young women to dance with men, in some cases as prostitutes as well as dancing partners.

But social dancing, public and private, was part of the lives of respectable people. Big, formal dances, elaborate in decoration, were associated with groups such as the volunteer firemen or the lodges, resplendent in their uniforms. At masquerade balls, participants displayed a range of impersonations. Private dances for elite groups featured a hired orchestra of three to five musicians. Dance clubs met in private homes or in rented facilities, with late-night dancing, sometimes including novelty features, such as the requirement that dancers wear a particular article of clothing, or themes, such as holiday dances or moonlight parties on a platform in the countryside outside of town. Quadrilles, waltzes, polkas, gallops, and reels—all were popular at one time or another, as were square dances for town dwellers and their rural neighbors.[90]

Theatre in the towns was balanced between traveling professional troupes who performed at local entertainment halls, usually for a week at a time, and the performances of local amateur groups, who presented their plays at the same halls or in churches, schools, or lodges. Both churches and schools organized skits, theatrical programs, and tableaux to build interest in drama among town dwellers, either as participants or as the audience. Those

THEATRE. As the hostility of the Protestant churches waned during the nineteenth century, local groups of artists of various kinds emerged, including actors. The theatre shown here, in Canandaigua, New York, was in fact a church. But notice the sign at upper left which indicates that this group is presenting the "cleanest show." [International Museum of Photography, George Eastman House]

who attended the productions of the local dramatic clubs could be lavish with their praise, quite stern in their disapproval of moral improprieties contained in any play, and quite critical of poor performances. The Protestant churches were divided (in the usual manner) in their attitudes toward theatre, and townspeople commonly considered professional actors as suspicious characters of questionable morals and untrustworthy habits. Yet professionals provided a measure of ability for the town dwellers who attended their performances, and this measure helped the same people appraise amateur productions.

The plays of both professional and amateur groups had to be morally proper to be acceptable to these audiences. The most favored plays were those with strong action and noble dialogue, with plots containing sympathetic characters threatened by villains. The audience was expected to hate the nasty characters and fear for the well-being of the good ones. Villains were punished and good people were rewarded. Minor characters brought comic relief. Female leads were the most popular. Christian virtues were stressed, restricting the language, behavior, and choice of subject. Thus did popular art reinforce prevailing morality and become a vehicle for buttressing virtue.[91]

Recitations and readings of well-known poetry or fiction and speeches on subjects of current interest were popular forms of verbal art in nineteenth-century towns. The emphasis given to the spoken word indicated a rather weaker interest in the printed word. Private and public libraries became a standard feature of the towns' cultural life during the century, however, and every substantial town had a variety of literary societies, reading clubs, and debating teams.[92]

The towns themselves typically provided the setting for nineteenth-century fiction. The most popular form of fictional writing, as was the case in drama and song, was melodramatic and sentimental and was usually the product of women writers who grew up in the towns. Harriet Beecher Stowe (*Oldtown Folks*, 1869), Sarah Orne Jewett (*Deephaven*, 1877), Rose Terry Cooke (*Somebody's Neighbors*, 1881, and *Root-bound and Other Sketches*, 1885), and Alice Brown (*Meadow Grass*, 1895, and *Tiverton Tales*, 1899) were all New England authors who wrote stories sympathetic to the towns, which were portrayed as places of pleasant intimacy and secure retreat.[93]

The technological developments that transformed communications and transportation during the twentieth century had a profound effect on the way town dwellers experienced artistic activity. Radio, beginning in the 1920s, and television, beginning in the 1950s, brought art and entertainment directly into the homes of those who lived in the towns, everything from the highest forms of the arts to the most popular kinds of entertainment. Phonograph records, compact discs, video and audio tapes, and the Internet all extended the penetration of art and entertainment into domestic space. The effect of such technologically generated artistic activity was to greatly diminish the incentive for individuals and families to develop their own artistic talents, to play or sing their own music, to do their own dancing, to draw and paint and sculpt and act. Ordinary town dwellers were far more apt to be the audience for art and entertainment in their own homes than they were to learn to be their own artists and to entertain themselves.

As might be expected, this shift was accompanied by a sharp decline in the number and variety of local organizations whose members engaged in artistic activity and entertainment. Home technology vied with traveling arts and entertainment groups, not in the towns but in the nearest urban centers, where a motorized public was able to gather. Traveling artists and entertainers toured the cities, confident they could draw on a public spread through a large hinterland (including town dwellers) who could attend via motor or rail transportation.

In the course of the century, town dwellers lost control over the content of the art and entertainment to which they, like everyone else, had relatively easy access. The moral restrictions on artistic endeavors in the nineteenth century gave way to looser media "codes" and judicially interpreted "community standards"—which meant the standards of an increasingly urbanized and heterogeneous society, not local town societies dominated by Protestant Christians.

The catch-all entertainment centers (or "opera houses") of the nineteenth century fell into disuse as traveling arts and entertainment groups confined their tours to urban centers. Only two standard conduits for the dissemination of culture in the towns remained. One was the public library, which continued to provide the most popular books for the local reading public, and which enhanced its access to the world of publications with the development of interlibrary loan systems. The other was the movie house. Until the development of television in the 1950s, films were shown not privately in homes but publicly in movie theatres—the only art and entertainment form that town dwellers still experienced collectively, in their own communities, in public places. As such, movie theatres were the descendants of the "opera houses" of yore. Feature films were not a new art with respect to their content. They conveyed visually the same kinds of stories that written fiction and theatrical drama had. But the stories were conveyed via a new technology, one that kept moviegoing, if not the other arts, a public activity.

Movies evolved from travelog slide shows and itinerant theatrical presentations. They were preceded by nickelodeon exhibitors who packaged programs in redecorated store buildings or in semi-abandoned "opera houses" and offered viewers educational and uplifting film subjects: scenic panoramas, depictions of industrial and manufacturing processes, informative newsreels, biblical imagery, and historical tableaux. Moviemakers went on, by the 1910s, to the making of "feature films," which were dramatic rather than informational productions. The more substantial towns converted old "opera houses" or built new theatres for a rapidly growing local audience. In a reaction reminiscent of the nineteenth century, conservative religious groups objected to the showing of worldly films and sometimes presented sanitized movies in their own churches rather than totally oppose this new form of art and entertainment.[94] But with the mass ownership of automobiles and access to bus lines, town dwellers gradually abandoned their local movie theatres and traveled to those located in nearby urban centers, where they were able to choose from a much greater range of films.

Public recitations and readings of published poems and stories declined dramatically during the twentieth century, replaced to some extent by the dramatic productions on network radio and television. In the 1940s published stories became available in relatively inexpensive paperback editions. For town dwellers who read fiction, their own communities—the towns themselves—continued to provide the typical setting for that fiction, at least until the 1930s, after which an increasing majority of people across the continent lived in urban, not rural, communities.[95]

During the early twentieth century, the towns continued to be portrayed positively in novels and stories, but some writers questioned the values of the small local communities they had grown up in but had left. William Allen White, as a newspaper editor in Emporia, Kansas, from the 1890s to the 1930s, became the most widely read journalistic spokesman for the towns anywhere in the country. He was also a popular novelist who portrayed the towns as comforting havens for a troubled, increasingly urbanized American people who could be regenerated through contact with the towns, where life was stable, values were traditional and sound, and people were fundamentally good.[96] Similarly, Booth Tarkington, in *The Gentleman from Indiana* (1900), described the people of Plattville, Indiana, as "one big, jolly family," a place where everybody belonged. Zona Gale, in *Friendship Village* (1908) and *Friendship Village Love Stories* (1909), celebrated the "togetherness" of the towns.[97]

But other writers of fiction, usually men who had left their towns, took a more sober, less sentimental and melodramatic view of town life. In Willa Cather's *O Pioneers!* (1913), Edgar Lee Masters's *Spoon River Anthology* (1915), Hamlin Garland's *A Son of the Middle Border* (1917), Sherwood Anderson's *Winesburg, Ohio* (1919), and Sinclair Lewis's *Main Street* (1920) and *Babbitt* (1922), the town shifts from a symbol of innocence to one of crassness, ugly materialism, cultural aridity, and mindless conformity. For these authors, town dwellers who were sensitive or creative or artistic had to live "buried lives." Or, if they escaped, as Thomas Wolfe wrote in the 1930s, such individuals wandered the earth, ever marked by their upbringing in the towns but filled with longing, anguish, or wild and despairing searches for meanings that would take them beyond their roots.[98]

After the 1930s, writers of fiction turned increasingly to urban settings. Town dwellers who read fiction gradually had to accustom themselves to accounts of urban life, the kind of community setting where most people actually lived. No longer could they commonly find fictional portrayals of their own communities. No longer were there significant numbers of storytellers who conveyed the nature of life in the towns. No longer were the towns the primary local community for most of the population across the North American continent.[99] Town dwellers experienced fiction the way they did all the other arts: through an urban sensibility, over radio and television and through attendance at itinerant performances and exhibitions in nearby urban centers.

## · IV ·

NATIVE TRIBAL LIFE was marked by seasonal rituals. Among the European colonists who settled in the Americas from the sixteenth through the eighteenth centuries, the Catholic settlers from Spain, Portugal, and France also celebrated annual rituals, or festivals, based upon a calendar of saints' days that had been developed by the Catholic church. The English Protestant settlers, by contrast, were confined to fast and penitence days sporadically declared by their ministers at times of calamity or of important community events. Whether Catholic or Protestant, such commemorations were special occasions when town dwellers were asked to mark a time of religious significance, something larger than their mundane lives.

Not until the nineteenth century, with the growing separation between work and leisure, did town dwellers across the North American continent develop commemorations in the form of holidays on fixed dates during the calendar year. These holidays continued to mark days of religious significance but also of secular, national significance as well. Christmas and Easter became major Christian celebrations, but so did the Fourth of July and Memorial Day emerge as great national holidays.

Christmas became the climax of a small holiday season. Local schools were dismissed for as long as a week. College and university students and distant relatives arrived at home to spend a vacation with their families. Schoolchildren learned songs and recitations for their Christmas programs. Churches featured decorated trees and held special Christmas services. Christmas was also a family celebration, and homes were decorated as well. Gift-giving and St. Nicholas (transformed into Santa Claus) also received growing attention. For Easter, women in the towns grew flowers with which to decorate the churches. Easter church services were combined with special music and new dresses and hats for the women parishioners. Special sunrise services were usually held in groves. Children dyed Easter eggs or joined egg hunts.

Other holidays were Christian in origin but turned secular in character. St. Valentine's Day became the day to celebrate love, and many towns sponsored dances while individuals sent greeting cards that were sentimental or humorous. All Hallow's Eve was marked by pageants and awards sponsored by service clubs for those in ghoulish costumes; but youths also engaged in vandalism and pranks. Thanksgiving, a church-initiated celebration, was set in the fall, at harvest time, with special church services, but it also became a major family feast day. New Year's Day, at the beginning of the Christian calendar, became a time of celebration—parties and drinking for less respectable town dwellers, dinners or oyster suppers or New Year's Eve "watch" parties at the churches for more respectable elements. Some town governments sponsored public receptions on the New Year. Many lodges sponsored dances. Individuals sometimes presented cards at the front door, stayed for a brief visit, and were served refreshments.

Still other holidays were completely secular in origin and involved the commemoration and celebration of the nation. The Fourth of July was observed with public prayers, readings of the Declaration of Independence, patriotic speeches by an "orator of the day," public dinners at which officials drank patriotic toasts, and, throughout the century, increasingly elaborate forms of entertainment and recreation, buttressed by gun salutes and fireworks. Fourth of July celebrations could go awry, as C. W. Goodlander recalled from his boyhood in mid-nineteenth-century Fort Scott, Kansas: "Just as the procession moved, by accident or otherwise, our fireworks caught fire and it was fun to see how the procession broke ranks and scattered in all directions to evade sky-rockets, Roman candles, whirligigs and serpents that were charging in all directions."[100]

The nation was made sacred through such ritualistic celebration, just as religious holidays replenished faith in God. Townspeople bonded with their nation by this annual rite, commemorating not God but the nation. In other secular holidays with a national focus, Civil War veterans associations started Memorial Day, in the late spring, to honor the nation's war dead, with ceremonies usually involving the decoration of the graves of those who gave their lives in the nation's wars; Washington's Birthday, honoring the nation's first president, was marked with parades, speeches, and dances.[101]

As these holidays became widely celebrated in towns across the conti-

HOLIDAYS. Among the national and secular holidays, none called forth a greater variety of celebrations than the Fourth of July. Here girls in an orphanage in Cooperstown, New York, literally wrap the flag around themselves. [New York State Historical Society]

nent, they were made legal by the federal or state governments and increasingly became nonwork days in wage contracts. During the course of the twentieth century, holidays came more to resemble rest days than days of celebration and commemoration. They also became linked to special forms of commerce, as celebrants at home or at public events were encouraged to buy Christmas gifts, Easter clothing, Halloween costumes, Thanksgiving food, New Year's alcoholic beverages, and Fourth of July trinketry. In the process, the connection between these annual holidays and their original, transcendent religious or secular purposes gradually weakened. Public ceremonies that concentrated on the meaning of these special occasions receded as they became opportunities for private leisure or recreation.

Town dwellers commemorated more than their nation and their God, however. By the early nineteenth century they also began to celebrate themselves, their own communities. The Puritans who founded the early New England towns believed they were establishing very special communities, with a transcendent purpose. Their descendants in the earliest towns began to write "histories" of what had become, by the 1820s and 1830s, communities that were nearly two hundred years old. As towns aged elsewhere on the East Coast, others, though more sporadically, wrote histories. By mid-century, still others scattered through the Midwest, the South, the Rocky Mountains, and the Pacific coast wrote histories of towns that were not even very old—a clear reflection of the growing strength of the antiquarian impulse to record the past. By the late nineteenth century, local history was reduced to a kind of formula, and publishers (most of them in Chicago) hired "hack writers" for historical sketches of towns and counties.

These amateur local histories (except for the formulaic ones) were usually written by scions of old and prominent families who appealed to other similarly situated town dwellers for historical materials and financial support. The histories were routinely published by subscription and were supported by those of the "core" population who identified strongly with "their" community and sought to apply gloss to their own position in accounts of their town's history, in which their families had played a prominent role. Those who subscribed typically were also commemorated by the inclusion of a biographical sketch, in a large section following the "history." When publishers later in the century organized local histories to a set formula, they sent salesmen with biographical sketch forms to be filled in by subscribers who agreed to buy the promised history. When published, the historical sketches were followed by large sections of biographical profiles of current-day supporters who sought to enshrine their prominence as part of their town's "history." Atlases of the towns, in published or cadastre (or wall) form, typically were surrounded by illustrations of the houses or businesses of prominent subscribers.

Amateur local histories were chiefly listings of information culled from surviving documents. Most of their authors lacked the capacity to create coherent narratives; they were more interested in information about their ancestors than they were in crafting the story of an enduring community. That the town had in fact survived seemed enough. Many of the antiquarians had founded the local historical society and became passionate to preserve evidence pertaining to the town and its core families.

Many, though far from all, of the amateur local histories were published—sometimes under the sponsorship of a town's government—on centennial or bicentennial anniversaries—by the twentieth century, even tricentennial. In some towns, official celebrations marked such dates; in others, the local historical society sponsored annual days marking the town's existence. These celebrations were sometimes daylong affairs with as much variety as Fourth of July activities: readings and recitations, oratory, poems, odes, music, parades. In some cases the commemoration of a town's birthday rivaled that of the nation itself.[102]

Interest in celebrating the past was so strong that in many of the newer towns in the Midwest and West, Old Settler Associations were formed shortly after towns were founded. These associations were enormously popular among older town dwellers. Like veterans organizations after wars, the pioneer settlers of the towns gathered annually as long as any remained alive to commemorate the founding and settlement of the towns. People sometimes talked of building and equipping pioneer cabins, and old settlers sometimes baked corn pone, displayed old newspapers, and exhibited relics of the early days. Their annual gatherings might take place at the county seat, with a morning oration followed by a basket dinner, and then music, games, reminiscences of the past, and a reading of the names of those who had died during the preceding year. At their most expansive, such reunions rivaled the old soldier encampments that veterans organizations sponsored. Both could last for three or four days and embrace a large territory, attracting two thousand to five thousand people who took advantage of excursion rates on rail lines. Both were large outdoor events and, at their largest, as big as revivals.[103]

In the twentieth century, this huge antiquarian enterprise lost energy as the towns ceased to be the primary community for most of a mobile but increasingly urban population. Town governments still sponsored the writing of histories to commemorate their town's founding, but those histories were far slimmer than their nineteenth-century predecessors and were often abundantly illustrated. Authors showed less interest in the massive collection of evidence that antiquarians of the previous century had reveled in. Towns sponsored historical pageants to mark such anniversaries, with a dramatic story line borrowed from books, radio, and television, eschewing the more varied and demanding ceremonies of earlier times. More and more towns held annual "town days," commemorating the town, but with a commercial emphasis, offering recreational programs to lure people who might also buy goods at sidewalk sales but who cared little about marking the town's existence.[104] In some cases the impulse to celebrate a town's past disappeared altogether as ethnic and racial groups promoted their own annual festivals, evidence that they were more interested in perpetuating their identities than in commemorating their town's founding.[105] This development perfectly mirrored the increasingly diverse multi-ethnic, multi-racial society throughout the continent.

## • V •

IN ADDITION TO commemorating their past during the nineteenth and twentieth centuries, town dwellers also tried to improve the quality of life in their communities. The impulse did not lead to alterations in their social and economic arrangements. Only the communitarian groups sought to reorient a capitalist society at the local level; only they sought to establish and sustain small communities where property was owned in common, where divisions of class, gender, and race did not exist. For most townspeople, the urge to improve the quality of life found a physical focus; improvement had an aesthetic definition. To improve one's town meant to enhance its appearance, its look and feel and smell and sound.

The "village improvement" movement of the last half of the nineteenth century combined art and nature, and revealed a growing popular awareness that towns occupied a middle ground in the cultural landscape. In this perception, towns were positioned somewhere between the harmony and beauty of nature and agriculture, on the one hand, and, on the other, the rape of the earth and the ugliness that extractive and industrial activity represented, and the obliteration of nature that urban settings signified. Ordinary town dwellers formed voluntary committees in hundreds of towns in the Northeast and, with their own labor and money or with the assistance of town governments, carried out physical improvements—laying sidewalks and curbs; fencing cemeteries and public grounds; planting trees along commercial and residential streets; installing storm drains, sanitary sewers, public water lines, street crossings, and street lights; and instituting such public services as street sprinkling, snow plowing, street lighting, and litter control.

The village improvement societies were influenced by Andrew Jackson Downing, a pioneering landscape architect who wrote on the importance of overall design and planning in enhancing the physical appearance of homes and towns. Village improvement societies developed comprehensive programs, but because of their voluntary character and their (and their town government's) limited financial resources, such plans often took decades to execute. "Village improvers" were progressives in the towns, but they looked to a better future through physical beautification not political, economic, or social reform. As a result of their efforts, hundreds of towns were transformed from what Downing had called "graceless villages" into what Henry James later called "elm-shaded villages."[106]

By the late nineteenth century the rural population that town dwellers served was in rapid numerical decline. Farmers themselves formed many local farmers' institutes, social organizations that kept individualistic family farmers informed of common concerns. Progressive reformers believed that the quality of life of this farm population could also be dramatically enhanced and improved, just as that of townspeople had been. But these reformers were not farmers, not "natives" in the way that village improvers were themselves town dwellers. Reformers of rural America helped create agricultural experimental stations affiliated with publicly funded state universities and after 1900 started what came to be called the "country life" movement. They were of the urban middle class, highly educated, and made what they thought of as "scientific" prescriptions for the improvement of rural living through surveys, reports, and scholarly studies. Their chief advocates were the presidentially appointed Commission on Country Life (1908) and, in the Protestant churches, a rural version of the social gospel. Both secular and religious advocates argued that the rural population needed to be more efficient, more modern, and more technologically progressive. Proposals that would have the greatest direct impact on town dwellers were the consolidation of both churches and schools.

But farmers did not support the changes advocated by country life reformers, and the movement declined rapidly after World War I. Not until the 1920s were there signs that the rural population was itself aware of the shortcomings of farm life, in contrast to town or city life. This awareness brought discontent and, finally, a desire for change. Farmers began to feel their isolation, began to think their life was dreary and without modern conveniences or technologies—the very qualities that country life reformers had pointed to. The onset of motorized transportation and radio only accentuated the farmers' sense of deprivation. In the 1920s farmers formed their own organizations—the Farm Bureau and the Farmers' Union—to deal with the need for improvements in rural life. A broad-gauged reform movement thus narrowed into efforts by a special interest—farmers—to find solutions to their own problems.[107]

Through the twentieth century, the towns became more integral a part of a mass society with a continental and even global scale of life. Towns became progressively more like cities, only smaller and slower to adapt to change. One consequence of this change was that the towns shared with cities problems of a physical character: suburban sprawl (on the edge of town), commercial strips on roads leading out of town, shopping malls at the outer perimeters, abandoned or defaced Main Street "cores." In the face of such physical decay and distortion, a new "improvements" movement emerged by the 1960s, as significant as the earlier "village improvement" associations' efforts but profoundly different in nature.

The new reformers hoped to preserve the physical heritage of the towns, not necessarily to improve their appearance. The movement was past-oriented, and its advocates acted as preservationists, concerned that the physical past of the towns be restored or maintained. They didn't like what was happening and were anxious about the future. To them, the real town was the old town, a physical construct from the past that was now threatened with decay and destruction. The historical town was all that remained of what was truly a town, for current town life was increasingly indistinguishable from life in the urban centers that absorbed ever greater percentages of the population.

Nothing more clearly mirrors the changing position of the towns in the larger society than this shift from the nineteenth-century village improvement associations, with their positive outlook and focus on the future at a time when the towns were still the primary community center for a still heavily rural population, to the preservationists of the later twentieth century, with their nostalgic focus on a past that was threatened and must at least be physically restored or maintained. In a larger sense, however, both movements equated the reform and improvement of the towns with their physical appearance. Neither group sought to tamper with basic economic, social, or political arrangements; both groups came out of the middle class. Both had a proprietary interest in improving the physical appearance and thus the aesthetic appeal of "their" communities. At bottom, what both advocated were aesthetic reforms.

The federal government first responded to the preservationist impulse in 1949 when it chartered the National Trust for Historic Preservation, which aimed to preserve for public benefit the "heritage" sites of America. A National Register of Historic Sites was compiled and was broadened in 1966 under new legislation to include properties of state and local as well as national significance. By 1976 (the time of the national bicentennial) the number of such sites had grown to twelve thousand. Within that number were more than a thousand historical districts, sections of towns and cities with houses and buildings of historical interest. By 1976 the National Trust had received so many inquiries from towns whose preservationists wished to restore their Main Streets that it launched a demonstration program to explore the connections between economic development and historic preservation. The thought was that the physical enhancement of central business districts might result in economic as well as aesthetic improvement. Towns as varied as Ipswich, Massachusetts; Essex and Old Lyme, Connecticut; Corning, New York; Hudson and Chillicothe, Ohio; Madison, Indiana; Woodstock and Galesburg, Illinois; and Hot Springs, South Dakota, were all involved in such projects.[108]

At its extreme, the preservationist impulse involved the creation of museum villages, newly created historic "towns" filled with historic houses and buildings moved to new sites, or replicas of such structures. The public was charged admission to these communities, which invariably contained period furnishings and were sometimes staffed with people who were costumed and acted in a manner consistent with the age of the "town." Williamsburg, Virginia; Old Sturbridge, Massachusetts; and Greenfield Village in Dearborn, Michigan, were among the best known. But by the late twentieth century, there were dozens of these usually well-attended museum villages dotting the landscape, a testament to the popularity of the belief that the purest, truest towns were those that stood outside of time, outside of history, exempt from the dynamics of real political, economic, social, and cultural change.[109]

The most compressed form of the physically idealized town was the theme park, in particular Disneyland in California and Disney World in Florida. In both, the town was reduced to a Main Street with a railroad station and a public square, reminiscent of Walt Disney's own hometown, Marceline, Missouri, at the turn of the nineteenth century. These theme park renderings reduced the town to a visual symbol, a cleaned-up version of the old town, without its unpaved, dusty, or rutty streets, equine latrines, banks of telephone wires, and signs over sidewalks. The popularity of the Disney theme-park towns was a reflection of a longing for a past America. The town was the archetypal, shared experience for mainstream Americans.[110]

With such theme parks, the idealized town became a shorthand symbol for the historical town, one charged with meaning and emotion. Towns as idealized physical symbols were now capable of being infinitely replicable— just as real towns had been during the prolonged orgy of town building across the North American continent during the seventeenth, eighteenth, and nineteenth centuries. The real physical town, which for so long had been the primary community for a rural population, became, in the twentieth century, in its most idealized physical form, a still-potent symbol of something that was still real but whose time of importance had irrevocably passed.

# CONCLUSION

# The Town in Myth and Reality

THE VAST MAJORITY of Americans have never lived in a town. As communities, towns have been the home for a fairly small minority of the European migrants and their descendants who settled on the North American continent over the last four centuries. Until the twentieth century, most Americans lived in rural settings, outside any community. Most were farmers, some were fishermen, loggers, and miners. But all *needed* communities as a place to engage with others in economic, social, cultural, and political activities. Towns emerged in all parts of the continent during the seventeenth, eighteenth, and nineteenth centuries because of this need. They functioned as "service centers" for an overwhelmingly rural population.

Those who lived in the towns were real estate agents (who bought and sold house and building lots), millers (who transformed grain into flour and logs into board by means of waterpower), craftsmen (who handcrafted products that farmers, miners, and fishermen could not or chose not to make for themselves), merchants and storekeepers (who sold goods made from afar and exported those made locally), and, by the nineteenth century, wage-laboring machine operators (who made mass-produced goods in water-powered factories). In the more substantial towns one could also find professionals (doctors, lawyers, teachers, ministers, editors), and, by the nineteenth century, bankers and businessmen.

Most towns were agricultural service centers, but there were also fishing villages and mining and lumber camps. This meant that most towns grew

292

out of economic needs. But the location of government and political instrumentalities in existing towns, or in towns founded expressly as sites for such agencies, also resulted in the creation of service centers. These were centers of a different kind, whose governmental focus overlay the town's ordinary functions. Religion too generated the development of towns. Some Christian sects founded their own towns in order to live together, apart from the larger population, in isolation and purity. Finally, some ethnic groups (such as German-speaking immigrants) and racial groups (such as black migrants after the end of slavery during the Civil War) sought to retain their unity in the midst of a hostile or strange society by founding and developing their own towns.

All the settlements that were scattered across the North American continent from the seventeenth to the nineteenth centuries overlaid territory in which the native population had lived for centuries. The continent and, within it, a rapidly expanding nation state afforded the newer settlers vast space, room to settle wherever and whenever they wanted to, and with whomever they preferred. This astonishing freedom over so extensive a terrain over so long a time led to a prolonged orgy of town building and to the creation of several thousand small local communities.

Most town dwellers developed communities that mirrored the characteristics of the larger society of which they were a part. Like both the rural and the fledgling but rapidly growing urban populations, town dwellers established a hierarchical society with exceptional social mobility for white men; a democratic political system, again for white men; economic activity that included distinctive forms of milling and industrial work (long before they could be found in urban centers) as well as craft and commercial enterprises (though the cities had a far greater range and variety of either); and a culture that long lacked the more sophisticated forms of art (cities being the main cultural centers) and that only slowly developed an affinity even for entertainment, as work gradually separated itself from leisure.

Only a tiny minority of town dwellers tried to create communities whose basic arrangements of life constituted a rival model, an alternative society, even on a small scale. These so-called communitarians were religious groups (Mennonites, Shakers, Mormons) or early socialist groups (Owenites or Fourierists) who founded towns based upon the common ownership of property, and who sought thereby to create small utopian societies whose members lived in peace, harmony, and cooperation rather than in competition, division, and hostility. In a fundamental way, these utopians carried the values of town dwellers everywhere to their logical extreme. The people of the towns favored togetherness, loyalty, neighborliness, and egalitarian sentiment, a community where everyone knew and cared for one another. Why not create a town where there was *perfect* cooperation, where *everyone* agreed on the best way to live and behave, where all shared everything—values, activities, property, material goods?

In the minds of communitarians, the perfect town was cleansed of the half-measures of ordinary town dwellers who sustained the prevailing arrangements of American society. Communitarians argued that those arrangements, when tested against their alternative model, were terribly flawed and ought to be abandoned. The Puritans were the first large group to exhibit this utopian impulse, but they made serious compromises in the application of the communitarian principle in their large-scale town-building enterprises. Their successors—groups such as the Mormons and Shakers, or the followers of Owen or Fourier—were much purer but far less successful in attracting large numbers to the creation of "perfect" towns.

As Americans abandoned farming, mining, lumbering, and fishing, and as the rural population hemorrhaged away, once again the towns failed to attract the majority of the population. Americans moved from the country into the city. The population in urban areas grew rapidly as the rural population engaged in agriculture rapidly declined. At the close of the eighteenth century, more than 90 percent of Americans listed farming as their primary occupation. By the end of the twentieth century that figure had declined to the astonishingly low figure of less than 2 percent. Most Americans lived in rural areas or towns in the nation's early years, but during the nineteenth century urban centers mushroomed, and by the twentieth century they became the places where most Americans lived. Just as the mechanization and commercialization of farming led to the development of large-scale farms, so too the introduction of steam and then electrical power led to the centralization of industry in cities.

In the nineteenth century, many town founders hoped their towns would grow into cities. They wanted continuous economic and demographic growth. Some towns, usually those with favorable transportation links, did grow into cities, proclaimed as such by state governments when they reached a certain level of population. But other towns far from urban centers failed, were abandoned, fell into disuse, or became ghost towns, usually when the single-source economic basis for their existence vanished (whether agricultural or extractive) or when motorized transport made them redundant for a population able to access the services of larger centers. Whether they grew, failed, or stabilized, few towns exhibited the special cluster of circumstances that led to the development of large urban centers.

Town dwellers became quite ambivalent in their attitude toward cities. Some tried to copy the wealth-seeking, individualist emphasis they saw urbanites eagerly embracing. Others became increasingly aware of urban innovations of all kinds—the latest technological developments, the latest fashions of class and status, the latest leisure-time activities. But town dwellers also continued to embrace those values they believed defined their communities and made them different from urban life: togetherness, neighborliness, loyalty, egalitarian sentiments, a sense that everyone knew everyone else and that everyone looked after one another in times of crisis. For these townspeople, cities were places filled with strangers, filled with environmental degradation, social division, and pervasive crime. The ambivalence with which town dwellers perceived cities led to a form of mass schizophrenia: cities both attracted and repelled them.

Various town dwellers recalled this feeling. Eliza Wiggin remembered that in mid-nineteenth-century Waverly, Kansas, when as a child she visited a city, "my mind was full of joyful anticipation tempered somewhat by the memory of my mother's parting admonition not to stare about open mouthed, not point to anything strange, nor in any other way expose my rusticity to the unsympathetic smiles and jeers of the scornful city populace."[1]

But in the late nineteenth century, when the railroads organized excursions that allowed town dwellers to visit cities, Burns Fuller remembered that "countless natives had their first look at the big city by way of these excursions. . . . What a thrill to be leaving the routine of village life for that teeming, exciting bustling life in the great metropolis. . . . For many, it was the 'highlight' of the year."[2]

By the early twentieth century, town dwellers themselves seemed to some observers to have lost their vitality in an era of increasing urban domination. In Hartford, Michigan, for instance, Willis Dunbar remembered that life "consisted of work, and [the] only escape was neighborhood gossip. Ambition was dead in many, even the younger people. There was little to create an expectation of better things ahead. The pioneer spirit was a thing of the past. The town had been built up about as much as it appeared it ever would be. People were plain bored."[3]

By the late twentieth century, towns had become pale copies of cities, though slower to accept change and much smaller. Town dwellers no longer lived in communities that differed substantially from urban centers, both because of great advancements in transportation and communications and the concurrent emergence of a mass society with a greatly enlarged scale of life in all its dimensions. As a consequence, the isolation that in earlier centuries had made small local communities the primary community for most of the population now faded away. A population with private and public access to motorized transport could live anywhere and commute to work wherever it lived. Electrical power provided energy for industry located anywhere there were favorable economic circumstances. Towns increasingly attracted urban commuters, became vacation spots or resorts for an urban population, or turned into places of retirement for urbanites who yearned for their hometowns or for farmers who had given up farming.

The overall character of life in the towns gradually became indistinguishable from that of the cities, though smaller in scale, range, and variety. As American society afforded women and nonwhites legal and political equality, so too did the towns—but more slowly, for they had typically been more conservative, more homogeneous, and less open to change and variety. As the American economy became large in scale and mechanized, so too did the towns—but more falteringly, for the tradition of local enterprise was deep and long. As the American polity became more democratic, tolerant of gender, ethnicity, class, and race among its citizens, so too did the towns—though tardily, for they had been inhabited by a less varied population. As American society embraced ever greater varieties of religious adherents (and even those of no active affiliation), so too did the towns—but more hesitatingly, for their Christian and especially Protestant orientation had been so strong.

In an urbanized society, some towns continued to have a special orientation, to be the sites for particular kinds of institutions and activities that skewed their functioning as a community. In the late twentieth century the countercultural (or "hippie") communes of the 1970s echoed the communitarian impulse, which had expressed itself so forcefully (though always among very small numbers) from the seventeenth to the nineteenth centuries. Military-base towns were a post–World War II echo of the government-controlled frontier forts and garrisons of earlier centuries. College towns were dominated by institutions of higher learning in the same way other towns had been a location for social institutions such as prisons, insane asylums, poorhouses, orphanages, and private schools. Resort and theme-park and vacation towns were later versions of nineteenth-century spas. "Retirement villages" were new creations of what many towns had at least partially already become.

In short, the impulse for Americans to live in or to locate their activities and institutions in small local communities was still a vital one. But most people, most activities, and most institutions were situated in fast-spreading urban settings. Even those that chose to locate in towns were greatly affected by developments initiated in the cities.

In the twentieth century, when most Americans came to live in urban areas, they resisted defining the city as their "community." Instead they searched for other identities and definitions of themselves that were of a more human scale. Perhaps the greatest legacy of the town, from the time it was the primary community for a largely rural population, was that urbanized Americans continued to define community in terms of "smallness." In the process, they greatly altered the very definition of what a community is.

This new sense of community expressed itself in a number of ways. For example, Americans identified themselves with the statistical categories they fell into. People identified their income level with their "class," their IQ level with their "intelligence," their stance in a public opinion poll as the basis of their values, views, or beliefs. These were attenuated "communities," filled with strangers, like the cities themselves—but they were strangers connected by a statistical commonality.

Another way this new sense of community expressed itself was through the equation of the groups one belonged to with one's "community." One's ethnicity, race, occupation, class, language, religion, gender, sexual orientation, and age all became the basis of group identities, of one's "communities." Similarly, institutions (such as hospitals and universities) and work or leisure places (offices, production and retail facilities, resorts) created short-term or continuing "communities." This pervasive practice of associating one's affiliations and sources of identity with one's "community" revealed the urbanite's profound need for a community with a small scale.

So when towns ceased to be their primary community, Americans still longed for small places. And though most people no longer lived in such places, Americans responded to symbolic representations such as museum villages and theme parks. The "town" resonated in the psyche of a largely urbanized population.

In a profound sense, the most important thing about the towns is their history. They were the primary local community for Americans from the seventeenth to the nineteenth centuries, and their partisans continue to argue for their intimacy, neighborliness, and human scale. Those who do not like them point to their record of intolerance, their narrow-mindedness, dullness, and tendency to exclude those who do not fit in. But the critics of cities are just as emphatic about pollution, social divisiveness, the frequent breakdown of civility, and the high incidence of crime in settings filled with strangers. Advocates of cities focus instead on their tolerance, variety, innovation, and excitement.

Either type of community, if organized in its most extreme form, brings calamity. The purest of towns—as indicated by the experience of the communitarians—can lead to a small group that is isolated from the ebb and flow of human life. The most sprawling of cities, those without planning and order, can become chaotic and stressful for people and the environment. The town's importance may indeed lie in the past, but the relationship of Americans to both their towns and cities suggests that the quest for desirable communities will endure for as long as humans are social animals.

# *Notes*

## Preface

1. This view of the nature of town "boundaries" is an elaboration of Edmund DeS. Brunner, Gwendolyn S. Hughes, and Marjorie Patten, *American Agricultural Villages* (New York: George H. Doran, 1927), 72–95; Edmund deS. Brunner and J. H. Kolb, *Rural Social Trends* (New York: McGraw-Hill, 1933), 98–101; and, for a more recent example, Everett M. Rogers, Rabel J. Burdge, Peter F. Korsching, and Joseph F. Donnermeyer, *Social Change in Rural Societies* (Englewood Cliffs, N.J.: Prentice-Hall, 1984), 115–118.

## 1. Foundings

1. Ruth Sutter, *The Next Place You Come To: A Historical Introduction to Communities in North America* (Englewood Cliffs, N.J.: Prentice-Hall, 1973), 17–28.

2. *Ibid.*, 38, 88.

3. *Ibid.*, 49–50.

4. *Ibid.*, 50.

5. David Hackett Fischer, *Albion's Seed: Four British Folkways in America* (New York: Oxford University Press, 1989), *passim*. See especially the charts on pages 787 and 813–815.

6. Edward T. Price, *Dividing the Land: Early American Beginnings of Our Private Property Mosaic* (Chicago: University of Chicago Press, 1995), 331–339. On the Southern landed elite: Rhys Isaac, *The Transformation of Virginia, 1740–1790* (Chapel Hill: University of North Carolina Press, 1982), 19–22.

7. The founders of Plymouth Colony, in 1620.

8. The founders of Massachusetts Bay Colony, in 1630.

9. Bruce C. Daniels, *The Connecticut Town: Growth and Development, 1635–1790* (Middletown, Conn.: Wesleyan University Press, 1979), 9–34.

10. Charles E. Clark, *The Eastern Frontier: The Settlement of Northern New England, 1610–1763* (New York: Knopf, 1970), 199–206.

11. John Frederick Martin, *Profits in the Wilderness: Enterpreneurship and the Founding of the New England Town in the Seventeenth Century* (Chapel Hill: University of North Carolina Press, 1991), 202, 205. Martin's fine study deals with a sample of 63 of the 120 to 140 towns that had been founded in New England by 1700.

12. *Ibid.*, 9–45.

13. *Ibid.*, 46–110.

14. *Ibid.*, 9–28.

15. *Ibid.*, 139–142.

16. *Ibid.*, 186–216. Charles Clark's account of the founding of towns in northern New England, mainly those in southeastern New Hampshire, does not conflict in any substantial way with Martin's later account, though Clark emphasizes the work of the proprietors in surveying the land granted to them. Clark, *The Far Eastern Frontier*, 180–188.

17. Kenneth A. Lockridge, *A New England Town, The First Hundred Years: Dedham, Massachusetts, 1636–1736* (New York: Norton, 1970), 3–22.

18. Stephen Innes, *Labor in a New Land: Economy and Society in Seventeenth-Century Springfield* (Princeton, N.J.: Princeton University Press, 1983), 123–124.

19. John Reps, *Town Planning in Frontier America* (Princeton, N.J.: Princeton University Press, 1969), 390–399.

20. *Ibid.*, 113.

21. Isaac, *The Transformation of Virginia*, 58–68, 88–98, 104–114.

22. Lois Green Carr, "'The Metropolis of Maryland': A Comment on Town Development Along the Tobacco Coast," *Maryland Historical Magazine*, 1974, vol. 69, no. 2, 142–144.

23. Joan Niles Sears, *The First Hundred Years of Town Planning in Georgia* (Atlanta: Cherokee Publishing Co., 1979), 23–24.

24. Reps, *Town Planning in Frontier America*, 107–111.

25. Edward M. Riley, "The Town Acts of Colonial Virginia," *Journal of Southern History*, vol. 16, no. 3 (August 1950), 306–323; John C. Rambolt, "The Absence of Towns in Seventeenth-Century Virginia," *Journal of Southern History*, vol. 35, no. 3 (1969), 343–360; Reps, *Town Planning in Frontier America*, 116–117.

26. *Ibid.*, 115–117.

27. Joseph Brown Thomas, Jr., "Settlement, Community, and Economy: The Development of Towns on Maryland's Lower Eastern Shore, 1660–1775," Ph.D. dissertation, University of Maryland, 1994.

28. Reps, *Town Planning in Frontier America*, 224–227.

29. *Ibid.*, 132–144.

30. *Ibid.*, 124.

31. L. Jeffrey Perez, "'Promises Fair to Be a Flourishing Place': Virginia Town Establishment in the 1780s and the Emergence of a New Temperament," *Locus*, vol. 6, no. 2 (Spring 1994), 135–149.

32. Reps, *Town Planning in Frontier America*, 227–232.

33. *Ibid.*, 238–250.

34. Carl Bridenbaugh, *Myths and Realities: Societies of the Colonial South* (Baton Rouge, La.: Louisiana State University Press, 1952), 147–152.

35. Christopher Edwin Hendricks, "Town Development in the Colonial Backcountry—Virginia and North Carolina," Ph.D. dissertation, College of William and Mary, 1991.

36. Carr, "'The Metropolis of Maryland'. . . ," 142–144.

37. Earle Carville and Ronald Hoffman, "Staple Crops and Urban Development in the 18th-Century South," *Perspectives in American History*, vol. 10 (1976), 7–11.

38. James T. Lemon, *The Best Poor Man's Country: A Geographical Study of South-eastern Pennsylvania* (Baltimore: Johns Hopkins University Press, 1972), 98–109. Also: Lucy Simler, "The Township: The Community of the Rural Pennsylvanians," *Pennsylvania Magazine of History and Biography* vol. 106, no. 1 (1982), 48–51.

39. Stephanie Grauman Wolf, *Urban Village: Population, Community, and Family Structure in Germantown, Pennsylvania, 1683–1800* (Princeton, N.J.: Princeton University Press, 1976), 12.

40. Lemon, *The Best Poor Man's Country*, 111–117.

41. *Ibid.*, 130–131.

42. *Ibid.*, 131–133.

43. *Ibid.*, 142.

44. Peirce F. Lewis, "Small Town in Pennsylvania," *Annals of the Association of American Geographers*, vol. 62 (June 1972), 323–351.

45. Bernard L. Herman, *Architecture and Rural Life in Central Delaware, 1700–1900* (Knoxville, Tenn.: University of Tennessee Press, 1987), 79–81.

46. Philip L. White, *Beekmantown, New York: Forest Frontier to Farm Community* (Austin, Tex.: University of Texas Press, 1979), 3–27.

47. William Wyckoff, *The Developer's Frontier: The Making of the Western New York Landscape* (New Haven, Conn.: Yale University Press, 1988), 2.

48. *Ibid.*, 16–20.

49. *Ibid.*, 59–60.

50. *Ibid.*, 75–78.

51. *Ibid.*, 84–86, 90–94.

52. Paul Cross Morrison, "A Morphological Study of Worthington, Ohio," *Ohio Journal of Science*, vol. 34, no. 1 (January 1934), 31–32.

53. Reps, *Town Planning in Frontier America*, 41.

54. *Ibid.*, 47–69.

55. Marc Simmons, "Settlement Patterns and Village Plans in Colonial New Mexico," in Daniel J. Garr, ed., *Hispanic Urban Planning in North America* (New York: Garland, 1991), 7–19. Also: Daniel Garr, "Planning, Politics, and Plunder: The Missions and Indian Pueblos of Hispanic California," *Southern California Quarterly*, vol. 54, no. 4 (1972), 291–312.

56. Reps, *Town Planning in Frontier America*, 69.

57. *Ibid.*, 85–105.

58. Lewis Atherton, *Main Street on the Middle Border* (Bloomington, Ind.: Indiana University Press, 1954), 3. More particularly, in the corn and wheat belts of the plains, villages were spaced every four, five, or six miles, wherever grain elevators were located along rail lines. Clarence Burt Odell, "The Functional Pattern of Villages in a Selected Area of the Corn Belt," Ph.D. dissertation, University of Chicago, 1939, 47.

59. Eliza J. Wiggin, *Impressions of Early Kansas* (Wichita, Kans.: Grit Printing, 1915), 5–6.

60. Ralph Gregory, "Count Baudissin on Missouri Towns," *Missouri Historical Society Bulletin*, vol. 27, no. 2 (January 1971), 115.

61. Don Harrison Doyle, *The Social Order of a Frontier Community: Jacksonville, Illinois, 1825–70* (Urbana, Ill.: University of Illinois Press, 1978), 19.

62. Robert Dykstra, *The Cattle Towns: A Social History of the Kansas Cattle Trading Centers: Abilene, Ellsworth, Wichita, Dodge City, and Caldwell, 1867 to 1885* (New York: Knopf, 1968), 11–15.

63. *Ibid.*, 31–32.

64. *Ibid.*, 41–45.

65. *Ibid.*, 56–57.

66. *Ibid.*, 63–64.

67. Richard Lingeman, *Small Town America: A Narrative History, 1620–The Present* (New York: G. P. Putnam's Sons, 1980), 108–110, for a description of town jobbing.

68. Harriet Bonebright-Closz, *Reminiscences of Newcastle* (Des Moines, Iowa: Historical Department of Iowa, 1921), 106.

69. Walters, "Early Western Illinois Town Advertisements: A Geographical Inquiry," *Western Illinois Regional Studies*, vol. 8, no. 1 (1985), 5–15.

70. Bernard C. Peters, "Early Town Site Speculation in Kalamazoo County," *Michigan History* vol. 56, no. 3 (1972), 200–215.

71. Stuart F. Voss, "Town Growth in Central Missouri, 1815–1880: An Urban Chaparral," *Missouri Historical Review*, vol. 64, nos. 1 and 2 (1970–1971), 64–80, 197–217.

72. John W. Reps, *Cities of the American West: A History of Frontier Urban Planning* (Princeton, N.J.: Princeton University Press, 1979), 391–436.

73. Ricky L. Roberts, "Chelsea: An Anthropological Study of a 19th-Century Western Frontier Town," Ph.D. dissertation, University of Kansas, 1985, 41–45.

74. Timothy R. Mahoney, *River Towns in the Great West: The Structure of Provincial Urbanization in the American Midwest, 1820–1870* (New York: Cambridge University Press, 1990), 273–274.

75. Stuart Seely Sprague, "Town Making in the Era of Good Feelings: Kentucky, 1814–1820," *Register of the Kentucky Historical Society*, vol. 72, no. 4 (1974), 337–341, and "Alabama Town Production During the Era of Good Feelings," *Alabama Historical Quarterly* vol. 36, no. 1 (1974), 15–20.

76. William D. Walters, "Unsurpassed Locations: Gulf Coast Townsite Advertisements: 1835–1837," *Pioneer America Society Transactions*, vol. 12 (1989), 65–72.

77. Raleigh A. Suarez, "Bargains, Bills, and Bankruptcies: Business Activity in Rural Antebellum Louisiana," *Louisiana History*, vol. 7, no. 3 (1966), 189–206.

78. John C. Hudson, *Plains Country Towns* (Minneapolis: University of Minnesota Press, 1985), 26–38.

79. John Mack Faragher, *Sugar Creek: Life on the Illinois Prairie* (New Haven, Conn.: Yale University Press, 1986), 121–129, 156–170.

80. Hudson, *Plains Country Towns*, preface.

81. Barbara Ruth Bailey, *Main Street, Northeastern Oregon: The Founding and Development of Small Towns* (Portland: Oregon Historical Society, 1982), 39–62.

82. Kathleen Underwood, *Town Building on the Colorado Frontier* (Albuquerque, N.M.: University of New Mexico Press, 1987), 7–9.

83. Odie B. Faulk, *Tombstone: Myth and Reality* (New York: Oxford University Press, 1972), 73–78.

84. The two best brief summaries of an extensive literature are John C. Hudson, "Towns of the Western Railroads," *Great Plains Quarterly*, vol. 2, no. 1 (1982), 43–44, and Richard Harold Smith, "Towns Along the Tracks: Railroad Strategy and Town Promotion in the San Joaquin Valley, California," Ph.D. dissertation, University of California, Los Angeles, 1976, 11–12.

85. Paul Wallace Gates, *The Illinois Central Railroad and Its Colonization Work* (Cambridge, Mass.: Harvard University Press, 1934), 121–148; Smith, "Towns Along the Tracks," 1–3.

86. Donald B. Oster, "The Hannibal and St. Joseph Railroad, Government and Town Founding, 1846–1861," *Missouri Historical Review*, vol. 87, no. 4 (1993), 411–415.

87. Reps, *Cities of the American West*, 526–533.

88. *Ibid.*, 535–540.

89. *Ibid.*, 544–547.

90. *Ibid.*, 559–576.

91. *Ibid.*, 576–583.

92. *Ibid.*, 593–631.

93. James A. Sherow, "Rural Town Origins in Southwest Reno County," *Kansas History*, vol. 3, no. 2 (1980), 99–100.

94. H. Roger Grant, "Iowa's New Communities: Townsite Promotion Along the Chicago Great Western Railway's Omaha Extension," *Upper Midwest History*, vol. 2 (1982), 53–55.

95. Harold E. Briggs, "The Great Dakota Boom, 1879–1886," *North Dakota Historical Quarterly*, vol. 4 (January 1930), 78–108.

96. Hudson, *Plains Country Towns*, 70–85.

97. Smith, "Towns Along the Tracks," 347–359.

98. Reps, *Cities of the American West*, 199, 206.

99. Ray Allen Billington, *The Far Western Frontier, 1830–1860* (New York: Harper and Brothers, 1956), 235–236.

100. Reps, *Cities of the American West*, 459, 466, 475, 485.

101. *Ibid.*, 491, 493–494.

102. *Ibid.*, 507, 510.

103. *Ibid.*, 513, 515, 516, 522.

104. James B. Allen, *The Company Town in the American West* (Norman, Okla.: University of Oklahoma Press, 1966), 14–32.

105. *Ibid.*, 33–49.

106. *Ibid.*, 50–69.

107. Joan Niles Sears, *The First Hundred Years of Town Planning in Georgia* (Atlanta: Cherokee Publishing Co., 1979), 11–31.

108. Page Smith, *As a City Upon a Hill: The Town in American History* (New York: Knopf, 1968), 19.

109. Laurie Ann Kattner, "From Immigrant Settlement into Town: New Braunfels, Texas, 1845–1870," *Americastudien*, vol. 36, no. 2 (1991), 155–161.

110. Albert J. Petersen, "German-Russian Catholic Social Organization," *Plains Anthropologist*, vol. 18, no. 59 (1973), 27.

111. Reps, *Cities of the American West*, 287, 290–291, 299, 302, 304, 313.

112. Zachary Cooper, *Black Settlers in Rural Wisconsin* (Madison, Wisc.: State Historical Society of Wisconsin, 1977), 4–7, 26–27; Shirley Jean Motley Carlson, "The Black Community in the Rural North: Pulaski County, Illinois, 1860–1890," Ph.D. dissertation, Washington University, 1982, 135–138.

113. Peter C. Smith and Karl B. Raitz, "Negro Hamlets and Agricultural Estates in Kentucky's Inner Bluegrass," *Geographical Review*, vol. 64, no. 2 (1974), 217–234.

114. Mozell Hill, "The All-Negro Communities of Oklahoma: The Natural History of a Social Movement," *Journal of Negro History*, vol. 31 (1946), 254–268;

Arthur L. Tolson, "The Black Towns of Oklahoma," *Black Scholar*, vol. 1 (April, 1970), 18–22; and Thomas Knight, "Black Towns of Oklahoma: Their Development and Survival," Ph.D. dissertation, Oklahoma State University, 1975, 67–68.

115. Kenneth Marvin Hamilton, *Black Towns and Profit: Promotion and Development in the Trans-Appalachian West, 1877–1915* (Urbana, Ill.: University of Illinois Press, 1991), 6, 45, 100, 120, 138.

116. Norman L. Crockett, *The Black Towns* (Lawrence, Kans.: Regents Press of Kansas, 1979), 40–42.

117. Hamilton, *Black Towns and Profit*, 4.

118. As quoted in Crockett, *The Black Towns*, 43, 44, 46, 47.

119. Smith, *As a City Upon a Hill*, 18, 27–30.

120. Dolores Hayden, *Seven American Utopias: The Architecture of Communitarian Socialism, 1790–1975* (Cambridge, Mass.: MIT Press, 1976), 16.

121. Smith, *As a City Upon a Hill*, 20–26.

122. William E. Leuchtenburg, *Franklin D. Roosevelt and the New Deal, 1932–1940* (New York: Harper and Row, 1963), 123, 140–141.

123. Shirley F. Weiss, *New Town Development in the United States: Experiment in Private Entrepreneurship* (Chapel Hill, N.C.: Center for Urban and Regional Studies, University of North Carolina, 1973), 5–10.

## 2. Sites

1. *Historical Atlas of the United States: Centennial Edition* (Washington, D.C.: National Geographic Society, 1988), 34–35.

2. Reps, *Town Planning in Frontier America*, 3–6, 25–29.

3. *Ibid.*, 20–24.

4. Anthony N. B. Garvan, *Architecture in Colonial Connecticut* (New Haven, Conn.: Yale University Press, 1951), 38–44.

5. Clark, *The Far Eastern Frontier*, 184–188.

6. Joseph S. Wood, "Elaboration of a Settlement System in New England," *Journal of Historical Geography*, vol. 10, no. 4 (1984), 331–356.

7. Daniels, *The Connecticut Town*, 156.

8. Clark, *The Eastern Frontier*, 206–219. Clark mistakenly believed that southern New England settlements were typically compact, but so did everyone else at the time he wrote. Joseph Wood has attempted to explain the widespread belief that early New England towns were planned and compact. Joseph S. Wood and Michael P. Steinitz, *The New England Village* (Baltimore: Johns Hopkins University Press, 1997), 135–154.

9. Wood and Steinitz, *The New England Village*, 2–8. Reps, *Town Planning in Frontier America*, 145–183, is inaccurate when he refers to fully formed villages as having been typical of the colonial or agricultural era. Reps relied on nineteenth-century amateur local histories, which were themselves inaccurate in their cartographical ascription to the colonial period of the *later* physical layout of sizable service centers from their own century. Wood is quite persuasive on this point.

10. *Ibid.*, 118–129, 229–235.

11. *Ibid.*, 129–144.

12. *Ibid.*, 240–245.

13. Sears, *The First Hundred Years of Town Planning in Georgia*, 13, 32–53.

14. Lemon, *The Best Poor Man's Country*, 99–102.

15. Wolf, *Urban Village*, 23–28.

16. Lemon, *The Best Poor Man's Country*, 99–102, 132–134; Reps, *Town Planning in Frontier America*, 204–216.

17. Turpin C. Bannister, "Early Town Planning in New York State," *Journal of the American Society of Architectural Historians*, vol. 3, no. 2 (January–April 1943), 37–40.

18. William J. Murtagh, *Moravian Architecture and Town Planning* (Chapel Hill, N.C.: University of North Carolina Press, 1967), 9–20.

19. Reps, *Town Planning in Frontier America*, 41–47. For a more detailed description: Zelia Nuttall, "Royal Ordinances Concerning the Layout Out of New Towns," *Hispanic American Historical Review*, vol. 5 (1922), 249–254.

20. Reps, *Town Planning in Frontier America*, 78–104.

21. Wood and Steinitz, *The New England Town*, 127–128.

22. Lemon, *The Best Poor Man's Country*, 193–216.

23. Isaac, *The Transformation of Virginia*, 58–65.

24. *Ibid.*, 88–94.

25. *Ibid.*, 299–322.

26. Wood and Steinitz, *The New England Town*, 71–84; John Demos, *A Little Commonwealth: Family Life in Plymouth Colony* (New York: Oxford University Press, 1970), 25–29; Clark, *The New England Frontier*, 193–198, 220–225.

27. Stephanie Wolf, *Urban Village: Population, Community, and Family Structure in Germantown, Pennsylvania, 1683–1800* (Princeton, N.J.: Princeton University Press, 1976), 34–37.

28. Darrett B. and Anita H. Rutman, *A Place in Time: Middlesex County, Virginia, 1650–1750* (New York: Norton, 1984), 65–69.

29. Isaac, *The Transformation of Virginia*, 30–42.

30. Demos, *A Little Commonwealth*, 36–51.

31. Reps, *Town Planning in Frontier America*, 390–400.

32. Wood and Steinitz, *The New England Village*, 2, 5–6, 88–104, 115–116, 122.

33. *Ibid.*, 71–84, 123, 125.

34. *Ibid.*, 127–128.

35. Wilbur Zelinsky, "The Pennsylvania Town: An Overdue Geographical Account," *Geographical Review*, vol. 67, no. 2 (1977), 127–147. Zelinsky surveyed 234 towns, a sizable sample.

36. Stuart Blumin, *The Urban Threshold: Growth and Change in a Nineteenth-Century Community* (Chicago: University of Chicago Press, 1976), 16–17.

37. Lisa Carol Tolbert, "Constructing Townscapes: Architecture and Experience in Nineteenth-Century County Seats of Middle Tennessee," Ph.D. dissertation, University of North Carolina (Chapel Hill), 1994.

38. Sears, *The First Hundred Years of Town Planning in Georgia*, 14–22, 56–57, 157–160.

39. *Ibid.*, 58–65.

40. Anthony F. C. Wallace, *Rockdale: The Growth of an American Village in the Early Industrial Revolution* (New York: Norton, 1978), 13–15.

41. John R. Stilgoe, *Common Landscape of America, 1580 to 1845* (New Haven, Conn.: Yale University Press, 1982), 99–107.

42. Reps, *Town Planning in Frontier America*, 269–271.

43. *Ibid.*, 273–275.

44. *Ibid.*, 279–282.

45. *Ibid.*, 299–303.

46. John A. Jakle, Robert W. Bastian, and Douglas K. Meyer, *Common Houses in America's Small Towns: The Atlantic Seaboard to the Mississippi Valley* (Athens, Ga.: University of Georgia Press, 1989), 22–63.

47. Edward T. Price, "The Central Courthouse Square in the American County Seat," *Geographical Review*, vol. 58 (January, 1968), 30–60.

48. As quoted in Marian M. Ohman, *A History of Missouri's Counties, County Seats, and Courthouse Squares* (Columbia, Mo.: University of Missouri, Columbia, 1983), 38.

49. *Ibid.*, 19–24.

50. *Ibid.*, 28–40.

51. *Ibid.*, 41–57.

52. *Ibid.*, 59–90.

53. Hudson, *Plains Country Towns*, 88–90.

54. Richard V. Francaviglia, "Victorian Bonanzas: Lessons from the Cultural Landscape of Western Hard Rock Mining Towns," *Journal of the West*, vol. 33, no. 1 (1994), 53–56.

55. Allen, *The Company Town in the American West*, 80–93.

56. Lowry Nelson, *The Mormon Village: A Pattern and Technique of Land Settlement* (Salt Lake City, Utah: University of Utah Press, 1952), 35, 38–39.

57. Reps, *Town Planning in Frontier America*, 414–420.

58. *Ibid.*, 400–410.

59. Glenn T. Trewartha, "The Unincorporated Hamlet: One Element in the American Settlement Fabric," *Annals of the Association of American Geographers*, vol. 33, no. 1 (March 1943), 38–75.

60. Richard V. Francaviglia, *Main Street Revisited: Time, Space, and Image Building in Small Town America* (Iowa City: University of Iowa Press, 1996), xviii–xxi, 6–7; Andrew Gulliford, "Vernacular and Small Town Architecture of Northwest Ohio," *Northwest Ohio Quarterly*, vol. 58, no. 4 (1986), 110–120.

61. *Ibid.*, 110–114.

62. Hermon W. De Long, *Boyhood Reminiscences* (Dansville, N.Y.: F. A. Owen Publishing Co., 1913), 6.

63. Anne A. Dodge, *Recollections of Old Stonington* (Stonington, Conn.: Pequot Press, 1966), 3–4.

64. Bailey, *Main Street*, 100–121.

65. Atherton, *Main Street on the Middle Border*, 43–44.

66. *Ibid.*, 217–222, 233–240.

67. John A. Jakle, *American Small Towns* (Hamden, Conn.: Archon Books, 1982), 46–48.

68. Philip L. White, *Beekmantown, New York*, 114–115.

69. Wiggin, *Impressions of Early Kansas*, 17.

70. Rose Wilder Lane, *Old Home Town* (New York: Longmans, Green, 1935), 6.

71. Doyle, *The Social Order of a Frontier Community*, 94–95.

72. Allen, *The Company Town in the American West*, 84–85.

73. Lingeman, *Small Town America*, 280–286.

74. Doyle, *The Social Order of a Frontier Community*, 128–155.

75. Lingeman, *Small Town America*, 291–292.

76. Willis F. Dunbar, *How It Was in Hartford* (Grand Rapids, Mich.: Eerdmans, 1968), 153.

77. Lane, *Old Home Town*, 7.

78. Pamela West, "The Rise and Fall of the American Porch," *Landscape*, vol. 20 (Spring, 1976), 42–47.

79. Hayden, *Seven American Utopias*, 43–45.

80. *Ibid.*, 149–150.

81. *Ibid.*, 225.

82. Leslie Stewart-Abernathy, "Urban Farmsteads: Household Responsibilities in the City," *Historical Archaeology*, vol. 20, no. 2 (1986), 5–8.

83. Lane, *Old Home Town*, 8.

84. Daniel J. Boorstin, *The Americans: The Democratic Experience* (New York: Random House, 1973), 274–280.

85. *Ibid.*, 288–289.

86. Weiss, *New Town Development in the United States*, 5–7.

87. Reps, *Cities of the American West*, 565–568.

88. Boorstin, *The Americans: The Democratic Experience*, 289–291.

89. But this was not the case in all towns. In Chilton, Wisconsin, subdivisions consisted of extensions of various grids. Similarly, in Grundy City, Iowa, the town's single grid of streets was extended in both north and south directions. And, Petersburg, Illinois, continued to have a relentless grid pattern. Jakle, Bastian, and Meyer, *Common Houses in America's Small Towns*, 23–63.

90. Lingeman, *Small Town America*, 462.

91. Jakle, Bastian, and Meyer, *Common Houses in America's Small Towns*, 170–173.

92. *Ibid.*, 183–184; West, "The Rise and Fall of the American Porch," 42–47.

### 3. Political Life

1. William Cronon, *Changes in the Land: Indians, Colonists, and the Ecology of New England* (New York: Hill and Wang, 1983), 37–38, 63–65.

2. *Ibid.*, 59.

3. Neal Salisbury, *Manitou and Providence: Indians, Europeans, and the Making of New England, 1500–1643* (New York: Oxford University Press, 1982), 42.

4. *Ibid.*, 43.

5. Cronon, *Changes in the Land*, 60.

6. Michael Zuckerman, *Peaceable Kingdoms: New England Towns in the Eighteenth Century* (New York: Knopf, 1970), 24.

7. *Ibid.*, 11–19, 32–33; Daniels, *The Connecticut Town*, 75–78; Bruce Daniels, *Dissent and Conformity on Narragansett Bay: The Colonial Rhode Island Town* (Middletown, Conn.: Wesleyan University, 1983), 24–25.

8. Martin, *Profits in the Wilderness*, 217–253.

9. Daniels, *The Connecticut Town*, 66.

10. *Ibid.*, 66.

11. Zuckerman, *Peaceable Kingdoms*, 140–146; Daniels, *The Connecticut Town*, 36.

12. Lockridge, *A New England Town*, 109.

13. Innes, *Labor in a New Land*, 125–128.

14. Daniels, *The Connecticut Town*, 34–36.

15. Zuckerman, *Peaceable Kingdoms*, 185–186.

16. Daniels, *The Connecticut Town*, 66–68.

17. Lockridge, *A New England Town*, 37–56, 119–138.

18. Innes, *Labor in a New Land*, 17–43.

19. Edward Cook, *Fathers of the Towns: Leadership and Community Structure in Eighteenth-Century New England* (Baltimore: Johns Hopkins University Press, 1976), 165–183.

20. Zuckerman, *Peaceable Kingdoms*, 215–219.

21. Daniels, *The Connecticut Town*, 87–90.

22. *Ibid.*, 90.

23. White, *Beekmantown, New York*, 174.

24. Lemon, *The Best Poor Man's Country*, 25.

25. Langdon G. Wright, "In Search of Peace and Harmony: New York Communities in the 17th Century," *New York History*, vol. 61, no. 1 (1980), 5–21.

26. Wolf, *Urban Village*, 187–188.

27. Lemon, *The Best Poor Man's Country*, 111.

28. Wolf, *Urban Village*, 162.

29. *Ibid.*, 201–202.

30. Isaac, *The Transformation of Virginia*, 91.

31. *Ibid.*, 134.

32. Daniels, *Dissent and Conformity of Narragansett Bay*, 69–71.

33. Daniels, *The Connecticut Town*, 69.

34. *Ibid.*, 69–70.

35. Wright, "In Search of Peace and Harmony," 5–21.

36. Wolf, *Urban Village*, 177–178.

37. Isaac, *The Transformation of Virginia*, 93.

38. Sears, *The First Hundred Years of Town Planning in Georgia*, 55–156.

39. Lemon, *The Best Poor Man's Country*, 130–140.

40. Gilbert R. Cruz, *Let There Be Towns: Spanish Municipal Origins in the American Southwest, 1610–1810* (College Station, Tex.: Texas A&M University Press, 1988), 144–170.

41. *Commercial Atlas and Marketing Guide* (Chicago, New York, and San Francisco: Rand McNally, any recent year).

42. White, *Beekmantown, New York*, 181–182.

43. *Ibid.*, 188–192.

44. Lucy Simlar, "The Township: The Community of the Rural Pennsylvanian," vol. 106, no. 1 (1982), 53–64.

45. Merle Curti, *The Making of an American Community: A Case Study of Democracy in a Frontier County* (Stanford, Calif.: Stanford University Press, 1959), 261–262. This is a study of Trempealeau County, Wisconsin, from 1850 to 1880, and of the townships within it.

46. *Ibid.*, 262–265.

47. *Ibid.*, 281–286, 291–294.

48. Doyle, *The Social Order of a Frontier Community*, 195.

49. *Ibid.*, 195–212, 217–223.

50. *Ibid.*, 223–226.

51. Dykstra, *The Cattle Towns*, 207–253.

52. Dunbar, *How It Was in Hartford*, 43, 18, 87.

53. Lingeman, *Small Town America*, 123; Boorstin, *The Americans: The National Experience* (New York: Random House, 1965), 165–167.

54. Ohman, *A History of Missouri's Counties, County Seats, and Courthouse Squares*, 19–23.

55. *Ibid.*, 157–160.

56. Doyle, *The Social Order of a Frontier Community*, 19.

57. Curti, *The Making of an American Community*, 361–376.

58. Hamilton, *Black Towns and Profit*, 141, 110.

59. Allen, *The Company Town in the American West*, 94.

60. George B. Lockwood, *The New Harmony Movement* (New York: Appleton, 1905), 4–5.

61. Charles Nordhoff, *The Communistic Societies of the United States* (New York: Harper and Brothers, 1875), 279.

62. Gwendolyn S. Hughes, "Village Politics," in Brunner, *et al.*, *American Agricultural Villages* (New York: George H. Doran, 1927), 241–244.

63. *Ibid.*, 255–257.

64. Brunner and Kolb, *Rural Social Trends*, 285–298.

65. James West, *Plainville, U.S.A.* (New York: Columbia University Press, 1945), 216–219.

66. Lowry Nelson, *The Minnesota Community: Country and Town in Transition* (Minneapolis: University of Minnesota Press, 1960), 107.

67. Arthur J. Vidich and Joseph Bensman, *Small Town in Mass Society: Class, Power and Religion in a Rural Community* (Princeton, N.J.: Princeton University Press, 1958), 113, 139–140. "Springdale" is a pseudonym for a real town in upstate New York in the Finger Lakes area.

68. *Ibid.*, 110–118, 128–132, 150–153.

69. Don Martindale and R. Galen Hansen, *Small Town and the Nation: The Conflict of Local and Translocal Forces* (Westport, Conn.: Greenwood, 1969), 149–159.

70. Kenneth D. and Katherine D. Rainey, "Local Government," in Thomas R. Ford, ed., *Rural U.S.A.: Persistence and Change* (Ames, Iowa: Iowa State University Press, 1978), 126–128.

71. *Ibid.*, 128–133.

72. *Ibid.*, 133–135.

73. *Ibid.*, 135–137.

74. *Ibid.*, 137–138.

75. *Ibid.*, 138–139.

76. *Ibid.*, 141–142.

77. *Ibid.*, 139–140.

78. *Ibid.*, 140–141.

79. *Ibid.*, 142–144.

## 4. Economic Life

1. Salisbury, *Manitou and Providence*, 30–34; Cronon, *Changes in the Land*, 60–67.

2. For a penetrating analysis of some of these points: *Ibid.*, 67–77.

3. *Ibid.*, 37–40.

4. Martin, *Profits in the Wilderness*, 28–37.

5. Wolf, *Urban Village*, 58–95.

6. Cronon, *Changes in the Land*, 34–156.

7. Christine Leigh Heyrman, *Commerce and Culture: The Maritime Communities of Colonial Massachusetts, 1690–1750* (New York: Norton, 1984), 31.

8. For a description of such activity in New England, at least: William F. Robinson, *Abandoned New England: Its Hidden Ruins and Where to Find Them* (Boston: New York Graphic Society, 1976), 76–80, 93–112.

9. Lemon, *Best Poor Man's Country*, 200–205.

10. Bridenbaugh, *Myths and Realities*, 147–152.

11. Wolf, *Urban Village*, 106–107.

12. Lemon, *The Best Poor Man's Country*, 114–115.

13. *Ibid.*, 119; Daniels, *The Connecticut Town*, 141.

14. *Ibid.*, 145–146.

15. Lemon, *The Best Poor Man's Country*, 118–122, 137–138.

16. Amos Long, Jr., "The Rural Village," *Pennsylvania Folklife*, vol. 29, no. 3 (1980), 125.

17. Hendricks, "Town Development in the Colonial Backcountry," *passim*; Thomas, "Settlement, Community, and Economy," *passim*; Carr, "The Metropolis of Maryland," 142–144.

18. Sears, *The First Hundred Years of Town Planning in Georgia*, 157–160.

19. Heyrman, *Commerce and Culture*, 52; Daniels, *The Connecticut Town*, 141.

20. Lemon, *Best Poor Man's Country*, 27–29.

21. Isaac, *The Transformation of Virginia*, 27–29; Breen, *Tobacco Mentality*, 62.

22. Carville and Hoffman, "Staple Crops and Urban Development in the 18th-Century South," 7–11, 26–39, 51–62.

23. Innes, *Labor in a New Land*, 3–122.

24. Daniels, *The Connecticut Town*, 147–148.

25. Lemon, *The Best Poor Man's Country*, 27–29.

26. *Ibid.*, 29–31.

27. *Ibid.*, 169, 179, 216–217.

28. As quoted in Isaac, *The Transformation of Virginia*, 35.

29. *Ibid.*, 38–42.

30. T. H. Breen, *Tobacco Culture: The Mentality of the Great Tidewater Planters on the Eve of the Revolution* (Princeton, N.J.: Princeton University Press, 1985), 84–123; Eugene Genovese, *Roll, Jordan Roll: The World the Slaves Made* (New York: Random House, 1975), 3–7.

31. Lockridge, *A New England Town*, 69.

32. Laurel B. Ulrich, *Good Wives: Image and Reality in the Lives of Women in Northern New England, 1650–1750* (New York: Oxford University Press, 1982), 13–14; Susan Geib, "Changing Works: Agriculture and Society in Brookfield, Massachusetts, 1785–1820," Ph.D. dissertation, Boston University, 1981, 121–131.

33. Daniels, *The Connecticut Town*, 156.

34. *Ibid.*, 157.

35. Rutman, *A Place in Time*, 205–206.

36. Daniels, *The Connecticut Town*, 147–148, 153–156.

37. Philip J. Greven, *Four Generations: Population, Land, and Family in Colonial Andover, Massachusetts* (Ithaca, N.Y.: Cornell University Press, 1970), 41–71, 125–172, 222–258.

38. Lemon, *The Best Poor Man's Country*, 71–97.

39. Wolf, *Urban Village*, 58–95.

40. Isaac, *The Transformation of Virginia*, 116–117.

41. Reps, *Town Planning in Frontier America*, 66–68; Kutsche and Van Ness, *Canones*, 36–38.

42. White, *Beekmantown, New York*, 29–56.

43. Jeremy W. Kilar, *Michigan's Lumbertowns: Lumbermen and Laborers in Saginaw, Bay City, and Muskegon, 1870–1905* (Detroit: Wayne State University Press, 1990), 14–17, 21–48, 300–305.

44. Allen, *The Company Town in the American West*, 14–32.

45. Richard Hogan, *Class and Community in Frontier Colorado* (Lawrence, Kans.: University Press of Kansas, 1990), 49.

46. Allen, *The Company Town in the American West*, 33–49.

47. *Ibid.*, 50–69.

48. *Ibid.*, 79–139.

49. Gary Kulik, Roger Parks, and Theodore Z. Penn, eds., *The New England Mill Village, 1790–1860* (Cambridge, Mass.: MIT Press, 1982), xxiii–xvi. This collection of documents has a fine introduction on the subject.

50. *Ibid.*, xxviii–xxix.

51. Thomas Dublin, *Women at Work: The Transformation of Work and Community in Lowell, Massachusetts, 1826–1860* (New York: Columbia University Press, 1979), 14–22.

52. *Ibid.*, 75–85.

53. Wallace, *Rockdale*, 14.

54. Robert Doherty, *Society and Power: Five New England Towns, 1800–1860* (Amherst, Mass.: University of Massachusetts Press, 1977), 23.

55. Kulik, Parks, and Penn, *The New England Mill Village*, xxvii.

56. *Ibid.*, xxix–xxxi; Wallace, *Rockdale*, 356–365; Dublin, *Women at Work*, 86–107.

57. Lingeman, *Small Town America*, 145–147.

58. Daniel J. Boorstin, *The Americans: The Democratic Experience*, 326–331.

59. Peirce Lewis, "Small Town in Pennsylvania," 340–341.

60. Boorstin, *The Americans: The National Experience*, 30–33.

61. Roderick Turnbull, *Maple Hill Stories* (Kansas City, Mo.: [no publisher], 1961), 47

62. Dunbar, *How It Was in Hartford*, 193.

63. Smith, *As a City Upon a Hill*, 105–106.

64. *Ibid.*, 90–91.

65. Geoffrey Rossano, "A Subtle Revolution: The Urban Transformation of Rural Life—New Gloucester, Maine, 1775–1930," Ph.D. dissertation, University of North Carolina, 1980, 375, 379, 386–387.

66. Richard Holmes, *Communities in Transition: Bedford and Lincoln, Massachusetts, 1729–1850* (Ann Arbor, Mich.: UMI Research Press, 1980), 83–84.

67. Hal S. Barron, *Those Who Stayed Behind: Rural Society in Nineteenth Century New England* (New York: Cambridge University Press, 1984), 63–68.

68. James Oakes, *The Ruling Race: A History of American Slaveholders* (New York: Knopf, 1982), 91–94.

69. Hubert Humphreys, "A History of the Village of Grayson, Louisiana and Adjacent Settlements, 1892–1992," *Journal, North Louisiana Historical Association*, vol. 23, no. 4 (1992), 108.

70. Faragher, *Sugar Creek*, 62–66, 184.

71. *Ibid.*, 199.

72. *Ibid.*, 102–105.

73. Lane, *Old Home Town*, 2.

74. Dykstra, *The Cattle Towns*, 74–100, 149–206.

75. Elvin Hatch, *Biography of a Small Town* (New York: Columbia University Press, 1979), 15.

76. Odell, "The Functional Pattern of Villages in a Selected Area of the Corn Belt," 17–26, 35.

77. Hudson, "The Plains Country Town," in Brian W. Blouet and Frederick Luebke, *The Great Plains: Environment and Culture* (Lincoln, Nebr.: University of Nebraska Press, 1979), 101, 105.

78. Boorstin, *The Americans: The Democratic Experience*, 317–321, 326–327. Gustavus Swift and Philip Armour were key figures in the development of refrigerated transport and processing assembly lines.

79. Boorstin, *The Americans: The National Experience*, 123; Doyle, *The Social Order of a Frontier Community*, 5–6, 63–64.

80. The preeminent boosters were William B. Ogden (Chicago), Daniel Drake (Cincinnati), and William Larimer (Pittsburgh, Omaha, Denver), all of whose towns did mushroom into cities. But there were many other boosters whose communities, while growing, remained towns, or at best small cities. Boorstin, *The American: The National Experience*, 116–121.

81. Blumin, *The Urban Threshold*, 52.

82. For an example of the railroad-building frenzies that could link the more favorably situated towns in a given area once railroad construction was relatively standardized by the 1840s and 1850s: Larry Lowenthal, "Railroad Rivalry in the Connecticut River Valley," *Historical Journal of Western Massachusetts*, vol. 20, no. 2 (1992), 109–132.

83. Doyle, *The Social Order of a Frontier Community*, 79–85.

84. Jakle, Bastian, and Meyer, *Common Houses in America's Small Towns*, 22–63.

85. Doherty, *Society and Power*, 40–45.

86. Doyle, *The Social Order of a Frontier Community*, 97–108.

87. Curti, *The Making of an American Community*, 65–83.

88. Faragher, *Sugar Creek*, 100–101.

89. Russell B. Nye, *Society and Culture in America, 1830–1860* (New York: Harper and Row, 1974), 267.

90. Atherton, *Main Street on the Middle Border*, 48.

91. *Ibid.*, 62.

92. Boorstin, *The Americans: The Democratic Experience*, 315–316, 321–322.

93. Jakle, Bastian, and Meyer, *Common Houses in America's Small Towns*, 29–32, 40.

94. Blumin, *The Urban Threshold*, 14–16.

95. Barron, *Those Who Stayed Behind*, 52–53.

96. Mahoney, *The River Towns in the Great West*, 258.

97. Barron, *Those Who Stayed Behind*, 71–75.

98. Curti, *The Making of an American Community*, 232–233.

99. Rodney O. Davis, "Prairie Emporium: Clarence, Iowa, 1860–1880," *Mid-America*, vol. 51, no. 2 (1969), 135–136.

100. Blumin, *The Urban Threshold*, 15.

101. Doris D. Fanelli, "William Polk's General Store in Saint George's, Delaware," *Delaware History*, vol. 19, no. 4 (1981), 212–222.

102. Dunbar, *How It Was in Hartford*, 62.

103. Atherton, *Main Street on the Middle Border*, 44–47.

104. Barron, *Those Who Stayed Behind*, 52.

105. C. W. Goodlander, *Memoirs and Recollections* (Fort Scott, Kans.: Monitor Printing Co., 1900), 93.

106. Doyle, *The Social Order of a Frontier Community*, 88–90.

107. Mahoney, *River Towns in the Great West*, 257.

108. Curti, *The Making of an American Community*, 223–231.

109. Atherton, *Main Street on the Middle Border*, 34.

110. *Ibid.*, 33–34.

111. *Ibid.*, 37–39.

112. *Ibid.*, 40, 57–58.

113. *Ibid.*, 50–54.

114. Crockett, *The Black Towns*, 115–145; Hamilton, *Black Towns and Profit*, 110, 125, 141.

115. Kattner, "From Immigrant Settlement into Town," 165, 169–170.

116. Hine, *California's Utopian Colonies* (New Haven, Conn.: Yale University Press, 1966) 6–7, 168.

117. Nordhoff, *The Communistic Societies of the United States*, 33; William Alfred Hinds, *American Communities and Cooperative Colonies* (Chicago: C. H. Kerr, 1908; original, 1878), 49.

118. Lingeman, *Small Town America*, 321, 443.

119. Ford, *Rural U.S.A.*, 8; Jim Hightower, "Corporate Power in Rural America," *W.I.N.*, vol. 8, no. 12 (July 1972), 8–10, reprinted in Richard D. Rodefield, ed., *Change in Rural America* (St. Louis: C. V. Mosby, 1978), 156–157.

120. Boorstin, *The Americans: The Democratic Experience*, 330–331.

121. Gwendolyn S. Hughes, "The Village as a Farm Service Station," in Brunner, Hughes, and Patten, *American Agricultural Villages*, 113–136.

122. C. E. Lively, "The Decline of Small Trade Centers," *Rural America*, vol. 10 (March 1932), 5–7; reprinted in Rodefeld, ed., *Change in Rural America*, 303–304.

123. Ford, *Rural U.S.A.*, 6–8.

124. Hart, "Small Towns and Manufacturing," *Geographical Review*, vol. 78, no. 3 (1988), 285.

125. Allen, *The Company Town in the American West, passim*; Patricia Duane Beaver, *Rural Community in the Appalachian South* (Lexington, Ky.: University Press of Kentucky, 1986), 29.

126. Hine, *California's Utopian Colonies*, 6–7.

127. Beaver, *Rural Community in the Appalachian South*, 29.

128. Jakle, Bastian, and Meyer, *Common Houses in American's Small Towns*, 46–52, 55–58.

129. Martindale and Hansen, *Small Town and the Nation*, 91–92.

130. Atherton, *Main Street on the Middle Border*, 217–221.

131. Burns Fuller, *Burns Fuller Remembers* (Fenton, Mich.: Independent Print Co., 1966), 30.

132. Dunbar, *How It Was in Hartford*, 69.

133. *Ibid.*, 199.

134. As quoted in Norman Moline, *Mobility and the Small Town, 1900–1930: Transportation Change in Oregon, Illinois* (Chicago: University of Chicago, Department of Geography Research Paper No. 32, 1971), 124.

135. Atherton, *Main Street on the Middle Border*, 220.

136. *Ibid.*, 237–238; Moline, *Mobility and the Small Town*, 126.

137. Charles Luther Fry, *American Villagers* (New York: George H. Doran, 1926), 42.

138. As quoted in Moline, *Mobility and the Small Town*, 130, 134, 138.

139. Brunner and Kolb, *Rural Social Trends*, 160–161.

140. David Ross Jenkins, *The Growth and Decline of Agricultural Villages* (New York: Teachers College, Columbia University, 1940), 4.

141. Glenn V. Fuguitt, "The Small Town in Rural America," *Journal of Cooperative Extension*, vol. 8, no. 1 (1965), 19–25, reprinted in Rodefield, *Change in Rural America*, 313.

142. Moline, *Mobility and the Small Town*, 156–158.

143. Brian L. Shulz, "Where Is Main Street?: The Commercial Landscape of Four Oklahoma Small Towns," *Chronicles of Oklahoma*, vol. 71, no. 1 (1993), 92–93.

144. Boorstin, *The Americans: The Democratic Experience*, 146–147.

145. *Ibid.*, 127–128.

146. *Ibid.*, 110–111.

147. *Ibid.*, 430–433.

148. Nancy Burns, "The Collapse of Small Towns on the Great Plains: A Bibliography," *Emporia State Research Studies*, vol. 31, no. 1 (Summer 1982), 7–8; David C. Mott, "Abandoned Towns, Villages, and Post Offices of Iowa," *Annals of Iowa*, vol. 17 (October 1930), 434–465; (January 1931), 513–543; (April 1931), 578–599; vol. 18 (July 1931), 42–69; (January 1932), 189–220.

149. Hudson, "The Plains Country Town," 107–109; Lofstgard and Voelker, "Changing Rural Life in the Great Plains," *Journal of Farm Economics*, vol. 45 (1963), 1110–1117, reprinted in Rodefield, *Change in Rural America*, 59–60.

150. Matti Kaups and Cotton Mather, "Eben: Thirty Years Later in a Finnish Community in the Upper Peninsula of Michigan," *Economic Geography*, vol. 44, no. 1 (June 1968), 59–61.

151. Lingeman, *Small Town America*, 446–447, 458. The statistics of this phenomenon have been much analyzed, perhaps most notably by Calvin L. Beale, "The Revival of Population Growth in Non-Metropolitan American," *Economic Research Service*, USDA. #605 (Washington, D.C., 1975), reprinted in Rodefield, *Change in Rural America*, 518–525.

152. Glenn V. Fuguitt and Donald W. Thomas, "Small Town Growth in the United States: An Analysis by Size, Class, and Place," *Demography*, vol. 3, no. 2 (1966), 526; Calvin L. Beale, "Quantitative Dimensions of Decline and Stability Among Rural Communities," in L. R. Whiting, ed., *Communities Left Behind: Alternatives for Development* (Ames, Iowa: Iowa State University Press, 1974), 3–21, reprinted in Rodefield, *Change in Rural America*, 71–75.

153. Jakle, Bastian, and Meyer, *Common Houses in American's Small Towns*, 22–63.

154. Lingeman, *Small Town America*, 465–467; P. D. Converse and Romona J. Russell, "Why City Workers Live in Agricultural Villages," *Current Economic Comment*, vol. 121 (August 1950), 37–46, reprinted in Rodefield, *Change in Rural America*, 368.

## 5. Social Life

1. Salisbury, *Manitou and Providence*; 42–47; Cronon, *Changes in the Land*, 59.

2. Lockridge, *A New England Town*, 69–71, 151.

3. Daniels, *The Connecticut Town*, 162.

4. Lockridge, *A New England Town*, 151; Daniels, *The Connecticut Town*, 162.

5. Lemon, *The Best Poor Man's Country*, 10–11.

6. Wolf, *Urban Village*, 124.

7. Daniels, *The Connecticut Town*, 147–148, 162.

8. Innes, *Labor in a New Land, passim.*

9. Daniels, *The Connecticut Town*, 162, 165.

10. For a good overall assessment: Isaac, *The Transformation of Virginia*, 11–138.

11. Heyrman, *Commerce and Culture*, 65–67, 79–80, 234–235, 259–265.

12. Zuckerman, *Peaceable Kingdoms*, 107–108.

13. Lemon, *Best Poor Man's Country*, 43–49.

14. Wolf, *Urban Village*, 127–129.

15. For a good description of these divided communities: Isaac, *The Transformation of Virginia*, 30–42, 65–87.

16. For an assessment of the "strata" of a rural area, Middlesex County, Virginia: Rutman, *A Place in Time*, 128–163.

17. For an assessment of the planter's life as a social elite: Isaac, *The Transformation of Virginia*, 34–42, 58–79, 88–135. For the mercantile elite: Innes, *Labor in a New Land*, 18. For an overall portrait with an emphasis on gentility as an ideal: Richard L. Bushman, *The Refinement of America: Persons, Houses, Cities* (New York: Knopf, 1992), 30–138.

18. As quoted in Isaac, *The Transformation of Virginia*, 43.

19. Innes, *Labor in a New Land*, 82–117. Also: Wolf, *Urban Village*, 121–123.

20. Greven, *Four Generations*, 175–221.

21. Daniels, *The Connecticut Town*, 8–44; Martin, *Profits in the Wilderness, passim.*

22. Isaac, *The Transformation of Virginia*, 116.

23. Lemon, *Best Poor Man's Country*, 71–83.

24. Wolf, *Urban Village*, 76–80.

25. Zuckerman, *Peaceable Kingdoms*, 123–153; Lockridge, *A New England Town*, 103–116. Zuckerman sees these activities as indicating a desire to "heal the divisions," whereas Lockridge presents them as indications of division.

26. For example: Innes, *Labor in a New Land*, 147–148; Heyrman, *Commerce and Culture*, 274–303; Paul Boyer and Stephen Nissenbaum, *Salem Possessed: The Social Origins of Witchcraft* (Cambridge, Mass.: Harvard University Press, 1974), 37–80.

27. *Ibid.*, 80–109; John Demos, *Entertaining Satan: Witchcraft and the Culture of Early New England* (New York: Oxford University Press, 1982), 275–312, 368–386.

28. Innes, *Labor in a New Land*, 128–150.

29. Heyrman, *Commerce and Culture*, 226–230, 261–265, 316–329.

30. Boyer and Nissenbaum, *Salem Possessed*, 37–109.

31. Gerald W. Mullin, *Flight and Rebellion: Slave Resistance in Eighteenth-Century Virginia* (New York: Oxford University Press, 1972), *passim.*

32. The best account of Puritan communalism is Zuckerman, *Peaceable Kingdoms*, 46–186.

33. Isaac, *The Transformation of Virginia*, 305–308.

34. Lemon, *The Best Poor Man's Country*, 84–85.

35. For a good case study: Jean F. Hankins, "A Cage for John Sawyer: The Poor of Otisfield, Maine," *Maine History*, vol. 34, no. 2 (1994), 96–115.

36. Wolf, *Urban Village*, 124–126, 189–191, 235–236, 316.

37. *Ibid.*, 127–153.

38. Lockridge, *A New England Town*, 11–12.

39. On the planters: Breen, *Tobacco Culture*, 95–97; Genovese, *Roll, Jordan Roll*, 3–7. On the merchants: Innes, *Labor in a New Land*, 18.

40. John Blassingame, *The Slave Community* (New York: Oxford University Press, 1972, revised ed.), 223–283. Blassingame deals with the antebellum period, but master-slave work relations did not fundamentally change from the colonial period to the antebellum period.

41. Clark Knowlton, "Changing Spanish-American Villages of Northern New Mexico," *Sociology and Social Research*, vol. 53, no. 1 (1969), 457–463; Paul Kutsche and John R. Van Ness, *Canones: Values, Crisis, and Survival in a Northern New Mexico Village* (Albuquerque, N.M.: University of New Mexico Press, 1981), 71–99. For indications that town dwellers in the towns founded by Spanish colonists or worker villages founded by modern Mexican or Chicano immigrants continued to exhibit these characteristics: John R. Van Ness, *Hispanos in Northern New Mexico: The Development of Corporate Community and Multicommunity* (New York: AMS Press, 1991), and Gilbert G. Gonzalez, *Labor and Community: Mexican Citrus Worker Villages in a Southern California County, 1900–1950* (Urbana, Ill.: University of Illinois Press, 1994).

42. Doherty, *Society and Power*, 46–50.

43. Blumin, *The Urban Threshold*, 39.

44. *Ibid.*, 52–56, 78–95.

45. Doyle, *The Social Order of a Frontier Community*, 103–108.

46. *Ibid.*, 262–263.

47. *Ibid.*, 119–155.

48. Curti, *The Making of an American Community*, 65–73, 223–248.

49. *Ibid.*, 78.

50. Kathleen Underwood, *Town Building on the Colorado Frontier* (Albuquerque, N.M.: University of New Mexico, 1987), 75–77.

51. Oakes, *The Ruling Race*, 37–68.

52. *Ibid.*, 69–95.

53. Faragher, *Sugar Creek*, 185.

54. *Ibid.*, 266.

55. Dykstra, *The Cattle Towns*, 108–109. For an unusually full and nuanced description of "class" in the cattle towns: C. Robert Haywood, *Victorian West: Class and Culture in Kansas Cattle Towns* (Lawrence, Kans.: University Press of Kansas, 1991), 13–60.

56. White, *Beekmantown, New York*, 29–52, 95–108.

57. Allen, *The Company Town in the American West*, 94–139.

58. Wallace, *Rockdale*, 44–65.

59. Fuller, *Burns Fuller Remembers*, 48.

60. Atherton, *Main Street on the Middle Border*, 148–151.

61. *Ibid.*, 151–153.

62. *Ibid.*, 153–160.

63. *Ibid.*, 161–168; Boorstin, *The Americans: The National Experience*, 124–134.

64. Atherton, *Main Street on the Middle Border*, 168–176.

65. Wiggin, *Impressions of Early Kansas*, 13.

66. Dunbar, *How It Was in Hartford*, 80.

67. *Ibid.*, 79–80.

68. Wiggin, *Impressions of Early Kansas*, 19, 46, 49, 50.

69. As quoted in Crockett, *Black Towns*, 55.

70. Roderick Turnbull, *More Maple Hill Stories* (Kansas City, Mo.: Lowell Press, 1974), 31.

71. Bushman, *The Refinement of America*, 182–186, 273–279, 420–425, 431–434.

72. Wallace, *Rockdale*, 63; Dublin, *Women at Work*, 183–197.

73. David J. Rothman, *The Discovery of the Asylum* (Boston: Little, Brown, 1970), *passim*.

74. Alma W. Swinton, *I Married a Doctor* (Marquette, Mich.: [no publisher], 1965), 372.

75. Smith, *As a City Upon a Hill*, 132–144.

76. Atherton, *Main Street on the Middle Border*, 163.

77. David J. Russo, *The Origins of Local News in the U.S. Country Press, 1840s–1880s* (Lexington, Ky.: Journalism Monographs No. 65, February 1980).

78. Dunbar, *How It Was in Hartford*, 70, 149.

79. As quoted in Atherton, *Main Street on the Middle Border*, 165–166.

80. *Ibid.*, 65–88.

81. Kilar, *Michigan's Lumbertowns*, 300–302.

82. Dykstra, *The Cattle Towns*, 100–107; C. Robert Haywood, *Victorian West*, 18–32; Gary L. Cunningham, "Gambling in the Kansas Cattle Towns: A Prominent and Somewhat Honorable Profession," *Kansas History*, vol. 5, no. 1 (1982), 9; Carol Leonard, Isidor Wallimann, and Wayne Rohrer, "Prostitution and Changing Morality in the Frontier Cattle Towns of Kansas," *Kansas History*, vol. 2, no. 1 (1979), 39.

83. *Ibid.*, 39–41, 52–53.

84. Charles L. Sonnichsen, *Billy King's Tombstone* (Tucson, Ariz.: University of Arizona Press, 1972), 93–94.

85. *Ibid.*, 46.

86. Cunningham, "Gambling in the Kansas Cattle Towns," 4–21.

87. Blake Gumprecht, "Whiskey Towns of Oklahoma Territory, 1889–1907," *Chronicles of Oklahoma*, vol. 74, no. 2 (1996), 146–164.

88. *Ibid.*, 165–169; Dykstra, *The Cattle Towns*, 239–292.

89. For accounts of ordinary temperance crusades in typical agricultural service centers: White, *Beekmantown, New York*, 162–169; Barron, *Those Who Stayed Behind*, 115–120.

90. Atheron, *Main Street on the Middle Border*, 88–95.

91. Wiggin, *Impressions of Early Kansas*, 34–35.

92. Swinton, *I Married a Doctor*, 9.

93. Dunbar, *How It Was in Hartford*, 91.

94. Fred Lape, *A Farm and Village Boyhood* (Syracuse, N.Y.: Syracuse University Press, 1980), 64, 90.

95. Barron, *Those Who Stayed Behind*, 115–120.

96. Atherton, *Main Street on the Middle Border*, 100–105.

97. Turnbull, *More Maple Hill Stories*, 33.

98. As quoted in Atherton, *Main Street on the Middle Border*, 103.

99. John M. Gorman, *I Remember Manzaner* (Bishop, Calif.: Pinon Press, 1967), 12.

100. Dunbar, *How It Was in Hartford*, 71–72.

101. Crockett, *The Black Towns*, 140; Carlson, "The Black Community in the Rural North," 137.

102. Nordhoff, *The Communistic Societies of the United States*, 105.

103. Mark Holloway, *Heavens on Earth: Utopian Communities in America, 1680–1880* (New York: Library Publishers, 1951), 19, 213–214.

104. Ford, ed., *Rural U.S.A.*, 8–9.

105. Thomas J. Durant, Jr., and Clark S. Knowlton, "Rural Ethnic Minorities," in *Ibid.*, 145–166.

106. Atherton, *Main Street on the Middle Border*, 267–280.

107. Albert Blumenthal, *A Sociological Study of a Small Town* (Chicago: University of Chicago Press, 1932), 144–174.

108. West, *Plainville, U.S.A.*, 120–127.

109. *Ibid.*, 97–99.

110. Joseph Bensman and Arthur J. Vidich, *Small Town in Mass Society*, 52–71.

111. *Ibid.*, 71–78.

112. *Ibid.*, 86–98.

113. Martindale and Hansen, *Small Town and the Nation*, 62–80.

114. Hatch, *Biography of a Small Town*, 83.

115. *Ibid.*, 102.

116. Carolyn Ellis, *Fisher Folk: Two Communities on Chesapeake Bay* (Lexington, Ky.: University Press of Kentucky, 1986), 129–140.

117. Salisbury, *Manitou and Providence*, 47–48.

118. For a detailed account of one town, Brookfield, Massachusetts: Geib, "Changing Works," 96–97, 167–171.

119. *Ibid.*, 162–165, 172–174.

120. For a description of Sugar Creek, a rural neighborhood in Illinois: Faragher, *Sugar Creek*, 135–136.

121. Gary Koerselman, "The Quest for Community in Rural Iowa: Neighborhood Life in Early Middleburg History," *Annals of Iowa*, vol. 41, no. 5 (1972), 1006–1020.

122. Zuckerman, *Peaceable Kingdoms*, 173–176.

123. Bushman, *The Refinement of America*, 185; Isaac, *The Transformation of Virginia*, 95.

124. *Ibid.*, 98–104.

125. As quoted in *ibid.*, 102.

126. Bushman, *The Refinement of America*, 160–164.

127. Daniels, *The Connecticut Town*, 150.

128. Ulrich, *Good Wives*, 51–60.

129. Elizabeth Donaghy Garrett, *At Home: The American Family, 1750–1870* (New York: Abrams, 1990), 39–60; Bushman, *The Refinement of America*, 273–279.

130. Barbara Berg, *The Remembered Gate: Origins of American Feminism: The Woman and the City, 1800–1860* (New York: Oxford University Press, 1978), 75–94.

131. Lape, *A Farm and Village Boyhood*, 66.

132. Atherton, *Main Street on the Middle Border*, 57–59.

133. Lane, *Old Home Town*, 11–13.

134. For the continuation of gender divisions: Faragher, *Sugar Creek*, 168. For the breaking down of those divisions: Isaac, *The Transformation of Virginia*, 164–172, 314–316.

135. Atherton, *Main Street on the Middle Border*, 59–60.

136. Haywood, *Victorian West*, 179–180.

137. Dunbar, *How It Was in Hartford*, 102.

138. Haywood, *Victorian West*, 220–226; also: Robert K. Gilmore, *Ozark Baptizings, Hangings, and Other Diversions: Theatrical Folkways of Rural Missouri, 1885–1910* (Norman, Okla.: University of Oklahoma Press, 1984), 103–110.

139. Haywood, *Victorian West*, 220–226.

140. Turnbull, *Maple Hill Stories*, 113–114.

141. For instance, in Tombstone, on the Arizona frontier, in the 1880s: Faulk, *Tombstone*, 123–125. Or in Sugar Creek, on the Illinois frontier, in the 1840s: Faragher, *Sugar Creek*, 153. Or in western Iowa, in the 1880s: Raymond A. Smith, Jr., "Sports and Games in Western Iowa in the Early 1880s," *Palimpsest*, vol. 65, no. 1 (1984), 9–16.

142. Lape, *A Farm and Village Boyhood*, 98–99.

143. Smith, "Sports and Games," 9–16; Haywood, *Victorian West*, 189–195. Even in the relatively isolated, wholly owned company towns of the mountainous West, corporate owners typically built "recreation halls" and other outdoor recreational facilities so that their employees could use a site built specifically for the purpose. Allen, *The Company Town in the American West*, 98–99.

144. Haywood, *Victorian West*, 170–178; Atherton, *Main Street on the Middle Border*, 128–135.

145. As quoted in *ibid.*, 131.

146. *Ibid.*, 135–142; Willis F. Dunbar, "The Opera House as a Social Institution in Michigan," *Michigan History Magazine*, vol. 27 (October–December 1943), 661–667.

147. Haywood, *Victorian West*, 133–138.

148. Atherton, *Main Street on the Middle Border*, 209–212.

149. Blumin, *The Urban Threshold*, 150–165.

150. Goodlander, *Memoirs and Recollections*, 35.

151. For example: White, *Beekmantown, New York*, 155–156.

152. *Ibid.*, 156–157.

153. Doyle, *The Social Order of a Frontier Community*, 186.

154. Leonard, Walliman, and Roher, "Groups and Social Organizations in Frontier Cattle Towns in Kansas," 61.

155. Doyle, *The Social Order of a Frontier Community*, 182–192.

156. Haywood, *Victorian West*, 244–248.

157. Cooper, *Black Settlers in Rural Wisconsin*, 18; Charles T. Banner-Haley, "An Extended Community: Sketches of Afro-American History in Three Counties Along New York's Southern Tier, 1890–1980," *Afro-Americans in New York Life and History*, vol. 13, no. 1 (1989), 13; Hamilton, *Black Towns and Profit*, 28, 68–69, 110, 128–129, 141; Crockett, *The Black Towns*, 146, 148–149.

158. Allen, *The Company Town in the American West*, 98–99.

159. Michael L. Berger, *The Devil Wagon in God's Country: The Automobile and Social Change in Rural America, 1893–1929* (Hamden, Conn.: Archon Books, 1979), *passim*.

160. *Ibid.*, 125; Moline, *Mobility and the Small Town*, 148–157.

161. For an examination of the phenomenon in one state: David D. Dawson, "Baseball Calls: Arkansas Town Baseball in the Twenties," *Arkansas Historical Quarterly*, vol. 54, no. 4 (Winter 1995), 409–426.

162. Moline, *Mobility and the Small Town*, 148–157.

163. Atherton, *Main Street on the Middle Border*, 248, 291.

164. For a study of activity of this kind in one state: Catherine E. Rymph, "'Keeping the Political Fires Burning': Republican Women's Clubs and Female Political Culture in Small-Town Iowa, 1928–1938," *Annals of Iowa*, vol. 56, nos. 1–2 (1997), 118.

165. Marjory Patten, "Village Social Organization," in Brunner, Hughes, and Patten, *American Agricultural Villages*, 191–192.

166. Brunner and Kolb, *Rural Social Trends*, 242–243.

167. Lingeman, *Small Town America*, 409–410.

168. Atherton, *Main Street on the Middle Border*, 247, 290–293.

169. Demos, *A Little Commonwealth*, 80, 184.

170. Daniels, *The Connecticut Town*, 158–159.

171. Jane C. Nylander, *Our Own Snug Fireside: Images of the New England Home, 1760–1860* (New York: Knopf, 1993), 38–39; Garrett, *At Home*, 240.

172. Ulrich, *Good Wives*, 127–129, 135–136, 144, 157–158; Garrett, *At Home*, 229; Nylander, *Our Own Snug Fireside*, 27–32.

173. Demos, *A Little Commonwealth*, 62–81, 107–117.

174. *Ibid.*, 100–106.

175. Zuckerman, *Peaceable Kingdoms*, 73–74; Demos, *A Little Commonwealth*, 139–140, 145–150.

176. *Ibid.*, 150–170; Wolf, *Urban Village*, 232, 255–262; Ulrich, *Good Wives*, 122–123.

177. Demos, *A Little Commonwealth*, 82–99; Ulrich, *Good Wives*, 13–50.

178. Demos, *A Little Commonwealth*, 174–178.

179. Nylander, *Our Own Snug Fireside*, 39–40.

180. Kutsche and Van Ness, *Canones*, 114–127; Knowlton, "Changing Spanish American Villages of Northern New Mexico," 460–461.

181. White, *Beekmantown, New York*, 110–111.

182. Faragher, *Sugar Creek*, 88–90.

183. John Coombs, "The Health of Central Wisconsin Residents in 1880: A New View of Midwestern Rural Life," *Wisconsin Magazine of History*, vol. 68, no. 4 (1985), 291–300, 308–310.

184. Faragher, *Sugar Creek*, 90–91.

185. Evelyn Bernetti Ackerman, "The Activities of a Country Doctor in New York State: Dr. Elias Cornelius of Somers, 1794–1803," *Historical Reflections* [Canada], vol. 9, nos. 1–2 (1982), 181–193.

186. *Ibid.*; White, *Beekmantown, New York*, 109.

187. Atherton, *Main Street on the Middle Border*, 153–160.

188. Dunbar, *How It Was in Hartford*, 48–49.

189. For example: Haywood, *Victorian West*, 139–145.

190. Fuller, *Burns Fuller Remembers*, 29.

191. Atherton, *Main Street on the Middle Border*, 71–72, 85–86, 91–92.

192. Dunbar, *How It Was in Hartford*, 100.

193. Lingeman, *Small Town America*, 268–269.

194. Haywood, *Victorian West*, 145–152.

195. Patricia G. Lane, "Birth, Marriage, and Death: Past and Present Customs in East Tennessee," *Tennessee Folklore Society Bulletin*, vol. 50, no. 2 (1984), 58–62.

196. Haywood, *Victorian West*, 152–157.

197. *Ibid.*, 256–274; Lingeman, *Small Town America*, 270–271.

198. Wiggin, *Impressions of Early Kansas*, 20, 33.

199. Dunbar, *How It Was in Hartford*, 79–80.

200. Wiggin, *Impressions of Early Kansas*, 15.

201. Haywood, *Victorian West*, 157–160.

202. Lane, "Birth, Marriage, and Death," 64.

203. Michael L. Berger, "The Influence of the Automobile on Rural Health Care, 1900–1929," *Journal of the History of Medicine and Allied Science*, vol. 28, no. 4 (1973), 319–331; Berger, *The Devil Wagon in God's Country*, 200–202.

204. On this particular point: August B. Hollingshead, *Elmtown's Youth and Elmtown Revisited* (New York: Wiley, 1975), 384–385.

205. West, *Plainville, U.S.A.*, 60–67, 165–205. For a similar report: Blumenthal, "A Sociological Study of a Small Town," 211–264.


## 6. Cultural Life

1. Salisbury, *Manitou and Providence*, 43.

2. *Ibid.*, 35.

3. Lockridge, *A New England Town*, 23–33.

4. Outbreaks of witchcraft, or belief that particular individuals were satanically possessed, created social tensions within a significant number of Puritan towns. But this phenomenon was dealt with in a formal, legal manner and did not lead to the permanent division of congregations into new and different churches. See Boyer and Nissenbaum, *Salem Possessed, passim*, and Demos, *Entertaining Satan, passim.*

5. Zuckerman, *Peaceable Kingdoms*, 61–65; Demos, *A Little Commonwealth*, 8–9.

6. Daniels, *The Connecticut Town*, 94–101.

7. Lockridge, *A New England Town*, 33–36.

8. Daniels, *The Connecticut Town*, 101–104.

9. Heyrman, *Commerce and Culture*, 281–301.

10. Isaac, *The Transformation of Virginia*, 58–65.

11. *Ibid.*, 161–167, 312–315.

12. Lemon, *The Best Poor Man's Country*, 112–113.

13. Wolf, *Urban Village*, 203–242.

14. Isaac, *The Transformation of Virginia*, 168–171.

15. Smith, *As a City Upon a Hill*, 233.

16. Knowlton, "Changing Spanish American Villages in Northern New Mexico," 462.

17. Smith, *As a City Upon a Hill*, 21.

18. *Ibid.*, 23–24.

19. Doyle, *The Social Order of a Frontier Community*, 158, 165–167.

20. Barron, *Those Who Stayed Behind*, 18–21, 114.

21. White, *Beekmantown, New York*, 117–145.

22. Faragher, *Sugar Creek*, 156–165.

23. Doyle, *The Social Order of a Frontier Community*, 157, 167–169.

24. Curti, *The Making of an American Community*, 127–131.

25. Hamilton, *Black Towns and Profit*, 18, 28, 68–69, 130.

26. Cooper, *Black Settlers in Rural Wisconsin*, 8.

27. Atherton, *Main Street on the Middle Border*, 168–174.

28. Stilgoe, *Common Landscape of America*, 231–238.

29. P. Jeffrey Potash, *Vermont's Burned-Over District: Patterns of Community Development and Religious Activity, 1761–1850* (Brooklyn, N.Y.: Carlson Publishing, 1991), 183–184.

30. Barron, *Those Who Stayed Behind*, 113–114.

31. White, *Beekmantown, New York*, 139–140.

32. Faragher, *Sugar Creek*, 162–164. Similarly, in the countryside in Trempealeau Township in Wisconsin, camp meetings during the summers of 1859 and 1860 drew, at their peak, more than a thousand people. Curti, *The Making of an American Community*, 128.

33. Doyle, *The Social Order of a Frontier Community*, 162–163.

34. For a detailed account of the cattle towns: Haywood, *Victorian West*, 90–111.

35. Wiggin, *Impressions of Early Kansas*, 40.

36. Margaret L. Johnson, *My Grandmothers and Other Tales of Old Woodstock* (Woodstock, Vt.: Woodstock Historical Society, 1957), 60.

37. Lape, *A Farm and Village Boyhood*, 83.

38. Fuller, *Burns Fuller Remembers*, 50.

39. Dunbar, *How It Was in Hartford*, 131.

40. Fuller, *Burns Fuller Remembers*, 50.

41. Goodlander, *Memoirs and Recollections*, 80.

42. Dunbar, *How It Was in Hartford*, 127.

43. Atherton, *Main Street on the Middle Border*, 186–189.

44. For a detailed account of the cattle towns: Haywood, *Victorian West*, 90–111.

45. Berger, *The Devil's Wagon in God's Country*, 144.

46. Roberts, Burdge, Korsching, and Donnermeyer, *Social Change in Rural Societies*, 166–167.

47. *Ibid.*, 163–165.

48. For instance, in "Springdale," New York: Vidich and Bensman, *Small Town in Mass Society*, 231–239.

49. *Ibid.*, 243.

50. Smith, *As a City Upon a Hill*, 81.

51. Vidich and Bensman, *Small Town and Mass Society*, 229–231.

52. Atherton, *Main Street on the Middle Border*, 256, 259–262.

53. Vidich and Bensman, *Small Town in Mass Society*, 228–229.

54. Wolf, *Urban Village*, 192.

55. Zuckerman, *Peaceable Kingdoms*, 72–79.

56. Demos, *A Little Commonwealth*, 142–144.

57. Wolf, *Urban Village*, 306.

58. Daniels, *The Connecticut Town*, 108–110.

59. Lemon, *The Best Man's Country*, 113–114.

60. Wolf, *Urban Village*, 193, 307.

61. *Ibid.*, 191–193, 239–241.

62. For a brief treatment: Atherton, *Main Street on the Middle Border*, 65–72, 174–180.

63. White, *Beekmantown, New York*, 223–232, 239, 251–252.

64. Faragher, *Sugar Creek*, 123–128.

65. Doyle, *The Social Order of a Frontier Community*, 34–35, 133, 152, 203–208.

66. Curti, *The Making of an American Community*, 282–283, 379–388, 404–415.

67. Haywood, *Victorian West*, 112–126.

68. *Ibid.*, 126–132.

69. Andrew Gulliford, "Country School Legacy in Wyoming," *Annals of Wyoming*, vol. 54, no. 2 (1982), 13.

70. Lane, *Old Home Town*, 3–4.

71. *Ibid.*, 13–17.

72. Gilmore, *Ozark Baptizings, Hangings, and Other Diversions*, 24–67.

73. Enid Bern, "Memoirs of a Prairie School Teacher," *North Dakota History*, vol. 42, no. 3 (Summer 1975), 11.

74. Spencer J. Maxcy, "The Teacherage in American Rural Education," *Journal of General Education*, vol. 30, no. 4 (1979), 267–273.

75. Hamilton, *Black Towns and Profit*, 66–68, 111–114.

76. Cooper, *Black Settlers in Rural Wisconsin*, 8.

77. Berger, *The Devil's Wagon in God's Country*, 171; Rogers, Burdge, Korsching, Donnermeyer, *Social Change in Rural Societies*, 141–143.

78. West, *Plainville, U.S.A.*, 76–77.

79. Martindale and Hansen, *Small Town and the Nation*, 116.

80. Berger, *The Devil's Wagon in God's Country*, 172; Berger, "Reading, Roadsters, and Rural America," *Journal of Library History*, vol. 12, no. 1 (1977), 42–47.

81. Atherton, *Main Street on the Middle Border*, 265–269, 300–305; West, *Plainville, U.S.A.*, 78–81; Martindale and Hanson, *Small Town and the Nation*, 115–118.

82. Arthur Versluis, *Native American Traditions* (Rockport, Mass.: Element Books, 1994), 73–74.

83. Atherton, *Main Street on the Middle Border*, 135–141.

84. Swinton, *I Married a Doctor*, 206.

85. Willa Cather, "The Incomparable Opera House," *Nebraska History*, vol. 49, no. 4 (1969), 373–378.

86. Atherton, *Main Street on the Middle Border*, 143–145; Boorstin, *The Americans: The National Experience*, 237–239.

87. Christopher S. Crary, *Pioneer and Personal Reminiscences* (Marshalltown, Iowa: Marshall Printing Co., 1893), 19.

88. Fuller, *Burns Fuller Remembers*, 58.

89. Atherton, *Main Street on the Middle Border*, 145–148. For a study of band master R. B. Hall and bands in Maine: Gordon Wingate Bowie, "R. B. Hall and the Community Bands of Maine," Ph.D. dissertation, University of Maine, 1993, *passim*. For a description of music in the cattle towns of Kansas: Haywood, *Victorian West*, 199–211.

90. *Ibid.*, 211–218.

91. *Ibid.*, 163–168, 218–220. For the Ozarks: Gilmore, *Ozark Baptizings, Hangings and Other Diversions*, 94–102.

92. Atherton, *Main Street on the Middle Border*, 145–146.

93. Smith, *As a City Upon a Hill*, 260–262; Anthony Channell Hilfer, *The Revolt from the Village, 1915–1930* (Chapel Hill, N.C.: University of North Carolina Press, 1969), 12–15.

94. Kathryn H. Fuller, *At the Picture Show: Small Town Audiences and the Creation of Movie Fan Culture* (Washington: Smithsonian Institution Press, 1996), xii–xiii.

95. Smith, *As a City Upon a Hill*, 258–259.

96. Edward Gale Agran, "William Allen White's Small Town America: A Literary Prescription for Progressive Reform," *Kansas History*, vol. 17, no. 3 (1994), 167–174.

97. Hilfer, *The Revolt from the Village*, 19–24.

98. *Ibid.*, 27–29; Smith, *As a City Upon a Hill*, 262–277.

99. For accounts of fiction with town settings after the 1930s: Herman Nibbelink, "Novels of American Rural Life, 1963–1984," *North Dakota Quarterly*, vol. 53 (Fall

1985), 167–172; and Walter Hobling, "Open Spaces and Narrow Minds: Soil, Soul, and Intellect in Recent U.S. Writing," *North Dakota Quarterly*, vol. 60, no. 1 (1992), 147–160.

100. Goodlander, *Memoirs and Recollections*, 47.

101. For a general account of holiday celebrations: Atherton, *Main Street on the Middle Border*, 193–206, 214–216, 312–318. For the cattle towns in Kansas: Haywood, *Victorian West*, 236–244. For the Ozarks: Gilmore, *Ozark Baptizings, Hangings, and Other Diversions*, 113–124. For the role of such celebrations as a device for spreading patriotism and assimilating new immigrants: Mary Lou Nemanic, "The Fourth of July on the Minnesota Iron Range: Small Town America and Working Class Nationalism, 1892–1992," Ph.D. dissertation, University of Minnesota, 1996.

102. The above account is based upon David J. Russo, *Keepers of Our Past: Local Historical Writing in the United States, 1820s–1930s* (Westport, Conn.: Greenwood, 1988), 27–61, 79–108, 149–164.

103. Atherton, *Main Street on the Middle Border*, 206–209; Gilmore, *Ozark Baptizings, Hangings, and Other Diversions*, 125–131.

104. Atherton, *Main Street on the Middle Border*, 309–310.

105. Esther Romeyn and Jack Kugelmass, "Community Festivals and the Politics of Memory: Postmodernity in the American Heartland," *European Contributions to American Studies*, vol. 32 (1995), 197–215.

106. Richard Ross Cloues, "Where Art Is Combined with Nature: Village Improvement in Nineteenth-Century New England," Ph.D. dissertation, Cornell University, 1987, 1143–1172; Stilgoe, *Common Landscape of America*, 202–208; 262–264.

107. William L. Bowers, *The Country Life Movement in America, 1900–1920* (Port Washington, N.Y.: Kennikat Press, 1975), 15–16, 24–35, 62–65, 84–85, 128–134; Barron, *Those Who Stayed Behind*, 41–50; Merwin Swanson, "The Country Life Movement in the American Churches," *Church History*, vol. 46, no. 3 (1977), 358–373; Dorothy Schweider, "Rural Iowa in the 1920s: Conflict and Continuity," *Annals of Iowa*, vol. 47, no. 2 (1983), 104–115.

108. Alice Cromie, *Restored Towns and Historic Districts of America: A Tour Guide* (New York: Dutton, 1979), xi–xii; Patricia Leigh Brown, "Main Streets Get Wise," *Historic Preservation*, vol. 31, no. 1 (1979), 29–34; Arthur P. Ziegler, Jr., and Walter C. Kidney, *Historic Preservation in Small Towns: A Manual of Practice* (Nashville: American Association for State and Local History, 1980), *passim*.

109. Kathleen Norris, "Gatsby on the Plains: Small Town Death Wish," *North Dakota Quarterly*, vol. 53, no. 4 (1985), 44–61; Cromie, *Restored Towns and Historic Districts of America*, *passim*.

110. Richard V. Francaviglia, "Main Street U.S.A.: A Comparison/Contrast of Streetscapes in Disneyland and Walt Disney World," *Journal of Popular Culture*, vol. 15, no. 1 (1981), 141–156.

## Conclusion: The Town in Myth and Reality

1. Wiggin, *Impressions of Early Kansas*, 54.

2. Fuller, *Burns Fuller Remembers*, 53.

3. Dunbar, *How It Was in Hartford*, 182–183.

# Bibliography

*This bibliography is restricted to items referred to in the text.*

AUTOBIOGRAPHICAL WRITINGS

Enid Bern, "Memoirs of a Prairie School Teacher," *North Dakota History*, vol. 42, no. 3 (Summer 1975), 5–16.

Harriet Bonebright-Closz, *Reminiscences of Newcastle* (Des Moines, Iowa: Historical Department of Iowa, 1921).

Christopher S. Crary, *Pioneer and Personal Reminiscences* (Marshalltown, Iowa: Marshall Printing Co., 1893).

Hermon W. De Long, *Boyhood Reminiscences* (Dansville, N.Y.: F.A. Owen Publishing Co., 1913).

Anne A. Dodge, *Recollections of Old Stonington* (Stonington, Conn.: Pequot Press, 1966).

Willis F. Dunbar, *How It Was in Hartford* (Grand Rapids, Mich.: Eerdmans, 1968).

Burns Fuller, *Burns Fuller Remembers* (Fenton, Mich.: Independent Print Co., 1966).

C. W. Goodlander, *Memoirs and Recollections* (Fort Scott, Kans.: Monitor Printing Co., 1900).

John M. Gorman, *I Remember Manzaner* (Bishop, Calif.: Pinon Press, 1967).

Ralph Gregory, "Count Baudissin on Missouri Towns," *Missouri Historical Society Bulletin*, vol. 27, no. 2 (January 1971), 114–123.

Margaret L. Johnson, *My Grandmothers and Other Tales of Old Woodstock* (Woodstock, Vt.: Woodstock Historical Society, 1957).

Rose Wilder Lane, *Old Home Town* (New York: Longmans, Green, 1935).

Fred Lape, *A Farm and Village Boyhood* (Syracuse, N.Y.: Syracuse University Press, 1980).

Charles L. Sonnichsen, *Billy King's Tombstone* (Tucson, Ariz.: University of Arizona Press, 1972).

Alma W. Swinton, *I Married a Doctor* (Marquette, Mich.: [no publisher], 1965).

Roderick Turnbull, *Maple Hill Stories* (Kansas City, Mo.: [no publisher], 1961).

————, *More Maple Hill Stories* (Kansas City, Mo.: Lowell Press, 1974).

Eliza J. Wiggin, *Impressions of Early Kansas* (Wichita, Kans.: Grit Printing, 1915).


BOOKS AND ARTICLES

Evelyn Bernetti Ackerman, "The Activities of a Country Doctor in New York State: Dr. Elias Cornelius of Somers, 1794–1803," *Historical Reflections* [Canada], vol. 9, nos. 1–2, 181–193.

Edward Gale Agran, "William Allen White's Small Town America: A Literary Prescription for Progressive Reform," *Kansas History*, vol. 17, no. 3 (1994), 162–177.

James B. Allen, *The Company Town in the American West* (Norman, Okla.: University of Oklahoma Press, 1966).

Lewis Atherton, *Main Street on the Middle Border* (Bloomington, Ind.: Indiana University Press, 1954).

Barbara Ruth Bailey, *Main Street, Northeastern Oregon: The Founding and Development of Small Towns* (Portland, Ore.: Oregon Historical Society, 1982).

Charles T. Banner-Haley, "An Extended Community: Sketches of Afro-American History in Three Counties Along New York State's Southern Tier, 1890–1980," *Afro-Americans in New York Life and History*, vol. 13, no. 1 (1989), 5–18.

Turpin C. Bannister, "Early Town Planning in New York State," *Journal of the American Society of Architectural Historians*, vol. 3, no. 2 (January–April 1943), 36–42.

Hal S. Barron, *Those Who Stayed Behind: Rural Society in Nineteenth Century New England* (New York: Cambridge University Press, 1984).

Patricia Duane Beaver, *Rural Community in the Appalachian South* (Lexington, Ky.: University Press of Kentucky, 1986).

Joseph Bensman and Arthur J. Vidich, *Small Town in Mass Society: Class, Power, and Religion in a Rural Community* (Princeton, N.J.: Princeton University Press, 1958).

Barbara Berg, *The Remembered Gate: Origins of American Feminism: The Woman and the City, 1800–1860* (New York: Oxford University Press, 1978).

Michael Berger, *The Devil's Wagon in God's Country: The Automobile and Social Change in Rural America, 1893–1929* (Hamden, Conn.: Archon, 1980).

———, "The Influence of the Automobile on Rural Health Care, 1900–29," *Journal of the History of Medicine and Allied Science*, vol. 28, no. 4, 319–335.

———, "Reading, Roadsters, and Rural America," *Journal of Library History*, vol. 12, no. 1 (1977), 42–49.

Ray Allen Billington, *The Far Western Frontier, 1830–1860* (New York: Harper and Brothers, 1956).

John Blassingame, *The Slave Community* (New York: Oxford University Press, 1972, revised ed.).

Albert Blumenthal, *A Sociological Study of a Small Town* (Chicago: University of Chicago Press, 1932).

Stuart Blumin, *The Urban Threshold: Growth and Change in a Nineteenth Century American Community* (Chicago: University of Chicago Press, 1976).

Daniel J. Boorstin, *The Americans: The National Experience* (New York: Random House, 1965).

———, *The Americans: The Democratic Experience* (New York: Random House, 1973).

Paul Boyer and Stephen Nissenbaum, *Salem Possessed: The Social Origins of Witchcraft* (Cambridge, Mass.: Harvard University Press, 1974).

Gordon Wingate Bowie, "R. B. Hall and the Community Bands of Maine," Ph.D. dissertation, University of Maine, 1993.

William L. Bowers, *The Country Life Movement in America, 1900–1920* (Port Washington, N.Y.: Kennikat Press, 1975).

T. H. Breen, *Tobacco Culture: The Mentality of the Great Tidewater Planters on the Eve of the Revolution* (Princeton, N.J.: Princeton University Press, 1985).

Carl Bridenbaugh, *Myths and Realities: Societies of the Colonial South* (Baton Rouge, La.: Louisiana State University Press, 1952).

Harold E. Briggs, "The Great Dakota Boom, 1879–1886," *North Dakota Historical Quarterly*, vol. 4 (January 1930), 78–108.

Patricia Leigh Brown, "Main Streets Get Streetwise," *Historic Preservation*, vol. 31, no. 1, 29–34.

Edmund deS. Brunner, Gwendolyn S. Hughes, and Marjorie Patten, *American Agricultural Villages* (New York: George J. Doran, 1927).

Edmund deS. Brunner and J. H. Kolb, *Rural Social Trends* (New York: McGraw Hill, 1933).

Nancy Burns, "The Collapse of Small Towns on the Great Plains: A Bibliography," *Emporia State Research Studies*, vol. 31, no. 1 (Summer 1982), 5–23.

Richard L. Bushman, *The Refinement of America: Persons, Houses, Cities* (New York: Knopf, 1992).

Shirley Jean Motley Carlson, "The Black Community in the Rural North: Pulaski County, Illinois, 1860–1900," Ph.D. dissertation, Washington University, 1982.

Lois Green Carr, "The Metropolis of Maryland: A Comment on Town Development Along the Tobacco Coast," *Maryland Historical Magazine*, vol. 69, no. 2 (1974), 124–145.

Earle Carville and Ronald Hoffman, "Staple Crops and Urban Development in the 18th Century South," *Perspectives in American History*, vol. 10 (1976), 7–62.

Charles E. Clarke, *The Eastern Frontier: The Settlement of Northern New England, 1610–1763* (New York: Knopf, 1970).

Richard Ross Cloues, "When Arts Combined with Nature: Village Improvement in Nineteenth Century New England," Ph.D. dissertation, Cornell University, 1987.

*Commercial Atlas and Marketing Guide* (Chicago, New York, and San Francisco: Rand McNally, any recent year).

Edward Cook, *The Fathers of the Towns: Leadership and Community Structure in Eighteenth Century New England* (Baltimore: Johns Hopkins University Press, 1976).

John Coombs, "The Health of Central Wisconsin Residents in 1880: A New View of Midwestern Rural Life," *Wisconsin Magazine of History*, vol. 68, no. 4 (1985), 284–311.

Zachary Cooper, *Black Settlers in Rural Wisconsin* (Madison, Wisc.: State Historical Society of Wisconsin, 1977).

Norman L. Crockett, *The Black Towns* (Lawrence, Kans.: Regents Press of Kansas, 1979).

Alice Cromie, *Restored Towns and Historic Districts of America: A Tour Guide* (New York: Dutton, 1979).

William Cronon, *Changes in the Land: Indians, Colonists, and the Ecology of New England* (New York: Hill and Wang, 1983).

Gilbert R. Cruz, *Let There Be Towns: Spanish Municipal Origins in the American Southwest, 1610–1810* (College Station, Tex.: Texas A&M University Press, 1988).

Gary L. Cunningham, "Gambling in the Kansas Cattle Towns: A Prominent and Somewhat Honorable Profession," *Kansas History*, vol. 5, no. 1, 2–22.

Merle Curti, *The Making of an American Community: A Case Study of Democracy in a Frontier Community* (Stanford, Calif.: Stanford University Press, 1959).

Bruce Daniels, *The Connecticut Town: Growth and Development, 1635–1790* (Middletown, Conn.: Wesleyan University Press, 1979).

———, *Dissent and Conformity on Narragansett Bay: The Colonial Rhode Island Town* (Middletown, Conn.: Wesleyan University Press, 1983).

Rodney O. Davis, "Prairie Emporium: Clarence, Iowa, 1860–1880: A Study in Population Trends," *Mid America*, vol. 51, no. 2 (1969), 130–139.

David D. Dawson, "Baseball Calls: Arkansas Town Baseball in the Twenties," *Arkansas Historical Quarterly*, vol. 54, no. 4 (Winter 1995), 409–426.

John Demos, *Entertaining Satan: Witchcraft and the Culture of Early New England* (New York: Oxford University Press, 1982).

————, *A Little Commonwealth: Family Life in Plymouth Colony* (New York: Oxford University Press, 1970).

Robert Doherty, *Society and Power in Five New England Towns, 1800–1860* (Amherst, Mass.: University of Massachusetts Press, 1977).

Don Harrison Doyle, *The Social Order of a Frontier Community: Jacksonville, Illinois, 1825–1870* (Urbana, Ill.: University of Illinois Press, 1978).

Thomas Dublin, *Women at Work: The Transformation of Work and Community in Lowell, Massachusetts, 1826–1860* (New York: Columbia University Press, 1979).

Willis F. Dunbar, "The Opera House as a Social Institution in Michigan," *Michigan History Magazine,* vol. 27 (October–December 1943), 661–672.

Robert Dykstra, *The Cattle Towns: A Social History of the Kansas Cattle Trading Towns: Abilene, Ellsworth, Wichita, Dodge City, and Caldwell, 1867 to 1885* (New York: Knopf, 1968).

Carolyn Ellis, *Fisher Folk: Two Communities on Chesapeake Bay* (Lexington, Ky.: University Press of Kentucky, 1986).

Doris D. Fanelli, "William Polk's General Store in Saint George's, Delaware," *Delaware History,* vol. 19, no. 4 (1981), 212–228.

John Mack Faragher, *Sugar Creek: Life on the Illinois Prairie* (New Haven, Conn.: Yale University Press, 1986).

Odie B. Faulk, *Tombstone: Myth and Reality* (New York: Oxford University Press, 1972).

David Hackett Fischer, *Albion's Seed: Four British Folkways in America* (New York: Oxford University Press, 1989).

Thomas R. Ford, ed., *Rural U.S.A.: Persistence and Change* (Ames, Iowa: Iowa State University Press, 1978).

Richard V. Francaviglia, *Main Street Revisited: Time, Space, and Image Building in Small Town America* (Iowa City, Iowa: University of Iowa Press, 1996).

————, "Victorian Bonanzas: Lessons from the Cultural Landscape of Western Hard Rock Mining Towns," *Journal of the West,* vol. 33, no. 1 (1994), 53–63.

Charles Luther Fry, *American Villagers* (New York: George H. Doran, 1926).

Kathryn H. Fuller, *At the Picture Show: Small Town Audiences and the Creation of a Movie Fan Culture* (Washington, D.C.: Smithsonian Institution Press, 1996).

Glenn V. Fuguitt and Donald W. Thomas, "Small Town Growth in the United States: An Analysis by Size, Class, and Place," *Demography,* vol. 3, no. 2 (1966), 513–527.

Daniel Garr, ed., *Hispanic Urban Planning in North America* (New York: Garland, 1991).

Elizabeth Donaghy Garrett, *At Home: The American Family, 1750–1870* (New York: Abrams, 1990).

Anthony Garvan, *Architecture and Town Planning in Colonial Connecticut* (New Haven, Conn.: Yale University Press, 1951).

Paul Wallace Gates, *The Illinois Central Railroad and Its Colonization Work* (Cambridge, Mass.: Harvard University Press, 1934).

Susan Geib, "'Changing Works': Agriculture and Society in Brookfield, Massachusetts, 1785–1829," Ph.D. dissertation, Boston University, 1981.

Eugene Genovese, *Roll, Jordan, Roll: The World the Slaves Made* (New York: Random House, 1975).

Robert K. Gilmore, *Ozark Baptizings, Hangings and Other Diversions: Theatrical Folkways of Rural Missouri, 1885–1910* (Norman, Okla.: University of Oklahoma Press, 1984).

Gilbert G. Gonzalez, *Labor and Community: Mexican Citrus Worker Villages in a Southern California County, 1900–1950* (Urbana, Ill.: University of Illinois Press, 1994).

H. Roger Grant, "Iowa's New Communities: Townsite Promotion Along the Chicago and Great Western Railway's Omaha Extension," *Upper Midwest History*, vol. 2 (1982), 53–63.

Andrew Gulliford, "Country School Legacy in Wyoming," *Annals of Wyoming*, vol. 54, no. 2, 10–19.

———, "Vernacular and Small Town Architecture of Northwest Ohio," *Northwest Ohio Quarterly*, vol. 58, no. 4 (1986), 107–121.

Blake Gumprecht, "Whiskey Towns of Oklahoma Territory, 1889–1907," *Chronicles of Oklahoma*, vol. 74, no. 2 (1996), 146–173.

Kenneth Marvin Hamilton, *Black Towns and Profit: Promotion and Development in the Trans-Appalachian West, 1877–1915* (Urbana, Ill.: University of Illinois Press, 1991).

Jean F. Hankins, "A Cage for John Sawyer: The Poor of Otisfield, Maine," *Maine History*, vol. 34, no. 2 (1994), 96–115.

Elvin Hatch, *Biography of a Small Town* (New York: Columbia University Press, 1979).

Dolores Hayden, *Seven American Utopias: The Architecture of Communitarian Socialism, 1790–1975* (Cambridge, Mass.: MIT Press, 1976).

C. Robert Haywood, *Victorian West: Class and Culture in Kansas Cattle Towns* (Lawrence, Kans.: University Press of Kansas, 1991).

Christopher Edwin Hendricks, "Town Development in the Colonial Backcountry—Virginia and North Carolina," Ph.D. dissertation, College of William and Mary, 1991.

Bernard L. Herman, *Architecture and Rural Life in Central Delaware, 1700–1900* (Knoxville, Tenn.: University of Tennessee Press, 1987).

Christine Leigh Heyrman, *Commerce and Culture: The Maritime Communities of Colonial Massachusetts* (New York: Norton, 1984).

Anthony Channell Hilfer, *The Revolt from the Village, 1915–1930* (Chapel Hill, N.C.: University of North Carolina Press, 1969).

Mozell Hill, "The All-Negro Communities of Oklahoma: The Natural History of a Social Movement," *Journal of Negro History*, vol. 31 (1946), 254–268.

William Alfred Hinds, *American Communities and Cooperative Colonies* (Chicago: C. H. Kerr, 1908; original 1878).

Robert V. Hine, *California's Utopian Colonies* (New Haven, Conn.: Yale University Press, 1966).

*Historical Atlas of the United States: Centennial Edition* (Washington, D.C.: National Geographic Society, 1988).

Walter Hobling, "Open Spaces and Narrow Minds: Soil, Soul, and Intellect in Recent U.S. Writing," *North Dakota Quarterly*, vol. 60, no. 1 (1992), 147–160.

Richard Hogan, *Class and Community in Frontier Colorado* (Lawrence, Kans.: University Press of Kansas, 1990).

August B. Hollingshead, *Elmtown's Youth and Elmtown Revisited* (New York: Wiley, 1975).

Mark Holloway, *Heavens on Earth: Utopian Communities in America, 1660–1880* (New York: Library Publishers, 1951).

Richard Holmes, *Communities in Transition: Bedford and Lincoln, Massachusetts, 1729–1850* (Ann Arbor, Mich.: UMI Research Press, 1980).

John C. Hudson, "The Plains Country Town," in Brian W. Blouet and Frederick Luebke, eds., *The Great Plains: Environment and Culture* (Lincoln, Nebr.: University of Nebraska Press, 1979), 99–117.

———, *Plains Country Towns* (Minneapolis: University of Minnesota Press, 1985).

———, "Towns of the Western Railroads," *Great Plains Quarterly*, vol. 2, no. 1 (1982), 41–54.

Hubert Humphreys, "A History of the Village of Grayson, Louisiana, and Adjacent Settlements, 1892–1992," *Journal of the North Louisiana Historical Association*, vol. 23, no. 4 (1992) 99–143.

Stephen Innes, *Labor in a New Land: Economy and Society in Seventeenth Century Springfield* (Princeton, N.J.: Princeton University Press, 1983).

Rhys Isaac, *The Transformation of Virginia, 1740–1790* (Chapel Hill, N.C.: University of North Carolina Press, 1982).

John A. Jakle, *American Small Town* (Hamden, Conn.: Archon Books, 1982).

John A. Jakle, Robert W. Bastian, and Douglas K. Meyer, *Common Houses in America's Small Towns: The Atlantic Seaboard to the Mississippi Valley* (Athens, Ga.: University of Georgia Press, 1989).

David Ross Jenkins, *The Growth and Decline of Agricultural Villages* (New York: Teachers College, Columbia University, 1940).

Laurie Ann Kattner, "From Immigrant Settlement into Town: New Braunfels, Texas, 1845–1870s," *Americastudien*, vol. 36, no. 2 (1991), 155–177.

Matti Kaups and Cotton Mather, "Eben: Thirty Years Later in a Finnish Community in the Upper Peninsula of Michigan," *Economic Geography*, vol. 44, no. 1 (1968), 57–70.

Walter C. Kidney, *Historic Preservation in Small Towns: A Manual of Practice* (Nashville, Tenn.: American Association of State and Local History, 1980).

Jeremy W. Kilar, *Michigan's Lumbertowns: Lumbermen and Laborers in Saginaw, Bay City, and Muskegon, 1870–1905* (Detroit: Wayne State University Press, 1990).

Thomas Knight, "Black Towns in Oklahoma: Their Development and Survival," Ph.D. dissertation, Oklahoma State University, 1975.

Clarke S. Knowlton, "Changing Spanish-American Villages of Northern New Mexico," *Sociology and Social Research,* vol. 53, no. 4 (1969), 455–474.

Gary Koerselman, "The Quest for Community in Rural Iowa: Neighborhood Life in Early Middleburg History," *Annals of Iowa,* vol. 41, no. 5 (1972), 1006–1020.

Gary Kulik, Roger Parks and Theodore Z. Penn, *The New England Mill Village, 1790–1860* (Cambridge, Mass.: MIT Press, 1982).

Paul Kutsche and John R. Van Ness, *Canones: Values, Crisis, and Survival in a Northern New Mexico Village* (Albuquerque, N.M.: University of New Mexico Press, 1981).

Patricia G. Lane, "Birth, Marriage, and Death: Past and Present Customs in East Tennessee," *Tennessee Folklore Society Bulletin,* vol. 50, no. 2 (1984), 58–67.

James Lemon, *The Best Poor Man's Country: A Geographical Study of Southeastern Pennsylvania* (Baltimore: Johns Hopkins University Press, 1972).

Carol Leonard, Isidor Walliman, and Wayne Rorher, "Groups and Social Organizations in Frontier Cattle Towns in Kansas," *Kansas Quarterly,* vol. 12, no. 2 (1980), 59–63.

William E. Leuchtenburg, *Franklin D. Roosevelt and the New Deal, 1932–1940* (New York: Harper and Row, 1963).

Pierce Lewis, "Small Town in Pennsylvania," *Annals of the Association of American Geographers,* vol. 62 (June 1972), 323–351.

Richard Lingeman, *Small Town America: A Narrative History, 1620–Present* (New York: G. P. Putnam's Sons, 1980).

Kenneth Lockridge, *A New England Town/The First Hundred Years: Dedham, Massachusetts, 1636–1736* (New York: Norton, 1970).

George Lockwood, *The New Harmony Movement* (New York: D. Appleton, 1905).

Amos Long, Jr., "The Rural Village," *Pennsylvania Folklife,* vol. 29, no. 3 (1980), 124–132.

Larry Lowenthal, "Railroad Rivalry in the Connecticut River Valley," *Historical Journal of Western Massachusetts,* vol. 20, no. 2 (1992), 109–132.

Don Martindale and R. Galen Hanson, *Small Town and the Nation: The Conflict Between Local and Translocal Forces* (Westport, Conn.: Greenwood, 1969).

Timothy R. Mahoney, *River Towns in the Great West: The Structure of Provincial Urbanization in the American Mid-West, 1820–1870* (New York: Cambridge University Press, 1990).

John Frederick Martin, *Profits in the Wilderness: Entrepreneurship and the Founding of New England Towns in the Seventeenth Century* (Chapel Hill, N.C.: University of North Carolina Press, 1991).

Spencer J. Maxcy, "The Teacherage in American Rural Education," *Journal of General Education*, vol. 30, no. 4 (1979), 267–274.

Norman T. Moline, *Mobility and the Small Town, 1900–1930: Transportation Change in Oregon, Illinois* (Chicago: University of Chicago, Department of Geography and Research Paper No. 132, 1971).

Paul C. Morrison, "A Morphological Study of Worthington, Ohio," *Ohio Journal of Science*, vol. 34 (January 1934), 31–45.

David C. Mott, "Abandoned Towns, Villages, and Post Offices of Iowa," *Annals of Iowa*, vol. 17 (October 1930), 434–465; (January 1931), 513–543; (April 1931), 578–599; vol. 18 (July 1931), 42–69; (October 1931), 117–148; (January 1932), 189–220.

Gerald W. Mullin, *Flight and Rebellion: Slave Resistance in Eighteenth Century Virginia* (New York: Oxford University Press, 1972).

William J. Murtagh, *Moravian Architecture and Town Planning* (Chapel Hill, N.C.: University of North Carolina Press, 1967).

Lowry Nelson, *The Minnesota Community: Country and Town in Transition* (Minneapolis: University of Minnesota Press, 1960).

————, *The Mormon Village: A Pattern and Technique of Land Settlement* (Salt Lake City, Utah: University of Utah Press, 1952).

Mary Lou Nemanic, "The Fourth of July on the Minnesota Iron Range: Small Town America and Working Class Nationalism, 1892–1992," Ph.D. dissertation, University of Minnesota, 1996.

Herman Nibbelink, "Novels of American Rural Life, 1963–1984," *North Dakota Quarterly*, vol. 53 (Fall 1985), 167–172.

Charles Nordhoff, *The Communistic Societies of the United States* (New York: Harper and Brothers, 1875).

Kathleen Norris, "Gatsby on the Plains: The Small Town Death Wish," *North Dakota Quarterly*, vol. 53, no. 4 (1985), 44–61.

Zelia Nuttall, "Royal Ordinances Concerning the Laying Out of New Towns," *Hispanic American Historical Review*, vol. 5 (1922), 249–254.

Russel B. Nye, *Society and Culture, 1830–1860* (New York: Harper and Row, 1974).

Jane C. Nylander, *Our Own Snug Fireside: Images of the New England Home, 1760–1860* (New York: Knopf, 1993).

James Oakes, *The Ruling Race: A History of American Slaveholders* (New York: Knopf, 1982).

Clarence B. Odell, "The Functional Patterns of Villages in a Selected Area of the Corn Belt," Ph.D. dissertation, University of Chicago, 1937.

Marian M. Ohman, *A History of Missouri's Counties, County Seats, and Courthouse Squares* (Columbia, Mo.: University of Missouri Press, 1983).

Donald B. Oster, "The Hannibal and St. Joseph Railroad, Government and

Town Founding, 1846–1861," *Missouri Historical Review,* vol. 87, no. 4 (1993), 403–421.

L. Jeffrey Perez, "'Promises Fair to Be a Flourishing Place': Virginia Town Establishment in the 1780s and the Emergence of a New Temperament," *Locus,* vol. 6, no. 2 (Spring 1994), 135–149.

Bernard C. Peters, "Early Town Site Speculation in Kalamazoo County," *Michigan History,* vol. 56, no. 3 (1972), 200–215.

Albert J. Petersen, "German-Russian Catholic Social Organization," *Plains Anthropologist,* vol. 18, no. 59 (1973), 27–32.

P. Jeffrey Potash, *Vermont's Burned-Over District: Patterns of Community Development and Religious Activity, 1761–1850* (Brooklyn, N.Y.: Carlson Publishing, 1991).

Edward T. Price, "The Central Courthouse Square in the American County Seat," *Geographical Review,* vol. 58 (January 1968), 30–60.

————, *Dividing the Land: Early American Beginnings of Our Private Property Mosaic* (Chicago: University of Chicago Press, 1995).

John W. Reps, *Cities of the American West: A History of Frontier Urban Planning* (Princeton, N.J.: Princeton University Press, 1979).

————, *Town Planning in Frontier America* (Princeton, N.J.: Princeton University Press, 1969).

Edward M. Riley, "The Town Acts of Colonial Virginia," *Journal of Southern History,* vol. 16, no. 3 (August 1950), 306–323.

Ricky Lyman Roberts, "Chelsea: An Anthropological Study of a 19th Century Western Frontier Town," Ph.D. dissertation, University of Kansas, 1986.

William F. Robinson, *Abandoned New England: Its Hidden Ruins and Where to Find Them* (Boston: New York Graphic Society, 1976).

Richard D. Rodfeld, ed., *Change in Rural America* (St. Louis: C. V. Mosby, 1978).

Everett M. Rogers, Rabel J. Burdge, Peter F. Korsching, and Joseph F. Donnermeyer, *Social Change in Rural Societies* (Englewood Cliffs, N.J.: Prentice-Hall, 1984).

Esther Romeyn and Jack Kugelmass, "Community Festivals and the Politics of Memory: Postmodernity in the American Heartland," *European Contributions to American Studies,* vol. 32 (1995), 197–215.

Geoffrey Louis Rossanno, "A Subtle Revolution: The Urban Transformation of Rural Life, New Gloucester, Maine, 1775–1930," Ph.D. dissertation, University of North Carolina, 1980.

David J. Rothman, *The Discovery of the Asylum* (Boston: Little, Brown, 1970).

David J. Russo, *Families and Communities: A New View of American History* (Nashville, Tenn.: American Association for State and Local History, 1974).

————, *Keepers of Our Past: Local Historical Writing in the United States, 1820s–1930s* (Westport, Conn.: Greenwood Press, 1988).

————, *The Origins of Local News in the U.S. Country Press, 1840s–1880s* (Lexington, Ky.: Journalism Monographs No. 65, February 1980).

Catherine E. Rymph, "Keeping the Political Fires Burning: Republican Women's Clubs and Female Political Culture in Small Town Iowa, 1928–1938," *Annals of Iowa*, vol. 56, nos. 1–2 (1997), 99–127.

Darrett Bruce and Anita H. Rutman, *A Place in Time: Middlesex County, Virginia, 1650–1750* (New York: Norton, 1984).

Dorothy Schweider, "Rural Iowa in the 1920s: Conflict and Continuity," *Annals of Iowa*, vol. 47, no. 2 (1983), 104–115.

Joanna Niles Sears, *The First One Hundred Years of Town Planning in Georgia* (Atlanta: Cherokee Publishing, 1979).

James R. Sherow, "Rural Town Origins in Southwest Reno County." *Kansas History*, vol. 3, no. 2 (1980), 99–111.

Brian L. Shulz, "Where Is Main Street?: The Commercial Landscape of Four Oklahoma Small Towns," *Chronicles of Oklahoma*, vol. 71, no. 1 (1993), 88–103.

Lucy Simler, "The Township: The Community of the Rural Pennsylvanian," *Pennsylvania Magazine of History and Biography*, vol. 106, no. 1 (1982), 41–68.

Page Smith, *As a City Upon a Hill: The Town in American History* (New York: Knopf, 1968).

Peter C. Smith and Karl B. Raitz, "Negro Hamlets and Agricultural Estates in Kentucky's Inner Bluegrass," *Geographical Review*, vol. 64, no. 2 (1974), 217–234.

Raymond A. Smith, Jr., "Sports and Games in Western Iowa in the Early 1880s," *Palimpsest*, vol. 65, no. 1, 9–16, 25.

Richard Harold Smith, "Towns Along the Tracks: Railroad Strategy and Town Promotion in San Joaquin Valley, California," Ph.D. dissertation, University of California at Los Angeles, 1976.

Stuart Seely Sprague, "Town Making in the Era of Good Feelings: Kentucky, 1814–1820," *Register of the Kentucky Historical Society*, vol. 72, no. 4 (1974), 337–341.

Leslie C. Stuart-Abernathy, "Urban Farmsteads: Household Responsibilities in the City," *Historical Archaeology*, vol. 20, no. 2 (1986), 5–15.

John R. Stilgoe, *Common Landscape of America, 1580 to 1845* (New Haven, Conn.: Yale University Press, 1982).

Raleigh A. Suarez, "Bargains, Bills, and Bankruptcies: Business Activity in Rural Antebellum Louisiana," *Louisiana History*, vol. 7, no. 3 (1966), 189–206.

Ruth Sutter, *The Next Place You Come To: A Historical Introduction to Communities in North America* (Englewood Cliffs, N.J.: Prentice-Hall, 1973).

Merwin Swanson, "The 'Country Life Movement' and the American Churches," *Church History*, vol. 46, no. 3 (1977), 358–373.

Joseph Brown Thomas, Jr., "Settlement, Community, and Economy: The Development of Towns on Maryland's Eastern Shore, 1660–1775," Ph.D. dissertation, University of Maryland, 1994.

Lisa Carol Tolbert, "Constructing Townscapes: Architecture and Experience in Nineteenth Century County Seats of Middle Tennessee," Ph.D. dissertation, University of North Carolina, 1994.

Arthur L. Tolson, "Black Towns of Oklahoma," *Black Scholar,* vol. 10, no. 6 (1970), 18–22.

Glenn T. Trewartha, "The Unincorporated Hamlet: One Element of the American Settlement Fabric," *Annals of the Association of American Geographers,* vol. 33, no. 1 (March 1943), 32–81.

Laurel Thatcher Ulrich, *Good Wives: Image and Reality in the Lives of Women in Northern New England, 1650–1750* (New York: Oxford University Press, 1982).

Kathleen Underwood, *Town Building on the Colorado Frontier* (Albuquerque, N.M.: University of New Mexico Press, 1987).

John R. Van Ness, *Hispanos in Northern New Mexico: The Development of Corporate Community and Multicommunity* (New York: AMS Press, 1991).

Arthur Verluis, *Native American Traditions* (Rockport, Mass.: Element Books, 1994).

Stuart F. Voss, "Town Growth in Central Missouri, 1815–1880: An Urban Chaparral," *Missouri Historical Review,* vol. 64, no. 1 and no. 2 (1970–1971), 64–80, 197–217.

Anthony F. C. Wallace, *Rockdale: The Growth of an American Village in the Early Industrial Revolution* (New York: Norton, 1978).

William D. Walters, Jr., "Early Western Illinois Town Advertisements: A Geographical Inquiry," *Western Illinois Regional Studies,* vol. 8, no. 1 (1985), 5–15.

————, "Unsurpassed Locations: Gulf Coast Townsite Advertisements: 1835–1837," *Pioneer America Society Transactions,* vol. 12 (1989), 65–72.

Shirley Friedlander Weiss, *New Town Development in the United States: Experiment in Private Entrepreneurship* (Chapel Hill, N.C.: Center for Urban and Regional Studies, University of North Carolina at Chapel Hill, 1973).

James West, *Plainville, U.S.A.* (New York: Columbia University Press, 1945).

Pamela West, "The Rise and Fall of the American Porch," *Landscape,* vol. 20 (Spring 1976), 42–47.

Philip L. White, *Beekmantown, New York: Forest Frontier to Farm Community* (Austin, Tex.: University of Texas Press, 1979).

Stephanie Wolf, *Urban Village: Population, Community, and Family Structure in Germantown, Pennsylvania, 1683–1800* (Princeton, N.J.: Princeton University Press, 1976).

Joseph S. Wood, "Elaboration of a Settlement System: The New England Village in the Federal Period," *Journal of Historical Geography,* vol. 10, no. 4 (1984), 331–356.

Joseph S. Wood and Michael P. Steinitz, *The New England Village* (Baltimore: Johns Hopkins University Press, 1997).

Langdon G. Wright, "In Search of Peace and Harmony: New York Communities in the 17th Century, *New York History,* vol. 61, no. 1 (1980), 5–21.

William Wyckoff, *The Developer's Frontier: The Making of the Western New York Landscape* (New Haven, Conn.: Yale University Press, 1988).

Wilbur Zelinsky, "The Pennsylvania Town: An Overdue Geographical Account," *Geographical Review,* vol. 67, no. 2 (1977), 127–147.

Michael Zuckerman, *Peaceable Kingdoms: New England Towns in the Eighteenth Century* (New York: Knopf, 1970).

# Index

A & P (Great Atlantic and Pacific Tea
Company), 172
Adult education, *265*, 268
Agriculture: cattle ranching, 104–105,
143–144, 191, 202; colonial era, 122–130;
cotton growing, 141–142; fairs, 222–224,
*223*; farm buildings, 54, 57–58, 82–83;
farmers in town, *165*; gender work
divisions, 128–129, *147*, 148; mechanization
of, 140–141, 143; Midwest, 29, 141,
142–144, 191; mills, 56, 120–122, *121*,
138–139; Native American agriculture,
117–118; New England, 128–130,
140–141; plantation layout, *59*; and railroad
towns, 31–32; and social life, 182, 190–191,
211–213; Southeast, 11, 15–16, 124–128,
140, 141–142, 190, *223*; Southwest, 132,
*223*; transient workers, 146–148; twentieth
century, 160, 164. *See also* Farmers; Rural
areas.
Alcohol: crusades against, 201–205; social
aspects, 201–205, 212, 214–215
Amusement parks, 227
Anglican churches, 244–245, 246–247, *247*
Annapolis, Md., planning, 52
Anti-Masonic party, 224–225
Anti-slavery towns, 28, 33
Anti-vice crusades, 201–205
Architecture, 49; courthouses, 69, *101*; houses,
80–81, 86–88; nineteenth century, 69, 74,
80–81, 275, 288; twentieth century, 86–88.
*See also* Building types; Layout; Town
planning.
Arizona: settlements, 30–31; social life, 203

Arts, 273–283; cities vs. towns, 242–243,
274–275, 282–283; colonial era, 273–274;
dancing, 278; Mid-Atlantic, *279*; Midwest,
275; music, 276–278, *277*; Native American
settlements, 273; nineteenth century,
274–280; performance arts, 275, 278–282,
*279*; and religious life, 273, 274, 278–279;
technology's effect on, 280–282; twentieth
century, 280–283; visual arts, 275–276;
writing, 280, 282–283, 285–287. *See also*
Architecture.
Atchison, Kans., 75
Automobiles, 168, *169*, 294; cultural life
affected by, 281–282; economic life affected
by, 168–170; health care affected by,
239–240; retail trade affected by, 170–172;
schools affected by, 271–272; social life
affected by, 227; town layout affected by,
85–86, 119

Ballou, Adin, 42
Bands, 276–278, *277*
Bankers, 193
Banks, 193, *195*
Baptisms, *255*
Baptist churches, 249
Barber shops, *162*, 216–217
Baseball, 221
Bauddisin, Count (quoted), 25–26
Beekman, William, 17–18
Beekmantown, N.Y., 17–18, 78
Bees, 211–214, 218
Benson, Minn.: political life, 112; schools,
272; social life, 209–210

Social life (*cont.*)
  201–205; gender divisions, 203, 212,
  214–218, 224–228, 236–238, 240–241;
  government, 187–188, 199–200; health
  care, 229–230, 232–234, 239–240; and
  industrialization, 193–197; leisure life,
  211–228, *218–219, 221*; lumber towns, 192;
  marriage, 230–231, 241; mill towns, 192;
  music, 276–278, *277*; Native American
  settlements, 176–177; newspapers, 194,
  200–201; nineteenth century, 178, 188–207,
  212–214, 232–239; political aspects, 212;
  poor people, 185–186, 197, 238; prejudice,
  183–184; prostitution, 201–205; Puritan
  settlements, 182–185; racism, 41–42, 197,
  207–208, 226–227; and schools, 85, 114,
  201, 266, 268, 269–270, 272–273;
  segregation, 226–227; social mobility,
  185–186; Spanish settlements, 188, 232;
  twentieth century, 207–211. *See also*
  Communal towns; Cultural life; Holidays;
  Religious life; Religious towns; Schools;
  *individual areas by name.*
Social mobility, 185–186
South Carolina, 13. *See also* Carolina colony.
South Dakota, 34, 38
Southeast, 11–16, 29; agriculture, 11, 15–16,
  124–128, 140, 141–142, 190, *223*; black
  freedmen settlements, 40–42, 271; building
  types, 56–58, *101, 106, 247*; Carolina
  colony, 13; communal towns, 42; economic
  aspects of towns, 11–12; economic life,
  124–126, 131–132, 138, 141–142, 153,
  166–167; factories, 167; fires, *87*; Florida,
  21–22; French settlements, 55; Georgia,
  14–15, 39, 52, 62–63; Kentucky, 67, *87,
  106, 149, 223*; layout, *59*, 62–63, 85;
  Louisiana, 22, 23; Maryland, 12–13, 52;
  mill towns, 138, 166–167; Mississippi, 41,
  *145*; North Carolina, 11, 14, 60; planning,
  52, 55, *59*, 62–63, 67; political life, 93, 98,
  99–100; port towns, 124–126, 141–142;
  religious life, 246–248, *247*; social life, 180,
  181–182, 183, 185, 190, 210; stores, 153;
  types of towns, 11–16. *See also* Virginia.
Southern Pacific railroad, 36
Southwest: agriculture, 104–105, 132,
  143–144, 191, 202, *223*; Arizona, 30–31,
  203; Colorado, 30, 37, 42, *277*; economic
  life, 132, 143; mining towns, 38–39, 43,
  70–72, 134; New Mexico, 22, 35; political
  life, 100–101; social life, 188, 191, 203, 208;
  Texas, 22, 34–35, 39–40; types of towns, 22.
  *See also* Railroad towns.

Spanish settlements, 20–22; economic life,
  132; planning, 55; political life, 100–101;
  public spaces, 55; religious life, 250; social
  life, 188, 232
Speculation: town formation as, 17–18, 25–26,
  32–33, 44–46, 106–108, 119–120. *See also*
  Land companies; Railroad towns.
Sports, *219*, 220–221, 227
"Springdale" (fictional town), 111–112, 209,
  260–261
Springfield, Mass., 126, 180
St. Louis, Mo., 28
"Starckey" (fictional town), 210
State governments, 101–102; Depression Era
  role, 110; public schools, 264–271; state-
  founded towns, 39
State-founded towns, 39
Stewart, David, 17
Stillwater, Minn., shops, *162–163*
Stillwell, Arthur, 35
Stone, Amos, 30–31
Stores, 153–156, *155, 157, 162–163*;
  automobiles' effect on, 170–172; chain
  stores, 172; franchises, 172; general stores,
  153–154, *155*; mail order, 172; mercantile
  elites, 180; social status of storekeepers, 196
Strawn's Opera House, *221*
Street signs, 78
Streets: Main Streets, 74–78, *75, 77*; rural
  areas, 115; street signs, 78; surfaces, 77, 78.
  *See also* Automobiles; Layout;
  Transportation.
Suburban developments, 83–89
Sugar Creek, Ill., 232–233, 254–256, 266
Surfaces of streets, 77, 78
Swinton, Alma W. (quoted), 205, 275

Tacoma, Wash., 84
Tarkington, Booth, 282
Taverns, 214–215. *See also* Alcohol; Saloons.
Taxes: to fund town foundings, 12; and rural
  political life, 112–113
Teachers, 194–196, 265–266, 270, 272. *See also*
  Schools.
Technology: arts affected by, 280–282;
  economic life affected by, 164–170,
  294–298; electricity, 78, 132–133, 139, 166,
  167–168; nineteenth century, 78, 132–133,
  136–141; power machinery, 132–133,
  136–137; religious life affected by, 259;
  telephones, 168–169; twentieth century,
  164–170. *See also* Factories; Factory towns;
  Mill towns.
Telephones, 168–169

# A NOTE ON THE AUTHOR

David J. Russo is emeritus professor of history at McMaster University. Born in Greenfield, Massachusetts, he studied at the University of Massachusetts and at Yale University, where he received a Ph.D. in history. He has pursued wide-ranging work in American local history, and his other books include *Families and Communities*, *Keepers of Our Past*, and *Clio Confused*. He lives in Hamilton, Ontario.